About this Book

The people of the Congo, as this book shows, have suffered cruelly throughout the past century from a particularly brutal experience of colonial rule; and, following independence in 1960, external interference by the United States and other powers, a whole generation of patrimonial spoliation at the hands of Mobutu (the dictator installed by the West in 1965), and periodic warfare, which even now continues fitfully in the East of the country. But, as this insightful political history of the Congolese democratic movement in the 20th century decisively makes clear, its people have not taken these multiple oppressions lying down. Instead, the Congolese people have struggled over the years to improve their conditions of life by trying both to establish democratic institutions at home and to free themselves from exploitation from abroad; indeed, these cannot be separated one from the other.

The author of this book, Professor Nzongola-Ntalaja, is one of the country's leading intellectuals. Despite being forced into long years of exile (during which he taught political science in the United States and elsewhere), he has played a part at significant moments in his country's political struggle. His deep knowledge of personalities and events, and his understanding of the underlying class, ethnic and other factors at work, make his book a compelling, lucid, radical and utterly unromanticized account of his countrymen's struggle. In acknowledging their defeat, he sees it and the crisis of the post-colonial state as the result of the breakdown of the anti-colonial alliance between the masses and the national leadership after independence.

This book is essential reading for understanding what is happening in the Congo and the Great Lakes region. It will also stand as a milestone in how to write the modern political history of Africa.

About the Author

Georges Nzongola-Ntalaja is a renowned scholar of African politics and an international consultant specializing in public policy, governance and conflict-related issues. His distinguished scholarly career has included tenure as the James K. Batten Professor of Public Policy at Davidson College in North Carolina (1998–99); Professor of African Studies at Howard University (Washington DC) from 1978 to 1997; lectureships in the Congo (1970–75) and Nigeria (1977–78); and a visiting professorship at El Colegio de Mexico (summer 1987). He has also served as President of the African Studies Association (ASA) of the United States, 1987–88; Member of the Executive Committee of the International Political Science Association (IPSA), 1994–97; and President of the African Association of Political Science (AAPS) from 1995 to 1997.

In the political sphere, he has played a role in his own country's difficult transition from the Mobutu dictatorship – in 1992 he was a delegate to the Sovereign National Conference of Congo/Zaire; serving thereafter as Diplomatic Adviser to the Transitional Government of Prime Minister Etienne Tshisekedi; and in 1996 as Deputy President of the National Electoral Commission of the DRC and chief representative of the democratic opposition on the Commission.

His publications include:

The State and Democracy in Africa, co-editor (AAPS Books, Harare, 1997; Africa World Press, Trenton, 1998)

The Oxford Companion to Politics of the World, co-editor (Oxford University Press, New York, 1993, 2001)

Conflict in the Horn of Africa (African Studies Association Press, Atlanta, 1991)

Revolution and Counter-Revolution in Africa (Zed Books, London, 1987)

The Crisis in Zaire: Myths and Realities, editor (Africa World Press, Trenton, 1986)

The Congo from Leopold to Kabila
A People's History

Georges Nzongola-Ntalaja

Zed Books
LONDON AND NEW YORK

The Congo from Leopold to Kabila: A People's History was first
published by Zed Books Ltd, 7 Cynthia Street, London N1 9JF, UK and
Room 400, 175 Fifth Avenue, New York, NY 10010, USA in 2002.

Distributed in the USA exclusively by Palgrave, a division of St Martin's
Press, LLC, 175 Fifth Avenue, New York, NY 10010, USA

Second Impression 2003

Map on p. xvi reproduced by courtesy of the Africa Institute of South Africa
Cover designed by Andrew Corbett
Set in Monotype Dante by Ewan Smith, London
Printed and bound in Great Britain by Bookcraft Ltd, Midsomer Norton

A catalogue record for this book is available from the British Library
Library of Congress Cataloging-in-Publication Data: available

ISBN 1 84277 052 7 cased
ISBN 1 84277 053 5 limp

Contents

Preface and Acknowledgements

§ I started writing this book in December 1999, following a request from Hakim Ben Hammouda of Codesria. But this work is based on my ongoing research on the Congo since 1968. My main interest then was mass participation in politics, with particular emphasis on the mass factor in the independence struggle and the student movement in the 1960s. The focus of research changed to the state in 1980, with a 14-year research project largely supported by three Howard University grants on the Mobutu regime, its external connections and its consequences for the Congolese people. A contract was signed with Zed Books for a book on the subject, and this was to follow the 1987 publication there of my *Revolution and Counter-Revolution in Africa*. As I became increasingly involved in the activities of the Congolese democracy movement from 1987 to 1996, this project was never completed.

I am very grateful to Codesria and Zed Books for giving me the opportunity to add another publication to the impressive list of works of synthesis on Congolese political economy, which include Mbaya Kankwenda's *Zaïre: Vers quelles destinées?*, my own edited volume entitled *The Crisis in Zaire: Myths and Realities*, Jacques Vanderlinden's *Du Congo au Zaïre, 1960–1980: Essai de bilan*, and *The Rise and Decline of the Zairian State* by Crawford Young and Thomas Turner. Familiarity with these four texts, which are rich in data and helpful in elucidating the past, should give the serious student of Congolese politics the background information needed for a better appreciation of this book.

My own contribution to the analysis of Congolese political realities is that of a scholar-activist. As a Congolese patriot who came of age during the great awakening of the national liberation struggle, I cannot be dispassionate or neutral in examining the political history of my country. As most people of my generation, I was forced to take a keen interest in politics as a teenager, and later on in life I took an active part in some of the events described in this book. Thus, in addition to using the historical and sociological methods of political economy, this study has also benefited from my own personal experience as a participant observer.

This experience spans four decades, from student activism in the

1960s to more recent involvement in Congolese civil society attempts to find a peaceful solution to the present crisis in the Great Lakes region. My baptism of fire in Congolese politics occurred in April 1960, when I was expelled from secondary school for participation in pro-independence activities. Four years later, I joined the Union générale des étudiants congolais (UGEC) and the editorial staff of its USA–Canada section organ, *La Voix des étudiants congolais (LAVEC)*. As chief editor of *LAVEC* between September 1965 and January 1967, I was challenged to keep up with political developments back home to be able to provide the best services possible as an opinion leader within the Congolese community in North America. Following three years of university teaching, administration and research in Mobutu's Zaire, between February 1971 and December 1973, I became convinced that the Mobutu regime was useless or dysfunctional for the Congo, and this is a position that I defended in my 1975 doctoral dissertation. The only logical thing to do, I thought, was to fight against it.

By 1979, this position had become sufficiently widespread among Congolese intellectuals in the United States that it was possible to found a research and political action NGO for those professionals and students interested in finding an alternative to the Mobutu regime, the Centre d'études et de recherches sur le Zaïre/Center for Research on Zaire (CEREZ). I was honoured to serve as the Center's executive director between 1981 and 1991. In addition to promoting socially or politically relevant research among our compatriots, CEREZ sponsored at least one panel on the Congo each year at the annual meetings of the African Studies Association of the United States. On top of this, four major achievements can be credited to CEREZ during this period: (1) pressure on the US Department of State to help obtain the liberation of Ernest Wamba-dia-Wamba, a founding member of CEREZ, who was detained in Kinshasa for nearly one year between 1981 and 1982; (2) an international research workshop on 'Myths and Realities of the Zairian Crisis' at Howard University in 1984; (3) work with the Rainbow Lobby, a progressive US political advocacy group in support of Etienne Tshisekedi and the democracy movement in the Congo, beginning with Tshisekedi's visit to the United States in 1987; and (4) the organization of a major conference on 'Prospects for Democracy in Zaire', held at Howard University with Tshisekedi and other Congolese democracy activists, in November 1990. In addition to CEREZ, I became an active member of the Mouvement national congolais/Lumumba (MNC-L) of the diaspora in 1984. In 1991, I was elected chair of the Brussels Conclave, from 28 February to 1 March, which took important decisions on the party's role in the democratic transition in the Congo. At a subsequent meeting in June 1991 in Metz, France, I was designated as one of the persons to go back home as part of a fact-finding and party reunification mission, which I did two months later, in August, along with Etienne-Richard Mbaya and Patrice Mosamete. As a result of all this pro-democracy activity, I was co-opted by the delegates at the Sovereign National Conference to join them as one of seven 'internationally renowned' Congolese scholars, in April 1992.

Nothing in my previous or later political life can compare with the singularly exciting and learning experience of this national political reform and constitutional convention. In Kabila's Congo, one often hears disparaging remarks about people who are nostalgic about the national conference. I, for one, plead guilty as charged. I have tried to tell the story of the conference in Chapter 6, but there is no way to do justice to what I witnessed. After my own general policy speech on 14 May, I received nearly five hundred letters from all over the country, and I was the featured speaker at two to three public forums practically every weekend between June and October 1992 in Kinshasa. Afterwards, as diplomatic adviser to Prime Minister Tshisekedi, I also learned a lot in three of the major missions in which I was involved: the April 1993 independence referendum in Eritrea, the June 1993 OAU summit in Cairo, and that year's UN General Assembly session in New York. While I served as a bona fide government representative in the United Nations Mission to Observe the Referendum in Eritrea (UNOVER), our delegation lost the credentials battle to Mobutu at the OAU and UN assemblies. In 1996, I was back home as deputy president of the National Electoral Commission, in which I also served as head of the democratic opposition. I resigned from the commission after eight months of service on 3 September, mostly to protest against the sabotage of its work by Mobutu's cronies, particularly Prime Minister Léon Kengo wa Dondo and Gérard Kamanda wa Kamanda, the interior minister. Working at close range with the Kengo government, the opposition leadership and representatives of the international community, I was able to gain valuable insights in the bankruptcy of the first group, the incompetence of the second, and the cynicism of the third.

All of this personal experience was invaluable in determining the content of this book. Given the multiplicity of my organizational affiliations and the very long time it took me to write it, the book owes its existence to the generous support and kind assistance of several organizations and many people, too numerous to be mentioned here. However, acknowledgement must be made of the support from the Faculty Research Program in the Social Sciences, Humanities and Education at Howard University from the Office of the Vice-President for

Academic Affairs, which allowed me to carry out research on the Congo in Belgium in 1980, 1986, 1993 and 1994, and at the United Nations Archives in New York in 1986 and 1987. I am also grateful to the Social Science Research Council of the United States, for a 1984 state-of-the-art research workshop grant, which permitted me to bring to Howard a number of distinguished scholars for an intellectual exchange on the economic and social crisis in the Congo.

Much of the chapter on the second independence movement was written in 1985 as part of the 'Alternative Futures for Africa' project of the Third World Forum (TWF) with funds from the United Nations University (UNU). Samir Amin, the TWF African coordinator, and the then UNU Vice-Rector Kinhide Mushakoji deserve credit for this project, which gave support to the growing interest of the African Association of Political Science (AAPS) in examining the issue of democracy in Africa, long before it became fashionable to do so. Five years later, at an AAPS–TWF workshop on popular movements and political conflict held near Mombasa, Kenya, Pablo Gonzales Casanova, the world-renowned Mexican sociologist, reinforced my interest in the mass factor in political change with very interesting examples from Latin America.

Intellectually and politically, the writing of this book has benefited greatly from discussions within CEREZ, the public fora that I was asked to address in Kinshasa in 1992 and 1996, and debates within AAPS. With respect to the Congo, AAPS held two outstanding workshops in Kinshasa on the politics and the economics of the democratic transition in August 1995 and February 1996, respectively. On the individual level, I am particularly grateful to Mbaya Kankwenda, a renowned Congolese economist and intellectual, for having taken the time to read the entire manuscript and for his very helpful critical comments, which resulted in major improvements to the text. I must also thank Gauthier de Villers and Erik Kennes, who made helpful comments on parts of the manuscript. The remarks by Robert Molteno of Zed Books and an anonymous reader for Codesria were also useful. Needless to say, I alone am entirely responsible for any weaknesses and errors throughout the book.

In the course of the events described here, I have spent long periods of time away from my closest relatives. Lubamba, Anna and Meta, who reside in the United States, have bravely borne the burden of having for their father a scholar-activist who spends a lot of time in Africa. For the extended Nzongola family in the Congo, the problem is my long stay in America. In spite of this, their love and understanding have been a source of strength for me.

In 1992, my brother Pierre, who is the eldest in the family, 20 years older than I am and is mistaken by some to be my father, came to see me in Kinshasa, 19 years after the last time we had seen each other. I was a bit apprehensive when he started delivering what he said was the message he brought for me from folks back home in the Kasai region. The message, to my surprise and delight, was that they were all behind my fight against the Mobutu regime and proud of me. Nothing could have energized me as much as this vote of confidence from people I love and admire greatly.

My wife, Margaret Carol Lee, has been an indispensable fountain of inspiration and a source of indefatigable support during the last five years. As my best friend and intellectual companion, she has exerted considerable moderating influence on my actions and a beneficial impact on my thoughts. This book could not have been completed in its present form without her love and encouragement. It is therefore dedicated to her.

Finally, I finished writing this book in my spare time while working for the United Nations Development Programme (UNDP) as senior technical adviser for governance in Nigeria. The views expressed in this book are my own and do not reflect those of the United Nations and its specialized agencies.

Georges Nzongola-Ntalaja
Abuja, Nigeria

Abbreviations and Acronyms

Abako	Alliance des Bakongo
AFDL	Alliance des forces démocratiques pour la libération du Congo
AGEL	Association des étudiants de Lovanium
AIA	Association internationale africaine
AIC	Association internationale pour le Congo
ANC	Armée nationale congolaise
APCM	American Presbyterian Congo Mission
APL	Armée populaire de libération
Balubakat	Association générale des Baluba du Katanga
BCK	Chemin de fer du Bas-Congo au Katanga
BSAC	British South African Company
CCCI	Compagnie du Congo pour le commerce et l'industrie
Cerea	Centre de regroupement africain
CFL	Compagnie des chemins de fer du Congo supérieur aux Grands Lacs
CFS	Congo Free State
CNE	Commission nationale des élections
CNL	Conseil national de libération
CNS	Conférence nationale souveraine
Conakat	Confédération des associations tribales du Katanga
CRA	Congo Reform Association
CSK	Comité spécial du Katanga
DRC	Democratic Republic of the Congo
DSP	Division spéciale présidentielle
EJCSK	Eglise de Jésus Christ sur la terre par le prophète Simon Kimbangu
FAC	Forces armées congolaises
FAR	Forces armées rwandaises (Habyarimana's army)
FAZ	Forces armées zaïroises (Mobutu's army)
FLNC	Front de libération nationale congolais
FPC	Forces politiques du conclave (Pro-Mobutu coalition)
HCR-PT	Haut-Conseil de la République / Parlement de transition

MARC	Mouvement d'action pour la résurrection du Congo
MLC	Mouvement de libération congolais
MNC	Mouvement national congolais
MPR	Mouvement populaire de la révolution
ONUC	Opération des Nations unies au Congo
Palu	Parti lumumbiste unifié
PDSC	Parti démocrate social-chrétien
PNP	Parti national du progrès
PSA	Parti solidaire africain
RCD	Rassemblement congolais pour la démocratie
RCD-ML	Rassemblement congolais pour la démocratie-Mouvement de libération (also known as RCD-Kisangani or RCD-Bunia)
RPA	Rwandese Patriotic Army
RPF	Rwandese Patriotic Front
SGB	Société générale de Belgique
TCL	Tanganyika Concessions Limited
UDI	Union des démocrates indépendants
UDPS	Union pour la démocratie et le progrès social
Uféri	Union des fédéralistes et des républicains indépendants
UGEC	Union générale des étudiants congolais
UMHK	Union minière du Haut-Katanga
UPDF	Ugandan People's Defence Force
Usor	Union sacrée de l'opposition radicale

Name Equivalency

Congo 1960	*Congo 2000*
Bakwanga	Mbuji-Mayi
Coquilhatville	Mbandaka
Elisabethville	Lubumbashi
Jadotville	Likasi
Léopoldville	Kinshasa
Luluabourg	Kananga
Paulis	Isiro
Port-Francqui	Ilebo
Stanleyville	Kisangani
Thysville	Mbanza-Ngungu

Mobutu's Zaire	
Bas-Zaïre	Bas-Congo
Haut-Zaïre	Haut-Congo
Shaba	Katanga

TO MARGARET

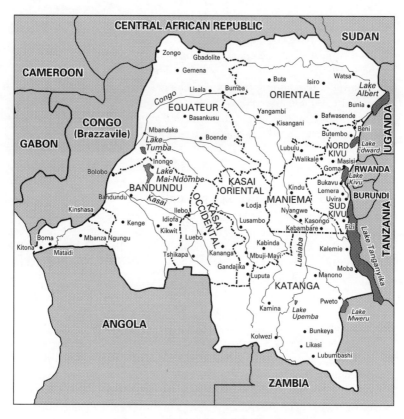

Democratic Republic of the Congo

Introduction

§ ON 4 August 1992, the overwhelming majority of the 2,842 delegates at the Congolese Sovereign National Conference in Kinshasa voted, to acclamation and standing ovation, to change the name of the country from 'Zaire' back to its original name of 'Congo'.[1] They also adopted a Transitional Charter or provisional constitution, according to which then President Mobutu Sese Seko was stripped of his executive powers but allowed to remain in office for two years as a ceremonial head of state. The international community chose to follow Mobutu in not recognizing these decisions as sovereign and binding on all parties. It chose to ignore them.

Five years later, on 17 May 1997, Laurent-Désiré Kabila changed all of this by a stroke of the pen. Having taken over Kinshasa by the force of arms after seven months of a virtually unchallenged long march, Kabila proclaimed himself president of a country he renamed the 'Democratic Republic of Congo'. This time, not only did the international community take notice of Mobutu's ouster and the change in the country's name, it moved quickly to recognize the new name and the new ruler.

The message that the world community of nations sent to the people of the Congo and Africa as a whole in these two instances is loud and clear. Changes through democratic means and the rule of law in Africa are not as deserving of unequivocal support as changes through the barrel of a gun. The first changes are slow and somewhat confusing, and seem to rely on universal principles of governance that some believe are not applicable to Africa. The second, on the other hand, are decisive and led by politically astute African leaders who are likely to establish stable political orders and market economies compatible with the interests of the developed North.

The preference for self-proclaimed rulers in place of democratically elected ones is symptomatic of the history of the Congo since its incorporation in the capitalist world economy in 1885. This is the year in which this vast country, more than 80 times the size of little Belgium, was ceded by the major world powers to King Leopold II of the Belgians as a personal possession. The system of personal rule with external backing established under the Leopoldian regime has been replicated in postcolonial Congo by Mobutu and Kabila, both of whom rose to power with foreign support.[2] In 40 years of existence as an independent state, the Congo has known only two democratically elected heads of government, Patrice Emery Lumumba and Etienne Tshisekedi wa Mulumba. They each held effective power as prime minister very briefly, Lumumba from 30 June to 13 September 1960, and Tshisekedi from 30 August to 30 November 1992. Both tenures were ended by a military takeover by Mobutu, on 14 September 1960 and 1 December 1992, respectively.

The Quest for Freedom and Prosperity

The negation of democracy and the popular will through Mobutu's usurpation of power in 1960, 1965 and 1992, and through Kabila's self-proclamation in 1997, were made possible by the external backing and/or endorsement that these actions obtained in the international community. For those external forces with a vested interest in the Congo's enormous size, geographical location and bountiful resource endowment, it is preferable to deal with rulers whom they can hope to influence and manipulate, rather than with democratically elected leaders who are accountable to their national constituencies. Given this reality, the struggle for democracy in the Congo is inextricably linked to the struggle for national liberation. It involves the quest for national sovereignty and genuine liberation from both colonialism and neo-colonialism in all its forms, as well as the ability of the Congolese people to freely determine their own destiny and to use their bountiful natural resources to improve their living conditions.

Did the country make any progress in this regard during the twentieth century? To this question, the people of the Congo can only answer in the negative. For they have known nothing but gross violations of their fundamental human rights since our country was established in 1885. Since then, the enormous wealth of the country has served not to meet the basic needs of the people but to enrich the country's rulers and their external political allies and business partners. The economic, social and moral decay of the Congo is thus a logical outcome of the country's integration, however imperfect, in the political economy of imperialism, on the one hand, and its rulers' insertion in the transnational networks of pillage and corruption, on the other.[3] In addition to Mobutu and Kabila, the rulers in question include the rebel warlords Jean-Pierre Bemba, Ernest Wamba-dia-Wamba and others. Under their control, the state has revealed itself as being primarily a simple tool of repression and wealth extraction for top officials and their foreign allies. It has been incapable of assembling the essential means and capabilities with which to generate economic growth and improve the living conditions of the masses.

This book is a study of the democracy movement in the Congo, from the standpoint of popular resistance to exploitation and repression, for a better social and political order. Although the initiative for political action and the intellectual leadership for it may come from outside the popular classes, it is always the latter's resistance that sustains the movement and enables it to weaken the enemy. The popular character of the struggle for democracy is often manifested through its reliance on memories of earlier resistance to oppression and on the ideas and values of popular culture, which are frequently expressed through religion and magic. Magico-religious beliefs and practices have character-ized popular resistance to political and social oppression from the days of the colonial conquest to contemporary struggles against dictatorship and external aggression. More recent examples include practices by the Simba and Mai-Mai resistance fighters of the 1960s and 1990s, respec-tively,[4] and the religious discourse of politically inspired popular songs at the time of the CNS.[5]

The democracy movement in the Congo is a struggle for political freedom and economic prosperity. That these two go hand in hand has never been in doubt there, given the character of Belgian rule as a colonial trinity of the state, the Catholic Church and large companies, as well as the continuation of economic exploitation and political repres-sion after independence. Thus, the independence struggle of the 1950s, the popular insurrections for a 'second independence' in the 1960s, the fight against Mobutu's one-party dictatorship, and the current struggle against new forms of dictatorship and external oppression have, as a common denominator, the demand for expanded rights politically and for a better life economically.

By looking at the democracy movement in this way, the book also seeks to analyse the relationship between the national liberation struggle and the class struggle, in an attempt to show that the crisis of the postcolonial state in Africa today can be traced to the breakdown of the anticolonial alliance of the masses with their nationalist leaders after independence. My working hypothesis is that the movement has failed to fulfill the people's aspirations for democracy and economic development because these aspirations were in marked discordance with the narrow class interests and political culture of the leaders of the movement.

The history of the democracy movement in the Congo consists of four major periods: (1) the independence struggle, from 1956 to 1960; (2) the 'second independence' movement, from 1963 to 1968; (3) the fight against Mobutu's dictatorship and reign of terror, from 1969 to 1997; and (4) the current struggle against new forms of dictatorship and external aggression. As a popular movement against political and social oppression, it has consisted in four specific moments of resistance: resistance to colonial rule (analysed here in Chapters 1–2); resistance to neocolonialism (Chapters 3–4); resistance to Mobutu's dictatorship and reign of terror (Chapters 5–6); and resistance to foreign aggression and new forms of dictatorship internally (Chapter 7). The book examines the strengths and weaknesses of the movement in each of these four periods. Two chapters are devoted to each of the first three periods, with the first chapter providing the historical background necessary for understanding the period, and the second describing in greater detail the specific characteristics of the democracy movement at the time, the major problems faced, and the lessons learned. Given its novelty and limited duration in the last century, the current period is dealt with in one chapter only.

The analysis itself is based on the theoretical insights from the classics of African liberation by Frantz Fanon and Amilcar Cabral.[6] As I have pointed out elsewhere, none of the contributions of Fanon and Cabral to our understanding of the national liberation struggle and the post-colonial state has been superseded by radically different analyses in the last 30 to 40 years.[7] Their writings are still pertinent for understanding the political history of popular struggles for freedom and economic development in Africa today.

The Congolese Democracy Movement in Historical Perspective

Chapters 1 and 2 look at the first period, which corresponds to the imperialist context out of which the Congo emerged as a modern state. As Cabral has pointed out, this is a context in which the absence of national representatives in the colonial power structure facilitates 'the creation of a broad front of unity and struggle that is vital to the success of the national liberation movement'.[8] As the one class of colonized society that had learned how to manipulate the colonial state apparatus, the petty bourgeoisie was in most cases the only class capable of leading the struggle for independence. Lacking a revolutionary consciousness, it sought primarily to replace the colonialists in the leadership positions within the state apparatus. To this end, it used the mass factor and exploited the threat of mass violence as a leverage for successful negotiations with the colonialists. Popular participation in the struggle was for the most part limited to public rallies, demonstrations and electoral politics.

The analysis for this phase begins with the examination of the roots of the anticolonial alliance in the Belgian Congo in the people's resistance against an oppressive colonial system. This provides the historical background necessary for understanding the major aspirations of this alliance and why its rank and file ultimately turned to a struggle for a 'second independence' when those aspirations went unfulfilled, with the triumph of neocolonialism and the rule of the so-called moderate leaders. The colonial system of economic exploitation, political repression and cultural oppression was built on the legacy of the Leopoldian system of primitive accumulation and crimes against humanity. As a good capitalist, King Leopold had resolved to make his private investment a profitable one, so as to raise money for himself and for Belgium's economic development. Based on state-sponsored terrorism, the exploitation regime resulted in a holocaust of millions of Congolese, which ended only as a result of the first major international human rights campaign of the twentieth century, the Congo reform movement.

As Fanon has suggested for Africa as a whole, resistance to colonial rule remained strong in rural Belgian Congo.[9] And, consistent with Terence Ranger's thesis on connections between primary resistance and modern mass nationalism,[10] it was strongest in those areas that had known precedents such as armed resistance to colonial domination. For it is precisely in such areas that mothers could, with ease, 'croon in their children's ears songs to which the warriors marched when they went out to fight the conquerers'.[11] But a culture of political struggle would also arise in areas where prophetic religious movements and peasant resistance to colonialism were strongest, as in the case of the regions of Lower Kongo, the birthplace of Kimbanguism, and Kwango-Kwilu, respectively.[12] With the third largest number of wage-earners in Africa, the Belgian Congo produced a relatively strong working-class movement and a class of white-collar workers from which the leadership of the nationalist movement emerged among middle-class civil servants known as *évolués*. Labour stabilization and postwar urbanization also resulted in the emergence of that permanent and unruly segment of the informal sector known as the *lumpenproletariat*.[13] By and large, it was these four social groups – peasants, workers, the *évolués* and lumpen elements – that made up the anticolonial alliance in the Congo.

Thus it is only when the fight for expanded rights by the *évolués* found a positive articulation with the Kimbanguist struggle for religious freedom, the peasants' resistance to colonial oppression and the workers' demand for better wages and working conditions that a veritable demo-cracy movement was born in the Congo in 1956. This is also the year of the Egyptian victory over imperialism at Suez, the independence of Morocco, Sudan and Tunisia, and of the birth of the independence struggle in Angola and Guinea-Bissau. These and other emancipatory winds of change from around the continent brought a great political awakening to the Belgian Congo, the 'model colony'. A major contribu-ting factor in this regard was the All-African People's Conference held in December 1958 in Accra, Ghana, where Lumumba met other leading figures of the Pan-African liberation struggle such as Frantz Fanon, Gamal Abdel Nasser, and the conference's convener, Kwame Nkrumah. The Kinshasa uprising of 4 January 1959, which launched the strategic slogan of 'immediate independence', took place in the aftermath of the Accra conference. Shocked by the violence of their presumably happy subjects and lacking the political will for an Algerian-type colonial war in an international context in which decolonization was the order of the day, the Belgians opted for a negotiated independence.

Chapters 3 and 4 deal with the second major period of resistance to oppression, the struggle for a 'second independence'. The crisis of decolonization, or what is better known as the 'Congo Crisis' of 1960–65, provides the background to this important period of the popular struggle for democracy in the Congo. It is significant that the very concept of 'second independence' is not of academic origin or a theoretical construct by a professional intellectual. It came out of the popular classes, from their own organic intellectuals, in the Kwilu region of the Congo. As a concept, it is consistent with Cabral's notion of the liberation struggle as consisting of two phases: the national phase, in which all classes of colonial society unite to fight the colonial system; and the social phase of reconstruction and transformation, in which the essential aspect of the problem is the struggle against neocolonialism.[14]

With the enemy defined as being both internal and external, it was inevitable that the national struggle became part and parcel of the Cold War. The moderate leaders of the neocolonial regime in Kinshasa were supported by the United States and its traditional allies in the region, namely Belgium, France, Israel and racist South Africa, while the Lum-umbist leaders of the movement enjoyed the backing of the Soviet Union, its Eastern European allies, China, Cuba and progressive African governments such as those of Algeria, Egypt, Ghana and Tanzania. Ernesto Che Guevara, the Argentine-born Cuban revolutionary, spent seven months as an instructor in a guerrilla camp in the mountains along Lake Tanganyika in 1965.[15] Laurent-Désiré Kabila, the commander of the guerrilla fighters in question, visited the camp only once during this entire period, as he spent most of his time pursuing a life of pleasure in Dar es Salaam and Kigoma, Tanzania.

The failure of the 'second independence' movement owes as much to its own internal weaknesses as to the externally led counter-insurgency, which included Belgian military experts, anti-Castro Cuban pilots working for the US Central Intelligence Agency (CIA), and white mercenaries from Europe, South Africa and Zimbabwe. Except for Pierre Mulele, who led the insurrection in Kwilu, the top leaders of the movement were neither revolutionaries nor democrats. They were for the most part politicians who simply wanted to regain the power they had lost after Lumumba's assassination. Their failure to practise good governance in the liberated territories, their tendency to resort to the divisive politics of ethnicity to hold on to power, and their business-as-usual politics of nepotism, corruption and repression could only result in a major setback to the democracy movement in the Congo.

The third and longest period in the struggle for democracy in the Congo coincides with the Mobutu regime, and particularly from 1969, the year of the first major confrontation with the student movement,[16] to Mobutu's demise in 1997. Chapters 5 and 6 are devoted to this period. The first of the two chapters examines the Mobutu regime as an externally backed and autocratic kleptocracy. Consistent with Fanon's anatomy of the postcolonial state,[17] this regime gave rise to a 'bourgeoisie of the civil service', or state bourgeoisie, which used party and state institutions as means of self-enrichment and social control. Instead of following 'the path of revolution', the new class stepped into the shoes of the former colonizers in maintaining the system and its reliance on the export of raw materials. However, it went further towards decadence in investing in foreign bank accounts and real estate, and in spending lavishly on luxury cars, fabulous marble villas, and all kinds of debauchery. Mobutu played the role of a neopatrimonial leader so well that he became the 'screen between the people and the rapacious bourgeoisie', standing 'surety for the ventures of that caste' and closing 'his eyes to their insolence, their mediocrity, and their fundamental immorality'.[18]

The economic, social and moral decay that this system produced came to be known as the 'Zairian sickness'. This was the sum total of the inversion of values, the immorality and the corruption that were eating up the social and moral fabric of the country. Consequently, a major objective of the fight against Mobutu's dictatorship and reign of terror was to reestablish the scale of values and to restore moral judgments on good and evil, right and wrong, and so on, in all human endeavours. The reconstruction of the economic and social infrastructure was seen as going hand in hand with the restoration of democracy, moral values and good manners. Democracy, in other words, had to be seen not simply as a system of good governance and a process of expanding political space and basic rights, but also as a moral imperative.[19] While it was Mobutu himself who first advocated moral regeneration with his ideology of 'authenticity' in the 1970s, his sincerity was called into question in the stinging 52-page letter that 13 members of parliament sent him in 1980 demanding the restoration of multiparty democracy. Their action launched the most important phase of this period of the democracy movement, which culminated with the holding of the CNS in 1991–92. These and related events are discussed in Chapter 6.

Chapter 7 examines the historical and geopolitical contexts of the last and current period of resistance to tyranny, from the fall of Mobutu in May 1997 to the assassination of President Laurent-Désiré Kabila in January 2001. For all practical purposes, the Mobutu regime as a system of personal and dictatorial rule ended on 24 April 1990, when internal and external pressures finally convinced him to replace the one-party system with multiparty democracy. But the wily dictator was able to hang on for seven more years. This was due to a number of factors, among others, the weakness of the democratic opposition; the resistance of his kleptocratic entourage to losing their power and privileges; and an international environment marked by a violent backlash to democracy by authoritarian leaders in Africa, the genocide in Rwanda, and the lack of genuine support for democracy and human rights in Africa by the major world powers. These factors form the background to the crisis of the Great Lakes region, whose major effects include the fall of Mobutu, Kabila's rise to power, and the regional war that erupted in August 1998.

These events, the last two in particular, have interrupted the transition to democracy that began in 1990. Having no experience in governing a modern state, no political base in the country, no political organization, and no political programme or societal project, Kabila was catapulted to power on the bandwagon of the Rwandan Patriotic Army (RPA) in its drive against the *interahamwe* militia and the remnants of the old army, the Forces armées rwandaises (FAR), which had taken refuge in the Congo. Instead of capitalizing on his new-found fame as the man who overthrew Mobutu, he refused to collaborate with the internal democratic forces that emerged from the National Conference and preferred to surround himself with Rwandans and Congolese adventurers from the diaspora with little knowledge of public affairs. Major James Kabarebe (or Kabare for short), a Rwandan military officer who grew up in Uganda, was named chief of staff of the new national army, the Forces armées congolaises (FAC). An admirer of the Ugandan model of the no-party state and still under the influence of the Stalinist model of one-party rule with which he became familiar in the 1960s, Kabila sought to close the political space of civil liberties that the Congolese people had dearly won during the last seven years of Mobutu's rule. Although political parties were banned and human rights activists jailed on a frequent basis, the banner of democracy was still held high by the independent press and civil society organizations.

Despised by those who had placed him in power and isolated politically at home and abroad, the Congolese president seemed so vulnerable in mid-1998 that those who had been plotting against him felt that it was only a matter of weeks before they got rid of him. But when Rwanda and Uganda and their Congolese allies launched their drive to oust Kabila in early August 1998, Angola and Zimbabwe moved in to save him. The resulting war, with its multiple actors from within and without, transformed what used to be a one-track movement for democracy into a multidimensional drive against external aggression and internal dictatorship. By 1999, the democracy movement had expanded its agenda to the fight for national independence and territorial integrity, in the face of a creeping occupation of the country and the systematic pillage of its natural resources by external forces, particularly Rwanda and Uganda. Most of the external forces were financing their war effort in the DRC with revenues from the Congo's own resources. As a former colony that financed its own colonization by Leopold and the Belgians, the Congo was witnessing history repeat itself.[20] The struggle for democracy had once again become synonymous with the struggle for national liberation.

In concluding the book, a brief look is taken at the prospects for peace, democracy and development in the Congo. Can the peace process under the Lusaka Agreement succeed in ending war and destruction in the Congo basin? Is it possible to reconcile the different political factions in the country to put the democratic transition back on track? Is the dawn of the new millennium going to rekindle faith in the capacity of the Congolese people to fulfill their aspirations for freedom and development under local, regional and central governments that truly represent the will of the people and in which the latter have confidence?

These are some of the questions that the book attempts to answer in summarizing the lessons of resistance and repression in the struggle for democracy in the Congo during the twentieth century. The lessons learned with respect to the strengths and weaknesses of the movement are examined from the standpoint of the internal and external environments under which it evolved. In this context, a particular emphasis is placed on the political limitations of the movement and the opportunities missed by its leaders, as well as on the constraints that the international environment imposed on their praxis.

Notes

1. The conference will hereafter be referred to as CNS, the abbreviation for the French original, Conférence nationale souveraine.

2. Prime Ministers Cyrille Adoula and Moïse Tshombe, who held legitimate power because of parliamentary approval in 1961–64 and 1964–65, respectively, were also imposed from the outside: Adoula by the United States through the United Nations Congo Mission, as we shall see in Chapter 3, and Tshombe by the United States and Belgium. Contrary to parliamentary tradition, Tshombe was not even a member of parliament; in 1960, he had chosen to run for the Katanga provincial assembly.

3. For a succinct description of these networks, see the four-article collection in *Le Monde diplomatique* of April 2000, 'Dans l'archipel de la criminalité financière'.

4. *Simba*, or 'lion' in Kiswahili, is the name by which the fighters of the 'second independence' movement in eastern Congo were known (see Chapter 5). Mai-Mai, from the word *mai* or 'water' in many Bantu languages, is used to designate various groups of local self-defence forces mobilized against Rwandan and Ugandan occupation troops in eastern Congo. Newer groups calling themselves Simba also joined the Mai-Mai in the popular resistance against the invaders from the east.

5. See Ndaywel è Nziem, *La société zaïroise dans le miroir de son discours religieux (1990–1993)*.

6. Fanon, *The Wretched of the Earth*. The best collections of Amilcar Cabral's speeches and writings are *Revolution in Guinea* and *Unité et lutte*; English trans.: *Unity and Struggle: Speeches and Writings*. Surprisingly, the English edition does not have two seminal essays on the social structure of Guinea-Bissau and Cape Verde, respectively.

7. Nzongola-Ntalaja, 'The Role of Intellectuals in the Struggle for Democracy, Peace and Reconstruction in Africa', Presidential Address delivered at the 11th Biennial Congress of the African Association of Political Science, Durban, South Africa, 23–26 June 1997, in *African Journal of Political Science*, Vol. 2, No. 2 (December 1997), p. 5.

8. Cabral, *Unity and Struggle*, p. 132.

9. Fanon, *The Wretched of the Earth*, pp. 92–102.

10. Ranger, 'Connexions between "primary resistance" movements and modern mass nationalism in East and Central Africa'.

11. Fanon, *The Wretched of the Earth*, p. 114.

12. See Demunter, *Masses rurales et luttes politiques au Zaïre: le processus de politisation des masses rurales au Bas-Zaïre*, for Lower Congo; and Weiss, *Political Protest in the Congo*, for Kwango-Kwilu.

13. According to Karl Marx, *Class Struggles in France (1848–1850)*, p. 50, 'the *lumpenproletariat*, which, in all big towns form a mass strictly differentiated from the industrial proletariat, a recruiting ground for thieves and criminals of all kinds, living on the crumbs of society, people without a definite trade, vagabonds, *gens sans feu et sans aveu*, with differences according to the degree of civilization of the nation to which they belong ... thoroughly malleable, capable of the most heroic deeds and the most exalted sacrifices, as of the basest banditry and the dirtiest corruption'.

14. Cabral, 'The weapon of theory', in Cabral, *Unity and Struggle*, pp. 119–37.

15. See Galvez, *Che in Africa*.

16. For a brief analysis of this episode, see Nzongola-Ntalaja, 'Confrontation in Congo Kinshasa'.

17. Fanon, *The Wretched of the Earth*, Ch. 3: 'The pitfalls of national consciousness', pp. 148–205.

18. Ibid., p. 168.

19. For this notion of democracy, see Nzongola-Ntalaja, 'The state and democracy in Africa'.

20. Marx, *The Eighteenth Brumaire of Louis Bonaparte*, p. 15, writes that with respect to facts and individuals of great importance, history repeats itself, 'the first time as tragedy, the second as farce'. The second rape of the Congo may appear as a farce, with externally sponsored warlords pretending to be heads of state in their respective enclaves, but its enormous tragic consequences for the Congolese people cannot be discounted.

. . . .

CHAPTER I

Imperialism, Belgian Colonialism and African Resistance

§ THE struggle for democracy in the Congo is a continuation of the fight against foreign domination, which dates back to the confrontation between African societies and European intruders in Central Africa at the end of the nineteenth century. By 1900, virtually all the African societies of present-day Democratic Republic of the Congo had lost their independence as a result of European conquest and occupation in the era of imperialism. Attempts to regain that independence within the boundaries of precolonial societies were doomed to failure, given the material superiority of the intruders, the new relations of production based on colonial capitalism, and the ideology of white supremacy. The anticolonial resistance of the people of the Congo arose within a restructured social space in response to the economic, political and social burdens of the new order. Its aims, which are the same as those of the current democracy movement, were the conquest of freedom as a fundamental human right and the basis on which personal dignity and social welfare can be built.

This chapter examines the roots of the Congolese democracy movement in the African resistance to colonialism in the Congo Free State (1885–1908) and the Belgian Congo (1908–60). This is done in three parts. The first part of the chapter provides the historical background to Belgian colonialism through a survey of the incorporation of the Congo into the capitalist world system beginning with the establishment of the personal rule of King Leopold II of the Belgians in 1885. The second part focuses on Belgian colonialism as a legacy of the Leopoldian system, and on its overall impact on the people of the Congo. The third and final part of the chapter looks at three different forms of African resistance to colonial rule: primary resistance, religious protest and revolts by peasants and workers.

Imperialism and the Establishment of European Rule in the Congo

The incorporation of the Congo and other African countries into the capitalist world economy in the twentieth century was the culmination of the establishment of trade relations between the African continent and Europe more than four to five hundred years earlier, in the fifteenth century.[1] During the five centuries that followed the creation of this connection, African–European relations were dominated first by the Atlantic slave trade, which constituted the primary means of primitive accumulation in the emerging global economy,[2] and then by the trade in the raw materials needed for industrial production in Europe. Until the onslaught of the east African slave trade and the slave-like Leopoldian regime in the 1840s and 1890s, respectively, much of the country was not exposed to these two historical processes. The areas most exposed to the latter were the Lower Congo, which formed a part of the Kongo kingdom, and those parts of Bandundu, Kasai and Katanga that were incorporated in the Luso-African trading frontier centred in Angola. The country as we know it today resulted from the imperial dream of King Leopold, his quest for access to the rich natural resources of Central Africa, and the imperial rivalries of the European scramble for Africa.

The Congo in the European scramble for Africa The Congo is centrally located in a vast area of linguistically and culturally related peoples, the overwhelming majority of whom speak Bantu languages. The Bantu-speaking majority entered the area many centuries ago in a series of migrations, gradually displacing the original inhabitants, a pygmoid population found today in small numbers in a few remote forest areas. Approximately 250 different ethnic groups inhabit the Congo, but most of them share many cultural traits. In addition to the linguistic unity binding the majority of the peoples of Central Africa, the Congo's ties to its immediate neighbours are reinforced by the fact that many of its ethnic groups straddle national boundaries. Examples include the Kongo, who are also found in Angola and Congo-Brazzaville; the Ngbandi, in the Central African Republic; the Zande, in Sudan; the Alur, in Sudan and Uganda; the Hutu, Tutsi and Twa, in Rwanda and Burundi; the Bemba, in Zambia; and the Lunda, in Zambia and Angola.

With Lake Tanganyika, the second-largest lake in Africa and fifth-largest in the world, separating them, Tanzania does not share a land border with the Congo. However, there are deep historical ties between the two countries. In the 1840s and 1850s, the Swahili-Arabs of Zanzibar and their Nyamwezi partners from western Tanzania brought the east

African long-distance trade in ivory and slaves to the interior of Central Africa. Unknowingly, they 'prepared the ground for the colonial conquest that followed in their wake'.[3] In addition to introducing Islam and Kiswahili to the Congo, the Swahili-Arab traders sold thousands of people into slavery in the Indian Ocean region, the Arab world and the Orient.[4] In the mid-1850s, a Nyamwezi trader by the name of Msiri brought his caravan west of the Luapula River and settled in Katanga, where he founded the state of Garenganze, with its capital at Bunkeya. Being Bantu speakers, the settlers were rapidly assimilated as a local ethnic group under the name of 'Yeke'. The assassination of Msiri in 1891 by a Congo Free State military officer marked the real beginning of the incorporation of the mineral-rich region of Katanga in the Belgian colonial empire.

Even before the full story of the Congo's wealth was known, this vast and fabulously rich real estate had attracted the envy of ambitious empire builders such as King Leopold. The bearded monarch followed with great interest the travels and adventures of missionaries and people sent out on reconnaissance missions in the various areas of the continent. One of the adventurers who caught the king's attention was the British-born American journalist Henry Morton Stanley. Having become famous for finding the British missionary David Livingstone in November 1871 at Ujiji, on the shores of Lake Tanganyika, Stanley travelled across the continent from Zanzibar to the mouth of the Congo River between 1874 and 1877, with the aim of reclaiming the Congo basin for Great Britain. Since Britain showed no interest in Stanley's project, Leopold made it his own and enticed Stanley to become his agent in the drive to colonize the Congo.

Aspiring to become a modern-day pharaoh, King Leopold began his African venture in September 1876, with the Brussels International Geographical Conference. Convened by the king, the Conference established an association of business entrepreneurs, geographers and physicians whose declared objectives were to learn more about Africa and to fight against the slave trade. Formally the honorary president of the Association internationale africaine (AIA), Leopold was the effective leader of the association and coordinator of the activities of the national chapters. He used his cunning and great diplomatic skills in disguising his colonial enterprise as a humanitarian venture for scientific research and economic development in Central Africa.

Once he had lured Stanley to his side, he created yet another organization, a financial syndicate whose name sounded like a research group, on 25 November 1878. The Comité d'études du Haut-Congo[5] included among its members the Belgian banker Léon Lambert, and William

Mackinnon, a British shipping magnate and founder of the Imperial British East Africa Company.[6] The king himself served as president and Stanley was chosen as head of the expedition to Africa. A year later, in December 1879, the Committee became the Association internationale du Congo (AIC), something 'confusingly similar to the AIA but in fact a wholly Belgian operation under Leopold's exclusive control'.[7] The king is said to have warned that 'care must be taken not to make it evident that the Association du Congo and the Association Africaine are two different things'.[8]

Stanley returned to Central Africa in 1879 and organized a large expedition designed to acquire for the king of the Belgians 'a slice of this magnificent African cake'.[9] Using duplicity and/or force, Stanley obtained 'treaties' from African rulers who, by placing a thumb mark on a piece of paper, ceded their territories to the AIC and its flag, a blue standard with a single gold star in the middle.[10] Using dynamite to build a road through rocky mountain ranges in Lower Congo, where the Congo River is not navigable due to rapids, Stanley earned the name of *Bula Matari*, or 'the smasher of rocks'.[11] He went on to establish administrative and trading stations along the river from Boma to Kisangani. Construction of the Kinshasa station on the south bank of the Malebo Pool opposite the French station on the north bank (Brazzaville) was completed in March 1882, and Stanley reached the site that came to bear his name at Wagenia Falls on 1 December 1883.[12] Establishing the minimum infrastructure of empire would keep Stanley in the Congo until June 1884. His work succeeded in providing King Leopold with the empire-building record he needed to justify his claims to the territories and resources of the Congo basin in Central Africa.

Using his personal fortune and diplomatic skills, the king moved rapidly to reap the rewards of Stanley's achievements by seeking the recognition of his self-proclaimed sovereignty over African territories in Central Africa from Portugal and the major imperialist powers, namely, Britain, France, Germany and the United States. With the help of an old friend and confidant, the former US Ambassador to Belgium, 'General' Henry Shelton Sanford, Leopold obtained a sympathetic ear from US President Chester Arthur, who called upon Congress to support what the king's lobbyist had presented as a humanitarian venture. After a 'rather incoherent' debate on 11 April 1884, the US Senate adopted a resolution recognizing the AIC flag as the 'flag of a friendly government'.[13] On 22 April 1884, the United States became the first country in the world to recognize King Leopold's claims to the Congo through a declaration by Secretary of State Frederick Frelinghuysen.[14]

With its claims to the right bank of Malebo Pool and its overall interests in Equatorial Africa, France represented a clear and present danger for Leopold's colonial scheme for the Congo. The king outsmarted the French policymakers by offering France a first option on his Congolese possessions should the AIC at some point in the future decide to divest itself of these acquisitions. Convinced that the ambitious king would eventually fail for lack of finances and support from Belgium, the French took the bait. They agreed to recognize Leopold's sovereignty in the Congo in return for preemptive rights or the first option on claims to the territory should Leopold relinquish it. In 1960, on the eve of Congo's independence from Belgium, France had to renounce this right of imperial succession.

With Paris and Washington behind him, Leopold had to confront the more difficult task of winning the approval of Berlin and London for his colonial scheme. Although he was an ethnic German and a cousin to Queen Victoria of Great Britain, the king had a hard time overcoming both the disdain of German Chancellor Otto von Bismarck, who had little patience for Leopold's grandiose pretensions, and the hostility of the British government, which feared that Belgian protectionism would threaten free trade in Central Africa. This concern for free trade by the greatest imperial power at the time had led Britain to back Portuguese claims to the Congo. Outraged by the Anglo-Portuguese agreement and eager to improve relations with France, Bismarck took advantage of the French endorsement of Leopold's scheme to grant Germany's formal recognition of the sovereignty of the AIC on 8 November 1884. Eventually, between 22 April 1884 and 23 February 1885, the AIC succeeded in obtaining through bilateral treaties the recognition of all the powers represented at the Berlin Conference except Turkey.[15]

The Berlin West African Conference, whose major focus was the freedom of navigation and commerce in the Congo basin, was held between 15 November 1884 and 26 February 1885. It was attended by delegates from 14 countries, namely, Austria-Hungary, Belgium, Denmark, France, Germany, Great Britain, Holland, Italy, Sweden-Norway, Portugal, Russia, Spain, Turkey and the United States.[16] The interests of the AIC were effectively represented by the Belgian delegation, which remained in constant touch with King Leopold in Brussels. The American lobbyist Sanford also attended the conference as an observer for the king. Although absent, the Belgian monarch had his interests articulated by a well-orchestrated public relations campaign. At the closing ceremony, when Bismarck read a letter from the AIC informing the conference of its recognition as a sovereign state by all the powers that mattered, the delegates rose and applauded loudly.[17]

That international recognition nearly coincided with the Berlin Conference resulted in the myth that the conference formally recognized King Leopold's Etat indépendant du Congo (EIC), or Congo Free State (CFS).[18] There is no provision for this in the Berlin Act. However, the announcement and the standing ovation constituted a symbolically strong endorsement of Leopold's enterprise by the imperialist powers, which were relieved for having finally resolved the Congo question. It is evident that in addition to Leopold's ability to use money and diplomacy to achieve his aims, rivalry among the major powers, each of which did not want to lose the Congo to another major power, accounted for his victory. For them, it was preferable to cede this vast territory in Central Africa to the king of a weak and little country such as Belgium, so as to maximize the chances of having this area serve as a free-trade zone for the more developed countries. The main question then, as it has been in the postcolonial period, is not so much who controls this resource-rich country as who should be excluded from such control.

The king took advantage of this international triumph to set up his personal rule in the Congo in 1885. In April the Belgian parliament passed a resolution authorizing him to be sovereign of two independent states simultaneously. This was followed by a royal decree on 29 May proclaiming the existence of the CFS, and Leopold's official accession as king-sovereign of the Congo on 1 August. As history would repeat itself on 24 November 1965 and on 17 May 1997, the people of the Congo were never consulted, and played no role in the proclamation of their absolute ruler.

Contrary to another widespread myth, the African continent was not partitioned at the Berlin Conference, where Europeans presumably drew up arbitrary territorial boundaries for Africa as a whole.[19] However, while partition was not part of the official business of the conference, more important negotiations took place behind the scenes in what amounted to preliminary *partition on paper*.[20] The real scramble for Africa or *partition on the ground* took place after the Conference, as European powers rushed to annex African territory through conquest. They attempted to comply with a basic ground rule of the Berlin Act, according to which *effective occupation* was the empirical test for legitimate claims to a colonial territory.[21] In reality, effective military, economic and administrative presence was not established in many a hinterland until 1900. Consequently, many claims were settled through negotiations between the colonial powers, although some cases were determined by the balance of power, as in the British–French confrontation at Fashoda.[22] According to the British historian Ruth Slade, the ultimate significance of the Berlin Conference was the arrogant belief that 'European powers had the right to annex African territory for their own advantage'.[23] Only Ethiopia under Emperor Menelik II succeeded in checking this arrogance, by its historic victory over Italy in 1896 at the Battle of Adwa.

The Congo case illustrates both the lack of effective occupation at the time of partition and the arbitrariness of territorial boundaries. Stanley's expedition, on which King Leopold's claims were based, had covered the territory along the Congo River from Boma to Kisangani. But when the two men sat down to draw up the original map of the Congo on 7 August 1884 at Ostend,[24] it covered a vast territory in Central Africa stretching 'from the coast to Lake Tanganyika, from four degrees north of the Equator to six degrees south'.[25] This is the map that Germany had reluctantly accepted in its bilateral treaty with the AIC on 8 November 1884. Anticipating French objections to the inclusion in this map of the Kouilou-Niari or Pointe Noire region, Leopold went into his study on Christmas Eve, 1884, to ponder over changes in the design. By the stroke of a pencil he modified the map, giving up the said territory in the southwest and adding in compensation new lands in the southeast. He extended the map beyond six degrees south of the Equator and annexed the Katanga region.[26] Although the adjustments made ultimately resulted in the loss of areas whose rich oil reserves were not yet known, such as Pointe Noire and the Cabinda enclave, they represented a masterful stroke with respect to Katanga, which was to prove extremely rich in minerals, particularly in its 'pedicle'.[27]

The new boundaries did eventually win international recognition, thanks in part to indifference by France and Germany, and to a 'stupid blunder' in Britain. When the new map arrived as an attachment to the CFS declaration of neutrality for Britain's consideration in August 1885, Sir Percy Anderson, head of the African section of the Foreign Office, was on summer vacation. His inexperienced assistant clerk, J. W. Warburton, referred the document for advice to John Bolton, a cartographer who had attended the Berlin Conference as an adviser to the British delegation. The expert replied that he saw no problem with the map, since it was basically the same as the one approved in Berlin.[28] Because of this erroneous conclusion – for no maps were approved at the Conference – Warbuton recommended that Her Majesty's government accept the boundaries of the Congo 'as laid down in Article 10 of the General Act of the Conference of Berlin'.[29] Since there is no mention of the Congo's borders in Article 10, the assistant clerk's confusion arose because this is the article that allows for the declaration of neutrality, which Leopold had used as a means of unilaterally declaring the boundaries of his new state. When Sir Percy returned from his vacation, he learned that the Foreign Office had given approval to something they did not have to consider, let alone accept. It was, he concluded, a 'stupid blunder'.

The consequences of this mistake for British interests in Central Africa became clearer later on, when rich mineral reserves were discovered in Katanga. On 29 May 1891, Anderson met with two representatives of the British South Africa Company of Cecil John Rhodes, the business entrepreneur and politician who had dreamt of a British empire stretching from the Cape to Cairo. To their question of whether they could raise the Union Jack in Katanga and make a treaty with King Msiri of Garenganze, he showed them King Leopold's declaration of neutrality of 1 August 1885 with its map attachment, to which Britain had made no objections.[30] Rhodes and his business partners had reasons to be furious, for London's blunder would eventually prevent them and Britain generally from having unlimited access to the rich mineral reserves of the copperbelt, which was now split between Northern Rhodesia (Zambia) and the Congo. Since 1884, external interests in the rich natural resources of the Congo have fuelled conflicts in this country and constituted a major reason why the Congo question is frequently on the international political agenda.

King Leopold II and the Congo holocaust Having acquired this vast and rich real estate, over 80 times the size of his Belgian kingdom, Leopold was resolved to make it a profitable enterprise. Since he had invested a lot of money in pursuing his prize – the high cost of expeditions, including steamboats and armaments; expenses for lobbying and public relations – he needed money to repay loans and to invest in the economic development of Belgium. According to the Belgian historian Jean Stengers, Leopold owned the Congo just as John Rockefeller owned Standard Oil.[31] As a good capitalist, the king had to judge the success of his colonial enterprise in strictly business terms, that is, in terms of whether or not it was profitable. Given the low level of the development of productive forces in the Congo, the king and his agents, who included quite a lot of Italians and Scandinavians (Danes, Norwegians and Swedes), had to resort to primitive accumulation. This meant the use of torture, murder and other inhumane methods to compel the Congolese to abandon their way of life to produce or do whatever the colonial state required of them.

Colonial accumulation was based on forced labour, which took on aspects of slave labour in the CFS, a political unit that was supposedly created as a humanitarian venture against slavery. As Auguste Maurel points out, while he funded anti-slavery conferences in Europe for purposes of misleading other imperialist powers as to his true intentions in Central Africa, 'Leopold II directly encouraged slave raids'.[32] There is ample evidence for this from Stanley's and CFS collaboration with Hamed bin Muhammed el-Murjebi, the Zanzibari slave trader who is better known by his caravan name of Tippu Tip, who had assisted Stanley in his first travels across the Congo.

Recognizing the Swahili-Arab presence east of the Lualaba River, Stanley seems to have convinced King Leopold to leave this area out of their Ostend map of the Congo. He justified his respect for Arab authority by the fact that 'we have come in presence of a people who might with some justice present [a] counterclaim to the territory, were we to cross the Lualaba'.[33] Moreover, the king, on Stanley's advice, did collaborate with the Swahili-Arabs, as the latter provided the CFS with 'freed slaves' as labourers and soldiers in exchange for money, while the two sides were also united in exploiting rivalries between the major powers.[34] Competition over the control of ivory, and not humanitarian impulse, pushed Leopold to change his Arab policy from collaboration to confrontation. Thus, between 1892 and 1894, the war against Swahili-Arab economic and political power was disguised as a Christian anti-slavery crusade by a colonial state whose brutal regime exceeded the worst horrors of Arab slavery.

Contrary to the free trade provisions of the Berlin Act, King Leopold proceeded to establish an economy controlled by the royal family and a few powerful trusts, including the Société générale de Belgique (SGB) and the Baron Empain banking group.[35] Although his preference was for Belgian capital, the emerging globalization of capitalist exploitation and the king's own interest in maintaining good relations with the major powers did provide an entry to the vast riches of the Congo for the bourgeoisies of other imperialist countries. Given the time it takes to build railroads, harbours and mining facilities, the economic role of most trusts yielded dividends only in the post-Leopoldian era. During his tenure, the king derived much of his wealth from the collection of rubber and ivory through forced labour.

The invention of the pneumatic or inflatable rubber tyre by the Scottish veterinary surgeon John B. Dunlop in 1887–88 and Edouard Michelin's patent of the tyre in 1891 resulted in the mass production of bicycles and the much-needed supply of a major component for the motor vehicle. These two developments created a large market for rubber tyres in the world economy.[36] King Leopold sought to capitalize on the abundance of rubber trees in the Congo to reap the rewards of the high demand for rubber on the world market. The king used his powers of eminent domain to create large land holdings from which he could derive huge profits. Paying no attention to indigenous land tenure systems, he created the fiction of 'vacant lands' by declaring the land previously used for shifting cultivation and hunting as vacant and therefore part of the public domain. Much of the country became either 'Crown domain' or the 'private domain of the state'. As landowners, the king and the state were major beneficiaries of the revenues derived from the collection of rubber and ivory on these supposedly vacant lands.

Beginning in 1891, the Congolese were required by law to supply labour, rubber and ivory to Leopold's agents. The killing of elephants for their tusks, whose ivory was greatly in demand abroad for piano keys and other goods, was carried out on a very large scale. More than the ivory, however, it was the collection of wild rubber that resulted in the depopulation of entire villages and the perpetration of heinous crimes against humanity in the Congo.[37] Villages unwilling or unable to meet the assigned daily quotas of production were subject to rape, arson, bodily mutilation and murder. Although this violence did not meet the definition of *genocide* in international law as 'acts committed with intent to destroy, in whole or in part, a national, ethnic, racial or religious group',[38] it resulted in a death toll of holocaust proportions that is estimated to be as high as 10 million people. Adam Hochschild has shown, persuasively, that this death toll was caused by three interrelated causes: (1) murder; (2) starvation, exhaustion, and exposure; and (3) disease.[39] A fourth cause of population decline in areas ravaged by the rubber campaign was a plummeting birth rate.[40] A population that was estimated to be between 20 and 30 million people at the beginning of the colonial era, was reduced to 8.5 million in 1911 and 10 million in 1924, according to official census data.[41]

In addition to the Leopoldian state, a few private companies were involved in this cruel and inhumane enterprise. These are companies to which the king had leased land as a concession on which they had exclusive rights of exploitation of all natural and human resources. In the rubber trade, two of the most notorious concession companies were the Anglo-Belgian India-Rubber Company (ABIR) and the Compagnie du Kasaï. As private companies that had to share their loot with the state, these rubber companies used extreme force to maximize their output. European company agents and their African overseers or *kapita* were ruthless in their regimental control of African work gangs. They frequently used the *chicotte*, a whip made from raw, sun-dried hippopotamus hide, to administer punishment to people who resisted orders or did not accomplish the required tasks on time.

The total subjugation of the inhabitants to the state and the concession companies made the CFS an 'independent state' of a peculiar type. Here was a state where the inhabitants were not citizens with democratic rights, but enslaved subjects of a sovereign they never saw. During his entire 23-year tenure as the Congo's king-sovereign, Leopold never put his feet on Congolese soil. He ruled the country as an absentee landlord or the majority owner of a joint-stock company who leaves day-to-day affairs to professional managers. He did not respect his international legal obligations to guarantee freedom from slavery and to promote free trade in the Congo basin. The only freedom that existed in this realm was for the Belgian king, his business partners and his agents to plunder the country as they saw fit. The spoils of plunder constituted huge capital flows into Belgium.[42] Reader summarizes some of the uses to which Leopold put the money as follows:

> Leopold displayed exceptional generosity in the disbursement of his newfound wealth. The Congo profits were used to fund a grandiose policy of public works and urban improvement – in Belgium. The magnificent Arcade du Cinquantenaire in Brussels, the famous Tervuren Museum, extensions to the Royal Palace, public works at Ostend, various urban building schemes – all were funded by the Congo Free State.[43]

That a significant part of Belgium's economic growth and development was based on slave labour in the Congo raises the question of reparations for the economic plunder and political repression suffered by Africans for the benefit of Europeans. If it is morally right for Germany to pay reparations to Israel for the atrocities committed by the Nazis against Jews and to people who were coerced into slave labour during the Second World War, and if Iraq should be forced to pay reparations to some Persian Gulf countries because of the consequences of its invasion of Kuwait, why is it wrong for former colonial powers such as Belgium to pay reparations for the heinous crimes they committed in the African territories they administered?

The Congo reform movement King Leopold's impressive achievements were built as a result of slave labour and the crimes of rape, torture, bodily mutilation and murder. These crimes, as the fictional character Kurtz shows in Joseph Conrad's novel *Heart of Darkness*, were a necessary component of the plunder. This is what the African American historian and journalist George Washington Williams saw during his journey across the Congo in 1890. It is his testimony that brought to the world the first detailed account of King Leopold's holocaust of the Congolese people, atrocities that Williams himself characterized as 'crimes against humanity'.[44]

Another African American, the Reverend William Henry Sheppard, played a prominent role in the international human rights campaign against King Leopold's rule in the Congo. A Presbyterian missionary and co-founder with the Reverend Samuel Lapsley of the American Presbyterian Congo Mission (APCM) in 1891, Sheppard became actively involved, alone or with his white colleague William Morrison, in bearing witness to the world on the suffering of the Congolese people at the hands of the king's men. Their reports, together with those of the British consul and Irish nationalist Roger Casement, helped to launch the first major human rights organization and campaign of the twentieth century, the Congo Reform Association (CRA).[45] Led by Edmund Dene Morel, a young and dynamic British shipping clerk, the CRA did with very limited resources what organizations such as Amnesty International, Human Rights Watch and others are doing today to mobilize world public opinion against gross violations of human rights around the globe. In the United States, the CRA was ably represented by the writer Mark Twain, whose satirical book *King Leopold's Soliloquy* is a classic,[46] and the African American leaders Booker T. Washington and W. E. B. DuBois.[47] The American chapter of the CRA was organized through the Massachusetts Commission of Justice by Robert Ezra Park, who served as secretary of the CRA between 1904 and 1905.[48]

Sheppard and Morrison were sued for libel by the Compagnie du Kasaï for an article that Sheppard had published in the January 1908 issue of the *Kasai Herald*, the APCM newsletter, on the negative social consequences of company rule among the Kuba people of western Kasai.[49] The case became an international *cause célèbre* as the CRA, US newspapers, and progressive opinion generally came to the defence of the two missionaries. Emile Vandervelde, president of the Second International and the socialist leader in the Belgian parliament, went to Kinshasa to represent the defendants in court, *pro bono*. When the proceedings began in September 1909, charges were dropped against Morrison for refusing to retract the article. He was the leader of the APCM in Luebo and the newsletter editor.

While Vandervelde's defence was superb, Hochschild is correct in maintaining that 'it was politics, not Vandervelde's eloquence or the missionaries' prayers, that dictated the results'.[50] The judge acquitted Sheppard on a technicality, that his article accused charter companies in general and did not specifically mention the Compagnie du Kasaï. Since US authorities had made it known that the outcome of the trial might have a bearing on Washington's recognition of the transfer of authority from Leopold to Belgium, a warning that remained evident with the presence in the courtroom in Kinshasa of the American consul-general and vice-consul, the judge knew what Belgium expected of him. At the same time, he also protected his job by not condemning the company for its atrocious rule, although he forced it to pay court fees.[51]

Sheppard's trial won him praise at home as a hero of the Congo for his work in denouncing the abuses of the Leopoldian system. According to the *Boston Herald*, 'Dr. Sheppard has not only stood before kings, but he has also stood against them. In pursuit of his mission of serving his race in its native land, this son of a slave ... has dared to withstand all the power of Leopold.'[52]

Another hero of the Congo and pan-African solidarity in the human rights campaign against King Leopold was Hezekiah Andrew Shanu, a Nigerian.[53] Born in Lagos in 1858, Shanu was educated there at the Church Missionary Society's elementary school, where he also taught until 1884. He joined King Leopold's Congo service in 1884, first as a recruiter of soldiers for the Force publique in his homeland, and later as clerk and French–English translator in the office of the governor-general at Boma. He left state service to go into private business in 1893, and became one of the most successful African entrepreneurs in Boma, where he owned a well-stocked store, a tailor's shop, a laundry and a guest house.[54] During an 1894 trip to Europe, he lectured on the Congo in Belgium, and also visited England, France and Germany.

An independent whose businesses were heavily patronized by Europeans, Shanu was praised and decorated by state officials, who used his collaboration in checking and putting down unrest among Africans during the Boma army mutiny of 1900. By 1903, for reasons that remain unclear, Shanu changed camps and started to collaborate with Morel, sending to the CRA leader information and documents that Morel published with detailed analysis in British newspapers and in books and pamphlets, with devastating consequences for the Leopoldian enterprise in the Congo. In 1904, the police chief of Boma tricked Shanu into acting as liaison between him and Morel, and then denounced him as Morel's accomplice. Consequently, he was ostracized in Boma, and Europeans boycotted his businesses. Facing ruin, Shanu committed suicide at the end of July 1905. In a warm tribute to the Nigerian-Congolese in the *West African Mail* of 8 September 1905, Morel wrote that Shanu 'fell as a victim of the struggle for justice'.[55]

The major achievements of the Congo reform movement go beyond its success in bringing pressure on the major powers to end the Leopoldian regime in Central Africa. With limited financial resources but with abundant energy, E. D. Morel was a great organizer who succeeded in combining investigative journalism with humanitarianism into an effective tool of political action.[56] In addition to producing a remarkable amount of documents for the historical record, including photographs of mutilated people, the movement helped to keep alive a tradition of humanitarian concern by non-governmental organizations (NGOs) about human rights abuses anywhere in the world.[57]

Hochschild depicts the CRA as a radical movement that went beyond the concerns of today's human rights groups with *results* to talk about *causes*, namely, 'the theft of African land and labor that made possible Leopold's whole system of exploitation'.[58] While this is true, the CRA did not represent a radical departure from humanitarianism as a social practice, because Morel and his partners did not call into question the colonial and imperialist bases of that system of exploitation.[59] They were still dealing more with the *symptoms* of the Congo problem, the atrocities and a particular form of colonial practice responsible for them, rather than with its *root causes*, the subjection of a people's entire social process to foreign domination.[60] They were concerned with the question of *reforming* colonialism rather than *abolishing* it. Their triumph, the transformation of the Congo from Leopold's personal possession to a Belgian colony in 1908, did not represent a major advance for the Congolese people and their quest for freedom and self-determination. For no radical change took place as a result of the action taken by the Belgian parliament ending the king's exclusive rule and territorial rights. The Leopoldian system was replaced by a colonial regime that was just as oppressive, albeit in a less brutal manner.

The Belgian Colonial System

As a colony, the Belgian Congo was strongly marked by the Leopoldian legacy as a system of economic exploitation, political repression and cultural oppression. When Belgium took over the running of the Congo in 1908, the Belgian government had to operate on the basis of what had already been established economically and administratively since 1885. According to Roger Anstey:

> Belgium inherited not only a colony, but a colony possessed of a certain structure. The elements of that structure were a sparse population and a battered customary society; a vast territory which had not been properly administered; a system of direct economic exploitation, or an unfettered variant of the concessionnaire system, and, as a consequence at a further remove, abuse and atrocity. Thirdly, the fact that the Congo was a legacy meant that Belgium had no relevant tradition of policy to invoke, no positive aims regarding it.[61]

Anstey thus refutes the assertion of those who, like Jean Stengers, would have us believe that after 1908 'the special characteristics of the Congo

Free State disappeared or were effaced, giving way to grey-haired ortho-doxy' in colonial matters.[62] On the contrary, Anstey shows that the legacy of the Leopoldian regime was crucial in determining not only 'the early lines of Belgian conduct in the Congo', but also the subsequent trends in Belgian colonial rule. He writes that 'there was no major departure from the broad lines of the original Belgian comportment in the Congo which the legacy had done so much to determine, though certainly there was refinement of that comportment'.[63]

The first step towards this refinement, and one that was partially meant to mollify public opinion in Europe and North America, was the adoption of a colonial constitution, the *charte coloniale*, which was drafted by men presumably committed to 'grey-haired orthodoxy' in colonial affairs, some of whom were major shareholders in Belgian companies with interests in the colony. With a Catholic party in power in Brussels and major companies represented in the colonial policy process, it was evident that the second Belgian regime in the Congo would rely on the alliance of the state with the Catholic Church and large corporations to continue the triple mission of economic exploita-tion, political repression and cultural oppression in Central Africa. More clearly than elsewhere, it was in the Belgian Congo – the 'model colony' of imperialist propaganda during the 1950s – that a perfect fit obtained between the 'colonial trinity' and these three features of the colonial system under imperialism.[64]

Economic exploitation The Congo occupies an area of 2,345,409 square kilometres in the heart of Africa. It is landlocked, except for a coastline of 40 km containing the mouth and lower reaches of the Congo River, which connects the country to the Atlantic Ocean. The third largest country in Africa after Sudan and Algeria, it shares borders with nine other countries in Central, East and Southern Africa. Economically, the country has enormous wealth in natural resources. Known primarily as a minerals-producing country, it has such an ecological diversity that it is also rich in non-mineral goods, including forest and water resources. Approximately 77 per cent of the total land area of 2,2267,600 sq. km is made up of forests and woodlands, including the tropical rainforest in the equatorial zone; the Mayombe Forest near the west coast, another important source of marketable timber; and the productive woodlands and grasslands of the savannah zones north and south of the equator. The natural vegetation comprises many valuable tropical trees such as ebony and mahogany, which are indigenous, as are wild rubber trees, palm trees, grape-vines, plantain and banana trees. Coffee, tea and cotton plants are also major agricultural products.

The animal life of the Congo is as profuse as its vegetation. Large and small mammals, birds and reptiles are found all over the country, while rivers and lakes are stocked with many kinds of fish. There are seven great lakes in the country, four of which are located along the eastern border in the Great Lakes region, and hundreds of rivers and smaller lakes. The whole country is drained by the Congo River and its many tributaries. The second longest river in Africa and fifth longest in the world, the Congo is second in the world after the Amazon with respect to hydroelectric potential.

The Congo has a wide array of minerals, including copper, cobalt, tin, zinc, gold, diamonds, iron ore, silver, cadmium, uranium, europium, niobium (or columbite), tantalum and thorium. Some of these minerals are of great strategic value. Uranium, for example, has been used to manufacture nuclear weapons, while rare metals such as niobium and tantalum are greatly needed for space aeronautics in the twenty-first century. According to experts, Africa contains 15 per cent of the world's niobium reserves and 80 per cent of its tantalum deposits. Of these African reserves, the Congo alone has 60 per cent of the niobium and 80 per cent of the tantalum.[65] These metals, together with other highly valued resources such as methane gas from Lake Kivu, are concentrated in the northeastern region of the country, which also possesses large quantities of gold, diamonds, coffee, tea and timber. Although it is not a major oil producer, the Congo exploits some crude oil offshore, in its territorial waters along the 40-km strip of the Atlantic Ocean.

The fourth and most important mission of the Compagnie du Katanga in 1892 laid the foundation for mineral exploitation, thanks to the excellent prospecting work done by a young Belgian geologist, René Jules Cornet. His revelations of the immense mineral reserves of Katanga earned for the country as a whole its international notoriety as a 'veritable geological scandal'.[66] The real scandal, however, is that in 110 years of mineral extraction, the wealth of the country has not been used to the benefit of the great majority of its people. Since the days of King Leopold, it has gone to serve the interests of the country's rulers and those of their political allies and business partners in the international community. This is why public control of the country's resources and their utilization for the development needs of the people are two of the major demands of the national and democratic movement. They are part and parcel of the struggle for national liberation and democratic governance.

Economic exploitation in the Belgian Congo was built on the legacy of the Free State, according to which the Congo served as a major source of capital accumulation for Belgium. Having provided the revenue for the construction of public buildings, highways and other public projects dear to King Leopold, the colony rescued the metropolitan power out of financial troubles during and after both world wars. An eloquent testimony in this regard is provided by the following statement on the Congo's vital support for the moribund Belgian state during the Second World War by Robert Godding, the Belgian colonial affairs minister in 1945–46:

> During the war, the Congo was able to finance all the expenditures of the Belgian government in London, including the diplomatic service as well as the cost of our armed forces in Europe and Africa, a total of some 40 million pounds. In fact, thanks to the resources of the Congo, the Belgian government in London had not to borrow a shilling or a dollar, and the Belgian gold reserve could be left intact.[67]

The colony was able to do this because of the war effort (*l'effort de guerre*), which imposed severe hardships on the Congolese people. In normal circumstances, able-bodied men with no wage employment were required to work on public projects such as road maintenance, building guest houses for itinerant administrators, and so on, for a total of 60 days per year. During the war, this period of forced labour was extended to 120 days, and included some of the most hated tasks dating back to the CFS, such as porterage and the collection of wild rubber. The economic and social consequences for the people were devastating. Hunger, starvation and death were once again destroying entire families, as people were constantly harassed by the security forces and unable to find time and energy for food cultivation. Those who were old enough to suffer through these hard times remember the Second World War as a particularly painful episode in their lives, although they never understood what their suffering and the white man's war itself were all about.

Congolese soil and labour also contributed to the war effort of the anti-fascist alliance at the global level, by supplying the uranium that Americans used to make the first atomic weapons, the bombs they dropped at Hiroshima and Nagasaki. A major consequence of this development was that the United States found for itself a vital national interest in the strategic minerals of the Belgian Congo, including uranium, copper, cobalt and industrial diamonds. This strategic interest expanded in the postwar period to imply a Western stake in preventing the Soviet Union and its allies from gaining influence in Central Africa.

The uranium came from the Shinkolobwe mine of the Union minière du Haut-Katanga (UMHK), the giant mining company and the single most important business enterprise in the Congo's economy. Established on 18 October 1906 under King Leopold's rule and with direct ties to the royal family, the UMHK was a modern capitalist corporation built by a group of interlocking Belgian trusts under the leadership of the SGB and foreign interests. The oldest of the colonial companies created by this partnership was the Compagnie du Congo pour le commerce et l'industrie (CCCI), the dean of Congo trusts, established in 1887. A major holding, its control passed on to the SGB after 1928. Created to promote industry, commerce, agriculture, finance and public works, the CCCI had as its first priority the construction of the Lower Congo railroad. For this purpose, a subsidiary company, the Compagnie du chemin de fer du Congo (CFC) was created in 1890 with 60 per cent of the initial capital subscribed by Belgian, British and German private groups, and 40 per cent by the Belgian state.[68] Built at the cost of thousands of lives, including those of labourers imported from West Africa, Barbados and China, the railroad was completed in 1898.

Other major corporations established shortly before the transfer of power from the king to Belgium included the Compagnie des chemins de fer du Congo supérieur aux Grands Lacs (CFL), a major concession company for the Great Lakes region; the Société internationale forestière et minière (Forminière), which became involved in mineral and timber exploitation in Kasai; and the Compagnie du chemin de fer du Bas-Congo au Katanga (BCK), a railroad company with extensive land and mineral rights. The BCK was the second largest and most important company after the UMHK in Katanga, the most economically important region of the Belgian Congo. As a corporation, its economic and historical significance was twofold. First, the BCK Railroad provided a much-needed connection between the Katanga mining industry and the international ports of Matadi in the Congo, Lobito and Benguela in Angola, and Beira in Mozambique. This was done by way of river transportation on the Kasai from Ilebo to the Kinshasa–Matadi railroad; through the Benguela Railway from Dilolo; and through the Rhodesian and Portuguese rail systems from Sakania. Second, the BCK Railroad transformed the landscape along the line of rail and contributed immensely to the development of commercial and administrative towns along the entire length of the network, or 1,820 kilometres from Ilebo to Sakania, and 520 kilometres from Tenke to Dilolo.[69]

Imperial rivalries between Belgium and Great Britain over the control of this region and its economy played a major role in shaping the history of Katanga. In 1899, the establishment of the British South African Company (BSAC) with a royal charter to govern and exploit regions north of the Cape and the Transvaal, posed a threat to Leopold's Congo venture, inasmuch as Cecil Rhodes was known to dream of a second Rand north of the Limpopo River, extending all the way to

Katanga. Although Africans had exploited copper and iron before colonialism in Katanga, the persistent rumours among European travellers
focused instead on their gold fantasies. The king ordered the CCCI to
urgently send a mission to Katanga for purposes of establishing CFS
rule and prospecting for minerals.

Following the then current practice, the CCCI set up a concession
company with exceptional rights and powers to ensure the effective
occupation, administration and mineral exploration of Katanga. The
Compagnie du Katanga was thus created on 15 April 1891, with a
concession measuring one-third of the region's territory, the other two-
thirds remaining the exclusive property of the state, which received in
return 10 per cent of shares in the new company.[70] In the face of King
Msiri's categorical refusal to submit to the authority of the CFS, a
European officer shot and murdered him in cold blood on 28 December
1891. Having overcome the last African resistance to the imposition of
colonial rule in south Katanga, Leopold's agents could now go about
the business of finding ways and means for the extraction of copper
and other minerals.

Practical difficulties of organization and governance eventually led
the state and the company to put their assets together and entrust the
management of their joint venture to a new organization, the Comité
spécial du Katanga (CSK), in 1900. The CSK became the real landlord
and government of the Katanga province. Until independence in 1960,
the CSK was one of three major mixed economy corporations sharing
concessionary authority in land and mineral rights with the state. The
other two were the CFL and the Comité national du Kivu (CNKi).
The major achievement of the CSK was the creation of the UMHK.[71]
The number one firm in Katanga and the Congo, the UMHK, was
established as a compromise between King Leopold and the British
entrepreneur Robert Williams, owner of Tanganyika Concessions
Limited (TCL).

One of Rhodes's partners, Williams and his TCL had in 1899 begun
mineral prospecting in Zambia and negotiations with the Compagnie
du Katanga. When the UMHK was established, the TCL held 14.5 per
cent of the shares, as against 25.1 for the CSK; 4.5 per cent for the SGB,
Belgium's main financial holding company; and over 50 per cent for
other Belgian and foreign financial groups.[72] In addition to the CFS
participation through the CSK, several Belgian financial groups represented King Leopold's interests. On the other hand, 48 per cent of the
TCL shares belonged to British banks such as Barclay's, Midland, Baring
and Rothschild. In 1921, when its resources became tied up in the
construction of the Benguela Railway, the TCL share in the UMHK

stock dropped from 45 to 16 per cent, and the company passed under the control of the SGB.[73]

Although Leopold and his successors did their best, and with success, to give greater weight to a Belgian national interest in the Congo's economy in general and in the mining sector in particular, the tendency of capitalist exploitation to become transnational, or what is known today as globalization, did provide an entry to the vast riches of this country for the bourgeoisies of other imperialist countries. The British and their South African partners were actively involved in the life and work of the UMHK through companies such as the TCL and Robert Williams and Company, a labour recruitment firm that supplied white and black workers from Southern Africa to the UMHK.[74] The TCL was also the majority owner of the Benguela Railway, the best route for the mineral exports from Katanga through the Angolan ports of Lobito and Benguela. Just how significant this entry as well as the subsequent integration of the entire copper mining region in the Southern African economic complex would prove to be in the international class struggle was later demonstrated by the British and South African support for the Katanga secession (1960–63).

Other powers had their vested interests in the Congo, but to a much lesser degree than Britain. If the American stake became stronger after 1940, the Ryan and Guggenheim groups were already involved since 1906 with the Forminière in diamond mining, and the Rockefeller group had some interests in the CCCI. German concerns were also involved in the CCCI, and Australian prospectors played a major role in locating gold deposits in the northeast. As Maurel suggests, 'this tendency towards the internationalization of the Congo under the leadership of some world monopolies explains sufficiently the gravity of the 1960 crisis, which threatened the common financial interests of Belgian, British, American and French imperialisms'.[75]

As for its impact, colonial exploitation brought about the plunder of human and natural resources, and transformed African societies by subjecting them to capitalist relations of production. Peasant production was progressively subordinated to the export requirements of monopoly capital for agricultural raw materials. The traditional ruling class, formerly the chief beneficiary of rural surplus labour, was incorporated into the authority structure of the colonial state to facilitate its extractive and repressive tasks, including tax collection, labour recruitment, conscription and order maintenance. Artisanal or simple commodity production lost much of its indigenous character, becoming an appendage to the capitalist commodity market and service sector, with the bulk of its activities located in the so-called informal sector of the economy.

Whatever chances African merchants who were active in the precolonial trading frontiers had of developing into a comprador bourgeoisie were eventually destroyed both by the trading monopoly granted to concession companies and the discriminatory policies favouring European and Asian merchants and protecting them from African competition.

Political repression The political institutions of kingdom were the dominant forms of state in Central Africa at the time of European penetration and conquest. They corresponded to social formations based on agricultural production wherein central authorities played a crucial role in the promotion of long-distance trade. The political systems in what was to become the Congo had comprised the Kongo, Kuba, Luba, Lunda and other savannah kingdoms whose peoples had been actively involved in the Luso-African trading frontier that emerged in Angola in the sixteenth century. Their future compatriots to the north and the east were part of the Swahili-Arab or east African frontier, which made contacts with Angola through the Nyamwezi in the late 1850s. Later on, its impact was felt as far away as Kinshasa to the west, through the medium of the riverine trade on the mighty Congo, and the Kasai to the south, through the slave raids of Ngongo Lutete, Lumpungu and Mpania Mutombo.[76]

Belgian trading and administrative stations began to supersede the old trading frontiers by the end of the nineteenth century. The expansion of the administration went hand in hand with the expansion of trade and the progressive integration of the country in the capitalist world-economy.[77] The colonial state accelerated this process by bringing all the major African political systems under its effective control and by subjecting the population to new methods of exploitation and control, including taxes in labour and in money, concession companies exercising a trading monopoly throughout a wide geographical area, labour recruitment for work in mines and on railroads, and so on. As a system of economic exploitation based on forced labour, Belgian colonial rule constituted a classic case of colonialism in that a colony was able to finance not only its own affairs but also the economic development of the metropolitan power. There was continuity in this regard between Leopold's CFS and the Belgian Congo. In 1921, Louis Franck, then Belgian minister of colonial affairs, wrote quite honestly that the first major goal of Belgian colonialism in the Congo was to develop 'the economic action of Belgium'.[78] This meant that colonial administrators had to give as much attention to peasant agricultural production and to labour recruitment for large companies as they gave to maintaining law and order.

During the early period of Belgian colonialism, the state's authority was established through company rule in large parts of the country, which were ceded to concession companies. Contrary to what historians such as Stengers have suggested, company rule did continue beyond 1908. A good example in this regard is the situation that the Reverend Sheppard and other Presbyterian missionaries witnessed among the Kuba, where rule by the Compagnie du Kasaï lasted from 1905 to 1910. According to Jan Vansina, this period of company rule in the Kuba kingdom was a period of atrocities.[79] The company held a monopoly over trade, and it was the only buyer to whom people could sell rubber in order to pay their taxes. These were collected for the company by King Kot aPe, who played the role of company agent in order to maintain his throne. In 1908, the company itself employed about 285 *kapita* or auxiliaries, who acted as armed rubber buyers and collectors, with one *kapita* per village. These African mercenaries were quick to use the gun to oppress villagers and to force them to produce more rubber. During the same year, there was food shortage and widespread hunger throughout the area.

In addition to using African chiefs and *kapita* as auxiliary agents, concession companies employed European contractors to recruit labour for them, a task for which they obtained the assistance of the state and some Christian missionaries. Before railroad construction was completed in the late 1920s and early 1930s, all Africans so recruited for work in the mining and related industries from areas as distant as Maniema and Kasai, went to Katanga on foot.[80] Europeans, on the other hand, were carried in hammocks and continued to be so well treated long after porterage was officially outlawed in 1926. Estimates are still needed for the number of people who died during all these long marches and in the construction of railroads. People who were adolescents in the 1910s and 1920s have told horror tales concerning the kidnapping of villagers for slave labour, the brutality of labour-recruiting agents and work gang foremen, and the manner in which people living along the lines of rail were coerced into feeding those who worked on the railroads.

State rule, when it was finally established at the local level, did not differ significantly from company rule. In setting up its rule, the state itself brought along new exigencies. These included not only the usual requirements for labour and taxes, but also a whole new set of regulations governing virtually all aspects of one's life. Crawford Young points out that the Belgian colonial state distinguished itself from others by its deeper penetration and greater organization of the countryside:

More familiar, and most unpopular, was the agricultural officer, of which there was at least one per territory, seconded by several African *moniteurs* with rudimentary training to bring the administrative system in contact with virtually all the population. Legislation permitting 60 days per year (45 after 1955) of compulsory cultivation (or other public works) was generally applied until 1957 and was still legally authorized, although largely abandoned, in 1960.[81]

Eventually, the colonialists understood that the best way to bring the administrative system in contact with the rural population was to utilize traditional African rulers or chiefs. In the beginning, despite the recognition of the traditional political organization in the 1891 decree on local administration, the post-conquest period was characterized by a sharp decline in the prestige of customary chiefs. They were deposed at will by colonial officials, who did not trust them, and replaced by loyal clerks, soldiers or domestic servants. It did not take long for the Belgians to understand that colonialism, like any other form of alien rule, cannot succeed in maintaining effective control without reliable local allies. The colonial administration became preoccupied with the question of declining chiefly prestige, and a 1900 report to King Leopold described the new approach to local administration as that of finding a popular intermediary with enough influence on the masses to maintain their obedience. For the newly enlightened colonialists, that intermediary was the traditional chief, the only person then capable of generating such obedience.

In line with this new policy, a series of decrees on local colonial administration in 1906, 1910 and 1933 succeeded in progressively transforming the chiefs into subaltern functionaries of the colonial administration. Their major task was to ensure that their administrative units adequately met what was known in colonial discourse as their 'collective obligations to the state'.[82] These included compulsory cultivation of certain export crops, conscription, forced labour on public projects, labour recruitment and taxes. Fulfilling these obligations in a satisfactory manner meant hardships for ordinary people but political and economic rewards for the chiefs. It succeeded in setting the chiefs against their own people.

The chiefs and other customary officials were part of a political system that answered perfectly to definitions of the colonial state by James S. Coleman and Ruth First as a 'pure bureaucratic state'.[83] In the face of a distant political supervision by the Belgian parliament and colonial affairs ministers in Brussels, the colonial bureaucracy constituted the state and held the effective power of governance. However, it ruled in alliance with other representatives of the Belgian bourgeoisie who served as managers of large enterprises and in the hierarchy of the Roman Catholic Church. Representatives of these two groups, along with a few others from the liberal professions, sat in important advisory bodies such as the Conseil colonial, the Conseil de gouvernement and the Conseil provincial, the last two established in 1914.[84]

The governor-general of the colony, in Boma since the Free State days and in Kinshasa from 1929 to 1960, held nearly despotic powers under a strong prefectorial system of French inspiration.[85] He had both executive and legislative powers. Until the administrative reform of 1933, he was assisted by a vice-governor-general in Katanga, appointed by the CSK due to the special status of this province, and by vice-governors in the other provinces. A second vice-governor-general was appointed for Rwanda and Burundi, as these two territories were annexed to the Congo in 1925 as a unit of a single administrative entity known as 'Le Congo belge et le Ruanda-Urundi'. Having conquered with Congolese troops these two territories of German East Africa during the First World War, Belgium formally took over their administration as a mandatory power under the League of Nations in 1921. In 1945, it became the administrative authority under the United Nations trusteeship system.

As the last major change in the colonial administrative system before the decolonization period, the 1933 reform established the basic structures of prefectorialism in the Congo for the rest of the century. The division of the country into provinces, districts, and *territoires* (or subdistricts), with the administrative head at each level appointed by the central authority, has remained relatively stable. The only exception to this was the period from 1960 to 1966, during which provincial autonomy under both the Loi fondamentale, the independence constitution, and the Luluabourg Constitution of 1964 had given rise to useful experiments in decentralization. In the Belgian Congo, provincial governors, district commissioners and territorial administrators (*administrateurs de territoire*) were permanent representatives and incarnations of the state in their respective areas of jurisdiction. They were veritable proconsuls who exercised despotism and total control.

The governor dealt mostly with general policy questions regarding the province. The 1933 reform changed the power of district commissioners, who were formerly the mainstay of colonial administration, as in the British and French colonies. Given the enormous size of districts in the Congo, the commissioners were to serve mainly as coordinators and inspectors of the work of the territorial administrators under their control, in addition to having primary responsibility with respect to chieftaincy affairs.

Despotism and total control were thus most evident at the level of the *territoire*, generally a vast area comprising several traditional chiefdoms. Here, the administrator was virtually in charge of everything, including the essential tasks of record keeping, order maintenance, tax collection, labour recruitment, conscription, the administration of justice and public services. Relying on a few assistants at headquarters and a network of *chefs de poste* in strategically important locations such as major transportation and trading centres, he served as the indispensable eyes and ears of the colonial system and the primary agent of political repression. The gathering, analysis, and transmission to his superiors of all information pertaining to public order and security, including health, welfare and the general political climate or *l'état d'esprit de la population*, was a critical and most important aspect of the administrator's work.

The fear of popular revolts and the need to maintain a healthy and tranquil political atmosphere were such that the Belgians had put in place three types of operation by the colonial army or Force publique to deal with anticolonial resistance. The three were military occupation, military operation and police operation. As the terms themselves indicate, military occupation involved the deployment of troops in a troubled area and requiring the inhabitants to feed them and to do whatever the troops required of them. Military and police operations, on the other hand, involved putting down a rebellion and intimidating the population in order to keep it on its best behaviour, respectively. One kind of police operation involving a very muscular show of force was known as the *promenade militaire*. This meant not a leisurely stroll by the military in the countryside, but a veritable walkover by the Force publique, to repress and intimidate a defenceless population.

If military and police operations were meant for groups, the repression and intimidation of individuals took place chiefly through the continued use of the *chicotte*. This was usually inflicted in public near the flagpole twice a day, at 6 a.m. and at 2 p.m., upon prisoners and others who were unfortunate enough to run foul of colonial authority in one way or another. The association of the punishment each morning with the raising of the Belgian flag was a daily reminder to colonial subjects of their subordination and oppression. It contrasted sharply with the colonialists' paternalistic vision that 'Belgium shall have completed her colonial task when our natives live happily under the shadow of our flag'.[86] Ironically, prosperity and happiness are not what the red, yellow and black standard symbolized to the Congolese. For them, the flag's affinity with the whip is what they associated the most with colonialism in their mental representations of the system. This has been beautifully depicted in popular urban paintings in the

Congo, particularly Tshibumba Kanda-Matulu's masterpiece, *Colonie belge*.

Cultural oppression Cultural oppression is the negation and, where possible, the destruction of the cultural values and institutions of an enslaved or a politically dominated people. In the context of colonialism as a structure of domination, this negation is 'a necessity inherent in the colonial system'.[87] It is a necessity because indigenous culture is a potent means of resistance against colonialism.[88] In Africa, European military conquest due to the benefits of industrial development reinforced white supremacy and paved the way for economic exploitation and political domination. To rationalize their plunder and self-serving expansion in Africa, the imperialists came up with the ideology of a civilizing mission as a 'white man's burden' to bring Christianity and commerce to people that Europeans regarded as 'inferior races'. Invented as an ideological justification of the inferiorization of dominated people, racism was institutionalized as one of the pillars of the colonial system. A 'model colony' for generating huge metropolitan profits and running smoothly as a pure bureaucratic state, the Belgian Congo was also exemplary in the manner in which paternalism was institutionalized as a means of deepening domination while reducing the costs of repression.[89]

As with the other two features of the colonial system, cultural oppression in the Belgian Congo cannot be divorced from the legacy of the Leopoldian system. King Leopold had used all the public relations facilities that money could buy, including lobbyists, celebrities and ghost writers, to depict his business venture in Africa as a humanitarian endeavour against slavery, disease and ignorance. The fact that the international human rights campaign against his regime was led by British and American citizens was often portrayed in Belgium as an Anglo-Saxon plot to take away the king's precious possession. Throughout the colonial era, Belgian officials from top to bottom sang the praises of 'Congo's illustrious founder'.

The ultimate insult in this regard was the tribute that King Baudouin paid to his great-grand-uncle in his patronizing speech at the ceremony marking Congo's independence in 1960. According to Baudouin, the Congo's independence was the culmination of the civilizing mission begun in 1885 by Leopold. To set the record straight, Prime Minister Patrice Lumumba's unscheduled and now famous reply told the world how the Congolese experienced this mission: through forced labour; the denial of fundamental human rights; and racism, including calling Africans 'monkeys', or *macaques*.

Racism was institutionalized through a vast number of statutes and regulations imposing differential treatment on grounds of race, and through other forms of *de facto* racial segregation.[90] The legalized forms of restrictions and disciplinary measures against Africans included a ban on the consumption of hard liquors; a ban on circulation in the European residential area after dark, except for security personnel and domestics; limitations upon the sale and ownership of land; punishment for 'disrespect' towards Europeans; corporal punishment; segregated housing; and a separate regime of labour legislation. The *de facto* forms of the colour bar included racial segregation in public accommodations, including trains, hotels, restaurants and soccer stadiums; and an unofficial ban on interracial sex, which did not apply to white men. Although these discriminatory restrictions had no legal basis, 'they were practiced just as effectively'.[91]

These and other forms of injustice and oppression were an integral part of the political economy of colonialism, and they were given justification in the ideology of white supremacy. For the colonial ideologues, the Congo was, culturally speaking, a tabula rasa. The absence of writing and a written literature was interpreted to mean the absence of any culture, history and scientific knowledge. Europe's, or the white man's, mission was to introduce these and other aspects of Western civilization in Africa in order to bring it out of darkness and barbarism. Most Westerners, whether they were colonial administrators, company officials, or missionaries, shared this reading of the African situation. With the exception of outstanding intellectuals and scholars like Sheppard, African American missionaries tended to share this negative view of Africans, particularly in the earlier period of evangelization, as Walter Williams has shown:

> William Sheppard's positive attitudes remained exceptional among nineteenth-century black American missionaries. Even though several made complimentary statements, and many emphasized the *potential* for Africa's advancement, in general the evangelists had a low opinion of indigenous African cultures. They saw themselves as civilized people who were trying to bring civilization to Africans.[92]

Thus, independently of the social and cultural benefits of Christian missions – and these were real as far as education and healthcare were concerned – in the logic of colonialism, missionary work helped to undermine African cultural autonomy and to promote colonial domination. The missions helped the state in its fight against African religions and condemned African music and art forms as inferior, childish and barbaric. Meanwhile, both missionaries and state officials went on looting thousands of African art objects, to the point where the best African art today is to be found not in Africa, but in Europe's museums. In the case of the Congo, the best collection is at the Tervuren Museum in the Brussels metropolitan area. The return of this cultural patrimony of the Congolese people is just one of the many reparations that they have a right to demand from their former masters.

White supremacy affected the work of Christian missions in more ways than one. Although the Protestants were more enlightened and less partisan with respect to support for the colonial state than the Catholics, they shared the same world view in which whites were supposed to be superior to blacks and where the Congolese needed to know 'their place' in the social structure. Among the Presbyterians, for example, Lapsley and Sheppard were co-founders of the Congo mission. When Lapsley passed away, another white had to be found to replace him as mission chief.[93] The idea of a black leader for the mission community was too revolutionary not only for the Belgian colonialists but also for the Presbyterian Church, USA, then a predominantly white denomination below the Mason-Dixon Line.

Although they campaigned vigorously against human rights abuses, the Protestants were against the excesses of colonial practice and not the colonial system itself. Although they were not as well integrated in the colonial circles of Belgian administrators, company managers, Catholic missionaries and European settlers, the Protestants – mostly Americans but including Britons, Scandinavians and a few Belgians – believed in the intrinsic necessity of colonialism, albeit in a more humane form. They did not question the colour bar in employment and remuneration, or other forms of racial segregation, all of which were meant to impose and reinforce an inferiority complex among Africans. As a matter of fact, racial segregation was also practised on Protestant mission stations, which replicated the Manichaean geography of colonial towns, with racially separate residential areas.[94] Even seating arrangements inside the church were segregated, with a section reserved for the missionaries. Until 1960, most of them shared the dominant European view that the Congolese were not 'ready' for independence. In April 1960, the author was expelled from the Presbyterian-Methodist United Secondary School at Katubue in Kasai, following a pro-independence protest by Congolese students.

After the Second World War, the Belgians began taking steps to liberalize the system by assimilating the African petty bourgeoisie into colonial society. This was to be done by granting to its members the status of honorary Europeans and exempting them from racist regulations applying to Africans. Some type of assimilation had been provided for in colonial legislation since 1892. In 1938, the Commission permanente pour la protection des indigènes,[95] another advisory group on colonial policy in Belgium, recommended its implementation. However, it was only in 1948 that the colonial administration saw fit to introduce a 'social merit card' (*carte du mérite civique*), which was quickly superseded in importance by a new status called 'matriculation' (*immatriculation*) in 1952, for those Africans sufficiently 'evolved' culturally to be treated like Europeans.[96]

Qualifying for this status required a test of the candidate's level of Europeanization and a recommendation letter from his employer. The test involved a rather humiliating visit by an investigative commission whose tasks included examining the candidate's household items such as silverware and linen, and determining whether he ate at the table with his spouse and spoke with his children in French. Ironically, the limitations of the new status with respect to promotion and pay were such that instead of further integrating the *évolués* or 'civilized Africans' into the world of colonial power, prestige and privilege, it alienated them so much that they sought to terminate the colonial system. As we shall see in the next chapter, they were led to join the popular masses in the anticolonial alliance and the struggle for independence.

African Resistance to Colonial Rule

In their struggle against the imposition of colonial rule, the people of the Congo did not produce a warrior-king akin to Menelik II, Samori Touré or Chaka Zulu. This was due in part to the fact that by the time the Europeans decided to annex the Congo, the power of most of the centralized precolonial states had passed its peak. The major exceptions to this were the conquest states, such as Msiri's Garenganze; the Swahili zone of influence under Tippu Tip and his successors; the Mangbetu state; and the Zande federation of King Gbudwe.[97] Unlike these states, which were relatively well armed thanks to their trade in slaves, ivory and other goods, the major indigenous kingdoms were too weak to mount a sustained armed resistance against European-led armies.

Under these circumstances, much of the resistance against colonial domination took place within new structures that colonialism itself had created: the colonial army, workers' camps and compulsory agricultural labour.[98] The tax, conscription and labour recruitment systems were also a major source of discontent, as was the loss of political autonomy by traditional rulers or chiefs, some of whom rebelled against the new order. Some of the rebellions lasted until the First World War, as in the case of the Shi (1900–16), and that of the Luba-Katanga of Kasongo Nyembo (1907–17). As the colonial system consolidated itself and perfected its mechanisms of exploitation and control, African resistance increasingly took the forms of religious protest, peasant rebellions and workers' revolts. These forms of popular resistance against colonial tyranny were to influence not only the struggle for independence, but also the ongoing quest for genuine democracy in the Congo.

Primary resistance in the Congo Free State Primary resistance refers to the armed struggle waged by an African people or state against the imposition of colonial rule. Generally, traditional authorities, including religious leaders, led this struggle. In the Congo, the leadership of the resistance was taken up initially by professional warriors defending a conquest state or a trading frontier, between 1892 and 1894, and then by mutineers from the colonial army, from 1895 to 1908. The mutineers were joined by ordinary people and a few traditional rulers who refused to submit to foreign rule in what a student of the resistance has characterized as a veritable 'people's war' against colonialism.[99] With few exceptions, the major precolonial states and empires were not involved in the resistance, either because they were no longer the dominant players in interstate relations in Central Africa, or since their rulers had found it more advantageous to collaborate with the invaders in order to hang on to their thrones.

The Kongo kingdom, the best known of all the precolonial political systems of Central Africa and whose name was adopted for the new state, is typical in this regard. The kingdom owed its foundation in the fifteenth century to a prosperous economy based on agriculture and long-distance trade. Based on a system of tributes, the central authority exerted its control over this economy, and its writ ran around the entire land. Unfortunately, the kingdom's progressive integration into the world economy through its ties to Portugal and its participation in the European or Atlantic slave trade eventually undermined its unity and contributed to its demise. Effective Kongo unity ended in the middle of the seventeenth century, following the defeat of the national army by the Portuguese at the Battle of Ambuila in 1665. Afterwards, according to David Birmingham, 'no central government could effectively limit the powers of increasingly small and fragmented chiefdoms'.[100]

Another major precolonial state, the Luba empire, had lost its unity before its actual incorporation into the CFS. More than the Kongo, the Luba experienced a general process of national disintegration described by Samir Amin as regressing 'into a formless conglomeration of more or less related ethnic groups'.[101] This regression was a result of both internal weaknesses and the impact of external factors. The Luba state had emerged in the sixteenth century and extended its control over a major portion of the Katanga–Kasai trade network, whose major commodities included iron, salt, copper and fish. The rulers expropriated the surplus of both production and trade in the form of tribute. The empire disintegrated between 1860 and 1891 due to the combined effect of outside intervention in succession struggles and the encroachment on its central core and client states by ivory and slave traders. These comprised three major groups: the Swahili-Arab agents of Tippu Tip; the Yeke of Msiri's Garenganze; and the Ovimbundu traders from the Luso-African frontier in Angola. By the time the first Belgian-led expedition reached the Luba heartland in 1891, the empire had been dismembered, with the control of the centre over peripheral areas or new frontiers virtually nil.[102]

However, if the Luba were no longer capable of resisting the colonial conquest as a single political unit, remnants of the empire did put up some of the strongest and sustained resistance to colonial rule in the Congo. The Kanyok rose against the CFS in 1895. Under the politically shrewd leadership of Chief Lumpungu, the Songye put up an effective resistance against the colonial labour policy and the attempt to undermine the traditional political economy for purposes of establishing the new order.[103] And the Luba-Katanga kingdoms of Kabongo and Kasongo Nyembo took up arms against the colonial state between 1907 and 1917.

As for the Lunda and the Kuba, the other major precolonial states south of the equator, the survival of centralized rule did not offer them a comparative advantage with respect to resisting against colonial domination. The Lunda heartland and its client states in Zambia and Angola had been undermined by the Luso-African trading frontier and repeated raids by the Cokwe. However, the empire survived the colonial conquest and even the partition, as Lunda chiefs in Angola and Zambia continued to recognize the authority of the Mwaant Yaav or Lunda king at the royal capital of Musuumb in the Congo.[104] Relatively more sheltered from external contacts by its geographical location, the Kuba state did nevertheless involve itself in the Angola and Katanga trade networks by the eighteenth century. It exported luxury cloth and ivory, and imported slaves, copper, beads and salt.[105] This process of incorporation into intercontinental trade and a larger economy contributed to the destruction of its autonomy, particularly with rising European incursion, between 1870 and 1910.[106] In both states, as in other major traditional political systems across the country, the paramountcy and prestige conferred upon the king within a system of indirect rule helped to create a tendency towards collaboration rather than confrontation with the colonial regime.

Of all the rulers who refused to submit to colonial rule, the most famous with respect to Congolese historical memory is Msiri, the Nyamwezi king of the Yeke people of Katanga. David Levering Lewis gives the following account of a confrontation between him and agents of the Compagnie du Katanga, the concession company with 'land rights' to much of the region, in April 1891:

> They demanded that the ruler, Msiri, swear allegiance to Léopold and hoist the Free State flag from his palace. 'I am master here,' Msiri ('the mosquito') replied with dignity, before unceremoniously dismissing the Belgians, 'and so long as I live the kingdom of Garenganze shall have no other.'[107]

Between 1891 and 1908, the history of the CFS was above all a history of African resistance to the imposition of colonial rule. After settling scores with Msiri in 1891, from 1892 to 1894 the CFS waged war against the other rulers of Tanzanian origin in the Congo, who controlled much of the territory east of the Lualaba River. This is the area that Stanley had left out of the Ostend map out of respect for the Swahili agents of the Sultan of Zanzibar, who 'might with some justice present [a] counterclaim to the territory'.[108] Between 1882 and 1890, Tippu Tip had become a veritable head of state rather than a simple caravan leader.

In fact, it was because of Stanley's recognition of the Zanzibari's power and influence in the region that in 1887 he offered Tippu Tip the title of governor of Stanley Falls (Kisangani), with a modest annuity of 360 pounds.[109] Amused by the offer to govern in Leopold's behalf a territory that he already controlled, the Swahili chief took the opportunity to sabotage Stanley's Emin Pasha Relief Expedition and to consolidate his power in eastern Congo. Tippu Tip returned to his native Zanzibar for good in 1890. He was succeeded at the Swahili capital of Kasongo by his son Sefu, who shared the leadership of the Swahili-Arab estate with his cousin Mohara at Nyangwe; Muhammad bin Sa'id ('Bwana Nzige' or 'Master Locust') at Kabambare; and the legendary Rumaliza at Ujiji, east of Lake Tanganyika.[110]

Sefu made a costly mistake in alienating his father's former slave and experienced military commander Ngongo Lutete, who defected with many of his Congolese troops to the CFS side. Thanks in part to these troops, the CFS succeeded in defeating the Swahili forces and effectively incorporating the Maniema, Kisangani, and Tanganyika areas into the colonial state. Hopeful that a major obstacle to his Pharaonic dream of getting a foothold on the Nile had been removed, Leopold put a lot of energy into the race to Fashoda. But this dream turned into a nightmare. The arbitrary execution of Ngongo Lutete by a Force publique officer in 1893 and the hardships and injustices inflicted on black troops and auxiliaries resulted in their loss of confidence in white officers and in revolts which the CFS would spend a lot of resources to suppress between 1895 and 1908.

The internal dynamics of the colonial army constitute the background to the military revolts. The Force publique had three categories of Africans. The first was made up of *soldiers* in the strict sense of the word: enlisted men and noncommissioned officers up to the rank of sergeant. The second category consisted of *military workers*, or people retained for maintenance work and food growing in and around military camps.[111] The third and last category was that of *porters*, who were needed to transport equipment and supplies during military campaigns. White officers, many of whom were psychopaths, sadists and incorrigible racists, subjected all three categories to harsh treatment. They took great pleasure in torturing their African subordinates, meting out the statutory 100 lashes of the *chicotte* at the slightest provocation. Moreover, the pay was low and not regular, and food was usually inadequate, in both quality and quantity. Under the circumstances, the perception of gross injustice in a stressful context was the spark needed to ignite a revolt.

The revolts grew out of two of the three major mutinies in the Force publique under the CFS: the Kananga garrison mutiny of 4 July 1895; the Ndirfi mutiny of 14 February 1897; and the Shinkakasa garrison mutiny at Boma on 17 April 1900, already mentioned above in connection with the Nigerian entrepreneur Shanu. The first revolt is also the most politically important because of the memories of primary resistance to which it gave rise in later years. Coming in the wake of the war against the Kanyok, the mutiny itself was triggered by a situation in which the bonuses promised for victory in this war were not paid, while the garrison commander continued to abuse his troops with utmost cruelty.[112] With the allies that they were able to attract in a vast operational area between the Lulua and Lualaba rivers in Kasai and Katanga, the Kananga mutineers went on to resist colonial rule for 13 years.

From a military standpoint, the second revolt was very professionally organized; involved larger numbers, over six thousand soldiers and auxiliaries; and was more difficult to suppress. The mutiny from which it developed took place in northeastern Congo and involved the advance column of the Dhanis Nile Expedition under Captain Gustave Leroi, in which 2,500 men were forced to march for 150 days through the Ituri Forest without rest and with very little food.[113] For three years, Ndirfi rebels or *baoni*, as they were called in Kingwana,[114] roamed through a vast area of the country east of the Lualaba River between the north-eastern corner of the country, Kisangani, Nyangwe, and the Great Lakes. The heroes of the eastern zone, for whom better documentary evidence exists, include Mulamba, Kandolo, Munie Pore, Saliboko and Changuvu.[115] More than two thousand *baoni* from this group, including spouses and children, gave themselves up in August 1900 to German East African authorities, on the other side of Lake Tanganyika.

Several factors explain the popular character of this resistance against European rule. First, the population in its great majority shared the grievances of the *baoni* against colonial oppression and the arbitrary rule of the white man. Second, the rebels were operating from a terrain they knew well and in which they enjoyed the support of the people, from whom they recruited the volunteers needed to replenish their ranks. And third, the multi-ethnic character of the rebellion laid the foundation for national awareness and solidarity that radical mass movements were later to exploit in mobilizing support for independence.

A common denominator in both cases was the arbitrary nature of colonial authority, together with the fact that African lives meant nothing to Europeans. In the aftermath of the criminal murder of Ngongo Lutete, an ally who was unceremoniously dumped after he had rendered loyal and useful service to the colonial cause, Africans had come to conclude that Europeans could not be trusted to be fair, loyal or grateful. It was necessary to kill them before they killed you. Significantly, Sergeant Kandolo, a former bodyguard of Ngongo Lutete, and a man who enjoyed great prestige for having killed the Kanyok chief Kalenda in 1895, led the Kananga revolt. His associates, corporals Kimpuki and Yamba-Yamba, were to become legendary figures, along with Luba chief Kapepula, for their heroic deeds against the CFS. The corporals were killed in action in early 1908, while Kapepula gave himself up on 21 February, followed by the last rebels on 12 May 1908. Even on colonial maps, there were villages called Kapepula, Kimpuki and Yamba-Yamba,[116] a well-deserved tribute for more than twelve years of anticolonial resistance.

Contrary to a widespread myth, the Tetela as a group did not rise against the establishment and consolidation of colonial rule, and much of the rebel activity took place outside Tetela territory, although many of the rebels on either side of the Lualaba were Tetela.[117] Since the Force publique was made up of Congolese conscripts and West African recruits known as 'coastal volunteers' (*volontaires de la côte*), the main cleavage was between nationals and expatriates. Thus the rebels were for the most part Congolese, among whom a sense of nationhood and patriotism was emerging. West African troops, many of whom were referred to as 'Hausa', were often used as the last resort, when European officers could no longer count on the loyalty of their Congolese troops. The rebels came from all over the Congo, although the overwhelming majority of them came from the eastern half of the country, including the Kasai. In addition to the Tetela/Kusu people of Sankuru and Maniema, they comprised representatives from the Luba cultural group (Luba, Songye, Kanyok, and so on), from the North Tanganyika area, and 'from all imaginable origins'.[118] The latter included some of the former auxiliaries of the Swahili-Arabs from Nyangwe under the leadership of Munie Pore, whose personal agenda went beyond the immediate revolt against the CFS in calling for the total elimination of Europeans and the reconstitution of the Swahili zone of influence as it existed under Tippu Tip.[119]

The major strength of the rebellion was that it was a resistance movement of mutineers supported by a large portion of the population and those chiefs who were hostile to the colonial state. Unfortunately, the movement found it necessary to sell slaves in order to obtain arms from both Angola-based traders known as *pombeiros* and East African traders.[120] This diminished the emancipatory thrust of the movement, as slavery was accepted as a means of fighting against another form of enslavement, the imposition of colonial rule. A second weakness was that the rebels had not reached a level of political and material organization necessary for confronting the technical superiority of the Force publique in firepower as well as the imperialist basis of the colonial state. In spite of these limitations, the resistance did succeed in helping to weaken the Leopoldian system, by providing more evidence of CFS atrocities for the human rights campaign by the Congo reform movement, and in laying the historical foundation for Congolese nationalism. With the end of armed revolts by the First World War, the flame of resistance to colonial rule passed on to religious movements.

The Kimbanguist movement From the standpoint of their colonial ideology of paternalism, the Belgians sought to undermine African nationalism by distracting their Congolese subjects from politics with bread and circuses. This meant encouraging as many households as possible to own bicycles, phonographs and radios, and providing urban residents with lively entertainment in the form of bars or dancing halls with plenty of beer, and soccer matches. As slaveholders usually delude themselves, the Belgians were convinced that they had succeeded in establishing a model colony, where 'the natives have happy smiles'.

As a matter of fact, the colonial subjects were not happy to pay taxes to governors and administrators who were not their legitimate rulers; to cultivate any crops the colonialists imposed on them; to provide unpaid labour for road maintenance and other public projects; to worship underground for fear of being arrested for belonging to 'subversive movements'; and to have the state attempt to regulate their private life in the name of civilization. Whatever smiles the Congolese forced themselves to display in front of their masters, their resistance to colonial rule remained a reality, particularly in those areas where prophetic religious movements and peasant opposition to forced labour and the compulsory cultivation of certain crops were strongest. In such areas, resistance to colonial rule was often expressed through a religious discourse.

This was the case in Lower Congo, the central region of the pre-colonial Kongo kingdom, now split between Angola, Congo-Brazzaville and the DRC. In this region, there exists a rich tradition of political action through religious expression dating back to the eighteenth century. After 1665, the breakdown of the kingdom and the conflicting interests of large trading families, Catholic missionaries and Kongo princes did not erase the sense of nationhood, which had emerged during two centuries of a relatively homogeneous political entity. The emotional commitment to the Kongo nation gave rise to several attempts to restore the unity and stability of the kingdom. One such attempt was undertaken in 1700 by the Anthonian sect, a black-consciousness type messianic movement led by a young woman prophet by the name of Kimpa Vita, who is known in European history books as Dona Beatrix or the Congolese Joan of Arc. Her prophetic vision for a rebuilt homeland defined her mission as that of restoring the kingdom to its ancient glory and purity. Like her French counterpart, she was condemned for heresy and burned at the stake.[121]

This vision of African renaissance and black power would be shared and eventually transformed with up-to-date ideological materials by modern Kongo prophets, beginning with Simon Kimbangu. In 1921, this Baptist catechist from the village of Nkamba and onetime palm oil company worker in Kinshasa began a prophetic ministry that went on to influence the course of events leading to independence nearly forty years later. Given all the conflicting accounts of Kimbangu's life and work, it is difficult to present a brief summary of his vision, message and ministry.[122]

For our purposes, however, what is most important is his legacy for the independence struggle and the democracy movement in the Congo. Suffice it to say that God had appeared to Kimbangu in visions and spoken to him through voices, asking him to preach the gospel of liberation from all forms of oppression, including sorcery, other negative customs and white domination. Kimbangu started his ministry on 6 April 1921 with this radical message, in addition to performing miracles and speaking in strange tongues. As a result, thousands of workers abandoned their jobs in government agencies, private companies and white households, to see and hear the new prophet at Nkamba-Jerusalem talk about racial pride, liberation and self-reliance.

As one would expect, the colonial trinity of the state, the Catholic Church and major private companies reacted quickly and vigorously. Kimbangu was arrested for preaching the subversive ideas of Pan-Africanism, tried and condemned to death for sedition.[123] By royal decree, the sentence was reduced to life imprisonment, which the prophet served at the infamous Kasapa Prison at Lubumbashi until his death in 1951. His tenure of 30 years as a political prisoner appears to be a world record, three years longer than Nelson Mandela, who spent 27 years in jail.

There is historical evidence that Kimbangu was influenced by Pan-African ideas during his stay in Kinshasa between 1918 and 1920. As a growing urban centre with over twenty thousand residents, Kinshasa had a small but active African petty bourgeoisie consisting of approximately one thousand West Africans and about five hundred Congolese, most of whom were employed by the state, large companies and the Christian missions. As the most literate social category and a reference group for the Congolese, the West Africans (Ghanaians, Nigerians, Senegalese and Sierra Leoneans) included Garveyist intellectuals who regularly read the Universal Negro Improvement Association's paper, *The Negro World*. Kimbangu came into touch with this circle through André Yengo, leader of an underground organization of the Congolese élite known as 'Congomen'. This was also the time when the Belgian colonial press was attacking the Congolese Pan-Africanist Paul Panda Farnana, whose political activities in Belgium depended greatly on information from Garveyist circles in Kinshasa and inspired the latter.[124]

Marcus Garvey's message and his strategic goal of going 'back to Africa' was passed on to less-educated Congolese such as Kimbangu and even to illiterate masses through West Africans and the Congolese élite of Kinshasa. The message caught the imagination of the Kongo masses, who held the notion of *mputu* or the white world (Europe and America) as the place where African people go when they die. Now the relatives who had been taken as slaves to America had been transformed into powerful and resourceful people who were about to return home and use their skills to help establish the heavenly kingdom on earth, in Kongoland.[125] In this connection, the formation of the Black Star Line gave added urgency to this expectation of imminent deliverance from white rule, as Kimbanguists made frequent mention 'of a ship that would sail up the Congo River to save the Congolese'.[126] For Kimbangu and his followers, the realization of the Pan-African ideal of 'Africa for the Africans' was God's will, indeed.

According to Muzong Kodi, 'Kimbanguism had two concomitant goals: the salvation of the soul and the liberation of the Congo from Belgian colonialism.'[127] Thus, from the very beginning, Kimbangu's disciples urged their followers to engage in anticolonial resistance. Because of their political beliefs, thousands of Kimbanguists languished in relegation camps built in the remotest areas of the country. Agricultural labour camps known as *colonies agricoles pour relégués dangereux* were built at Ekafera (Equator Province), Kasaji (Katanga), Lubutu (Eastern Province) and Belingo (Bandundu) for banished people who were considered 'dangerous'. These concentration camps would later be used for other prisoners of conscience under the Mobutu regime.

Ironically, the detention centres served as relay stations for spreading the Kimbanguist message of liberation to all political prisoners and to other people with whom the faithful came into contact. In spite of Kimbangu's arrest and the persecution of his followers between 1921 and 1959, popular faith in his message continued to grow, and several politico-religious movements of Kimbanguist inspiration arose to occupy the political space. These included 'Ngounzaism (1935), Salvationism (1936–38), Mpadism or Khakism (1939–46) [and] Nzambi Malembe (1948)'.[128] The Kitawala movement, which originated from the African Watch Tower churches of Malawi and Zambia, also joined Kimbanguism in strengthening the hold of politico-religious movements on Congolese workers and peasants. From 1923 on, it spread rapidly in eastern Congo and greatly influenced African resistance to colonial rule. The two movements had many similarities, including their reliance on the Bible as the ultimate source of inspiration, their opposition to spiritual domination by foreign missionaries and their commitment to 'Africa for the Africans'.

On Christmas Eve, 1959, Belgium finally granted legal recognition to the Eglise de Jésus-Christ sur la terre par le prophète Simon Kimbangu (EJCSK).[129] Ten years later, in 1969, the EJCSK became a member of the Geneva-based World Council of Churches. Today, Kimbanguism is the third major religious community in the Congo after Catholicism and Protestantism. In addition to its wide appeal among the Kongo of Angola and Congo-Brazzaville, it has established missions in several countries in Central and Southern Africa. From a revolutionary movement, it has become an established church, and a conservative one. During the Mobutu regime, His Eminence Joseph Diangenda, then spiritual leader of the EJCSK, was a staunch ally of the dictator. When he died in a Swiss hospital in 1992, people were scandalized by seeing young people throw rocks at his funeral cortege from N'Djili International Airport to the church's main Temple in Kinshasa, very un-African behaviour.

At its birth, Kimbanguism was characterized by a radical questioning of oppressive authority, at a time when Catholicism was a pillar of the colonial system and Protestantism an advocate for mild reforms. Since the Sovereign National Conference, all three churches, along with the Orthodox Church and the Muslim community, have represented a voice of moderation in Congolese politics as major civil society actors. On the other hand, their respective justice and peace commissions, and some of the Catholic lay groups, tend to espouse progressive or radical positions, particularly with respect to the issues of peace, democracy, equality and economic justice. In this regard, they work in close collaboration with other civil society organizations, including human rights groups, development NGOs representing peasant interests and labour unions.

Peasants' and workers' revolts, 1900–45 In addition to primary resistance and religiously based protest, anticolonial revolts in the form of peasant uprisings and urban rebellions did play their part in consolidating a tradition of resistance that later proved useful for the independence struggle and the democracy movement in the Congo. Colonial economic exploitation had brought about the plunder of human and natural resources and transformed African societies by subjecting them to capitalist relations of production. Although peasants are not a class that belongs to the capitalist mode of production, forced labour and the compulsory cultivation of certain crops meant that peasant production, like that of the working class, was essentially designed to generate raw materials for the capitalist world market and surplus value for the Belgian bourgeoisie. People were compelled either to cultivate cash crops or earn wages from European firms, settlers and households in order to pay taxes, as failure to do so entailed harsh punishment from colonial officials. In the end, the use of force was necessary for the collection of ivory and rubber in the earlier years of colonialism and for cash crop production later on, as well as for the supply of labour to European mines, industries and plantations.

It was against this system of forced labour and its negative social and economic consequences that peasants rose in rebellion against colonial authority. Earlier revolts were tied to the compulsory collection of ivory and rubber, while later revolts were a manifestation of peasant rejection of the colonial system in its entirety. The refusal to conform to colonial economic, political and cultural measures took different forms, from passive resistance to armed rebellion.[130] One of the major rural revolts was the Pende uprising of 1931 in the Kwilu region, which claimed well over one thousand lives before it was put down.[131] The revolt was directly tied to the colonial political economy in general and to the economic hardships imposed by the two concession companies operating in the region, the Huileries du Congo Belge and the Compagnie du Kasaï, in particular.

Peasant unrest combined with discontent among company workers and the militancy of politico-religious movements to make the Kwilu one of the bastions of rural radicalism in the Belgian Congo. It is this radicalism that would later permeate the mass base of the Parti solidaire africain (PSA) of Antoine Gizenga and Pierre Mulele during the struggle for independence, and make it easier for Mulele to launch in Kwilu, between 1963 and 1968, 'the first real experience of revolutionary resistance in [postcolonial] Africa'.[132] Between 1992 and 1994, Mobutu's cronies in Bandundu Province tried their best to arouse the indigenous population against migrants from Kasai in an effort to replicate the ethnic cleansing then going on in Katanga, but failed. For the people of this province were sufficiently politicized and strongly committed to national unity to reject this kind of demagoguery.

In the urban and industrial centres, the poor living conditions of African workers contrasted sharply with the luxury enjoyed by the European bourgeoisie, petty bourgeoisie and labour aristocracy. The latter group was made up of skilled white workers from Europe and, in the mining centres of Katanga, Southern Africa. As already pointed out above, Africans were barred from stores and public accommodations reserved for Europeans and from the European section of town after dark. They were also required to carry passes for travel across provincial boundaries, and restricted as to how long they could stay as visitors in urban and mining centres. Their resentment against the colonial system thus went beyond parochial issues of wages, promotion and working conditions, although these were certainly central as sources of conflict and anticolonial sentiment.

Forms of resistance in urban areas included army mutinies and strikes and work stoppages by mining, industrial, transportation and public sector workers. Until 1945, the most important urban rebellions were the 1941 mineworkers' strike in Katanga, the 1944 insurrection in Kasai and Katanga, and the 1945 dockworkers' strike and demonstration in Matadi. Of the three, the first two were particularly significant for their implications for the nationalist movement and inter-ethnic politics later on. The first rebellion was the 1941 UMHK mineworkers' general strike over pay demands, which started on 4 December in Likasi and ended with the Lubumbashi massacre of 9 December 1941, with over one hundred strikers killed.[133] The paradoxical role played by African soldiers in the massacre served as a catalyst for the second rebellion, which started with a mutiny of the Kananga garrison on 20 February 1944. The insurrection was planned to involve soldiers, workers, peasants and white-collar employees of the state and the private companies along the line of rail from Kananga to Lubumbashi. It resulted in mutinies in army barracks in several towns, the sabotage of mining and industrial machinery and rail lines, and uprisings by peasants who joined mutineers in a manner reminiscent of the people's war of 1895–1908, which had also begun as a mutiny at Kananga.

The February–May 1944 insurrection was the first serious challenge to Belgian colonial rule since the days of primary resistance. It involved virtually all the social classes of the anticolonial alliance, with a minimum reform programme that white-collar employees, soldiers, workers and peasants could agree upon. John Higginson describes this programme as follows:

(1) an end to hunger and starvation; (2) the abolition of the forced cultivation of cotton and of the abusive power of government-appointed chiefs and rural social assistants; (3) reduction of the head tax, which, given African wages, was higher than similar taxes levied in South Africa; (4) better treatment by European officers and the abolition of racial epithets such as '*macaque*' and '*singe*'; (5) the abolition of corporal punishment in the prisons; (6) the abolition of the economic privilege of white skin.[134]

All three revolts were partially a result of the hardships imposed on the African population as part of the war effort between 1940 and 1945. But they were above all a response to colonialism as a system of exploitation and oppression. After their brutal suppression, which included massacres, the Belgians responded to their fear of urban unrest not only with the infamous *opérations policières* in African townships, but also with better economic and social services for their restless subjects, in the hope of keeping the public eye on bread and circuses. Fortunately, the improved standard of living in urban areas could not quench the thirst for an even better life of freedom and material abundance. Moreover, urban development attracted large numbers of young people from rural areas and small towns to the larger cities, where they eventually played a major role in the independence struggle. For it was this lumpenproletariat, together with the working class, that initiated the rebellion of 4 January 1959 in Kinshasa, which resulted in Belgium's decision to grant independence to the Congo.

Notes

1. The first known encounter between Europe and the Congo region occurred in 1482, when the Portuguese traveller Diego Cão arrived at the mouth of the Congo River. He mistook the local name for the river, 'Nzadi' (meaning 'great river' in Kikongo) for 'Zaïre'. Amazingly, this is what our country was called between 1971 and 1997, thanks to President Mobutu's decision that this was more 'authentic' than identifying the country with the Kongo kingdom and thus a single ethnic group. John Reader, *Africa: A Biography of the Continent*, p. 344, gives 1483 as the date of Cão's Congo adventure.

2. Primitive accumulation is the process by which great masses of people are forcibly divorced from their means of subsistence so their labour power can be exploited by their masters to acquire more wealth. Africa's role in the crucial phase of capitalist development through primitive accumulation was noted by Karl Marx in *Capital*, Vol. 1, p. 751. On the specific nature of primitive accumulation in the Congo, see Maurel, *Le Congo de la colonisation belge à l'indépendance*, pp. 129–44.

3. Shillington, *History of Africa*, p. 252.

4. In about 1870, one of these slaves, a young man from Maniema in eastern Congo, found himself in Bagamoyo as a house slave to an Arab who served as the Liwali or town chief under the authority of the Sultan of Zanzibar. Muhammad bin Ramiya went on to become the first copra trader in Bagamoyo; a free man; one of the first African petty bourgeois entrepreneurs in Tanzania; and the founder, in 1905, of the Muslim brotherhood al-Tariqa al-Qadiriyya in Bagamoyo. Shaykh Ramiya and the brotherhood played a prominent role in the leadership of the struggle against colonialism in Tanzania. See Nimtz, 'The Qadiriyya and political change'.

5. The Upper Congo Study Committee.

6. Maurel, *Le Congo*, p. 15.

7. Lewis, *The Race to Fashoda*, p. 36.

8. Ascherson, *The King Incorporated*, p. 117.

9. The phrase is King Leopold's. See Hochschild, *King Leopold's Ghost*, pp. 35–6.

10. According to Reader, *Africa*, p. 539, Leopold had chosen for his flag 'the motif of the old kingdom of Congo in Angola'. In the colonial discourse of the 'civilizing mission', the blue standard represented darkness; the star stood for the light of civilization; and the colour gold for the wealth of the Congo.

11. *Bula Matari* became the name by which people referred to Belgian administrators. Later on, it became synonymous with government and administration in Congolese languages.

12. As the first European to have navigated the Congo River from Wagenia

Falls (Kisangani) to Malebo Pool (Kinshasa), Stanley had the honour of having his name associated with both sites, as 'Stanley Falls' and 'Stanley Pool'. Whereas the city that grew around Stanley Falls became 'Stanleyville', the one at Stanley Pool was named by Stanley himself as 'Léopoldville', in honour of his Belgian boss. All these colonial names were replaced by the original African names in post-independence Congo.

13. Reader, *Africa*, p. 540. On the career and lobbying activities of Henry Shelton Sanford, who earned the honorary title of general for financial support to the Union Army during the American civil war, see Hochschild, *King Leopold's Ghost*, pp. 58–60 and 75–87.

14. Hochschild, *King Leopold's Ghost*, pp. 80–1.

15. See Stengers, *Congo mythes et réalités*, p. 87.

16. Austria and Hungary became separate states after the defeat of the Austro-Hungarian empire in the First World War. A Danish colony from 1523 to 1814, 'Norway was granted home rule in a union with Sweden, an arrangement that lasted until 1905'. Lars Mjøset, 'Norway', in *The Oxford Companion to Politics of the World* (Oxford University Press, New York, 2001), p. 610.

17. Hochschild, *King Leopold's Ghost*, p. 86; Reader, *Africa*, p. 543.

18. Stengers, *Congo mythes et réalités*, pp. 84–7.

19. Ibid., pp. 81–2.

20. Slade, *King Leopold's Congo*, p. 40.

21. Although this was meant to apply to coastal areas only, it became a general principle of colonial partition.

22. See Lewis, *The Race to Fashoda*.

23. Slade, *King Leopold's Congo*, p. 41.

24. Stengers, *Congo mythes et réalités*, p. 59.

25. Reader, *Africa*, p. 541.

26. Stengers, *Congo mythes et réalités*, p. 61.

27. This refers to the small footlike shape of the Congolese territory protruding into Zambia.

28. Stengers, *Congo*, p. 65.

29. Ibid., p. 66, citing Warburton's memo.

30. Ibid., p. 68.

31. Stengers, 'La place de Léopold II dans l'histoire de la colonisation', *La Nouvelle Clio*, IX, 1950, p. 527, cited in Slade, *King Leopold's Congo*, p. 176.

32. Maurel, *Le Congo*, p.33.

33. Stanley's memo to King Leopold II, cited in Stengers, *Congo mythes et réalités*, Note 87, p. 77.

34. Maurel, *Le Congo*, p. 33.

35. Joye and Lewin, *Les trusts au Congo*.

36. Lindqvist, *'Exterminate All the Brutes'*, p. 24; Reader, *Africa*, pp. 544–5.

37. See Morel, *Red Rubber*.

38. United Nations, *Convention on the Prevention and Punishment of the Crime of Genocide*, UN General Assembly Resolution 260A (III), 9 December 1948.

39. Hochschild, *King Leopold's Ghost*, pp. 225–34.

40. Ibid., pp. 231–2. For detailed information on this period, see Vangroenweghe, *Du sang sur les lianes*; Marchal, *L'Etat Libre du Congo*; Marchal, *E. D. Morel contre Léopold II*.

41. The first figure comes from Reader, *Africa*, p. 547, and the second from Hochschild, *King Leopold's Ghost*, p. 233.

42. On Leopold's huge fortune, which was distributed in different holdings and foundations such as the *Fondation de la Couronne*, see Marchal, *E. D. Morel contre Léopold II*, Vol. 2, pp. 431–3; Vangroenweghe, *Du sang sur les lianes*, p. 19, who gives the total sum of Leopold's profits as approximately BF6 billion in current francs, or a little over US$200 million.

43. Reader, *Africa*, p. 544.

44. See Hochschild, *King Leopold's Ghost*, pp. 111–12.

45. The most detailed study of this movement to date is the two-volume work by Jules Marchal, *E. D. Morel contre Léopold II*. Hochschild, whose own book on the subject is a bestseller, writes in a bibliographical note that Marchal's study is 'the best scholarly overview by far, encyclopedic in scope'. *King Leopold's Ghost*, p. 339.

46. See Twain, *King Leopold's Soliloquy*, originally published in 1905 and 1906 in New York and Boston, respectively.

47. For more information on the African American role in challenging imperialism in the Congo, see Skinner, *African Americans and U.S. Policy toward Africa, 1850–1924*, Ch. 6, pp. 215–43.

48. Williams, *Rethinking Race*, pp. 68–9.

49. For a detailed analysis of the 1905–10 period of company rule among the Kuba, see Vansina, 'Du royaume kuba au "territoire des Bakuba"'.

50. Hochschild, *King Leopold's Ghost*, p. 264.

51. Ibid., pp. 261–5.

52. Cited in ibid., p. 264.

53. The following information on Shanu was obtained from Marchal, *E. D. Morel contre Léopold II*, Vol. 1, especially pp. 330–2; Hochschild, *King Leopold's Ghost*, pp. 218–21.

54. He also ran a guest house in Matadi.

55. Cited in Marchal, *E. D. Morel contre Léopold II*, Vol. 1, p. 332.

56. Vangroenweghe, *Du sang sur les lianes*, pp. 178–83.

57. Hochschild, *King Leopold's Ghost*, pp. 304–6.

58. Ibid., p. 306.

59. The major exception to this was W. E. B. DuBois, a leader of the then emerging Pan-African movement.

60. This is how Cabral defines imperialist domination. See his essay 'The weapon of theory' in either *Unity and Struggle* or *Revolution in Guinea*.

61. Anstey, *King Leopold's Legacy*, p. 261.

62. Stengers, 'The Congo Free State and the Belgian Congo until 1914', p. 298.

63. Anstey, *King Leopold's Legacy*, p. 262. As Guy De Boeck points out in his outstanding chronicle of African resistance to the imposition of colonial rule, *Baoni: les révoltes de la Force publique sous Léopold II, Congo 1895–190*, p. 360, the dominant historiography speaks of King Leopold's Congo and the Belgian colony as though they were two different countries, when in fact the laws and regulations as well as colonial agents, settlers and administrators remained in place, and repression was carried on as usual.

64. The best analysis of these three defining characteristics of modern colonialism is to be found in Suret-Canale, *French Colonialism in Tropical Africa*. On the colonial trinity in the Belgian Congo, see Young, *Politics in the Congo*, p. 10.

65. See NCN Special Report, 'An Interim Report on the case of moving tantalum and niobium minerals from Congo to Rwanda', http://www.marekinc.com/NCNSpecialTantalum3.htm (9 July 1999).

66. Lekime, *La mangeuse de cuivre*, pp. 11–19.

67. Cited in Rodney, *How Europe Underdeveloped Africa*, p. 172. On the economic value of the Congo to Belgium, see, in addition to the outstanding works of Jules Marchal cited above, Stengers, *Combien le Congo a-t-il coûté à la Belgique?*; Joye and Lewin, *Les trusts au Congo*. The Congo is a classic example of a colony that financed its own subjugation.

68. Joye and Lewin, *Les trusts au Congo*, pp. 17–18.

69. An excellent example of the critical role of the railroad in urban development is provided by the history of the city of Kananga, formerly Luluabourg. The original site of the city was a station established on 8 November 1884 by the German colonial agent Herman Von Wissman on a hill overlooking the Lulua River, 15 kilometres from the site where the BCK railroad station would be built some 40 years later. In July 1928, the first train arrived at Lulua-Gare with King Albert and Queen Elizabeth of Belgium. Four years later, the state post was moved from Luluabourg/Malandji to Lulua-Gare, which became 'Kananga' in 1933 and the seat of the Administrative Territory of Kananga. As the town developed rapidly into a major commercial and transportation centre, the Kasai provincial capital was moved from Lusambo to Luluabourg in 1950. In 1971, the city's name was changed to 'Kananga', as the locals have always called the place. For more details on the urbanization of Kananga, see Nzongola-Ntalaja, 'Urban administration in Zaire: a study of Kananga, 1971–73', pp. 59–108. For information on the broader social and economic impact of the railroad, see Nicolaï and Jacques, *La transformation des paysages congolais par le chemin de fer*.

70. Joye and Lewin, *Les trusts au Congo*, pp. 24–5.

71. Saïd, *De Léopoldville à Kinshasa*, p. 59.

72. Ibid., p. 59.

73. Marchal, *Travail forcé pour le cuivre et pour l'or*, p. 97.

74. Ibid., Part One, pp. 7–195.

75. Maurel, *Le Congo*, p. 26. For a summary of British, French, American and German economic interests in the Belgian Congo, see Saïd, *De Léopoldville à Kinshasa*, pp. 102–13.

76. Brief surveys of the history and social structure of these political systems include Birmingham, *Central Africa to 1870*; Vansina, *Kingdoms of the Savanna*. Ngongo Lutete, a Tetela warlord, and Lumpungu, a Songye chief, were Congolese auxiliaries of the Swahili-Arab slavers from Zanzibar. Mpania Mutombo was Lumpungu's right-hand man between 1888 and 1890.

77. Vellut, 'Rural poverty in western Shaba, c. 1890–1930'.

78. Franck, 'La politique indigène'.

79. Vansina, 'Du royaume kuba', pp. 3–54.

80. Black mineworkers were also recruited from Angola, Rwanda, Burundi and the British territories of Rhodesia and Nyasaland. After the railroad from Southern Africa reached Lubumbashi in 1910, rail transportation eased the movement of mineworkers from the south to Katanga.

81. Young, *Politics in the Congo*, p. 11.

82. Magotte, *Les circonscriptions indigènes*, p. 49.

83. See Almond and Coleman, *The Politics of the Developing Areas*, p. 315; First, *Power in Africa*, p. 40.

84. Respectively the 14-member Colonial Council to advise the Belgian government, with eight members appointed by the king and six by parliament; the Government Council to advise the governor-general of the colony; and its counterpart at the level of the provincial governor.

85. On prefectorialism and prefectorial systems, see Robert C. Fried, *The Italian Prefects*; Spitzer, 'The bureaucrat as proconsul'.

86. From the 1946 farewell address by Governor-General Pierre Ryckmans, cited in Bustin, 'The Congo', p. 33.

87. Suret-Canale, *French Colonialism*, p. 369.

88. See Cabral, 'National liberation and culture', in Cabral, *Unity and Struggle*, pp. 138–54; Fanon, *The Wretched of the Earth*, Ch. 4: 'On national culture,' pp. 206–48.

89. Hodgkin, *Nationalism in Colonial Africa*, p. 53, offers an excellent description of Belgian paternalism, whose roots he finds in Plato's political philosophy.

90. Edouard Bustin, from whom this information is obtained, surprisingly asserts that 'racial discrimination was not institutionalized', in the very paragraph in which he gives numerous examples of ways in which racism was institutionalized in the Belgian Congo. See Bustin, 'The Congo', p. 36.

91. Ibid., p. 36.

92. Williams, *Black Americans and the Evangelization of Africa, 1877–1900*, pp. 123–4. Emphasis in the original.

93. The man chosen for this role was William Morrison, who did an outstanding job as a leader and as a linguist.

94. The notion of colonialism as a Manichaean world comes from Fanon, *The Wretched of the Earth*, pp. 41–2.

95. Standing Commission for the Protection of Natives.

96. Bustin, 'The Congo', p. 37.

97. See De Boeck, *Baoni*, pp. 71–84, on the Swahili-Arab or 'Gwana' zone of influence; and Lewis, *The Race to Fashoda*, pp. 60–72, on the Zande federation.

98. De Boeck, *Baoni*, p. 18.

99. Ibid., p. 356.

100. Birmingham, *Central Africa to 1970*, p. 65.

101. Amin, *The Arab Nation*, p. 81.

102. For a comprehensive account of Luba political history, see Reefe, *The Rainbow and the King*.

103. Higginson, *A Working Class in the Making*, pp. 23–5.

104. For more information on the Lunda, see Bustin, *Lunda under Belgian Rule*.

105. Vansina, 'The peoples of the forest', p. 97.

106. The best study on the Kuba is Vansina, *The Children of Woot*.

107. Lewis, *The Race to Fashoda*, p. 63. As it turned out, Msiri was the only master that Garenganze did know. His murder eight months later resulted in the dismantling of his realm, a territory larger than Great Britain.

108. See note 33 above.

109. Lewis, *The Race to Fashoda*, p. 65.

110. Ibid., p. 66.

111. De Boeck, *Baoni*, p. 45.

112. Ibid., pp. 91–104.

113. Ibid., pp. 173–90.

114. Kingwana is the local version of Kiswahili in eastern Congo.

115. The Kandolo of the eastern front was a traditional dignitary who commanded a group of auxiliaries for the colonial army, and should not be confused with Sergeant Kandolo of Kananga fame. In his outstanding book, *The Race to Fashoda*, David Levering Lewis refers to Mulamba as 'Malumba' and commits the error of identifying the rebels as 'Tetela'.

116. De Boeck, *Baoni*, p. 354.

117. Ibid., pp. 19–23, 71–89 and 211–17.

118. Ibid., p. 214.

119. Ibid., p. 216.

120. Ibid., p. 130 This was a general curse for Central Africa at this time. As Dennis D. Cordell points out, 'The use of firearms for offense made them imperative for defense. Even societies that did not engage in raiding searched

for arms to protect themselves from more aggressive neighbours. *But to procure arms, one had to sell slaves.* This led to even greater violence as societies were forced to take captives to ensure their own security.' See his 'The Savanna Belt of North-Central Africa', in Birmingham and Martin, *History of Central Africa,* Vol. One, p. 68. Emphasis added.

121. For details on this period of Kongo history, see Thornton, *The Kingdom of Kongo.*

122. Sources consulted include Asch, *L'Eglise du prophète Kimbangu*; Demunter, *Masses rurales et luttes politiques au Zaïre*; Kodi, 'The 1921 Pan-African Congress at Brussels'; Mahaniah, 'The presence of black Americans in the Lower Congo from 1878 to 1921'; MacGaffey, *Modern Kongo Prophets.*

123. Kimbangu and his assistants had actually gone underground following the order to arrest him on 6 June 1921, and continued to preach to large numbers in spite of a state of emergency declared for the Lower Congo areas most affected by his ministry on 12 August. They finally turned themselves in on 12 September, and Kimbangu was found guilty of sedition by a court martial sitting in Mbanza-Ngungu on 3 October 1921. See Kodi, 'The 1921 Pan-African Congress at Brussels', pp. 274–5.

124. Ibid., pp. 275–84. Mahaniah, 'The presence of black Americans in the Lower Congo', pp. 411–16, also speaks of the direct influence of African American workers at the oil palm factory where Kimbangu worked in Kinshasa, the Huileries du Congo Belge, but he does not provide much information as to how these diaspora Africans got there.

125. For this and other Kimbanguist prophecies, see MacGaffey, 'Kongo and the King of the Americans'.

126. Kodi, 'The 1921 Pan-African Congress at Brussels', p. 279.

127. Ibid., p. 279.

128. Asch, 'Contradictions internes d'une institution religieuse', p. 100.

129. The Church of Jesus Christ on Earth by the Prophet Simon Kimbangu.

130. One story I heard in 1972 in the Congo was that in one village people boiled cottonseeds before planting them, with the obvious result that no cotton grew on the land, to the puzzlement of Belgian officials.

131. Weiss, *Political Protest in the Congo*, p. 187. Martens, *Pierre Mulele ou la seconde vie de Patrice Lumumba*, p. 29, writes that although the official figure was 550, as many as 1,500 people may have died.

132. Chomé, *L'ascension de Mobutu*, p. 191.

133. See Higginson, *A Working Class in the Making*, pp. 185–208; Marchal, *Travail forcé pour le cuivre et pour l'or*, pp. 196–9.

134. Higginson, *A Working Class in the Making*, p. 198.

CHAPTER 2

The Struggle for Independence

§ A tradition of anticolonial resistance had grown in the Congo out of the people's war of 1895 to 1908, the politico-religious movements since 1921, and peasants' and workers' revolts from 1900 to 1945. It constituted a necessary condition for modern mass nationalism and the struggle for independence. But to wage this struggle successfully against the colonial system, an intellectual leadership was needed. In the Congo, as in other colonial territories in Africa, the people found a willing and interested leadership within the class of educated Africans commonly known in French as the *évolués*. For the protest of the peasantry against forced labour and a heavy tax burden, the demands of the working class for higher wages and better working conditions, and the struggle of the lumpenproletariat for the right to reside and earn a decent livelihood in the cities, had a common denominator with the cause of the *évolués*, in economic and social justice. As the 1944 insurrection had demonstrated, all of these classes of colonized society were each an integral part of a single national struggle for a better life socially and economically. The realization of this objective required the formation of an anticolonial alliance for political emancipation.

This chapter examines both the reasons why the *évolués* joined ordinary people in a common fight against colonial rule and how they led this popular alliance in a successful struggle for independence. A major question in this respect concerns the nature of the anticolonial alliance itself and how it materialized as a social force. These and related questions are dealt with in two parts, with the first part focusing on the social structure of the Belgian Congo in the context of postwar modernization, and the second on the different phases of the independence struggle.

The Social Basis of Decolonization in the Belgian Congo

Postwar modernization with rapid economic growth constitutes the background to the rise of modern mass nationalism and the independence struggle in the Belgian Congo. The major economic transformation took place in the urban and mining centres. There, three new social classes emerged as a political force within the structures of colonial capitalism and its contradictions. The first class was that of skilled and unskilled workers constituting the modern proletariat, one of the largest and most stable working classes in colonial Africa. The second class consisted of petty bourgeois employees and entrepreneurs, and included the Congolese élite or *évolués*. As for the last class, the lumpenproletariat, its appearance was inseparably linked to the processes of urbanization and proletarianization. Generally, this is a class made up of permanently urbanized and proletarianized masses who, unable to find steady wage employment or lacking the necessary skills or vocation for it, develop their own means of livelihood and survival through informal sector activities.

The involvement of the peasants, workers and lumpen elements in the independence struggle was basically a continuation of the popular resistance against colonial rule. In the context of postwar modernization and rapid economic growth, it was also a function of the class struggle, in which the *évolués* implicated themselves in a common quest for economic and social justice. For a better understanding of the strength and weaknesses of the nationalist movement and the political limitations of the independence struggle, it is necessary to examine the social basis of decolonization in the social structure of the Belgian Congo. There is no better place for such an analysis than the class structure, through which the interests and aspirations of the historical actors are articulated.

The class structure of the Belgian Congo can be delineated as follows:

- The *metropolitan or imperialist bourgeoisie*, physically absent but economically and politically dominant in the country, where it was represented by the top managers of large corporations, the higher echelons of the state apparatus, and the hierarchy of the Catholic Church.
- The *middle bourgeoisie*, made up of Belgian and other European settlers who owned their own means of production and employed a large number of wage workers in agriculture, commerce and manufacturing industry.
- The *petty bourgeoisie*, divided along racial lines, and made up of a number of fractions and strata: (1) the liberal professions, whose members were nearly all Europeans; (2) European and American missionaries; (3) middle-level company managers and state officials, all European; (4) European shopkeepers and artisans; (5) Asian shop-

keepers; (6) African white-collar employees (state, company, mission); and (7) African traders and artisans.

- The *traditional ruling class*, composed of kings, nobles, lords of the land, ancient warrior chiefs and religious authorities.
- The *peasantry*, that enormous mass of poor rural producers of food and cash crops to which the overwhelming majority of the African population belonged.
- The *working class*, consisting of the modern proletariat, and composed of two distinct fractions, one European and one African: (1) skilled white workers, employed in supervisory positions in the mines and large industries, and constituting a veritable labour aristocracy; and (2) black workers, skilled and unskilled, constituting the largest African proletariat outside of South Africa and Egypt, who were divided into two strata: urban and industrial workers on the one hand, and rural and agricultural workers, on the other.
- The *lumpenproletariat*, or that group of proletarianized masses without stable wage employment, made up for the most part of school leavers and rural migrants eking out a living through a variety of activities, legal and extralegal, within the informal sector.

The imperialist bourgeoisie The first and most powerful class in the colonial social structure was the Belgian imperialist bourgeoisie, which imposed its hegemony in the Congo through the colonial trinity. As an economic entity, the Congo remained virtually a monopoly of the Belgian bourgeoisie, led by the royal family and a few powerful trusts, including the SGB and other representatives of finance capital, already mentioned in Chapter 1. However, the tendency of capitalist exploitation to become transnational and King Leopold's desire to win influential friends for his colonial enterprise outside Belgium did provide an entry to the vast riches of the Congo for the bourgeoisies of the other imperialist countries. The most successful in this regard were the British who, through Robert Williams's TCL and other interests, played a significant role in the mining and industrial development of Katanga. Unfortunately, the fact that these interests were tied to the survival of white settler domination in Southern Africa was partly responsible for preventing the Belgian bourgeoisie from adopting an enlightened position on decolonization. Lack of political maturity made it join reactionary forces in an attempt to deprive the Congolese people of the fruits of their independence by supporting the Katanga secession.

All the top managers of the three sectors of the colonial system were members of the imperialist bourgeoisie, either by origin or through their politically strategic functions. Former high-ranking colonial officials were rewarded for their good services with directorships in major Belgian companies. On the other hand, bourgeois families in Belgium used their influence and connections to have their sons appointed to prestigious posts in the colonial system. The close relationship between the dominant class in Belgium and the governing élite in the Congo enhanced both interdependence and collaboration between the three sectors in their execution of the essential tasks of colonialism. To accomplish these tasks, or better to exploit and oppress African peasants and workers, the imperialist bourgeoisie relied on the support and assistance of three classes of intermediaries: the middle bourgeoisie, the petty bourgeoisie and the traditional rulers or chiefs.

The European middle and petty bourgeoisies Theoretically, the middle and petty bourgeoisies are distinguished by the manner in which they derive their respective incomes. The middle bourgeoisie belongs to the capitalist mode of production, and it is a fraction or a stratum of the capitalist bourgeoisie.[1] The petty bourgeoisie, on the other hand, is the class of owners/producers who do not directly exploit wage labour. Operating in the sphere of production as artisans and in that of commerce as shopkeepers or traders, petty bourgeois entrepreneurs use their own labour and that of their family members. They only occasionally or in a very limited way utilize hired labour.

On the other hand, there are groupings of individuals who do not fall into this category of the traditional petty bourgeoisie, but who do share the bourgeois aspirations and ideology of this class. The term 'new petty bourgeoisie' is used to designate these groupings, which comprise the liberal professions, civil servants, and the white-collar personnel of private enterprises and civil society organizations. The 'traditional' and 'new' petty bourgeoisies are the two major fractions of the petty bourgeoisie in contemporary society.

In the mid-1950s, the bulk of the European population of approximately 100,000 in the Belgian Congo belonged to the middle and petty bourgeoisies. This population was divided into four main categories: (1) the personnel of private enterprises, 45 per cent; (2) government officials and civil servants, 20 per cent; (3) colonists or settlers, 20 per cent; and (4) missionaries, including Americans, 15 per cent.[2] When white workers are excluded from the first group, and the top bourgeois managers from the first, second and fourth groups, the remainder of these three groups is made up of the new petty bourgeoisie, while the third or settler group is composed of middle bourgeois and petty bourgeois entrepreneurs. According to Crawford Young, the European population of 110,000 on the eve of independence 'included 10,000 civil servants, 1,000 military officers, 6,000 Catholic missionaries, and several thousand managers of colonial corporations'.[3]

If the distinction between the middle bourgeoisie and the petty bourgeoisie is theoretically clear, it is nevertheless not so easy to divide the settlers between these two classes. This difficulty is a function of the large number of economic activities in which the settlers were involved and, in particular, of the tendency of individual settlers to engage in more than one activity.[4] In spite of this difficulty, it is possible to determine that the middle bourgeoisie was essentially made up of Belgian settlers, who constituted nearly 60 per cent of all 24,000 white settlers in the Congo (9,284 heads of households and their family members) in 1956, while the petty bourgeoisie comprised mainly Greek, Portuguese and Italian shopkeepers.[5] Belgians were in a stronger position among the settlers because they received greater support from the state, including vocational training, financial aid and technical assistance.

A product of the colonial situation, the middle bourgeoisie owed its economic privilege and prosperity to this active support and assistance from the colonial state. The colour bar and other discriminatory practices prevented any real competition from African peasants and entrepreneurs, while taxation and forced labour were used to ensure a regular supply of cheap African labour for European enterprises. As farmers, ranchers and operators of quarries, sawmills and agro-industrial establishments, the settlers played a crucial role in the penetration of the countryside by the capitalist mode of production and in the proletarianization of the African peasantry.

With an abundant supply of cheap and unskilled labour, the middle bourgeoisie fulfilled its intermediary role as agent and/or subcontractor for large metropolitan firms in the import–export economy through wholesale trade and the processing of agricultural products. Given its relatively poor financial and technological resources, it could not develop itself economically to the point of becoming self-reliant. For unlike the settler bourgeoisies of South Africa and Zimbabwe, it did not have the political power required to retain a sizeable portion of the surplus for purposes of generating internal growth and economic development.

Although the exercise of democratic rights was severely curtailed in the Congo, even for Belgians, settler political organizations became very active after the Second World War. The settlers were politically organized to defend their interests and fight against African nationalism through a federation of settler associations, the Fédération des associations de colons du Congo Belge et du Ruanda-Urundi (FEDACOL), which maintained a permanent delegate in Brussels for lobbying purposes and published a newspaper, *Eurafrica*. With their strongest clusters in the Kivu and Katanga provinces, the settlers were greatly influenced by white-settler life and politics in Kenya and Southern Africa, respectively. The Union katangaise, the party of white settlers in Katanga, was instrumental in the preparation and execution of the Katanga secession.

Like the middle bourgeoisie, all the European fractions of the petty bourgeoisie and the small white labour aristocracy favoured the continuation of the colonial system. The extremely high standard of living that the colonial situation allowed them to enjoy was something they could hardly dream of in Belgium, let alone in the impoverished regions of Italy or in the then underdeveloped Greece and Portugal. This identity of interests was clearly understood by the African masses, who perceived the Greek, Italian and Portuguese shops as easy targets for their frustrations and anticolonial violence.

The African petty bourgeoisie Only a small number of Africans were successful as business owners, planters, ranchers and small-scale manufacturers. For example, a 1959 colonial information digest noted with pride the existence of 'a mechanized cabinet-making workshop employing some twenty people' in the village of Ngeba, a moderate-size village in the Lower Congo region.[6] Further east, as Edouard Bustin has written, Joseph Kapenda Tshombe built his family's fortune and 'the foundations of a small business empire by organizing the import of manioc from Kasai into Kapanga territory – hence the nickname of "Tshombe" (manioc) which he passed on to his elder son Moïse'.[7] Kapenda Tshombe went on to become the first Congolese millionaire, in Belgian francs, and he visited Belgium in 1948, at a time when there were severe travel restrictions for Africans in the Belgian Congo.

However successful individuals such as the Ngeba manufacturer and Kapenda Tshombe might have been, they were too isolated geographically and of insufficient importance numerically or otherwise to constitute a fraction, let alone a well-defined stratum, within the middle bourgeoisie. Given the limitations imposed by colonial racism and discriminatory practices with respect to their ability to accumulate capital, and given their own resistance to these limitations, they were part and parcel of the African petty bourgeoisie. In 1956, established African traders and artisans were estimated at 12,000 and 4,000, respectively.[8]

There were no African doctors, dentists, pharmacists or professional lawyers in the Belgian Congo. According to official statistics, the liberal professions category of the African petty bourgeoisie, or 'people who put their training and their intellectual gifts at the service of the community provided they can find reasonable remuneration',[9] consisted of approximately five hundred individuals, who were identified as accountants, journalists, musicians, painters, sculptors, and self-taught advocates who acted as counsels for the defence in the so-called native courts.

Three groups of Africans – Catholic priests or *abbés*, medical assistants, and agricultural assistants or agronomists – gained entry into professions that required post-secondary education, with the credentials of the first two categories being roughly equivalent to a university degree. As members of religious orders (the *abbés*) or salaried employees in the civil service and the private sector (medical assistants in mission and company hospitals), they constituted the upper stratum of the new African petty bourgeoisie.

The remainder of the petty bourgeoisie did not have such impressive credentials with respect to formal education. The maximum educational attainment in this group was a secondary school diploma, for which three to six years of post-primary education were needed, depending on the work qualifications required. It should be noted, however, that the intellectual credentials of the Congolese petty bourgeoisie were not exclusively a function of formal education achievements. Many of the *évolués* read a lot on their own or took correspondence courses. Patrice Lumumba, a prominent figure in élite circles and later on the Congo's first prime minister, was an autodidact whose formal education consisted only of four years of elementary school and one year of technical training at a school for postal clerks.

The Congolese petty bourgeoisie consisted of the following three categories of people: (1) *civil servants* (medical assistants, agronomists, clerks, nurses, teachers, soldiers, police officers, etc.); (2) *company personnel* (medical assistants, clerks, nurses, teachers, etc.); and (3) *mission employees* (medical assistants, priests/pastors, nurses, teachers, etc.). Along with the chiefs, these social categories played the role of intermediary between the colonial order and the African masses through the institutions of the state, the companies and the Christian missions. In addition to providing the colonial system with the support personnel required for it to operate effectively, they helped the system undermine the resistance of the masses to the culture and values of their oppressors.

Politically, the civil servants were the most important of all four groupings, given their position as junior representatives of the colonial authority structure and their indispensable role in implementing the extractive, regulatory and repressive tasks of the colonial state. Until 13 January 1959, the date on which a single civil service status for Europeans and Africans (the *statut unique*) was introduced, there were two separate and unequal groups in the civil service. The first group, or that of the *agents de l'Administration d'Afrique*, was exclusively white until token integration opened its lower ranks to blacks in 1957. The second, or Congolese group, was that of the *agents auxiliares de l'Administration*. There were four grade levels of functions and salaries in the European group. Members of the fourth and lowest grade earned a basic salary before allowances between 12,000 and 18,000 Belgian francs a month in 1957 (or US$240 to 360). This salary far exceeded the approximately 7,000 francs (or US$140) earned by the highest ranked Congolese, the medical assistants.[10]

Congolese medical assistants were an intermediate professional category between doctors and registered nurses. In spite of their professional training, qualifications and experience, they were ranked lower than European nurses and public health officers with lesser qualifications, and on the same level with adjunct public health agents. They could not supervise European nurses and public health workers, who often behaved in a racist manner towards the Congolese health specialists. Since their professional ethic was strongly in opposition to active political participation, their interest and involvement in nationalist politics were a direct result of the strains and frustrations they experienced because of their ambiguous status and the lack of opportunities for social advancement. In 1952, medical assistants established an association designed to articulate and defend their interests. As part of the petty bourgeois élite, they also belonged to the various associations that existed to promote the struggle of the *évolués* for freedom, equality and justice. For the denial of economic and social equality was the major grievance of the African petty bourgeoisie as a whole against the colonial system.

Just as there existed a radical difference between the European and African petty bourgeoisies, there was a clear-cut distinction between the petty bourgeois élite of the *évolués* and the lower strata of the African petty bourgeoisie. These strata comprised the thousands of schoolteachers and assistant nurses without a secondary school diploma, adjunct clerks, soldiers, police officers, evangelists and others. Like the bulk of African traders and artisans, these wage-earners did not have the education, material means and social rank required to achieve an élite status. They were nevertheless part of the petty bourgeoisie because the work in which they were regularly engaged was definitely outside the production process and principally related to the repressive and ideological functions of the colonial system. This is applicable not only to state and mission employees, but also to those employees such as nurses and teachers who were entrusted with the social welfare functions of private enterprises. They were distinguishable from sub-clerical and maintenance workers by their trade, education and interests.

Unlike the élite, the lower petty bourgeois strata had a standard of living that was moderately better than that of the average peasant, and not much different from that of the average worker. In fact, urban and industrial workers living in company towns or quarters enjoyed a higher standard of living than most of the lower petty bourgeois strata. The major economic cleavage among all African wage-earners below the petty bourgeois élite was between those who resided in large cities and well-equipped company towns or quarters and those who lived in small towns, mission stations and rural areas. Whereas the people in the first group enjoyed perhaps the best urban amenities of any colonial territory in Africa, those in the second group remained in closer contact and interaction with the traditional milieu. In this context, and due to low wages, the rural and partially urbanized lower petty bourgeois strata had to engage in agricultural production in order to become self-sufficient in food, in addition to relying on the labour of their spouses to make ends meet. The close social ties between the lower petty bourgeois strata and the other popular classes (peasants, workers and lumpen elements), with whom they formed the *working people* of the Congo, enhanced the value of these strata as sources of potential organizers for nationalist parties and revolutionary movements.

The traditional society: chiefs and peasants The penetration of the capitalist mode of production in the rural sector undermined the vitality of the precapitalist modes and accelerated their disintegration, but it did not result in their wholesale destruction. This is because those aspects of the precolonial political economy that were found useful for social welfare and for law and order were carefully preserved under colonialism. It is this dissolution/conservation tendency of colonial capitalism that made it possible for large numbers of peasants to enter the process of proletarianization without ever becoming proletarians, and to perform modern economic functions while remaining under the control of traditional authorities and ideologies.[11] Thus, if the changes due to the introduction of the head tax, cash crops and plantation agriculture did affect peasant life in an adverse manner, they did not succeed in radically transforming traditional social relations. This was due to several factors, including the weakness of the capitalist penetration itself, the mostly extractive nature of economic activities, and the survival of traditional leadership.

The transformation of traditional rulers into local agents of the colonial administration has already been described in Chapter 1. Suffice it to say that the very unpopular tasks they had to perform in this regard resulted in alienating them from their own subjects. As loyal collaborators, they were rewarded with longer tenure and distinguished service medals. Many of the paramount chiefs had become so comfortable with the colonial order that in 1959, they had no problem joining a state-created party designed to promote a conservative alternative to the nationalist leadership, the Parti national du progrès (PNP). For the anticolonial alliance, this organization of middle-level black civil servants and traditional chiefs was basically an anti-independence party. The contempt shown for the party in Congolese public opinion was expressed in derisively calling it on the basis of its acronym as the 'Parti des nègres payés'.[12]

As for the peasants, they did not improve their lot in 75 years of colonial rule, in spite of the hard work in which they engaged. Hardships such as compulsory cultivation of cotton, from which they gained very little revenue, a heavy tax burden and forced labour, meant that they were increasingly being impoverished instead of improving their standard of living. Table 2.1 shows the relative importance of the rural sector of the economy in the overall summary of the economic standing of the indigenous population during the 1950s, the decade of rapid economic growth in the Belgian Congo.

The low level of the marketed product of indigenous enterprises shows that although they were integrated in the money economy, the

Table 2.1 Indigenous enterprises and monetary income (in millions of francs; FC50 = US$1)

	1950	1954	1958
a) Gross national product	30,480	49,350	55,850
b) Marketed product of indigenous enterprises	3,600	4,950	6,230
c) b/a as %	12	10	11
d) Value of indigenous commercial activity	210	700	1,200
e) d/a as %	0.69	1.4	2
f) d/b as %	5.85	14	19
g) Monetary income of indigenous population	8,780	15,910	20,330
h) Wages paid to indigenous population	5,180	10,960	14,100
i) h/g as %	59	69	69
j) h/a as %	17	22	25

Sources: Bézy, 'Problems of economic development of Congo', p. 78, Table 8; Belgium, Belgian Congo and Ruanda-Urundi Information and Public Relations Office, *Belgian Congo*, Vol. II.

peasants did not enjoy an easy access to modern manufactured goods, because of their very low monetary income. If African commercial activity was not limited to retail traders, the peasants' part in it was very small indeed. Peasant farmers nevertheless sold part of their food output in rural and urban markets, but the colonial administration kept agricultural prices low, in order to ensure a higher rate of investment through forced saving. Fernand Bézy explains the reasons for this anti-people policy as follows:

> As a matter of fact, Congolese economic development has been financed to a large extent by the forced saving of a generation of workers, even of those of independent means. Indeed, economic policy has kept agri-cultural prices artificially low, for fear that a rise in the cost of living might bring with it an increase in wages. Thus, inflationary periods, as well as those following devaluation, have until recently, always worsened the position of peasants and workers, thus increasing – temporarily at least – the possible mobilization of forced saving.[13]

Thus, in addition to the accumulation mechanisms associated with the compulsory cultivation of export crops, the colonialists undermined the economic well-being of the peasants by depriving them of the ability to make a decent living through the sale of their food products. Rather than transforming rural society economically and culturally, they left it at almost the same level of economic and cultural life as at the time of conquest, but in a shattered and chaotic state. Consequently, pauperization and repression were to constitute a major source of peasant discontent and necessary conditions for their participation in the anticolonial alliance.

The proletariat and the lumpenproletariat Skilled and unskilled workers employed as wage earners in agriculture, mining, industry, construction, transportation and services constituted the proletariat of the Belgian Congo, one of the largest and most stable working classes on the African continent. On the whole, the Congo had the third-largest number of African wage earners after South Africa and Egypt. In 1952, for example, there were 1,078,000 wage earners in a population of 12 million people. This was roughly equivalent to the number of wage earners in the entire French empire in Black Africa and Nigeria taken together, or 1,080,000 wage earners for a population of 54 million people.[14] The figures in Table 2.2 give another example of the leading position of the Congo with regard to wage employment in Africa.

The Congolese wage-labour force comprised nearly 40 per cent of the adult male population in 1956. By sector, its structure was made up

Table 2.2 Number of African wage earners, 1954–57 (in thousands)

Congo	1,083
Algeria	1,035
Morocco	928
Southern Rhodesia (Zimbabwe)	610
Kenya	555
Tanganyika (mainland Tanzania)	431
Northern Rhodesia (Zambia)	263
Ghana	262

Source: Bézy, 'Problems of economic development of Congo', p. 76, Table 6.

as shown in Table 2.3. In the table, the category 'others' included state employees other than clerks, mission employees and domestic servants. The relatively large size of the Congolese proletariat was a function of the steady and rapid growth of the colonial economy since the First World War. Between 1920 and 1955, the GNP grew at an annual rate of 6 per cent. Coupled with this growth was the increasing share of industry in the gross domestic product (GDP). In 1956, the proportions of the GDP represented by agriculture and industry were 24 per cent and 39 per cent, respectively.[15]

However, if the share of industry in the Congolese economy was relatively high and comparable to rates found in highly developed economies, it should be noted that we are dealing here with an under-developed economy in which subsistence production was not included

Table 2.3 Structure of the Congolese wage-labour force, by sector

	1951	1956
Agriculture	243,714	300,791
Mining	112,268	105,503
Industry	150,316	133,542
Construction	100,109	124,319
Transportation	69,128	91,789
Commerce	72,655	81,548
Clerical	20,982	39,699
Others	254,368	322,705
Total	1,023,540	1,199,896

Sources: Bézy, Problèmes structurels de l'économie congolaise, pp. 128–55; Bézy, 'Problems of economic development', pp. 73–7; Inforcongo, Belgian Congo, Vol. II.

in the GDP figures. Moreover, the industrial production taking place remained basically at the primary stage. According to Bézy, the structure of industrial production in 1957 was made up as follows:

- mining, metal extraction, and basic refining: 51 per cent;
- industrial processing of agricultural products: 12 per cent;
- manufacturing industries, 21 per cent;
- construction and production of building materials, 16 per cent.[16]

Despite its limitations, industrial production, led and stimulated by the mining industry, was largely responsible for the relatively high degree of proletarianization in the Belgian Congo. The development of a large mining industry in a country lacking in basic infrastructure and in modern social services required that auxiliary enterprises be set up to facilitate the extraction, basic refining and evacuation of minerals to the sea for export, on the one hand, and to provide the labour force with those services and amenities that the state was not equipped to finance, on the other. The transportation, construction, manufacturing and service industries that resulted from this process combined with commerce and expanded state administration to generate rapid urban growth. By 1955, over 22 per cent of the African population was living outside its traditional milieu, while 8.5 per cent resided in 22 urban centres, including 14 cities with a population of more than 25,000 people each.

Increased demand for labour accounted for the fact that the proportion of the monetary income of the African population represented by wages was 59 per cent in 1950 and 69 per cent in 1954 and 1958.[17] It also contributed to the urbanization of the African population, which was in part stimulated by the Belgian policy of labour stabilization established under Colonial Affairs Minister Louis Franck in 1922. In addition to eliminating the high turnover so characteristic of migrant labour in Africa and increasing productivity, the policy eventually resulted in two significant developments.

The first was the progressive replacement of African workers from other colonies with workers from the Belgian Congo and Ruanda-Urundi. In Katanga, this meant the phasing out of black mineworkers from Southern Africa, as 'the Union Minière sought to rid itself of the "troublesome Rhodesias" and, at the same time, increase the number of Luba and Hutu workers'.[18] The second and related development was that a skilled African labour force grew in numbers and settled permanently in the urban centres. By making it possible for workers to bring spouses with them and raise families in urban and industrial centres, the policy of labour stabilization contributed to the emergence of a favourable urban demographic structure. In the Belgian Congo, urban demography exhibited a near equilibrium between the sexes and a better age structure than were found elsewhere on the continent, particularly in Southern Africa.[19]

The stabilization of labour in the UMHK copper mines, where the policy was initiated, contrasted sharply with labour practices across the border on the Zambian copperbelt, where the African personnel of the mining companies had to be renewed by 50 per cent each year in the early 1950s. The comparable figure for the UMHK from 1945 to 1950 was 3 per cent: three workers had to be recruited each year to maintain 100 people in the workforce. Of its 19,369 African workers in 1952, 9,786 or 50.5 per cent had at least ten years of continuous service.[20] This kind of labour stability and prolonged exposure to urban life tended to favour permanent urbanization in the Congo. As André Lux has shown in his study of the economic development of the urban centres of Kananga, Gandajika and Tshikapa, most of the people who had lived for some time in an urban centre did stay there or moved to another, generally larger, urban centre. They seldom returned to their villages of origin.[21] In this way, most of the inhabitants of large cities would 'have grown deep roots in the urban milieu', not only in the particular city in which they resided, 'but also throughout the succession of their inter-urban migrations'.[22]

This relatively high degree of labour and urban stabilization gave rise to a new class of proletarianized masses in the Belgian Congo: the lumpenproletariat. It consisted of three major groups: (1) young school-leavers unable to find clerical or other skilled work; (2) migrants from the rural sector unable to find wage employment or lacking enough income with which to set up a formal business; and (3) dropouts from the working class and the petty bourgeoisie. Generally, individuals in this class, particularly those in groups 1 and 2, did occasionally enter the wage sector for brief periods. The hard-core unemployed, on the other hand, shied away from the wage sector, because of repeated failure to succeed in it, better income-earning opportunities elsewhere, or both. On the whole, the specific occupations in or outside the wage sector tended to follow a sexual division of labour.

Lumpenproletarian women were mostly divorcees with little or no formal education and no marketable skills. Consequently, they were for the most part self-employed as prostitutes, who were fashionably known as *femmes libres*, or 'free women'. The women who preferred to keep their matrimonial options open did their best to avoid this 'freedom' and assisted their families in household and informal trading activities. Some did occasionally seek employment from Europeans for the one category of domestic service considered unsuitable for men, namely, childcare. For men, the range of self-help occupations among the young people who constituted the bulk of the lumpenproletariat included hawking, apprenticeship in the informal economy and crime. Intermittent wage employment for older and less entrepreneurial elements included gardening, sentry duty and a variety of unskilled and short-term jobs. In both cases, financial constraints and/or legal restrictions with regard to urban residence and access to a housing lot or *parcelle* required that these men and women be put up by relatives, find rental housing, or live in squatter settlements.

Economically and socially, the lumpenproletariat was clearly distinguishable from the other African social classes, by the manner in which its members earned their living and by the behavioural patterns associated with their adventurous and parasitical mode of life. The reality of the lumpenproletariat as a distinct class was evident to all, even at the level of sociocultural perceptions and discourse. Thus, regardless of any income-generating activity members of this class engaged in, they were almost invariably identified in the public mind and vocabulary as *chômeurs* (the unemployed). They were in this way distinguished from those classes and class fractions that were perceived as doing useful work: clerks (*commis*), traders (*commerçants*), workers (*travailleurs*), and villagers (*villageois*).[23]

This differentiation was cleverly exploited by the Belgian colonialists, who rather unsuccessfully attempted to eliminate the lumpenproletariat as a class by periodically deporting the *chômeurs* to their presumed villages of origin. For the young men involved, their dissatisfaction with the colonial political economy for its failure to absorb them in a meaningful way was exacerbated by the resentment against this sort of repression. More than any other popular class in the Belgian Congo, the lumpenproletariat was in a position to help mobilize the masses in the anticolonial struggle by providing a linkage between the rural and urban masses. It was in a perfect position to transmit modern revolutionary ideas to the countryside, where resistance to colonial rule had remained strong, and to bring back to the cities news of peasants' revolts and the latest 'revelations' of millennial prophets on the impending end of white rule. Belgian authorities had understood the destabilizing potential of the lumpenproletariat in the cities, and sought to preempt any collaborative action between it and the proletariat. In a country where so much of the marketed production depended on wage labour, even in agriculture, the fear of labour unrest was pervasive in official circles, particularly in view of the bloody events of 1941, 1944 and 1945.

Objectively, the economic and social conditions obtaining in the

Belgian Congo were more favourable than elsewhere in Africa to the development of a trade union movement. The high degree of economic concentration, with a small number of highly integrated large firms controlling 50 to 80 per cent of production or activity in their respective sectors, resulted in large concentrations of workers in urban and non-traditional areas. The promotion of Africans to skilled jobs in the mining, transportation and manufacturing industries, jobs that were reserved for whites south of the border in the Rhodesias and South Africa, combined with widespread general literacy to produce a proletariat capable of appreciating the value of trade union organization. In spite of all this, the Belgian Congo had one of the lowest numbers of unionized workers in Africa. Of the 1,146,000 African wage earners recorded at the end of 1954, only 7,500 (or less than one per cent) were unionized. This compared very unfavourably with 23 per cent in French West Africa, 25 per cent in Northern Rhodesia (Zambia), and 50 per cent in Nigeria.[24]

The principal obstacle to the expansion of the trade union movement in the Congo resided in colonial legal restrictions. Until December 1954, an African had to have worked for three years within the same craft to qualify for membership in a labour union. Only two kinds of trade union were allowed: craft unions, with all members having the same occupation or craft; and unions limited to a single firm, with all workers employed by the same employer. No one could belong to both kinds of union at the same time, and local, regional and national federations were forbidden. Moreover, all unions were required to have European advisers, and colonial administrators had the right to participate in all union meetings.[25] The Belgians had hoped that by having such a tight control over the unions, they would prevent the politicization of workers. Ironically, it was the politicization of the proletariat and other African social classes through the great nationalist awakening of the mid-1950s that eventually led to the relaxation of labour laws and the expansion of the trade union movement.

Also crucial in the development of working-class consciousness-raising and politicization was the political and organizational experience gained in pre-trade union forms of organization such as workers' lodges. These were voluntary associations created along ethnic or regional lines for solidarity, mutual assistance, the observance of traditional feasts and ceremonies, burial and other support in time of need. As John Higginson has shown in his excellent study of the mineworkers of Katanga, the lodges were instrumental since the 1920s in organizing boycotts, work stoppages and strike actions, while some of them were politically radicalized by the Kitawala movement.[26]

In the end, African participation in modern economic activities widened the social space, with labour migrations, the workplace, trade unions and urban life generally bringing together people of different backgrounds and ethnic groups. In this process, it brought together the popular classes and the petty bourgeois élite in an alliance against colonial rule, and created among them a sense of nationhood.[27] The four classes shared the common grievances of the colonized against colonial exploitation and oppression. Economic inequality, or the great disparity between their life chances and those of the European colonialists and settlers, was a major source of discontent and a salient factor of the colonial conflict. In the Belgian Congo, the average annual income per capita was estimated at US$77 in 1956, but only US$41 for Africans and US$29 for the 9 million people living in the rural sector.[28] In 1958, the Congolese share of the national income was approximately 58 per cent for some 13,540,182 people, while the European minority of 100,000 people had to itself over two-fifths or 42 per cent.[29]

By this time, the Congolese people had come to the realization that their economic rights could not effectively materialize without political rights. To obtain the latter, they joined together in an anticolonial alliance for political emancipation.

The Anticolonial Alliance and the Independence Struggle

To wage the struggle for independence in the Congo, peasants, workers and other proletarianized masses embraced the *évolués* or the petty bourgeois élite to form an anticolonial alliance. The previous chapter has described how this alliance was born in the African resistance against colonial rule, and the first part of the present chapter has examined the objective interests as well as the aspirations of each of the classes making up the alliance. The analysis that follows is an examination of how the anticolonial alliance succeeded in organizing and carrying out a successful struggle for independence from 1956 to 1960. This is done through an analysis of the critical role played by different social classes in the struggle, with particular emphasis on the petty bourgeoisie as the intellectual and political leaders of the national independence movement.

The petty bourgeoisie and independence Two conflicting theses have been advanced in the historiography of African nationalism on the origins of the struggle for independence. In his otherwise excellent study of national independence movements in Asia and Africa, Rupert Emerson asserts that colonialism was a school for democracy – when in fact it was a school for tyranny[30] – and that the largely illiterate masses had no clear understanding of the notion of people's sovereignty, as they were 'little aware of the complexities of the issues with which they were confronted'.[31] For him, only their educated élites were in a position to understand such issues:

> Colonial educational systems have frequently been attacked, with evident justice, for teaching the history of the metropolitan country or of Europe rather than local history – the stock image is that of children of French Africa or Madagascar reciting 'nos ancêtres les Gaulois' – but it was from European history that the lessons of the struggle for freedom could on the whole be most effectively learned. The knowledge of Western languages opened up vast bodies of literature teeming with seditious thoughts which the young men who came upon them were not slow to apply to their own problems.[32]

Thomas Hodgkin rejects this viewpoint, the manner in which it minimizes the role of the masses in the African independence struggle, and the idea that Africans could not learn the lessons of resistance to colonial rule from their own history:

> For large masses of Africans in a variety of colonial territories to say 'No' to the colonial system and 'Yes' to the ideas of 'freedom' and 'independence' it was not an essential pre-requisite that their leaders should have studied the Western political classics at Harvard, the Sorbonne, or the London School of Economics.[33]

Hodgkin supports Fanon's thesis that the masses, the peasants in particular, had a clear understanding of the critical issues, and that their attitude in the struggle for national liberation was more radical than that of their petty bourgeois leaders, who tended to be more moderate and preferred constitutional bargaining to a people-based war of liberation.[34] He adds that 'without the mobilization, and participation, of significant sectors of "the masses" – and in some critical situations, pressures on the national leadership to move more rapidly than it would have chosen to go – the African revolutions which we have experienced, and are experiencing, could never have occurred'.[35]

The historical evidence from the Belgian Congo supports Hodgkin's thesis.[36] The Congolese people had effectively learned the lessons of the struggle for freedom not from their petty bourgeois élite, but from their own history of anticolonial resistance from 1895 to 1945. It is no coincidence that the nationalist movement found a fertile ground for a high level of political mobilization and emotional involvement in the independence struggle in areas that had known either primary resistance or anticolonial revolts. As Fanon writes with reference to the former,

> the propaganda of nationalist parties always finds an echo in the heart of the peasantry. The memory of the anti-colonial period is very much alive in the villages, where women still croon in their children's ears songs to which the warriors marched when they went out to fight the conquerers.[37]

This was a resistance in which the masses, led by traditional rulers and organic intellectuals from their own ranks, took the initiative in fighting against the colonial system. And they did this without the benefit of knowledge derived from the Western classics, for the ideas of freedom and democracy are universal, and not an exclusive monopoly of the West.[38] Whatever their real situation might be, human beings every-where have a permanent aspiration for freedom and for a better social and political order. In crisis situations, this basic human need 'becomes a necessity, or even a *political demand for a new social project*'.[39] No great intellectual exercise was required for ordinary people to reject colonial-ism and to yearn for a better political order.

In the Congo, petty bourgeois intellectuals did not get involved in the resistance against colonial rule until the penetration of Garveyist and Pan-Africanist ideas in the 1920s in Kinshasa, and the 1944 insurrection. In Kananga, where the insurrection started as an army mutiny, a group of *évolués* actually attempted to take advantage of it by writing a memorandum to colonial authorities demanding to be treated a little better than the 'retarded and ignorant mass'. Crawford Young notes that this memorandum was 'the first public group petition for better treat-ment; the case for reform rested in part upon the claims that *évolués* had played a key intermediary role in limiting the impact of the mutiny'.[40] It is evident that in spite of their reading of Western classics as a mark of civilization, these *évolués* had no seditious thoughts or revolutionary ideas. The existence of such ideas in a particular historical period, according to Karl Marx and Frederick Engels, 'presupposes the existence of a revolutionary class'.[41]

The Congolese petty bourgeoisie, the only class with the intellectual skills required for systematizing the revolutionary notions and aspira-tions of ordinary people into revolutionary ideas and programmes, was reformist rather than revolutionary. Until 1956, its main interests re-volved around 'human relations' or its quest for full integration into the colonial or white society. Victims of the 'illusion of the epoch',[42] the idea of Europe's civilizing mission in Africa, the *évolués* embraced the vision of a Belgo-Congolese community in which they would become partners with the colonialists in ruling over the 'ignorant mass'. Even

Lumumba, who would later become the greatest hero and martyr of Congo's independence, was at this time one of the advocates of the dominant ideology.[43]

The illusion of a Belgo-Congolese community was strengthened by the assimilationist thrust begun in 1948 with the *carte de mérite civique*, together with the creation of Belgo-Congolese discussion clubs known as *amicales* and the entry of the Congolese élite in imported Belgian political parties and labour organizations.[44] Despite the strong endorsement they received during King Baudouin's 1955 visit to the Congo, these integrationist initiatives did not succeed in eliminating discrimination with respect to career and other economic opportunities, nor in ending the daily humiliations of colonial racism. Once they realized that equality and justice could not be obtained under the colonial situation, the *évolués*, like their élite counterparts elsewhere in colonial Africa, opted to join the mass-based anticolonial resistance and lead the struggle for independence.

The anticolonial alliance was made possible by the convergence of the interests of the working people with those of the *évolués* or petty bourgeois élite. All of the social classes involved were agents of history, inasmuch as they commonly identified the colonial or white society as the general obstacle to their economic and political emancipation, and sought to remove this obstacle for the sake of freedom and a better future for themselves and their children. Since political parties were not allowed in the Belgian Congo until the mid-1950s, the politically active *évolués* had to rely on élite clubs and ethnic associations to advance their interests. Of the two types of organization, it was the latter that provided them with a critical linkage to the mass of the people. And it is this linkage that made it possible for the democracy movement to arise as an interclass alliance for independence.

Within the alliance, it was the petty bourgeoisie, and particularly its élite fraction, which had the knowledge, experience and intellectual preparation needed for taking control of the state once colonialism was destroyed.[45] And it was within this class that national consciousness had developed the most, in addition to having made inroads among the proletarianized masses of the major urban and industrial centres. Thus, if the petty bourgeois élite was destined to become the standard-bearer of the independence movement in the Belgian Congo, the proletarianized masses were its active supporters, with the lumpenproletariat playing a particularly crucial role in the nationalist awakening.[46] Given their permanent resistance against colonialism, the peasants were readily available for political mobilization as an indispensable ally in the struggle for independence.

Three phases are distinguishable in the Congolese independence struggle: August 1956 to December 1958, the phase of political agitation; January 1959 to January 1960, the phase of the radicalization of the struggle; and February to June 1960, the phase of the precipitous transition to independence. The first phase corresponds to the birth of the democracy movement; the second to the increased role of the popular masses in defying colonial authority; and the third to the making of a fragile political revolution.

The birth of the Congolese democracy movement The year 1956 is an important landmark in the annals of the national liberation struggle in Africa. Already a crucial date internationally for two epoch-making events, the Khrushchev report on Stalin's crimes and the Franco-British-Israeli Suez expedition and its failure, it was equally a decisive turning point in African history.[47] In addition to the preservation of Egypt's independence, 1956 was the year of the independence of Morocco, Sudan and Tunisia; the setting in motion of the decolonization process in the French territories of West Africa, Equatorial Africa and Madagascar; and of the birth of the national independence movement in Angola, Guinea-Bissau and the Belgian Congo.[48] In the Congo, a democracy movement emerged as a result of intra-élite debate on the future of the country, the opening of the political space to African participation, and the impact of these developments on ordinary people.

The intra-élite debate revolved around a pamphlet originally written in 1955 in Flemish by a little-known Belgian professor at the Colonial University at Antwerp, A. A. J. Van Bilsen. Published in French translation in February 1956, Van Bilsen's 'thirty-year plan for the political emancipation of Belgian Africa' was a political bombshell in colonial and *évolué* circles.[49] If Van Bilsen was denounced by the defenders of the colonial order as a lunatic or subversive, the emancipation that he had wished to prepare so carefully came about only four years later in the Congo, 26 years ahead of schedule.

There were two notable reactions to the Van Bilsen plan in the Congo. The first came from a moderate group of African Catholic intellectuals calling itself Conscience africaine (African Consciousness). The group's membership included Joseph Malula, a Catholic priest who would later become the second African to attain the rank of a Roman Catholic cardinal in the twentieth century; Joseph Ileo, who was still active in the Congolese democracy movement until his death in 1994 as president of the Parti démocrate social chrétien (PDSC);[50] and Joseph Ngalula, whose entire political career since 1959 is best characterized by unadulterated opportunism. In a manifesto published in the 2 July

1956 issue of *Courrier d'Afrique*, a Kinshasa newspaper, the Conscience africaine group endorsed the Van Bilsen plan, which it found to be a good starting point for political debate on the country's future. By a curious coincidence, the text of a declaration by the Catholic bishops of the colony stating that the time had come for the Congolese to take part in running the country also appeared in the same issue of the newspaper.[51]

The second and more radical response came from the Alliance des Bakongo (Abako), which rejected the Van Bilsen plan as too timid. The group was led by Joseph Kasa-Vubu, a middle-level civil servant who was well known in colonial and élite circles. His 1946 lecture to an *évolué* club on 'the right of the first occupant' has been variously interpreted as an assertion of Congolese nationalism, Kongo nationalism, or of both.[52] What is indisputable is that by the time he took over the Abako presidency in 1954, Kasa-Vubu was determined to go beyond the cultural agenda of the organization to deal with the more general issues of social and political emancipation in the Congo. Abako was originally created in 1950 by Edmond Nzeza Nlandu as the Association des Bakongo pour l'unification, la conservation et l'expansion de la langue kikongo, a cultural association for the promotion of Kikongo, then rapidly losing ground in the capital region of Kinshasa to Lingala, a lingua franca of commerce and popular music also used by the Belgians in the Force publique. With a solid political base among the Kongo masses in Kinshasa and the Lower Congo, it became the spearhead of the Congolese independence movement.

The independence struggle in the Congo can be said to have begun on 23 August 1956. This is the day that Abako responded to the Van Bilsen plan and the Conscience africaine manifesto with a manifesto of its own at a public meeting, which marked the beginning of political agitation for Congolese independence. The Abako document, which was read in public by Kasa-Vubu, rejected the 30-year plan and called for the setting into motion of an orderly transition to self-government in a federal structure. Although the word used in the published version of the Abako counter-manifesto was *émancipation*, Kasa-Vubu publicly used the words *indépendance immédiate*.[53] With these two words, Abako defined the theme of revolutionary politics in the Congo for the next three-and-a-half years. Abako's overwhelming victory in the municipal elections of 1957 in Kinshasa showed that its radicalism was shared by non-Kongo Congolese. After the elections, Kasa-Vubu took the occasion of his inauguration on 20 April 1958 as mayor of the Dendale *commune* or municipality to deliver another public speech calling for the recognition of the Congo as a nation. He also chose to depict his swearing-in ceremony as the initial establishment of democracy in the Congo.[54]

The political reforms of 1957 led to the emergence of numerous political parties in 1958. In addition to the Abako and the PSA, the parties that were to play a major role in the politics of independence included the Mouvement national congolais (MNC), led by Patrice Lumumba; Balubakat, the political association of the Luba-Katanga under Jason Sendwe; the Centre de regroupement africain (Cerea) of Anicet Kashamura, which was based in Kivu; and the Confédération des associations tribales du Katanga (Conakat) of Moïse Tshombe.

The MNC split itself in two in 1959 over policy differences between the moderate leaders, former Conscience Africaine group members Ileo and Ngalula along with trade union chief Cyrille Adoula, and Lumumba. Under the influence of Belgian Catholic and liberal circles, they accused Lumumba of communistic and dictatorial tendencies. The dissidents failed in their attempt to remove him from the party presidency in July 1959, as Lumumba retained majority support in the national executive committee. The moderates then formed a separate wing with their candidate to replace Lumumba, the Kasai provincial leader Albert Kalonji. By October 1959, the two wings had become two separate parties known as Mouvement national congolais-Lumumba (MNC-L) and Mouvement national congolais-Kalonji (MNC-K), respectively. In spite of having prominent non-Luba leaders such as Adoula and Ileo among its founders, the MNC-K eventually became a predominantly Luba-Kasai party. Except for the MNC-L and the state-controlled PNP, all these parties were ethnically or regionally based.

If Kasa-Vubu's Abako can be said to be the first real political party in the Congo, Lumumba's MNC was the first truly national party, and one that played a crucial role in the political agitation for independence. Who is Patrice Lumumba and how did he come to play such a prominent role in the Congolese independence struggle and the birth of the democracy movement in the Congo? Born of humble origins on 2 July 1925 at Katako Kombe in the Sankuru district of Eastern Kasai, the young Lumumba rebelled against the paternalism and authoritarianism of both Catholic and Protestant missionaries in Sankuru and escaped to Bukavu to start a career as a clerical employee. Basically self-educated, he spent much of his adult life as a postal clerk in Kisangani, where he was also active in several civic associations. It was through the activities of these associations that he learned a lot about the world, together with the art of organizing. He also acquired in the process a strong commitment to the political emancipation and economic development of the Congo as a multiethnic state.

By the late 1950s, at a time of great nationalist upheavals across the

African continent, Lumumba had moved to Kinshasa, where he served as the publicity director of a brewery while engaging in political activism. In October 1958, he joined a few other prominent intellectuals to found the MNC, which grew rapidly by attracting support from all sections of the population and in all regions of the country. Lumumba was so well known for his political oratory that in December 1958, a hotel employee in Kinshasa took A. R. Mohamed Babu and Tom Mboya to meet him. The East African leaders had made a stopover in Kinshasa on their way to the All-African People's Conference in Accra, Ghana. Having determined that a country as strategically important as the Congo should be represented at this historic Pan-African gathering, they wanted to identify prospective Congolese participants. They were so impressed with Lumumba, with whom they communicated in Kiswahili, that they sought and obtained financial resources from back home to take him and two other Congolese leaders to Accra.[55] The other Congolese delegates were Gaston Diomi and Joseph Ngalula.

It was in Accra that Lumumba met Kwame Nkrumah, Frantz Fanon, Gamal Abdul Nasser, Ahmed Sékou Touré and many other leaders who would later support him in his struggle to uphold Congo's independence and territorial integrity. And it was from Accra that he brought back to the Congo new political perspectives, a mature nationalism, and a strong commitment to the African national project. The major components of that project, which continue to define Lumumbism as a political ideology and a heroic legacy in the Congo, are national unity, economic independence and pan-African solidarity. Upon his return home, Lumumba sought to mobilize all strata of the Congolese population to join the independence and Pan-African struggles through the MNC. On Sunday 28 December 1958, he held a very successful rally in the heart of the African section of Kinshasa to report to the nation on the results of the Accra conference. Several thousand people attended the rally, where they heard Lumumba call for a total and genuine independence.[56]

Fearing that he might be overshadowed by the new prominence of the MNC leader, Kasa-Vubu and his Abako lieutenants scheduled a rally of their own for the following Sunday, 4 January 1959. Rivalry between political leaders contributed to increasing mass participation in politics, as those aspiring to leadership positions had to prove their representativity by having a popular constituency, or a political base from which a mass following could be mobilized. With the notable exception of Lumumba and his MNC, political mobilization took place primarily along ethnic and regional lines. Such mobilization was also necessary for electoral competition, which was introduced through the municipal elections of December 1957 in Kinshasa, Lubumbashi and Likasi, and those of December 1958 in the other four provincial capitals (Bukavu, Kananga, Kisangani and Mbandaka). With mass political participation, a veritable democracy movement was born as the nationalist awakening in the Congo found a positive articulation with the fight for expanded rights by the *évolués* and the working people's aspirations for freedom and material prosperity.

The mass factor in the independence struggle   The political agitation begun by Kasa-Vubu in August 1956 was to culminate in Lumumba's mass rally of December 1958. Immediate independence had now become a national goal; the problem was how to obtain it. The working people of Kinshasa, including the lumpenproletariat, gave their solution on 4 January 1959.

The trouble began with the Belgian mayor of Kinshasa. On Tuesday 30 December 1958, the secretary of the local Abako section sent a letter to the mayor informing him of his party's intention to hold a meeting on the YMCA premises, not too far from the place where Lumumba had held his rally, on the following Sunday, 4 January 1959. The letter reached City Hall on Friday 2 January. On the pretext that the letter did not explicitly ask permission for the party meeting, the mayor's office replied on Saturday 3 January that if the proposed meeting did not have the 'private character' its planners seemingly intended, they would be held responsible for any consequences. As law-abiding *évolués* familiar with the political nuances of administrative correspondence, Abako leaders interpreted the mayor's letter as a ban. They decided to reschedule their meeting for 18 January, so as to obtain the necessary authorization and react to the anxiously awaited government policy statement on Congo's future, which Brussels had promised to release on 13 January 1959.[57]

When the crowd gathered as expected at the YMCA on Sunday, Abako leaders, including Kasa-Vubu himself, went over there to explain that since the meeting was not authorized, people should go home and reconvene in two weeks' time. The crowd refused to disperse peacefully, and responded with violence by throwing rocks at the police and attacking passing white motorists, European-owned shops, and all other symbols of white privilege and authority. The entire African section of Kinshasa joined the rebellion, which lasted three days.[58] Already on the first day, many of the 20,000 football (soccer) fans coming out of the main stadium late Sunday afternoon reinforced the ranks of the protesters. Although official figures obtained from hospitals and burial services indicated only 49 people dead, all Congolese, and 116 injured, including 15 Europeans, estimates of people killed were as high as three hundred. Many Africans were buried by relatives and friends without any formalities, and all the people injured did not seek hospital care.[59]

If 4 January is a public holiday in the DRC today as 'Independence Martyrs Day', it is because the mass action on that day in 1959 sounded the death knell of Belgian colonialism in the Congo. *Indépendance immédiate*, the slogan of the Kinshasa protesters, soon became a non-negotiable demand of the national independence movement all over the country. The revolt marked the beginning of a new and truly revolutionary phase in the movement, the phase of the radicalization of the struggle. This is a phase in which the initiative passed from the petty bourgeoisie to ordinary people. The Kinshasa revolt was entirely spontaneous, with the urban masses taking their own initiative to make the slogan 'immediate independence' a reality. The entire course of Congolese history was changed by their action.

The Belgians were extremely shocked by the violence of their presumably happy subjects. Faced with the people's demand for independence, the lack of political will in Belgium for an Algerian-type colonial war, and an international context in which decolonization was the order of the day, they had to accept the idea of a negotiated independence. This was the gist of two separate policy statements released on 13 January 1959 by both the Belgian king and government, with the royal declaration going much further in explicitly endorsing the idea of independence.

Also shocked by the violence, the *évolués* were 'thoroughly frightened by this destructive eruption'.[60] This is, according to Frantz Fanon, the typical reaction of nationalist leaders before negotiations have been started with the colonial power. They 'are not at all convinced that this impatient violence of the masses is the most efficient means of defending their own interests'.[61] Later on, however, they discover the usefulness of the threat of mass violence as a means of obtaining concessions from the colonialists. It was only after Kasa-Vubu and other Abako leaders were detained because of the Kinshasa incidents that some of his supporters went across the river to Brazzaville and threatened to organize a guerrilla movement. The only other major party to consider using violence if negotiations failed was the Gizenga/Mulele wing of the PSA. Other major parties, including Lumumba's MNC, declared themselves to be non-violent. Nevertheless, all parties used violence where it was of maximum profit to them: against their Congolese opponents in electoral competition. This is also a partial explanation for the intensification of ethnic conflicts during this period.

The masses not only initiated the decolonization process; they also influenced its pace. A major reason for the Belgian decision to grant independence in 1960 was the fact that several areas of the country had become totally ungovernable. For example, much of the population of the Lower Congo and Bandundu regions had ceased to recognize the authority of the colonial state, and were willing to take orders only from Abako and the PSA, respectively.[62] They refused to pay taxes and to respect administrative regulations. Some even refused to have any contact with the social services provided by the colonial state. The radicalization of the independence struggle intensified during the months of September 1959 to January 1960. In addition to the well-organized civil disobedience in Lower Congo, major incidents included the violent disturbances of 29–30 October 1959 at Kisangani, ethnic violence in Kasai and in the trust territory of Rwanda, and the widespread boycott of the local elections of December 1959.

The Kisangani incidents took place as a pro-independence protest in the wake of Lumumba's MNC party congress there from 23 to 28 October. The violence, whose gravity was comparable to that of the January events in Kinshasa, resulted in over twenty deaths and the arrest of Lumumba, who was sent to the notorious underground prison at Likasi. His detention made him a very popular figure and a rallying point for the independence struggle. When the Roundtable Conference of Belgian and Congolese leaders opened on 20 January 1960 in Brussels, the Congolese formed a common front and insisted on Lumumba's release from jail as a condition for pursuing the talks.

The Lulua–Baluba war erupted on the night of 11–12 October and the Hutu–Tutsi one on 2 November 1959.[63] As civil wars, these violent eruptions were not directed against the colonial state. However, they contributed greatly to undermining its authority, inasmuch as colonial authorities were perceived – and correctly so – as favoring one side against the other: the Lulua in Kasai, and the Hutu in Rwanda.[64] The massive deployment of the Force publique to deal with these emergencies at a time when its resources were stretched thin in the face of popular unrest and a climate of violence all over the country reduced the state's capacity for order maintenance.

Except perhaps for the traditional chiefs, most people, including nationalist leaders and the politicized masses, had lost interest in the December 1959 elections for local government councils. The colonialists were perceived as helping their PNP allies to do well in these elections, from which the Belgians hoped to find their Congolese interlocutors for constitutional negotiations leading to independence. The nationalist leaders, who already saw themselves as the *interlocuteurs valables*, saw the bottom-up approach of the Belgians as a deliberate move to slow down the decolonization process. Their impatience helped to fuel the growing popular defiance of colonial authority. Dealing with the latent and sometimes open rebellion against the colonial state meant either the use of coercion to obtain compliance with the law, or letting the situation deteriorate into anarchy, with negative consequences for all concerned. Since neither alternative was attractive, the Belgians opted for acceding to the popular demand for 'immediate independence'.[65] They convened the Roundtable Conference, which met from 20 January to 20 February 1960, and at which the decision was made for the Congo to obtain a total and unconditional independence on 30 June 1960.

The making of a fragile political revolution By the time independence was achieved, the national and democratic movement responsible for it was deeply rent by internal contradictions owing to its own weaknesses and the destablilizing actions of the Belgians. The *évolués* and other petty bourgeois elements displayed both their opportunism by jumping on the independence bandwagon without a clear understanding of where it was leading them to, and their inexperience in neglecting to deal with the economic aspects of the transfer of power. Whereas all major leaders attended the Political Roundtable Conference in January–February, Moïse Tshombe of Conakat was the only prominent politician who bothered to show up at the Economic Roundtable Conference, which met in Brussels between 26 April and 16 May 1960. Yet it was in this latter forum that the Belgians sealed the fate of the country. Negotiating with university students and other politically insignificant delegates relying on Belgian experts to make sense of the complex issues at stake, the Belgians laid the groundwork for transferring much of the enormous state portfolios in colonial companies to Belgium, through privatization, while leaving virtually all the public debt to the new state.[66] The Congolese leaders were evidently true believers in the Nkrumahist gospel of first seeking the political kingdom.

While they neglected to protect the country's economic assets, the newly elected leaders were more concerned with enjoying the material benefits that colonialism and the colour bar had denied them than with a radical transformation of the inherited system for purposes of meeting the people's expectations of independence. At the conclusion of the May elections, hundreds of petty bourgeois leaders went to Kinshasa, and to provincial capitals, as the representatives of the people. Their first official act, after they had fought each other for the important positions of leadership, was to accept not only the privileges that had been enjoyed by the Europeans before them, but also some new privileges of their own creation. Parliamentarians, for example, voted to raise their remuneration from 100,000 to 500,000 francs a year (US$2,000 to 10,000), in a country where the annual per capita monetary income for Africans was below US$50.

The other social classes, well aware of this development, asked for their fair share of the fruits of independence. Given the growing unrest of the emerging class struggle, the new rulers thought that they could count on the Force publique to keep the situation under control. The *évolués* were mistaken. They had failed to perceive, or if they did, to face up to the implications of independence for the other classes. It was precisely because of this failure that the mutiny of the army a few days after independence caught them by surprise. To the soldiers demanding change and immediate Africanization of all officer appointments, Lumumba and others preached patience, and showed their élitism by promising to provide additional training for the soldiers and non-commissioned ranks before they were given higher promotions. This was good logic but bad politics. It was the soldiers' turn to ask the politicians: 'If higher studies are required for promotions, what higher studies have *you* done to become what you are now?'[67] The soldiers rebelled. The teachers threatened not to return to their classrooms. To the working people of the Congo, the politicians had simply become 'liars'.

The alliance formed by the four classes of Congolese society against colonial rule was being broken in the birth of a new ruling class made up of former clerks, medical assistants and other petty bourgeois elements. The petty bourgeois élite had simply wished to de-Europeanize the existing system, without ever understanding, or willing to understand, that the other classes wanted fundamental change. If the end of colonial rule was a revolution in the sense that white rule disappeared to be replaced by black rule, this was 'rather a partial, *merely* political revolution which leaves the pillars of the building standing'.[68] Given its precipitous nature, the mass discontent with it, the international context in which it took place, and the crisis it brought about, the independence of the Congo was also a very fragile political revolution.

Notes

1. See Poulantzas, *Political Power and Social Classes*, pp. 84–5, for the distinction between class fractions and strata.

2. Belgium, Belgian Congo and Ruanda-Urundi Information and Public Relations Office (Inforcongo), *Belgian Congo*, Vol. I (Brussels, 1959), p. 392.

3. Crawford Young, 'Zaire: the anatomy of a failed state', p. 99.

4. Inforcongo, *Belgian Congo*, Vol. I, pp. 299 and 398–9. Other statistical data were obtained from the annual reports on the administration of the colony presented to the Belgian parliament, *Rapports sur l'Administration du Congo Belge*, which are part of colonial archives at the Bibliothèque Africaine of the Foreign Ministry in Brussels.

5. A number of Italians also owned construction firms, and some Italian Jewish families were among the most prominent members of the commercial bourgeoisie.

6. Inforcongo, *Belgian Congo*, Vol. I, p. 405.

7. Bustin, *Lunda under Belgian Rule*, p. 262, note 19.

8. Inforcongo, *Belgian Congo*, Vol. I, p. 405.

9. Ibid., p. 406.

10. de Craemer and Fox, *The Emerging Physician*, pp. 35–6.

11. In this regard, the notion of 'semi-proletarianized peasant' makes sense only when applied to such peasants, who were subject to compulsory cultivation of cash crops and/or found seasonal employment as wage earners on farms and plantations. It is inappropriate when applied to full-time agricultural workers living outside their traditional milieu and, even more so, to urban-based workers.

12. 'Party of Paid Niggers', instead of National Party of Progress.

13. Bézy, 'Problems of economic development of Congo', p. 82.

14. Bézy, *Problèmes structurels de l'économie congolaise*, p. 102, Table 37.

15. Bézy, 'Problems of economic development', pp. 74–5.

16. Ibid., p. 75.

17. Ibid., p. 78, Table 8.

18. Higginson, *A Working Class in the Making*, p. 94. By 1931, according to Higginson, the number of African workers from neighbouring colonies working in Katanga outnumbered the Congolese from other provinces by 2 to 1: by official count, 15,103 to 7,112, respectively (p. 114). Most of the foreign Africans were from the British territories of the Rhodesias and Nyasaland (Zambia, Zimbabwe and Malawi). For the mining giant UMHK, Higginson shows that the number of workers from Rwanda and Burundi, mostly Hutu, increased from 400 to 4,700 between 1926 and 1930, or from 3 to 30 per cent of the African workforce (p. 102, Table 4.5).

19. For detailed information on urbanization in the Belgian Congo, see Denis, *Le phénomène urbain en Afrique centrale*; Lux, *Le marché du travail en Afrique noire*; Lux, 'Migrations, accroissement et urbanisation de la population congolaise de Luluabourg'; Nzongola-Ntalaja, 'Urban administration in Zaire: a study of Kananga, 1971–73'; Pons, *Stanleyville*.

20. Bézy, *Problèmes structurels*, pp. 134–44.

21. Lux, *Le marché du travail*, p. 179.

22. Ibid., pp. 180–1.

23. On the congruence between the public vocabulary in the Congo and the more rigorous categories of class analysis, see Nzongola-Ntalaja, 'The bourgeoisie and revolution in the Congo'. In this article, I had erroneously confused the petty bourgeois élite of the *évolués* with the bourgeoisie.

24. Bézy, *Problèmes structurels*, p. 123, Table 43.

25. Ibid., p. 125.

26. Higginson, *A Working Class in the Making*, pp. 79–85 and 113–19.

27. See Nzongola-Ntalaja, 'The national question and the crisis of instability in Africa', p. 542.

28. See Bézy, *Problèmes structurels*, pp. 164–97, for a comparative analysis of African and European incomes in the Belgian Congo.

29. Bézy, 'Problems of economic development', p. 84, Table 11.

30. According to Ruth First, *Power in Africa*, p. 40: 'If there was any training and adaptation before independence, it was schooling in the bureaucratic toils of colonial government, *a preparation not for independence, but against it*. It could not be otherwise. *Colonialism was based on authoritarian command; as such, it was incompatible with any preparation for self-government.*' Emphasis added.

31. Emerson, *From Empire to Nation*, p. 227.

32. Ibid., p. 53.

33. Hodgkin, 'The relevance of "Western" ideas for the new African States', p. 60.

34. See Fanon, *The Wretched of the Earth*, pp. 92–102.

35. Hodgkin, 'The relevance of "Western' ideas", p. 61.

36. See Demunter, *Masses rurales et luttes politiques au Zaïre*; Weiss, *Political Protest in the Congo*.

37. Fanon, *The Wretched of the Earth*, p. 114.

38. Northcote Parkinson, *The Evolution of Political Thought*, p. 7, warns against the Eurocentric notion that 'all political thinking has been done in Europe and America'.

39. Nzongola-Ntalaja, 'The state and democracy in Africa', p. 11. Emphasis in the original.

40. Young, *Politics in the Congo*, p. 77.

41. Marx and Engels, *The German Ideology*, p. 65.

42. See ibid., pp. 57–8, on the historical impact of dominant ideologies and the 'illusion of the epoch'.

43. Lumumba, *Le Congo, terre d'avenir, est-il menacé?*, pp. 22 and 203–9.

44. On the other hand, the importation of Belgian political quarrels between Christian Democrats, Liberals and Socialists in the colony, such as the 1954 controversy over the establishment of public schools in the Congo, helped to widen the political horizons of the *évolués*, as did the presence of some of them at the 1958 Brussels World Fair.

45. This point, which Amilcar Cabral makes in his analysis of the social

structure of Guinea-Bissau, is generally applicable to all colonial territories in Africa. See Cabral, *Revolution in Guinea*, pp. 68–9.

46. The role of the lumpenproletariat in the political awakening of the Belgian Congo is noted by, among others, Demunter, *Masses rurales et luttes politiques au Zaïre*, p. 198; Vanderstraeten, *De la Force publique à l'Armée nationale congolaise*, p. 22. Hereafter referred to as *Histoire d'une mutinerie*.

47. On the historical significance of the year 1956, see Bénot, 'Amilcar Cabral and the international working class movement', p. 82.

48. The *loi-cadre* or political framework legislation adopted by the French parliament in 1956 at the initiative of colonial affairs minister Gaston Defferre with the support of health minister Félix Houphouet-Boigny set in motion processes that eventually led to the independence of the French territories in 1960, in spite of their 'no' vote in the 1958 referendum, in which Guinea-Conakry alone chose to break with France.

49. Van Bilsen, 'Un plan de trente ans pour l'émancipation politique de l'Afrique belge'.

50. The Christian Social Democratic Party.

51. Vanderstraeten, *Histoire d'une mutinerie*, pp. 19 and 489, note 2. Both texts were prominently featured on the front page.

52. The first view is found in Gilis, *Kasa-Vubu au coeur du drame congolais*, p. 63; the second view in Lemarchand, *Political Awakening in the Belgian Congo*, p. 181; and the third view in Artigue, *Qui sont les leaders congolais?*, 2nd edn, p. 133.

53. Gilis, *Kasa-Vubu*, pp. 79–80.

54. Vanderstraeten, *Histoire d'une mutinerie*, p. 20.

55. Personal communication from Mohamed Babu in London, September 1987.

56. Vanderstraeten, *Histoire d'une mutinerie*, p. 20.

57. Ibid., pp. 23–4.

58. The most detailed non-official account of the events is Marrès and de Vos, *L'équinoxe de janvier*. See also Gilis, *Kasa-Vubu*, pp. 121–4.

59. Vanderstraeten, *Histoire d'une mutinerie*, pp. 23–9.

60. Weiss, *Political Protest in the Congo*, p. 17.

61. Fanon, *The Wretched of the Earth*, p. 50.

62. For details, see Demunter, *Masses rurales et luttes politiques au Zaïre*, for Lower Congo; and Weiss, *Political Protest in the Congo*, for the Kwilu and Kwango districts of Bandundu.

63. I prefer to maintain the conventional designation of this war as 'Lulua–Baluba', rather than 'Lulua–Luba' or 'Luba–Lulua' because the Lulua, too, are a Luba people. However, in the context of this conflict, the word 'Luba' refers only to the Luba from southeastern Kasai, who are not Lulua.

64. These conflicts are dealt with later in this book, in Chapters 3 and 7, respectively.

65. That force was not a viable solution to civil disobedience in the Lower Congo was confirmed by Acting Governor-General André Schöller, after an inspection trip to the region in August 1959. Vanderstraeten, *Histoire d'une mutinerie*, p. 33.

66. On the economic swindle committed by Belgium against the Congo at the Economic Roundtable and in subsequent pre-independence agreements, see Saïd, *De Léopoldville à Kinshasa*, pp. 211–32.

67. This is a paraphrase of a passage in a letter by Congolese soldiers published in a Kinshasa newspaper, *Emancipation*, 19 March 1960, cited in Monheim, *Mobutu, l'homme seul*, p. 72.

68. Karl Marx, *Critique of Hegel's Philosophy of Right*, in Tucker, *The Marx–Engels Reader*, p. 20. Emphasis in the original.

CHAPTER 3

The First Congo Crisis

§   ON 4 February 2000, the United Nations Security Council authorized, for the second time in 40 years, the deployment of a UN peacekeeping force to the Congo. As in 1960, this decision was in response to the threat posed to international peace and security by violent conflict in Central Africa. For the Congo's strategic location in the middle of Africa and its fabulous natural endowment of minerals and other resources have since 1884 ensured that it would serve as a theatre for the playing out of the economic and strategic interests of outsiders: the colonial powers during the scramble for Africa; the superpowers during the Cold War; and neighbouring African states in the post-Cold War era. To prevent a direct confrontation between the United States and the Soviet Union, the Security Council deployed from 1960 to 1964 what was then the largest and most ambitious operation ever undertaken by the UN, with nearly 20,000 troops at its peak strength plus a large contingent of civilian personnel for nation-building tasks.[1]

This latter aspect of the Opération des Nations unies au Congo (ONUC) was a function of the fragile political revolution described in the previous chapter. The Congo won its independence from Belgium on 30 June 1960. Patrice Lumumba's MNC-L and its coalition of radical nationalist parties had captured a majority of seats in the lower house of parliament in the pre-independence elections in May. Lumumba became prime minister and head of government, while the Abako leader Joseph Kasa-Vubu became the ceremonial head of state. The victory of a militantly nationalist leader with a strong national constituency was viewed as a major impediment to the Belgian neocolonialist strategy and a threat to the global interests of the Western alliance.

Within two weeks of the proclamation of independence, Prime Minister Lumumba was faced with both a nationwide mutiny by the army and a secessionist movement in the province of Katanga bankrolled by Western mining interests. Both revolts were instigated by the Belgians, who also intervened militarily on 10 July, a day before the Katanga secession was announced. In the hopes of obtaining the evacuation of Belgian troops and white mercenaries, and thus ending the Katanga secession, Lumumba made a successful appeal to the UN Security Council to send a UN peacekeeping force to the Congo. However, the UN secretary-general, Dag Hammarskjöld, interpreted the UN mandate in accordance with Western neocolonialist interests and the US Cold War imperative of preventing Soviet expansion in the Third World. This led to a bitter dispute between Lumumba and Hammarskjöld, which resulted in the US- and Belgian-led initiative to assassinate the first and democratically elected prime minister of the Congo.

Thus what became known as the 'Congo crisis' of 1960–65 was in actual fact a crisis of decolonization. This is to say that the decolonization of the Belgian Congo did not follow the classical pattern of a relatively long period of initiation by the colonial rulers of their successors, preferably a group of moderate nationalists. Belgium's inability to apply this pattern, the collapse of its *pari congolais* and Brussels' failure to prevent a radical nationalist such as Lumumba from becoming prime minister created a crisis for the imperialist countries, which were determined to have a decolonization favourable to their economic and strategic interests with the help of more conservative African leaders. With Belgium's failure to transfer power in an orderly fashion to a well-groomed moderate leadership group that could be expected to advance Western interests in Central and Southern Africa, the crisis of decolonization in the Congo required US and UN interventions. Working hand in hand, Washington, New York and Brussels succeeded in eliminating Lumumba and his radical followers from the political scene and in replacing them with moderate leaders.

This is the historical background to the second period of the resistance to tyranny in the Congo, which corresponds to the struggle for a 'second independence', the subject matter of Chapter 4. The present chapter seeks to elucidate the reasons why decolonization eventually failed to meet the people's expectations of independence. This is done by looking at the major factors and manifestations of the first Congo crisis, together with the role that the United Nations played in it. Until the popular insurrections of 1964, which the crisis helped to generate, the mass democratic movement was undermined by the rise of ethnic and regional chauvinism, as the new rulers sought to depoliticize the masses and keep them under their control.

The Crisis of Decolonization, 1960–65

The first Congo crisis was a period of political instability and civil war that began with the mutiny of the armed forces on 5 July 1960 and ended with the military coup of 24 November 1965. It included, among other major events, the Katanga secession, Lumumba's assassination, and the consolidation of political power by Congolese moderates under the tutelage of Washington, New York and Brussels. The country paid a very high price, in both human lives and missed development opportunities, for the triumph of the moderates. Their external sponsorship and backing only deepened the crisis, as many of the people politicized by radical nationalist parties perceived the moderates as traitors to the national cause. An important determinant of the crisis of decolonization in the Congo was an ideological split between 'radicals' and 'moderates' in the nationalist movement.[2] The success of foreign interference in Congolese affairs, Mobutu's ascendancy, and the rise of the first organized opposition to the state system of which he became the effective chief beginning in September 1960, are all attributable to it.

The ideological split in the nationalist movement Of all the cleavages within the Congolese nationalist movement, the most important historically was the ideological split between radicals and moderates. The radicals were progressive nationalists who sought to create nationally oriented and mass-based political parties, and saw independence as an opportunity for some changes likely to benefit ordinary people economically and socially. In African and international politics, they espoused the pan-African ideal of African unity and the Bandung principle of 'positive neutralism' or non-alignment. For them, a strong central government in a unitary state was the most appropriate agency for fulfilling these aims. They were emotionally committed to obtaining genuine independence, politically and economically, although they were not very clear on how to achieve this goal.[3] Their popularity within the industrial working class, the most politically conscious sector among the masses, is best exemplified by the strong and consistent support that the important Luba-Kasai population of the mining and urban centres of Katanga gave to Lumumba and his MNC-L, even after the split between him and Luba-Kasai leader Albert Kalonji had become final in late 1959.

In addition to Lumumba, the most prominent radicals were Antoine Gizenga and Pierre Mulele, leaders of the Gizenga wing of the PSA, and Anicet Kashamura, president of the Cerea. A regionally based party, like the PSA, the Cerea sought to mobilize the people of the Kivu province in the drive for independence, and espoused unitarism, pan-Africanism and non-alignment. The fourth member of the radical coalition was the Katanga cartel of unitarist parties led by Balubakat. Although it was an ethnically based political organization, the Balubakat party earned its radical nationalist credentials for its fight against separatism and the secessionist movement in Katanga. The most prominent Balubakat leaders were Jason Sendwe, Prosper Mwamba Ilunga, Ildephonse Masengwo and Laurent Kabila.

The moderates, most of whom have already been mentioned in their respective political confrontations with radicals, were nationalists who tended on the whole to be conservative in their political outlook generally, whether they were unitarists or federalists. In addition to Kasa-Vubu, Tshombe, Kalonji, Ileo and Adoula, the principal moderate leaders included Cléophas Kamitatu, Victor Nendaka, Justin Bomboko and Joseph Mobutu. Given their readiness to accept Western tutelage, they did enjoy a high level of support from the Belgians and other Western government and corporate circles. This backing was clearly evident in the aborted attempt to make Kasa-Vubu head of government at independence; Western involvement in the Katanga secession; the UN endorsement of Kasa-Vubu's illegal dismissal of Lumumba as prime minister; and the US and Belgian roles in Lumumba's assassination.

Kasa-Vubu's nomination as prime minister-designate by the Belgian official in charge of the transition, African Affairs Minister Ganshof van der Meersch, was surprising because his initial base consisted of twelve Abako seats as opposed to 33 by the MNC-L out of the 137 seats in the House of Representatives. Moreover, Lumumba was better placed to produce a working majority with his coalition partners, Gisenga's PSA, Kashamura's Cerea and Sendwe's Balubakat. This is the formula that finally succeeded, once Kasa-Vubu failed to form a viable government. On the other hand, this attempt to block Lumumba's accession to the office of the prime minister and the manifold compromises that resulted in the formation of the first national regime with each of the opposing camps occupying a seat in the dual executive boded ill for the radical alliance. From then on, the moderates won the power struggle in all its decisive stages: Mobutu's return to active military duty as a result of the mutiny; the Kasa-Vubu's coup of 5 September 1960; the first Mobutu coup of 14 September 1960; Lumumba's fall and assassination; the elimination of the Lumumbists from the political scene; and the crushing of the second independence movement.

The mutiny of the armed forces With Lumumba in power, his enemies opted for destabilization. The first result of such activity was the mutiny of the armed forces less than one week following the proclamation of independence. It all started with General Emile Janssens, commander of the Force publique, the colonial army, who had been kept at his post by the new government of independent Congo. Given the climate of discontent for lack of promotions among noncommissioned officers and the rank and file described in the previous chapter, the general convened a meeting of the troops at the main army camp in Kinshasa on 4 July. On the big blackboard in front of the excited troops, he wrote the following words: 'before independence = after independence'. For the men in uniform, he told them, there would be no changes as a result of independence; discipline would be maintained as usual, and white officers would remain in command. Given the intelligence information at his disposal, Janssens's ill intent cannot be exorcised by any postmortem rationalization by the general himself or his apologists, including Louis-François Vanderstraeten, author of the most detailed work on the mutiny.[4]

Janssens's provocation and the patronizing promises by Prime Minister Lumumba that training would be made available to prepare the Congolese for promotions in the military only added fuel to the fire by convincing soldiers that they were being denied the fruits of independence. Consequently, the mutiny had become inevitable. The mutineers demanded promotions, salary increases and the dismissal of all Belgian officers. Some garrisons actually took it upon themselves to elect their own officers. If Janssens's intention in instigating the mutiny was to discredit Lumumba's leadership and to eventually push him out of power, the immediate results were the panic and flight of European civil servants and settlers, which deprived the economy and the state of most of their professional and technical cadres.

To calm the situation, Lumumba began the process of Africanizing the officer corps by appointing Victor Lundula, a medical practitioner who had served in the Force publique and as a burgomaster in Likasi, general and commander in chief of the armed forces, which he renamed the Armée nationale congolaise (ANC). He also appointed Mobutu, one of the two junior ministers in the prime minister's office, as colonel and chief of staff of the ANC. Both appointments were ill advised. Lundula did not have the necessary qualifications to manage a modern army. As for Mobutu, Lumumba made a serious blunder based on his overconfidence in commanding the loyalty of the people around him and his political naïvety. He refused to listen to apparently well-founded rumours about Mobutu's ties to the Belgian and American intelligence services. In appointing Mobutu to this sensitive position, he had unwittingly chosen his own Judas.

As the mutiny began to spread all over the country, President Kasa-Vubu and Prime Minister Lumumba made several trips into the interior with the hope of restoring law and order. They also considered several options with regard to foreign military assistance in order to achieve this goal. These included US military assistance, which was in fact requested without Lumumba's knowledge by the supposedly 'communist' Deputy Prime Minister Gizenga. The situation changed for the worse on 10 and 11 July, with Belgian military intervention and Tshombe's proclamation of the Katanga secession, respectively. On 12 July, Lumumba and Kasa-Vubu appealed to the United Nations for help, requesting the dispatch of UN troops to protect the country from external aggression and to restore its territorial integrity. This request for UN intervention re-inforced an earlier initiative by US Ambassador Clare Timberlake, who as early as 10 July was advocating the presence of UN troops as the best way of protecting Western interests in the Congo. Timberlake also hoped that the unilateral Belgian intervention could be legalized by placing it under a UN umbrella.[5] This idea of a UN cover for Western or specifically American interests became an integral part of US policy in the Congo.[6]

The Katanga secession Having lost control of the situation in the Congo, Belgium intervened militarily on 10 July 1960, under the pretext of protecting European lives and property. On the following day, 11 July, the Katanga province declared its secession from the Congo. This was not a pure coincidence. A clear indication of their true intentions was that the Belgians disarmed all non-Katangese soldiers and expelled them from the province, while retaining those who were native to the province for service in the Katanga Gendarmerie. That Belgium should participate in the criminal enterprise of ethnic cleansing that was so dear to Godefroid Munongo, Katanga's powerful interior minister and a descendant of the Nyamwezi King Mziri, shows just how desperate Brussels and its corporate allies were in trying to make the secession an African affair. In reality, Tshombe and Munongo served as the African front for the more powerful interests of mining companies and white settlers. A discussion of the Katanga secession is inadequate without reference to the colonial political economy and settler interests in the province.

As already shown in Chapters 1 and 2, the Katanga province was geographically and economically an integral part of the multinational corporate empire established in Southern Africa before the First World War under British hegemony. The integration of this mineral-rich province into the Southern Africa economic complex had laid the foundations for the Katanga secession. During the early years of mining exploitation in Katanga, most of the skilled workers were white settlers from the south. They brought with them values and behavioural patterns that greatly reinforced the racism of the Belgian colonial system. With white South Africans and Rhodesians as their reference groups, Belgian settlers sought to create a colonial settler system and to subordinate the political economy of the province to their interests. Settler political organizations became very active after the Second World War, but they were repulsed in their quest for state power by the Belgian imperialist bourgeoisie, which controlled the colonial state and did not wish to concede a higher portion of the economic surplus to the settlers.

Later on, however, the prospects of independence under a radical unitarist and nationalist government did bring a rapprochement between the imperialist bourgeoisie, which was represented on the terrain by the top management of UMHK and other SGB companies in Katanga, and the settler bourgeoisie and petty bourgeoisie. The Union katangaise, the party of white settlers, was instrumental in the preparation of the secession. But to bring it about and to give it credibility in an international environment marked by an overwhelming support for national self-determination, independence and majority rule, the settlers needed black allies to front for them. And these they found in Tshombe's and Munongo's Conakat.

Conakat was founded on the premise that the wealth of the mineral-rich Katanga province should benefit mainly the 'authentic Katangese' or those native to the province. It was ironic that a person such as Conakat leader Godefroid Munongo, a descendant of the Nyamwezi ruler Msiri, could consider himself more authentic as a Katangese than the Luba-Kasai, whose ancestral homeland is in Katanga. In reality, the major theoreticians and financial backers of the party worked behind the scenes and were to be found among white settlers. The settlers saw and used the party as a vehicle for their long-held dream of a separate political entity likely to close ranks with the white redoubt in Southern Africa: the Federation of Rhodesia and Nyasaland (Zambia, Zimbabwe and Malawi), the Portuguese colonies of Angola and Mozambique, South Africa, and Southwest Africa (Namibia). Conakat was a reactionary party from its very beginning. Whereas the majority of the *évolués* had followed the Conscience africaine group and Abako in rejecting the idea of a union with Belgium, the Katanga party advocated both a loose federation and the Belgo-Congolese community. A pro-secession party, Conakat was basically the voice of white settlers through African mouths.

Thus was an 'internal settlement' scheme imposed on the Katanga province, long before the white rebel government of Ian Smith coined the term to designate the agreement he signed with Bishop Abel Muzorewa, the Reverend Ndabaningi Sithole and Chief Jeremiah Chirau on 3 March 1978, for a limited measure of power sharing in Zimbabwe. With such a scheme, colonial settlers hoped to salvage their power and privileges through co-optation of a handful of reactionary black leaders. In the Katanga case, real power remained in the hands of former colonial officials, who received the full backing of the Belgian state, and who were assisted in their rape of the Congo and its resources by a host of white adventurers and mercenaries from all over Europe and Southern Africa.

Britain, France and apartheid South Africa gave active support to the secession, as their ruling classes shared the Belgians' fear of Lumumba's commitment to genuine independence and radical social change. In a region where colonial rule was being challenged head-on in all the ten countries south of the Congo and Tanzania, the white reactionary forces were determined to keep this mineral-rich province within a white-dominated Southern Africa, from Katanga to the Cape, and including the Federation of Rhodesia and Nyasaland, the Portuguese colonies of Angola and Mozambique, and the British High Commission Territories of Botswana, Lesotho and Swaziland. Needless to say, Namibia had simply become a fifth province of South Africa. The coming together of the white racists to defend this political project with the help of their allies in Western Europe and North America, including former colonial officials, fascist groups and US conservatives led by Senators Barry Goldwater, Thomas Dodd and their colleagues from Dixie, marked the high point of the counterrevolution in Central and Southern Africa. Despite their profession of faith against racism, the power élites of Britain, France and Belgium were an integral part of this counter-revolution.

The cynicism of the Western powers became evident once the major threat to their interests in the Congo was removed. After the assassination of Lumumba and the elimination of the Lumumbists from the political scene in Kinshasa, Belgium and the Western alliance determined that they could do profitable business in the Congo with the anti-communist and pro-Western moderates they had helped put in power. Given the worldwide disapproval of the Katanga secession, particularly in Africa and the Third World generally, there was no compelling reason to support it. They pulled the rug from under Tshombe's feet, and the secession was ended by UN military action in January 1963.

The secession of South Kasai Of all the secessions having to do with inter-ethnic conflict in Africa, the story of South Kasai is not as well known. Yet the events that took place in August 1960 in that little corner of the Congo were to have a major impact on the political history of the country. Following reports of massacres of unarmed civilians in and around the city of Mbuji-Mayi in late August, UN Secretary-General Dag Hammarskjöld characterized the atrocities then being committed by the ANC against the Luba-Kasai as an act of genocide. On 5 September, President Kasa-Vubu used this allegation as one of his reasons for dismissing Lumumba from his job as prime minister. The rest of Lumumba's story is known. He never again exercised his powers as a democratically elected head of government. He was placed under house arrest, imprisoned like a common criminal, and assassinated a few months later.

How did the secession of South Kasai come about to play such a decisive role in the first Congo crisis? It all began with the political exploitation of inter-ethnic conflict in the Kasai province by the leaders of the two wings of the MNC, Patrice Lumumba of the MNC-L and Albert Kalonji and Joseph Ngalula of the MNC-K. The conflict in question opposed two of the three subgroups of the Luba-Kasai, known as Lulua and Luba respectively. The two, along with the third subgroup, the Konji or Luntu, trace their origin to the precolonial Luba empire in Katanga; have the same material culture, social institutions and customs; and speak the same language, Tshiluba. The Lulua–Baluba conflict, which was briefly noted in Chapter 2, is seldom a subject of serious scholarly inquiry, in spite of its lessons for the Hutu–Tutsi conflict in Rwanda and Burundi. A brief historical background should help elucidate its strictly colonial origin.

A brief description of the rise and fall of the Luba empire already appears in Chapter 1. The ancient kingdom had emerged among people possessing a homogeneous culture, and whose family structures and religious practices survived well into the twentieth century.[7] Migrants from the Luba heartland in the seventeenth and eighteenth centuries helped to spread Luba cultural influence, including political ideologies and organizational principles, throughout the Katanga–Kasai savanna between Lake Tanganyika and the Kasai River. Although those who moved to the Kasai region never organized a single centralized state, they remained emotionally attached to the genesis myth and other ideologies stressing the unity of the Luba as a people, in spite of their division into closely related ethnic groups. These include the Luba-Kasai, already identified above; the Luba-Katanga, also divided into three separate groups under the royal lineages of Kabongo, Kasongo and Mutombo Mukulu, respectively; and several related groups. Numerically and politically, the most important of the Luba-related groups are the Songye, who built town-states, and the Kanyok, who were organized under a single precolonial kingdom. Like the Luba-Kasai, with whom they are commonly identified as 'Kasaians' in Katanga, they had migrated to Kasai long before colonial rule.

There is no better example of the invention of ethnicity or, in other words, of how artificial ethnic identities can be than the Lulua–Baluba conflict. Unlike the Hutu–Tutsi conflict, whose ideological configuration involves a myth of separate origins – the Hamitic myth – the two Kasai groups do not dispute their common origin, and are proud of their common culture and language. Father A. Van Zandijcke, a Belgian missionary and scholar, has shown that up to 1870, there was no generic term to designate the people who are now called Lulua. All of their separate groupings or chiefdoms used to identify themselves as Luba migrants from the south.[8] According to Jan Vansina, the Cokwe gave the name 'Lulua' to these groupings because of their settlement in the Lulua River valley.[9]

The Lulua–Baluba conflict arose in the context of ethnic identity construction and mobilization within the colonial political economy. Between 1880 and 1890, the Luba populations of southeastern Kasai were being decimated by the slave raids of the Cokwe and those of the Songye auxiliaries of the Swahili-Arab slavers under the command of Chief Lumpungu. After 1885, thousands of people fled to the safety of the Kananga and Luebo areas in central and western Kasai respectively. Among the Lulua, they were welcomed as kith and kin and given refuge and protection. Uprooted from their own region of origin, the newcomers were more readily available than the locals for recruitment to wage labour and for attending the churches and schools of the Christian missionaries who came to their assistance. A process of differentiation driven by colonial land and labour policies was set into motion and did result in the settlers and the locals forming two separate groups known respectively as 'Baluba' and 'Bena Lulua'. Between 1925 and 1930, for example, the Belgians proceeded with the regrouping of Luba settlers into separate villages on Lulua land.

To justify this policy of divide-and-rule, the colonialists invented the stereotype of the Luba as 'progressive' and 'hardworking' in contrast to the Lulua and other groups, who were said to be 'conservative' and 'lazy'. One colonial administrator even claimed that when it came to farming, one Luba was as productive as seven Lulua.[10] Having enlisted the Luba during the previous 60 years as their auxiliaries in all the three sectors of the colonial enterprise – business, government and evangelization – the Belgians began to fear them in the 1950s because of their unrelenting criticism of racism and discriminatory practices. For purposes of weakening the rising tide of opposition against the colonial system, Belgian authorities and the Catholic Church sought to deepen the process of ethnic polarization by developing a counterweight to the Luba élite. In 1952, they helped set up an exclusive ethnic association called Lulua Frères, with the double aim of improving the socio-economic position of the Lulua so they could 'catch up with the Baluba' and promoting a Lulua counter-élite. This organization eventually served as the brains trust for Lulua political activities, and provided overall direction for ethnic cleansing against the Luba in 1959–60.

The advent of political parties and electoral politics in 1958 helped to accelerate the antagonisms between the two groups, as membership in political parties and voting behaviour tended to follow the new lines of ethnic cleavage. In 1959, the discovery by a Luba clerk of a proposal by a Belgian provincial official to resettle Luba farmers from Lulua land in the economically booming centre of the province back to their impoverished homeland in southeastern Kasai was a spark that led to a poisoned atmosphere in intergroup relations. Luba opposition to the plan and other grievances resulted in violent demonstrations in August and the arrest and banishment of Albert Kalonji to a remote penal colony in the Sankuru district. In spite of the strained relations between them due to the split within the party being engineered by his rivals in Kinshasa, Lumumba went to Kananga, the Kasai provincial capital, to demand Kalonji's release.

After months of heightened tensions, the Lulua–Baluba war erupted on 11 October 1959. It lasted through the general elections of May 1960, which, according to Crawford Young, 'took on the aspect of an anti-Baluba plebiscite' throughout the Kasai province.[11] Although the MNC-K had won a plurality of 21 seats out of 71 in the provincial assembly, it failed to win control of the provincial government. For Lumumba was able to put together a coalition totalling 50 votes and hand over the provincial leadership to Barthélemy Mukenge, a Lulua. This was Lumumba's first major political blunder. As the number one national leader, he chose to side with one group in a bitter inter-ethnic conflict. Although this was fair game, democratically speaking, it sent a very bad message to Luba victims of ethnic cleansing, particularly those facing deadly violence from the Lulua and other groups in Kasai.

The defeat in the Kasai province came on top of Kalonji's failure to win an influential position in the national government. Ironically, Kalonji had rejected the agriculture portfolio in Lumumba's cabinet, a position that suited well his abilities as an agricultural engineer, and one that he accepted four years later in Tshombe's cabinet. In 1960, he and his top lieutenants were so bitter with frustration and political defeat that they confused their own narrow political interests with those of an entire group, the Luba of southeastern Kasai.[12] In Katanga, their support for Tshombe against Sendwe and his Balubakat party militated against the best interests of the Luba-Kasai settlers, who subsequently stood alone. On the one side, they were rejected by Tshombe's Conakat and its 'authentic Katangese' like Munongo, the architect of ethnic cleansing against Kasaians. On the other side, their Luba-Katanga kin, who were unitarists and Tshombe's political enemies, accused them of betrayal. In Kasai, the Luba leaders had earlier rejected the idea of repatriation contained in the Lake Munkamba accords of January 1960, which were endorsed by Luba traditional rulers under the pressure of colonial officials. By 14 June 1960, these same leaders were ready to put out an emotional call to the Luba scattered all over the Congo to return to their South Kasai homeland. Anti-Luba violence all over Kasai and in Katanga only reinforced this basically self-serving and opportunistic drive by politicians seeking to make up for their own political failures.

The original plan was for the creation of an additional province, whose legislature and government would consist of the MNC-K provincial representatives elected in May. However, Kalonji's personal ambition was such that although he was elected to the national parliament, he saw in the chaotic environment of the period the opportunity to realize his dream of becoming a supreme leader somewhere. On 8 August 1960, he proclaimed the secession of South Kasai from Lubumbashi, where he received encouragement and support from Tshombe and the Belgians. From the idea of a province that would seek parliamentary approval in Kinshasa, it was now a question of establishing the Autonomous State of South Kasai, a sovereign entity, with Kalonji as president and Ngalula as prime minister. Kalonji managed to find traditional rulers who were able to put him through rigorous rites of passage from the presidency to the throne as the new *mulopwe* or king of the Luba. That the Luba-Kasai had never known a single ruler in nearly two centuries did not seem to matter to the MNC-K leader, who now went by the name of Kalonji Ditunga, the last word in the royal nomenclature meaning 'country' or 'homeland'.

The creation of South Kasai coincided with the launching of a major drive by the ANC to move into the Katanga province for purposes of crushing the secession. From Kananga, one of the major military bases and transportation hubs in the Congo, the major means of surface communication with Katanga, including the line of rail, passed through the territory designated as the state of South Kasai. Whoever gave the ANC the order to crush the rebellion in South Kasai before moving on to Katanga – be it Lumumba or Mobutu – the entire chain of command, including Mobutu, Lumumba and Kasa-Vubu, must be held responsible for the heinous crimes against humanity committed by ANC troops against unarmed civilians. That Hammarskjöld could make reckless statements about genocide without any credible evidence, and that Kasa-Vubu could dismiss Lumumba illegally and get away with it internationally, shows how the secession of South Kasai provided Lumumba's enemies with the excuse they needed to get rid of him.

With Lumumba's fall and assassination, the moderate leaders in Kinshasa were in no hurry to take action against Kalonji's rebellion. After all, he was a member of their anticommunist and pro-Western club. He was so accommodating to his allies in Kinshasa that he turned Mbuji-Mayi, the South Kasai capital, into the preferred location for slaughtering Lumumba's followers and other progressives. Pierre Finant, the first governor of the Eastern province, and other prominent Lumumbists were sent there for extrajudicial executions. Relying on the export of diamonds and on highly motivated civil servants, South Kasai enjoyed two years of self-rule during which thousands of internally displaced persons were resettled in gainful employment and social services were relatively well run. All of this took place in the context of an increasingly militaristic regime, which waged war against all peripheral groups that were unwilling to accept Luba rule, the Kanyok in particular.

In September 1962, the secession was ended by a military revolt led by the chief of staff of Kalonji's own army, with the support of central authorities in Kinshasa. South Kasai became one of the 21 provinces established by law in 1962. In 1966, when President Mobutu reduced the number of provinces to eight, it was one of only two new provinces to survive, the other one being Lower Congo. However, the province was enlarged to incorporate the rest of the Kabinda district and the entire Sankuru district, and renamed as Eastern Kasai.

The fall of Patrice Lumumba Having failed to bring Lumumba down through the mutiny, his internal and external enemies used the secessions of Katanga and South Kasai as obstacle courses through which he could be entrapped. He was charged with the sin of communism in the first instance, and accused of the crime of genocide in the second. I have already shown how the latter accusation arose, and will examine the first charge in detail in the second part of the chapter, in connection with the role of the United Nations. Suffice it to say that in the face of considerable Western support for the Katanga secession and UN reluctance to use force to end it, Lumumba requested and received some military aid from the Soviet Union in August 1960. For his enemies in Washington and Brussels, this was, at least officially and for propaganda reasons, the straw that broke the camel's back. It provided them with an easy justification for removing from power and eventually assassinating a nationalist and revolutionary leader who threatened their neocolonial interests in Central Africa.

Lumumba's fall and assassination were the result of a vast conspiracy involving US, Belgian and UN officials on the one hand, and his Congolese political enemies, including Kasa-Vubu, Mobutu and Tshombe, on the other. In the United States, a Senate Committee headed by Senator Frank Church investigated the role of the Central Intelligence Agency (CIA) in the affair in 1975–76.[13] After detailing all that the Agency did in planning and helping Lumumba's political rivals in the Congo to kill him, the committee absolves the CIA, since it did not actually pull the trigger or carry out the very act of assassination. A very strange conclusion, indeed. In Belgium, new revelations on the role of Belgian authorities in the assassination by Ludo De Witte forced the government in December 1999 to approve the creation of a parliamentary commission of inquiry.[14] My own research in the United Nations Archives in New York has yielded data on the contempt for Lumumba by UN Under-Secretary-General Ralph Bunche, an African American and former professor of political science at Howard University; the anti-Lumumba activities of Andrew Cordier, another American UN official in ONUC; and the close collaboration between UN, US and moderate Congolese officials. Following is a reconstruction of the entire episode from 18 August 1960 to 17 January 1961.

US President Dwight D. Eisenhower met with his National Security Council on 18 August 1960. Following a briefing from his aides on the situation in the Congo, he asked them whether 'we can't get rid of this guy'. To Allen Dulles, the CIA boss, this was taken to be a presidential directive to assassinate Lumumba, as US presidents were then held by conventions of 'deniability' never to say such nasty things openly. Back at the CIA headquarters at Langley, Virginia, Dulles gave instructions to Sidney Gottlieb, the CIA's top scientist, to move expeditiously on implementing the presidential order. Gottlieb would later land in Kinshasa, equipped with a deadly substance made of cobra venom, to be applied to Lumumba's food or toothpaste. To Lawrence Devlin, the CIA station chief and the man who had recruited Mobutu for Uncle Sam between 1958 and 1960 in Brussels, this type of adventure *à la* James Bond appeared ludicrous. Who was going to penetrate Lumumba's security in order to poison him? For Devlin, the best course of action was to work with Lumumba's Congolese rivals to eliminate him politically and, maybe later, physically. This is the plan of action that was finally put in motion, in collaboration with Belgium.

By 1 September, ANC troops had successfully invaded South Kasai and were advancing towards Katanga. Frightened by reports of the boldness of these troops, Tshombe and Kalonji, the secessionist leaders, appealed to Kasa-Vubu, their moderate and federalist ally, to stop Lumumba's anti-secessionist drive. Two critical factors gave Kasa-Vubu the impetus he needed to make the move against Lumumba. The first was that ANC military action in South Kasai had resulted in massacres of innocent civilians in several locations, notably at Mbuji-Mayi and Kasengulu, near Tshilenge. With Hammarskjöld cynically exploiting these unfortunate killings by describing them as 'genocide' against the Kasai Luba, Kasa-Vubu found it convenient to blame the prime minister, while sparing ANC chief of staff Mobutu and the field commanders. The second factor was the presence in Kinshasa of Andrew Cordier. According to Thomas Kanza, who served as the Congo's first permanent representative at the United Nations, Cordier 'arranged things in favor of Kasavubu and the interests of the West'.[15] The man threw the weight and prestige of the UN behind the Western demand that Kasa-Vubu dismiss Lumumba.

On the evening of 5 September 1960, the Congolese were startled upon hearing the little and squeaky voice of President Kasa-Vubu on the airwaves announcing his dismissal of Lumumba.[16] The dismissal was based on a controversial and little-understood article of the interim constitution handed down by the Belgians, but it was clearly a civilian coup and therefore illegal. Both houses of parliament, where Lumumba still had a working majority, gave him a vote of confidence and rejected Kasa-Vubu's decision as null and void. Lumumba reacted by dismissing Kasa-Vubu, whom he had supported for the ceremonial presidency against Jean Bolikango for purposes of appeasing the strong Abako constituency in Kinshasa. Parliament also refused to remove Kasa-Vubu from office, in spite of his illegal action. By dismissing Lumumba illegally, Kasa-Vubu created a constitutional crisis for the young republic.

There were only two ways of resolving the constitutional crisis: either by reconciling Lumumba and Kasa-Vubu or by forcibly removing one of them from the political scene. Diplomats from a number of African countries and the new UN envoy Rajeshwar Dayal chose the first option, but failed. The path of reconciliation had already been made into an obstacle course by the good works of Andrew Cordier, the US Embassy in Kinshasa, Kasa-Vubu's Belgian advisers and Colonel Mobutu's CIA and UN friends, including CIA chief Devlin, UN force commander Carl von Horn of Sweden and his deputy, General Ben Hammou Kettani of Morocco. For a week, the political situation remained confused, while African diplomats tried their best to reconcile Lumumba and Kasa-Vubu. Mobutu's friends had been encouraging him to stage the third instalment of the drama, which he did on 14 September 1960. The young officer pulled off his first military coup with the help of the CIA and of General Kettani.

Officially, Mobutu declared his intention as that of temporarily *neutralizing* both Lumumba and Kasa-Vubu politically. Until the situation improves or returns to normal, he promised, the country was to be run by a college of commissioners made up of university graduates and students under the presidency of Justin Bomboko, foreign minister in Lumumba's cabinet. In reality, this was a coup against Lumumba. While he was virtually placed under house arrest, the apparently 'neutralized' Kasa-Vubu presided over the swearing-in ceremony for the young commissioners, and continued to discharge his official functions such as receiving foreign envoys. Bomboko, the first commissioner, was actually one of four ministers who had formally endorsed Kasa-Vubu's dismissal order. When the Kasa-Vubu delegation to the UN General Assembly won the credentials battle over the rival delegation representing Lumumba and his democratically elected government, the process of eliminating him from the political scene had won international endorsement, even as he remained extremely popular throughout the Third World.

Having succeeded in removing Lumumba from office, the anti-Lumumba alliance of UN officials, Belgian authorities, US diplomats and Congolese moderates was now preoccupied with how to prevent him from regaining state power. Timberlake, the US ambassador, was totally obsessed with this question, and sought UN approval for Lumumba's arrest. More elegant and diplomatic than the Yankee envoy, Hammarskjöld played for time, so as 'not to create the impression that he was "out to get Lumumba"'.[17] But his appeasement of the Belgians, his August 1960 agreement with Tshombe to station UN troops in Katanga without threatening the secession, and his slavish obedience of directives from Washington could not hide the fact that he was 'out to get Lumumba', as his American and Belgian allies did.

The Belgians had no scruples about their intentions. In a well-researched book and an outstanding contribution to the analysis of the Congo crisis, Belgian sociologist Ludo De Witte has shown, conclusively, that the Belgian ruling class and its representatives in the Congo were directly responsible for Lumumba's assassination.[18] As early as 10 September 1960, Foreign Affairs Minister Pierre Wigny wrote to his subordinates in Brazzaville that 'responsible authorities had the duty to render Lumumba harmless'.[19] In response to these instructions, Colonel Louis Marlière, Mobutu's Belgian adviser who spent a lot of time with other Belgian conspirators across the Congo River in Brazzaville, started making preparations for assassinating Lumumba as part of an operation called the Barracuda Plan. In a document signed in October 1960, the then Belgian minister for African affairs, Count Harold d'Aspremont Lynden, stated explicitly that Belgian interests required 'the final elimination of Lumumba'.

The Barracuda Plan, like the CIA cobra venom plan, was abandoned once Lumumba was placed under house arrest on 10 October, with a ring of Ghanaian blue helmets around his residence flanked by an outer ring of ANC troops. Following the credentials vote in the UN General Assembly on 24 November, Lumumba realized that the only way to regain power was through popular support and armed struggle led by the legitimist forces then gathering in Kisangani under the leadership of Antoine Gizenga, the deputy prime minister. He had to break out of his isolation as a prisoner in his own residence. On 27 November 1960, Lumumba fled Kinshasa in an attempt to reach his stronghold of Kisangani. US and Belgian intelligence services were quick to offer their assistance to Mobutu and security police chief Victor Nendaka in tracking Lumumba's movements. A Sabena helicopter was provided to Gilbert Pongo, Nendaka's deputy, for this purpose. Raymond Linard, pilot and co-owner of Air Brousse, an airline providing services to small airports in the Congo, also joined the chase.[20]

Lumumba was captured on 1 December at Lodi, on the left bank of the Sankuru River, and denied UN protection by the Ghanaian contingent at Mweka the next morning.[21] He was handed over to Pongo at Ilebo, and flown with the latter to Kinshasa on an Air Congo DC-3 airliner. After enduring more humiliation and brutal beatings at the Binza parachutist camp in Mobutu's presence and spending a miserable night in Nendaka's garage, Lumumba was transferred to the élite armoured brigade camp at Mbanza-Ngungu, in the Lower Congo. Even in jail, Lumumba continued to pose a threat to the moderate leadership in Kinshasa and to its Western backers. By January 1961, the Lumumbist government in Kisangani began expanding its control and authority in the eastern part of the republic and thus encouraged Lumumba's followers all over the country to continue the struggle for genuine independence, national unity and territorial integrity.

US and Belgian officials were greatly alarmed by these developments, with the US embassy in Kinshasa preoccupied by rumours of a pro-Lumumba coup. There was also fear among the moderate Congolese authorities that the soldiers guarding Lumumba at Mbanza-Ngungu might free him. For Washington and Brussels, the time to get rid of Lumumba physically had arrived, but there was need to get his Congolese enemies involved in the conspiracy to kill him. The Congolese conspirators were the moderate leaders in Kinshasa, including members of the college of commissioners, and the secessionist leaders of Katanga and South Kasai. Since Washington had limited ability to operate on the ground, direct responsibility for Lumumba's assassination was assumed by the Belgians, who carried out this odious act through a chain of command running from the ruling class in Brussels to Belgian non-commissioned officers in the Katanga gendarmerie.

According to De Witte, three separate levels of responsibility can be delineated in this chain. At the very top, there was a Congo committee chaired by Prime Minister Gaston Eyskens and including African Affairs Minister Harold d'Aspremont Lynden and Foreign Minister Pierre Wigny. It is the last two who orchestrated the entire assassination plan, through their assistants such as Major Jules Loos, military adviser to d'Aspremont Lynden. And it is this minister who gave the final order for Lumumba's transfer to Lubumbashi, which took place on 17 January 1961 in a Sabena DC-4 under the command of Captain Piet Van der Meersch.[22]

The second level comprised the major Belgian representatives in the Congo, both military and civilian. The military officers included Colonel Frédéric Vandewalle, former head of the security police in the Belgian Congo and coordinator of Belgian military affairs in Katanga; Colonel Louis Marlière, Mobutu's military adviser; Major Guy Weber, Tshombe's military adviser; Commander Armand Verdickt, a Belgian intelligence officer serving in Katanga; and Captain-Major René Smal, another member of the Katanga advisory team under Professor René Clemens. In addition to this *éminence grise* of the Katanga secession, the civilian advisers included Victor Tignée, Godefroid Munongo's chief of staff, Jacques Bartelous and Jacques Brassinne.

All of these senior officials played a crucial role in masterminding the assassination plot and giving orders to the third group, or those who had to execute the plan. These included police commissioners Frans Verscheure, Georges Segers and Gerard Soete; Captain Julien Gat, the chief executioner; plus Lieutenants Gabriel Michels and Claude Grandelet, and Lance-Sergeant François Son.

Stories that have long circulated as rumour in the Congo, but which were also told to the UN commission of inquiry, have now been proved to be historical facts. Lumumba and his two companions, Youth and Sports Minister Maurice Mpolo and Senate Vice-President Joseph Okito, were severely beaten on the plane ride to Katanga, in the presence of two Luba-Kasai members of the college of commissioners, Defence Commissioner Ferdinand Kazadi and Internal Affairs Commissioner Jonas Mukamba.[23] Not too far from the Luano airport in Lubumbashi,

Lumumba and his companions were tortured at the Brouwez villa some eight kilometres from downtown; personally assaulted by Munongo, other Katanga leaders and Belgian officers; and shot by an execution squad under the command of Captain Gat. Police Commissioner Soete and his brother removed the bodies from the burial site the next day and dissolved them in acid.[24] The Belgian parliamentarian inquiry should, if it is conducted in a more transparent manner than the Church committee whitewash in the US Senate, yield more useful information on Lumumba's assassination.

The United Nations and the Congo Crisis

For the plot against Lumumba to succeed, the support, or at the very least the neutrality, of the UN Secretariat was indispensable. At every critical juncture in Lumumba's drama, UN officials and troops were involved, by acts of commission or omission. After Kasa-Vubu's coup, Cordier, the US citizen who had replaced Bunche as acting representative of the UN secretary-general in the Congo, denied Lumumba access to the national radio station. He pretended that the ban was to prevent incendiary speeches by all involved, when Kasa-Vubu was free to cross the river and use the Brazzaville radio station under the control of his kinsman, the priest-president Youlou. As already indicated above, UN troops stood by as Lumumba was tortured by his captors at Ilebo on 2 December 1960, and at the Lubumbashi airport, when he was brought over to be handed to his executioners following severe beatings on the plane, on 17 January 1961. Having sided with Kasa-Vubu in the constitutional dispute, Hammarskjöld himself told the Security Council on 10 December 1960 that the UN could not do anything about Lumumba's arrest by Mobutu's troops since his arrest warrant was approved by the head of state.[25]

Thus, if the United Nations was not as directly involved in Lumumba's assassination as Belgium and the United States, it was nevertheless an accessory before the fact. This was a result of the very broad mandate that the Security Council had given to ONUC, the UN mission in the Congo, and Hammarskjöld's interpretation of that mandate in accordance with US and Western interests. Even after Hammarskjöld's death in a plane crash near Ndola, Zambia in September 1961, most UN officials were wittingly or unwittingly serving Western interests in the Congo.[26] As Timberlake had thought from the very beginning, the UN represented the best umbrella for US interests there.

The United Nations mission in the Congo (ONUC) The Congo crisis erupted in early July 1960, in an international context dominated by national liberation struggles and the Cold War. The situation was so tense that Hammarskjöld took the rare step of formally notifying the Security Council in accordance with Article 99 of the UN Charter that there was a potential threat to international peace and security in Central Africa.[27] With the United States convinced that the UN was the best instrument for protecting Western interests in the Congo and the Soviet Union attentive to the Afro-Asian solidarity with Lumumba, the Security Council approved the deployment of a UN peacekeeping force to the Congo.

Once ONUC was established, Hammarskjöld departed from previous practice, by which the Council itself kept direct control over peace-keeping operations, by centralizing management and supervision within the Secretariat. He named a special representative of the secretary-general (SRSG) as the overall manager of the UN operation, and the person to whom the force commander must report. Before a commander had arrived on the scene in the Congo, Ralph Bunche acted as both UN special representative and force commander.[28] In addition to the SRSG, a position of chief of civilian operations was also created for ONUC, in view of the importance of the nation-building component of its mandate.

A major dispute arose concerning the interpretation of this mandate by Lumumba and Hammarskjöld, whose views on the issue were diametrically opposed. The text of the mandate itself is quite clear. The Security Council directed the secretary-general to provide military assistance to the Congolese government to ensure the withdrawal of Belgian troops, to end the Katanga secession, and to restore law and order throughout the country. It also directed the Secretariat to provide technical assistance to the government for ensuring the smooth running of essential services.[29] For Lumumba, then, what ONUC was supposed to do was crystal clear: help his government send the Belgian troops home; end the Katanga secession, which was made possible by Belgian support; restore law and order; and train Congolese civil servants in running essential services. Hammarskjöld, on the other hand, saw matters differently. The most charitable explanation of his position is that he was convinced that the Belgians would leave without confrontation once UN troops had restored law and order and brought the situation under control.

While this was true for the rest of the country, it could not apply to Katanga, where Belgian soldiers and white mercenaries were backing the secession. Hammarskjöld was unwilling to use force to expel Belgian military advisers and white mercenaries from Katanga. He remained

adamant in this way, even after the Security Council implicitly authorized such action on 21 February 1961, in the wake of Lumumba's
assassination. Ironically, that resolution was actually the legal basis that
Hammarskjöld's own envoys in the Congo, deputy special representative
Mahmoud Khiary and the representative in Katanga, Conor Cruise
O'Brien, used for O'Brien's two bold attempts to end the secession by
force, Operation Rumpunch (28 August 1961) and Operation Morthor
(13 September 1961).[30] Neither operation succeeded, thanks in part to
vigorous protests by major Western powers, led by the United Kingdom.

Fearful of antagonizing the Western powers with a more forceful
stand against Tshombe and the secession, Hammarskjöld was mainly
interested in using the UN for maintaining law and order and running
essential services outside Katanga. He placed greater emphasis on these
law and order and nation-building components of the ONUC mandate,
since they were perfectly compatible with his grandiose vision of turning the United Nations into a world government. One positive outcome
of this vision for the Congo was that long before the second United
Nations Operation in Somalia (UNOSOM II), the Congo mission had
broken new ground in the evolution of UN peacekeeping with respect
to preventive diplomacy, peace enforcement, and the leading role of the
secretary-general in shaping the mandate of peacekeeping missions.[31]
The Security Council gave ONUC a very clear mandate to engage in
peace-building activities, and this resulted in the UN literally taking over
all public services in the Congo. Before that, UN peacekeeping operations involved mostly the monitoring of ceasefires in interstate conflicts
by keeping two well-defined belligerents apart. With the Congo, the
UN embarked on a new adventure in seeking durable solutions to
internal conflicts, with all the consequences that this entails for national
sovereignty and the pursuit of hidden agendas by external forces.

The danger of external interference in domestic affairs did materialize in the Congo. The secretary-general and his chief collaborators on
Congo matters shared a common Cold War outlook with Western
policymakers, and saw their mission in the Congo as that of preserving
the then existing balance of forces in the world. Two diplomats who
had great admiration for Hammarskjöld have testified as to his pro-
West bias. Kanza, the former Congolese representative at the UN, writes
that Hammarskjöld 'believed that the West had a sacred mission towards
Africa in generally, and especially the Congo'.[32] Dayal, the SRSG in the
Congo, reports that his boss 'had little respect for the Soviet Under-
Secretary, G. P. Arkadiev, and though Arkadiev's functions were political,
he was rather pointedly excluded from participation in the Congo
discussions'.[33] Dayal does not tell us why a senior UN political affairs

official was so excluded by a man he claims was committed to the philosophy of nonalignment.

This exclusion was all the more significant in view of the fact that these 'Congo discussions' in the UN Secretariat were a major responsibility of Hammarskjöld's American aides Ralph Bunche and Andrew Cordier, the Cold War crusader who played such a vital role in Kasa-Vubu's coup. Others who played key policymaking roles on the Congo included General Carl von Horn, Hammarskjöld's compatriot who served as force commander in the Congo, and the secretary-general's British assistant, Brian Urquhart. Did Hammarskjöld believe that only Arkadiev was incapable of dissociating his national interests from UN business, while the Americans and other Westerners were, like him, true international civil servants with no national or ideological bias? There was a commonality of views between Hammarskjöld, his collaborators and Western policymakers concerning Lumumba, whom they all distrusted, and on what needed to be done to preserve Western interests in the Congo.[34] For Congolese patriots, there is no ounce of doubt that Hammarskjöld's actions did serve Western interests in the Congo.

U Thant, his successor, was more honest as someone who knew on which side his toast was buttered. Given the new circumstances, the serene but sharp-tongued secretary-general ended up doing exactly what Lumumba had insisted upon, namely using force to end the Katanga secession. This became possible after President John F. Kennedy gave the UN a green light in December 1962 to end Tshombe's rebellion by force. In this regard, it should be noted that the so-called 'U Thant plan' for Katanga's reintegration in the Congo was entirely drafted by Congo experts at Foggy Bottom in Washington and sent to the top floor of the Secretariat through the US mission at the UN.

By then, maintaining the unity of the Congo had become more important for the West than the instability the secession would perpetuate. The Belgians and other Europeans who had feared a Congo under progressive nationalists such as Lumumba and his followers were relieved that the country was now securely in the hands of pro-Western moderates led by General Mobutu. For the UN managers in the Congo, force could be used because the Katanga problem was now seen 'as *per se* part of an external intervention by Belgians, so that the UN could take measures against the Katangese as needed to end the intervention without choosing sides in an internal conflict'.[35] If such a rationalization was needed for UN bureaucrats, the Belgians saw no problem in having Tshombe, their protégé, take a much-needed vacation in Spain before returning home later. He did so 'by the big door' 17 months later, to assume the post of Congo's prime minister. Tshombe's triumphant return in June 1964 coincided with the end of the first UN mission in the Congo.

The UN and US interests in the Congo What has been said concerning the relevance of the UN presence in the Congo for the West in general is even more applicable for the United States in particular. As the leader of the Western camp, the US wasted no time in getting involved in the Congo crisis. In the context of the Cold War, this involvement was part of a tradition established in the Middle East and Southeast Asia after the Second World War, by which Uncle Sam would intervene in a strategically important country where the former colonial power was unable to retain control over a turbulent situation. In the Congo, as in Vietnam, the United States replaced the former colonial power as the principal arbiter of the country's destiny. However, the complexity of the issues and the interests at stake did require that Belgium remain, along with France, Washington's major partner in an increasingly multilateral strategy of imperialism that sought to involve other Western powers, regional powers or clients, and multilateral lending and economic management agencies such as the International Monetary Fund (IMF), the World Bank and the Paris Club. Where there were no vital US interests, military intervention was best achieved through proxies, the best one being the United Nations.

Thus, during the first Congo crisis, the UN Secretariat was a key actor in the multilateral strategy of imperialism led by the United States. Neither Hammarskjöld nor the US government had any intention of collaborating with the legally and democratically constituted Lumumba government to resolve the crisis. US diplomats and intelligence officers were doing their best to undermine and subvert this government.[36] They were fortunate to have dedicated allies in ONUC. When Cordier became the acting head of the UN Congo mission between Bunche's departure on 28 August 1960 and Dayal's arrival on 8 September, there was no doubt as to the fact that the United Nations had become a simple instrument of US policy in the Congo. Cordier and US Ambassador Timberlake worked hand in hand to implement US policy objectives. Acting as a viceroy, Cordier helped engineer and execute the illegal overthrow of Lumumba from power, beginning with his active support of the Kasa-Vubu coup of 5 September.

Lumumba died for attempting to uphold the constitutional order, national unity and territorial integrity. The Katanga secession was the single most important issue in his bitter dispute with Hammarskjöld concerning the UN mandate. Because of UN reluctance to end it by force, Lumumba felt compelled to seek military assistance elsewhere, and he obtained some help from the Soviet Union. Both US and UN officials raised such a fuss about Soviet planes, trucks and supplies that it was largely forgotten that the first shipment of military equipment and supplies to the Congo was part of the Soviet contribution to the UN operation, which included the ferrying of Ghanaian troops from Accra to Kinshasa.[37] Moreover, as the Soviet government argued in a note to the UN secretary-general, 'the sending by the Soviet Union of help to the government of the Republic of the Congo – in the form of civil aircraft and motor vehicles – was not contrary to the terms of the resolutions of 14 and 22 July 1960, since the said resolutions set no limit on the right of the government to ask for or be given direct bilateral aid'.[38]

On 31 August 1960, when told of US concern over Soviet assistance in ferrying ANC troops to Kisangani for the campaign against the secession, Hammarskjöld reassured Washington 'that he had given strict orders not to permit any "unauthorized landings" by Soviet planes transporting Lumumba's troops to Katanga'.[39] This is a good example of how UN interference in the internal affairs of the Congo was part of the US strategy of indirect intervention. In this particular case of Soviet assistance to Lumumba, UN actions were also part of a wider propaganda campaign aimed at convincing world public opinion that Lumumba was bent on allowing Soviet expansion in the heart of Africa. As Kanza points out, this campaign was 'part of the necessary psychological preparation for a major coup in the Congo, a coup inspired and supported by the Western powers'.[40] For this coup to succeed, the support of the UN Secretariat was indispensable.

Having played a major role in Lumumba's fall, the UN was also useful in the American-led drive to eliminate his followers from the political scene. In the wake of Lumumba's assassination, the main US objective was to prevent Gizenga or any other prominent Lumumbist from becoming head of government. Everything had to be done to make sure that the radical nationalists would not dominate parliament and the government. Under UN auspices, the parliament was convened on the campus of Lovanium University (now the University of Kinshasa). The outcome was never in doubt, as those external forces controlling the situation had already decided that Cyrille Adoula was the best choice for the post of prime minister. US officials have described the entire process as 'really a U.S. operation but using outstanding UN personalities'.[41]

The pattern of US involvement in Congolese affairs changed in 1964, with the departure of the UN force from the country by 30 June.

Without the UN umbrella, the United States had to find another way of influencing the course of events in the Congo. Since a heavy American presence was excluded from the very beginning, the most appropriate strategy was that of multilateral Western involvement underwritten by the United States, with Belgium playing a leading role in coordinating the involvement and supplying the necessary personnel for its success on the ground. Given its vital interests in the Congo, its colonial experience and its familiarity with the country and its leaders, Belgium was perfectly suited to play this role. The nomination of Tshombe as prime minister in July 1964 and the US–Belgian collaboration in counter-insurgency were part and parcel of this strategy. For in order to protect Western interests and save the moderates, the two powers had to step in more forcefully to fill the 'internal security gap' created by the departure of UN troops, in the midst of popular insurrections for a 'second independence'.

Notes

1. According to Durch, 'The UN operation in the Congo', p. 336, 'ONUC reached its peak strength in July 1961, with 19,825 troops.' ONUC was the acronym for the operation's name in French, Opération des Nations unies au Congo.

2. This chapter is partly based on an earlier discussion of this theme in my article 'The continuing struggle for national liberation in Zaire'.

3. For the basically reformist ideological positions of the nationalist petty bourgeoisie as a whole, see in addition to Chapter 2 in this book Jean-Paul Sartre's preface to Van Lierde, *La pensée politique de Patrice Lumumba*.

4. Vanderstraeten, *De la Force publique à l'Armée nationale congolaise*, pp. 141–3, defends Janssens against accusations that he played the role of *agent provocateur*. The general's own version of events can be found in his memoirs, *J'étais le général Janssens*.

5. See Kalb, *The Congo Cables*, p. 7.

6. For an excellent study of this theme, see Weissman, *American Foreign Policy in the Congo 1960–1964*.

7. See Mukenge, 'Croyances religieuses et structures socio-familiales en société luba' on the strong connection between Luba religion and family structures.

8. Van Zandijcke, *Pages de l'histoire du Kasayi*, p. 7. See also Mabika Kalanda, *Baluba et Lulua*, pp. 91–5.

9. Vansina, *Kingdoms of the Savanna*, p. 221.

10. From an administrative report cited in Nicolaï and Jacques, *La transformation des paysages congolais par le chemin de fer*, p. 103.

11. Young, *Politics in the Congo*, p. 537.

12. See Ilunga Mbiye Kabongo, 'Ethnicity, social classes, and the state in the Congo, 1960–65: the case of the Baluba', for the most comprehensive study of the Luba-Kasai dilemma. Unfortunately, this unique and outstanding work on Luba–Kasai political history is still unpublished.

13. See US Congress, Senate, *Interim Report: Alleged Assassination Plots Involving Foreign Leaders*, by the Select Committee to Study Government Operations with Respect to Intelligence Activities, 94th Congress, 1st Session, 20 November 1975; the same committee's *Final Report: Foreign and Military Intelligence*, Book I, 94th Congress, 2nd Session, 26 April 1976.

14. De Witte, *L'assassinat de Lumumba*.

15. Kanza, *Conflict in the Congo*, p. 301.

16. As a veteran of municipal politics, Kasa-Vubu actually made a mistake in reading his prepared text by initially referring to Lumumba as *premier bourgmestre* (first burgomaster) instead of *premier ministre*.

17. Kalb, *The Congo Cables*, p. 137.

18. De Witte, *L'assassinat de Lumumba*.

19. This and other references to the Belgian plot are taken from the chronology in ibid., pp. 401–6.

20. See De Witte, *L'assassinat de Lumumba*, pp. 128–32.

21. For details of this episode, which included Lumumba's driver taking advantage of the lack of vigilance by his ANC guards to take the prime minister to the Ghanaian soldiers' camp, see ibid., pp. 127–35.

22. The full text of d'Aspremont Lynden's order of 16 January 1961 to transfer Lumumba to Katanga 'as quickly as possible' appears in ibid., p. 217.

23. Both Kazadi and Mukamba were to play prominent roles in South Kasai politics, and Mukamba went on to become one of the most powerful associates of President Mobutu, for whom he managed the diamond mines of Mbuji-Mayi for more than a decade until 1997.

24. De Witte, *L'assassinat de Lumumba*, pp. 237–324.

25. Nkrumah, *Challenge of the Congo*, pp. 91–2.

26. The major exceptions were Rajeshwar Dayal of India, who replaced Bunche and Cordier as special representative in September 1960; Mahmoud Khiary of Tunisia, his deputy; and Conor Cruise O'Brien of Ireland, who served as UN representative in Katanga.

27. Durch, *The Evolution of Peacekeeping*, p. 319.

28. See Hill and Malik, *Peacekeeping and the United Nations*, p. 38; Durch, *The Evolution of Peacekeeping*, p. 337.

29. Ratner, *The New UN Peacekeeping*, Table 1.1, p. 11.

30. See O'Brien, *To Katanga and Back*, for his own account of these events; and Kalb, *The Congo Cables*, pp. 287–99.

31. Contrary to what Michael Wesley states in his book *Casualties of the New*

World Order, p. 78, UNOSOM II was not the first UN attempt at peace enforcement.

32. Kanza, *Conflict in the Congo*, p. 220.
33. Dayal, *Mission for Hammarskjöld*, p. 308.
34. Kalb, *The Congo Cables*, pp. 17–35.
35. Ratner, *The New Peacekeeping*, p. 105.
36. US Congress, Senate, *Interim Report*, pp. 13–70.
37. Kalb, *The Congo Cables*, pp. 57–8.
38. Cited in Kanza, *Conflict in the Congo*, p. 282.
39. Kalb, *The Congo Cables*, p. 69.
40. Kanza, *Conflict in the Congo*, p. 284.
41. Cited in Weissman, *American Foreign Policy in the Congo*, p. 147.

CHAPTER 4

The Second Independence Movement

§ THE first major resistance against the postcolonial state in Africa took place between 1963 and 1968 in the Congo. A mass-based movement for genuine independence, this resistance was the work of a popular alliance of workers, peasants, the unemployed urban youth, students, lower civil servants and radical nationalist leaders. This chapter is a historical analysis of the struggle between the neocolonial state and this popular alliance, which was a revival through armed struggle of the mass democratic movement of the 1956–60 period. The objectives of the movement were basically the same during the two periods, namely, freedom from foreign control and expanded democratic and economic rights. Hence the label 'second independence', which ordinary people in the movement chose to designate their struggle. The chapter also provides an assessment of the strengths of the second independence movement in its confrontation with the neocolonial state, as well as its weaknesses in the face of the externally led counterinsurgency.

The Birth of the Second Independence Movement

Patrice Lumumba's martyrdom for the cause of genuine independence, national unity and territorial integrity gave rise to the first political opposition to the neocolonial state under the moderates. Even before Lumumba's death, the government established by his followers in Kisangani had begun expanding its control and authority in the eastern part of the country, with spectacular military victories in Kasai and northern Katanga. Instead of sapping their morale, Lumumba's death pushed them to try even harder. The moderates who had taken over the central government in Kinshasa rushed to conclude a military alliance with the very secessionist forces against which they were supposed to be fighting in Katanga and South Kasai. On 27 February 1961, Joseph Ileo, the interim prime minister, signed a military accord in Lubumbashi with Tshombe and Kalonji.[1] This was followed by regular meetings between Mobutu and high-level representatives of the two secessionist governments in Brazzaville and Lubumbashi, where another military agreement was signed in July 1961.[2]

The threat of a Lumumbist victory was finally averted when the US-backed manoeuvres of the UN Congo mission succeeded in arranging for the formation of a government of national unity in August 1961 under Adoula, as already mentioned in the preceding chapter. In spite of the hopes raised by the entry of Gizenga, Christophe Gbenye and others in the Adoula government, the latter was unable to resolve the contradictions between the two fractions of the political class. The Adoula government was unable to achieve a lasting reconciliation because it was basically a puppet regime, responsive to the pressures of General Mobutu, who had become a veritable kingmaker due to his external ties, and taking its directives from the US embassy in Kinshasa. Weissman has shown that the American government 'not only supported Adoula, it was, in many ways, part of his government'.[3] Having outmanoeuvred the Lumumbists at Lovanium, Adoula's tutors and advisers sought to diminish their influence in the new government, before having them dismissed.

Most of the prominent Lumumbists were eliminated from the political scene by October 1963. Some of them went into exile across the river in Brazzaville, where a revolution had replaced the conservative Youlou government with a more progressive leadership in August. It was in Brazzaville that practical steps were taken to launch an armed struggle for purposes of regaining state power. The leadership of a national opposition to the puppet regime had been constituted. But if this opposition was to present a serious threat to the neocolonial regime and state, it needed a mass base. A remarkable fact about this period is that not only did the masses adhere to the opposition movement in great numbers; they also brought to it its guiding thread conceptually, by calling it a struggle for a second independence.

The concept of 'second independence' The concept of 'second independence' was not coined by an academic, or by a 'traditional' intellectual in the Gramscian sense.[4] It was a product of the political beliefs and notions of ordinary Congolese in their attempt to make sense of the crisis of decolonization. In addition to this theoretically rich concept of second independence, virtually all of the guiding ideas and themes of the opposition movement were essentially the intellectual production of the masses and their organic intellectuals. These included their notions of state officials as 'liars' and as the 'new whites' and various magico-religious ideas concerning warfare.

Rather than being the product of pure imagination, these political notions were grounded in the material reality of their experience since independence. During the campaign for the independence elections of May 1960, politicians had promised to their constituents everything under the sun, including the abolition of taxes, houses in durable materials, piped water, electricity, free healthcare, free education, more jobs and better wages. After independence, people noticed that most of the promises had not been kept. There were no jobs, houses and modern amenities; the social services available were deteriorating rather than improving; and taxes of all kinds were still being collected. In some areas, people were still being required to do forced labour on public projects such as roads.

Politicians were liars, people said. In many local languages, it became fashionable to equate lying with 'doing politics'. Added to this was a general perception that little had changed. The whites were gone, but the blacks who had replaced them as rulers and administrators were just as bad, oppressive and at times cruel. They lived in the big colonial mansions or villas; drove nice cars and sometimes bigger and better cars than the colonialists; looked down on the people; and were quick to use the army and the police to repress any dissent or questioning of their authority. In many cases, their use of force was uncalled for and totally arbitrary. They were the 'new whites', black in skin but white in their thinking.

Moreover, the people found out that the new rulers could not hold on to power in the face of popular discontent without the help and support of the former colonial rulers. Military assistance, training and even intervention from their friends and allies abroad helped the new rulers retain control over unwilling subjects. Thus, to fight them also meant fighting against their backers in the international community. However difficult that might be, it had to be done if people were to have genuine freedom and to improve their standard of living. The first independence had failed. It was time to fight for a second independence.

Peasants and other ordinary people in the Kwilu district of Bandundu, who had been politicized by the PSA during the independence struggle, made the foregoing analysis. However, people elsewhere in the country shared the main outline of their assessment of independence and why it failed to meet their expectations. What is impressive in this analysis is the clarity of the popular vision of postcolonial politics, particularly the continuity in the functions of the state, its class basis and its neocolonial connection. This clarity resulted from the relatively high level of political consciousness among urban youth and among the people generally in those areas that were heavily politicized by the parties of the Lumumbist coalition. These were, for the most part, areas that also had historical memories of either primary resistance or anticolonial revolts, such as the districts of South Kivu, North Katanga, Maniema and Kwilu.

The concept of second independence is also consistent with Amilcar Cabral's notion of the liberation struggle as consisting of two phases: the national phase, in which all classes of colonial society unite to fight the colonial system; and the social phase of reconstruction and transformation, in which the essential aspect of the problem is the struggle against neocolonialism and its internal allies. Thus, translated into the language of political economy, the struggle for a second independence means a revolutionary class struggle by the popular alliance against the neocolonial state controlled by a power bloc comprising the metropolitan or imperialist bourgeoisie. Such a struggle is in the final analysis a struggle for national liberation. For national liberation in its fullest sense, according to Cabral, is a revolutionary process involving the complete overthrow of imperialist domination in its colonial and neocolonial forms.[5]

The 'new whites' in post-Lumumba Congo So who were the 'new whites' against whom the second independence movement was organized, and why was their mode of governance so bad that a complete overhaul of the state was necessary? Having won their confrontations with the radicals in 1960 and 1963, the moderates were definitely in charge of the Congolese state since the fall of Lumumba. They enjoyed strong support from Belgian, UN and US officials, as well as from other Western government and corporate circles. However, this support was not equally distributed among all major moderate leaders, and this had the effect of exacerbating conflicts within their camp, which was not monolithic. Some of these conflicts had their origins in the pre-independence division between unitarists and federalists. In the immediate post-Lumumba period, the most important conflict was between those moderates in continuous control of the central state apparatus and their counterparts in the provincial capitals, including the secessionist centres of Lubumbashi and Mbuji-Mayi. While the federalists (Tshombe, Kalonji, Kasa-Vubu, Kamitatu and Bolikango) were generally leaders of major regionally based political parties, the unitarists (Mobutu, Adoula, Nendaka and Bomboko) had no solid political base and, except for the latter, only secondary positions in the parties to which they belonged.[6]

The most important factor in the ascendancy of the unitarists in the moderate camp was their control of the central state machinery, particularly its key organs, which were closely linked to external sources of assistance and pressure. The most important of these organs were the military, the security police, the foreign ministry, the central bank and the internal affairs apparatus, which remained under the control of Mobutu, Nendaka, Bomboko, Albert Ndele and Damien Kandolo, respectively. These five men formed the nucleus of what came to be known as the Binza Group, so called because they usually met in the Kinshasa suburb of Binza, where they had private residences. This politically powerful clique worked closely with American, Belgian and UN officials, and imposed its will on President Kasa-Vubu and Prime Minister Adoula.

In accordance with American wishes, the Binza Group used all the means necessary, including pressure on Kasa-Vubu and Adoula, to eliminate the Lumumbists from the political scene. Gizenga, the deputy prime minister, was relegated to the island prison of Bula-Bemba in January 1962. By October 1963, most, if not all, of the ministers from the Lumumbist camp had been sacked. On 29 September 1963, Kasa-Vubu dismissed parliament for the second time during his tenure as head of state, so that he, Adoula and their Binza Group allies could exercise power unfettered by legislative oversight and the probing eye of the Lumumbist coalition. Four days later, the Lumumbists founded an umbrella organization designed to coordinate their struggle to regain state power, the Conseil national de libération (CNL).[7] The CNL moved to establish its headquarters across the river in Brazzaville, where a popular revolution in August 1963 had replaced the reactionary Youlou regime with a more progressive government. Here, the CNL sought to attract support for its struggle against the neocolonial regime from the progressive and socialist countries.

The political defeat of the Lumumbists in the externally orchestrated political manoeuvres of the Binza Group in 1962–63 coincided with the victory of the central government over the secessionists in South Kasai and Katanga. With the radical threat apparently out of the way, the authorities in Kinshasa knew that their external masters would no longer be displeased with the restoration of national unity and territorial integrity. Once the provincial status of South Kasai was established by law in July 1962, pressure was exerted on Kalonji to give up his rebellion. By then, he had lost the support of some of his former lieutenants, and it was the head of his own gendarmerie who ended his adventure in September. The former king of the Luba-Kasai went into exile in Franco's Spain, only to return in July 1964 as agriculture minister in Tshombe's national salvation government. Tshombe's own secession was too tall an order for Mobutu's army. The task of ending it was finally entrusted to UN troops in December 1962, and the Katanga secession was over by the end of January 1963. Tshombe, too, went into exile in Spain, where he spent a year and a half before returning home as prime minister of the Congo as a whole.

The double victory of the Binza Group over the Lumumbists and the secessionists also coincided with new political dynamics in the provinces, whose number rose from six to 21. With ample external aid, the control of funds needed for political manipulation and patronage, and the ability to arrest those provincial leaders they disliked, the group exploited the weakness of provincial governments to consolidate its ascendancy as the final arbiter of political rivalries in the Congo. This turned out to be a double-edged sword. The creation of new provinces had once again raised people's expectations with respect to the fruits of independence, or those promises for a better life made to them in 1960 by the politicians. As these politicians fought each other for power and influence and spent limited financial resources in enriching themselves, dispensing patronage and, rather infrequently, paying state employees, the promises were simply forgotten.

Instead of improving, all social services deteriorated. Instead of more jobs, old ones were disappearing and wage employment became rare, thus contributing to adding thousands of school-leavers and rural migrants to the ranks of the urban lumpenproletariat. In addition to these privations, the people were subject to unhealthy living conditions, a skyrocketing inflation due to the shortage of essentials and to specu-lation, and all kinds of extortion by security forces and other state employees. The result was a widespread popular discontent with the new provincial governments and, indirectly, the central government authorities sustaining them. This discontent served as a basis for an aspiration towards a new or real independence, one in which the leaders would be more people-oriented, rather than more interested in enriching themselves and serving their foreign masters.

Strengths and Weaknesses of the Second Independence Movement

The neocolonial situation involves the uninterrupted exploitation of the country's resources by the metropolitan bourgeoisie, but this time in collaboration with national ruling classes. The primary mission of the latter is to maintain the order, stability and labour discipline required for meeting the country's obligations to the international market. The essential reality of the neocolonial situation in Africa, according to Jean Ziegler, resides in 'tensions between a dissatisfied people and rulers essentially conservative, concerned above all with the preservation of their acquired privileges'.[8]

In the Congo, this situation gave rise to Africa's first national liberation struggle in the neocolonial context, with a mass-based movement comprising ordinary people and radical nationalists. Since the guiding ideas and themes of the struggle had already been produced by the popular masses, the task of revolutionary intellectuals such as Pierre Mulele was simply that of systematizing the popularly produced notions and ideas into the language of twentieth-century revolutionary theory and practice. Needless to say, the people's vision of a future of equality, justice and material prosperity was not new. It had already been given expression in various ways, notably in anticolonial revolts and through the activities of religious movements, as already shown in Chapter 1.

As Badiou and Balmès suggest with respect to the ideological resistance of ordinary people in general, the ideas of the popular masses against exploitation and oppression do not remain dormant until there appears a group of professional intellectuals or revolutionaries capable of guiding their materialization.[9] For the masses, too, have their own organic intellectuals. However, the rebellions through which ordinary people's ideas and sentiments are expressed have very little chance of changing the system radically in the absence of modern organizational resources necessary for a long and protracted struggle. These resources include a leadership capable of analysing the balance of forces correctly, and of charting an appropriate course of action. In the Congo, the only group that was well placed to play this leadership role was that of the radical and progressive nationalists, who were identified with the Lumumbist camp.

In this context, the political defeat of the Lumumbists in 1962–63 was a great blow to the popular alliance, as ordinary people were left with no organization to speak on their behalf. The only exception to this was the Union générale des étudiants congolais (UGEC), a national student organization founded in 1961 to fight tribalism and to carry out the progressive agenda that Patrice Lumumba had embraced for the country. The major components of this political project were national unity, economic independence and pan-African solidarity. Until it was banned by the Mobutu regime in 1968, UGEC remained the most stable and most vocal legal opposition grouping in the country. Its three national congresses, held in 1961, 1963 and 1966, represent three important phases in the development of a socialist consciousness within a predominantly élitist and careerist university student population.[10] Because of the limitations imposed on its political practice by élitism and careerism, UGEC was incapable of assuming the leadership of the mass movement.

Like the student movement, the labour movement was unable to organize the masses politically. Its leaders were basically reformists whose overall political outlook and practice smacked of economism and opportunism. Like most UGEC leaders, virtually all Congolese trade union leaders, including André Boboliko and Raphaël Bintou, were eventually co-opted by President Mobutu to serve at the highest levels of his regime.

Given this leadership vacuum, the masses had to await the regrouping of the Lumumbist politicians to find leaders who would guide them in the struggle against the neocolonial state. By the end of 1963, both Mulele and the CNL had decided to initiate the armed struggle in areas where the MNC-L, the PSA and other parties of the Lumumbist coalition were strongest. These comprised, for the most part, Bandundu in the west and the entire northeastern portion of the country, including the regions of Kisangani, Kivu, Maniema, Sankuru and North Katanga. However, given the difference in political itinerary and ideology within the leadership, the second independence movement developed as two separate liberation wars, with separate organizations, command structures and political strategies, with Mulele in Bandundu and the CNL in the east. The essential difference between the two consists in the more radical aims of Mulelism, which had a comprehensive programme of social transformation, as compared to the narrow class interests of the CNL politicians managing the eastern front from Brazzaville, Kigoma, or the relative safety of liberated Kisangani.

Pierre Mulele and the Kwilu Maquis Mulele was the first prominent Lumumbist to return to the Congo in 1963, and the first person to launch a revolutionary struggle against a neocolonial state in Africa.[11] After nearly fifteen months in Cairo as the external representative of the Gizenga government, Mulele went on to spend the next fifteen months in the People's Republic of China, where he received training in revolutionary guerrilla warfare between April 1962 and July 1963. Returning to Kwilu through Kinshasa, he spent nearly six months laying down the groundwork for a revolutionary struggle and training the first group of partisans.

Mulele attempted to systematize the ideas, notions and thoughts of the masses into a coherent analysis of the situation and a programme of action for purposes of changing it radically. His systemization was done through a Marxist-Leninist framework of class analysis together with a Maoist strategy of political education and guerrilla warfare.[12] Schoolteachers, nurses, state and company clerks and secondary school students formed the ranks of disciplined cadres that he trained for the struggle. They joined unemployed urban youths and peasants in what became a profoundly popular and rural insurrection.[13] Much of what is known about his teachings comes from the lecture notes taken by the trainees. A remarkable aspect of his doctrine was the insistence on discipline and exemplary behaviour by the guerrilla, whose objective is to destroy the old order and not to benefit from its material goods. Guerrillas were to respect the people with whom they came into contact. They were not to mistreat them or to deprive them of their property. The major task was the radical transformation of society from the bottom up, on the basis of well-tested values of solidarity in village life.

After several encounters with the repressive machinery of the neo-colonial state in late 1963, a full-fledged guerrilla war was launched in January 1964. At first, the Mulelist forces succeeded in controlling a major portion of Kwilu. Their earlier successes were so spectacular, including the killing of an army colonel and commander of the expeditionary force, that Mulele became a living legend all over the country. He became so famous that CNL fighters in the east believed that he had invented a magical formula for turning bullets into water, took what a CNL fetishist assured them was the real thing, and shouted the slogan *Mai Mulele* (Mulele water) when they came into direct contact with enemy fire. There is no evidence that Mulele's own guerrillas used this slogan, but controversy remains as to whether Mulele himself led people to believe that he was invulnerable to bullets.

His own forces depended so much on Molotov cocktails, hunting rifles and other traditional weapons, and such small quantities of modern arms and ammunition as could be captured from the enemy, that they were not in a position to expand and hold territory far away from their camps. They never succeeded in capturing Idiofa and Gungu, the two major urban centres in their operational zone, or in expanding this zone beyond the areas occupied by the two ethnic groups constituting the initial base of the insurrection, the Mbunda (Mulele's ethnic group), and the Pende (Gizenga's group).

In spite of these limitations, the core of the Mulelist maquis remained more or less intact until November 1967, and Mulele himself survived all counterinsurgency drives aimed at dislodging him from the Kwilu bush from August 1963 to August 1968. For five years, Mulele and his maquis held their ground against the neocolonial state and the Binza Group. He was so popular that despite a high government reward of approximately $10,000 for information leading to his capture, dead or alive, not a soul was found to betray him. It was only after he had gone to Brazzaville for medical treatment and for regrouping that the Mobutu regime lured him back home with false promises of amnesty and national reconciliation.

Under pressure from the Brazzaville authorities, who did not wish to have him on their soil, and hesitant about seeking political asylum in another country far away from the guerrillas he had left behind in Kwilu, Mulele reluctantly returned to Kinshasa with slim hopes of either working for genuine national reconciliation or resuming the struggle clandestinely. The messenger who presented the false amnesty offer on behalf of President Mobutu was none other than Binza Group member and perennial foreign minister, Bomboko. The treachery of the group became once again apparent when Mulele was murdered by Mobutu's generals shortly after his last return home. Having been proven right for his refusal to reconcile with Lumumba's murderers in 1961, Mulele was obviously overwhelmed by poor health and uncertainty to make such a fatal mistake in 1968. His assassination on 3 October 1968 marked the end of both the second independence movement and the second period of the resistance against tyranny in the Congo.

There are many lessons to draw from Mulele's revolutionary enterprise, but only few will be underlined here. The choice of his own region of origin as a revolutionary base, the lack of external sources of military supplies, and the absence of a dependable rear base in the neighbouring countries turned out to have the most negative consequences for the struggle. Although it did appear sensible for all revolutionaries to start the struggle in their own areas with the aim of eventually merging all of the revolutionary bases in a truly mass-based national struggle, the fact that a revolutionary leader of Mulele's stature was to be mainly identified with his and allied ethnic groups proved detrimental to the struggle, as other groups were encouraged to feel excluded from it by the enemies of the revolution. In the contemporary world, a revolutionary group facing a militarily superior enemy cannot hope to succeed without access to external sources of essential supplies, lethal and non-lethal.

On the positive side, it must be acknowledged that in spite of the limited space of his operational theatre, Mulele came to incarnate the entire second independence movement. The label 'Mulelist' was applied to all anti-government guerrillas, including CNL fighters, who actually looked upon Mulele as their patron saint. With so little physical achievement on the ground, Mulele earned this exalted position for at least two reasons. One is the natural sympathy that fair-minded people would have for someone who has been murdered in cold blood, especially after so much noise was made in the state media about the amnesty offer. The other and more important reason is that his was a principled struggle for general welfare and not for selfish gains such as political office and material benefits. The major lesson of Mulele's experience is the image he has left of a person so totally committed to the cause of liberation that nothing else mattered, including his or her own life. In Congo's history, the martyrdom of Pierre Mulele recalls that of Patrice Emery Lumumba.

The CNL and the eastern front The CNL was rent by ideological differences and personality conflicts from the very beginning. A group of revolutionary intellectuals from the PSA/Gizenga trained in China defended a mass line identical to that of Mulele, who had already started organizing his maquis when the CNL was created. This group was opposed to a more moderate MNC-L group led by Christophe Gbenye, the nominal leader of the MNC-L, whose radical credentials were already in doubt since he had signed the arrest warrant against Gizenga in January 1962, in his capacity as interior minister in the Adoula government. Gbenye and his friends wanted to enlist the support of progressive elements in the international community for another attempt at a government of national unity or 'public salvation' in Kinshasa, but one controlled by the Lumumbist majority in the parliament. However, that majority had been shown to be more fiction than fact when the US-sponsored manoeuvres of 'outstanding UN personalities' had found enough Lumumbist politicians ready to be bought so they could join the PSA/Kamitatu in supporting Adoula against Gizenga in July–August 1961 at Lovanium.

To the differences over strategy between those who opted for armed struggle and those who wanted to pursue the game of parliamentary politics was added a number of personality conflicts, the most significant of which opposed MNC-L leaders Gbenye and Davidson Bocheley. The latter was joined by PSA militants to form what became known as the CNL/Bocheley, whose plans included developing a broad-based guerrilla struggle by linking the Mulele maquis to revolutionary fronts to be created in the east and elsewhere in the west. However, an attempt to establish a maquis in the Lake Maindombe district and from there link up with Mulele ended in failure.

The CNL/Gbenye, on the other hand, went on to become the largest and militarily the more successful front of the second independence movement. Once it opted for armed struggle in 1964, it became preoccupied with recapturing state power in a vast area of the country formerly under the control of Lumumbists and covering more than the entire eastern half of the Congo minus South Kasai and the southern portion of Katanga. This is basically what the Gbenye group accomplished in spectacular fashion when, under the pressure of people such as Gaston Soumialot and Laurent Kabila, it decided to use violence.

Soumialot and Kabila had been designated since Brazzaville to co-ordinate the struggle in the east, and they went to Burundi in January 1964 to start preparations for the armed struggle. The insurrections that they helped organize began later on 15 April, with the first victory against Mobutu's army being registered on 15 May when Soumialot's forces took over the city of Uvira.

Unlike the Mulelist maquis, which attempted to train cadres for a protracted war, the CNL opted for quick and large-scale military operations for the control of cities and towns, including provincial capitals and major commercial centres. Relying primarily on the youth branches of the MNC-L and allied parties, CNL commanders used surprise attacks by lightly armed but mostly drugged gangs of youths to over-power army and police garrisons and took over urban and industrial centres in rapid succession.

The fighters, who called themselves *Simba* (lions in Kiswahili), had virtually no modern weapons, except for those they captured or picked up from the defeated or fleeing enemy. Their basic arsenal consisted of traditional weapons and magico-religious resources that supposedly ensured their invincibility. These included an immunization ritual with drops of the magic water called *Mai Mulele* (see above), various fetishes, and the observation of a strict code of conduct involving sexual ab-negation and certain dietary restrictions on the eve of battle. They would charge poorly motivated and frightened security forces in such large numbers that, regardless of high casualties among the rebels, government troops would be so intimidated by the advancing multitude that they, too, eventually came to believe in the invulnerability of the *Simba* to their bullets. After a few major victories, all CNL commanders had to do was to send a telegraph to the next city or town announcing their impending arrival, and all the garrisons would be deserted by the security forces. The announcement over the wire or by other means of communication provoked such a panic among government troops that they ran away, leaving their arms behind to be picked up by the fighters.

The rapid breakdown of state authority throughout the entire region created an administrative and military vacuum that the CNL had to fill with its liberation army, the Armée populaire de libération (APL), under the command of General Nicolas Olenga. Within two months and a half, the APL was in control of North Katanga, Maniema, Sankuru, the entire Eastern province and portions of Equateur province. By November 1964, the CNL had succeeded in taking control over more than half of the national territory. The biggest victory of the campaign came on 4 August 1964, when Kisangani fell to the APL. A month later, Gbenye established a people's republic there on 5 September, with himself as president, Soumialot as defence minister, Olenga as armed forces commander, and Thomas Kanza as foreign minister.

Having established its rule in seven of the 21 provincial capitals and in numerous towns and rural districts, the CNL now had the opportunity to show how well it could help fulfill the people's expectations of independence, or replace the 'flag' independence of 1960 with a more genuine second independence. Preoccupied more with regaining the power they had lost to the moderates that with organizing a genuine liberation struggle, CNL leaders clearly lacked the will and the ability to play the role of revolutionary intellectuals. Their goals, as exemplified by their mode of governance, were not different from those of the neo-colonial ruling clique in Kinshasa. The following assessment of the brief tenure of the CNL regime in the east by Jules Gérard-Libois gives an apt description of some of the major weaknesses of the eastern front:

> The revolution also soon ran into trouble from within its own leadership. The common phenomenon in the Congo of fragmentation and conflict among leaders and groups was once again repeated ... all these negative features were powerfully enhanced, with more arbitrary arrests and ruthless repression, with hoarding by some leaders, with the demagogic exploitation of xenophobia and primitive beliefs, and with a reckless wastage of young lives in ill-prepared operations.[14]

Like their counterparts in Kinshasa and elsewhere in the Congo, CNL leaders were above all concerned with settling scores with their political enemies. Once they took over provincial or district headquarters, the first item of business was to occupy the official mansion and to enjoy the privileges of office, which included money, tradable commodities such as gold, and a life of pleasure. They also began fighting among themselves for the spoils of victory. Every imaginable weapon, including appeals to ethnic loyalty and the assassination of rivals, was used in the process.

Given the lack of political preparation, the spontaneous mobilization of partisans, and the rapid turn of events, CNL leaders could not control their middle cadres effectively. These were recruited from among clerks, primary schoolteachers, ex-soldiers, ex-policemen and leaders of the *jeunesses* or party youth wings. For most of these partisans, as for their leaders, the concept of 'second independence' meant their turn to enjoy the fruits of independence formerly monopolized by the Kinshasa- and foreign-backed moderate leaders they had removed from power. With their mostly undisciplined hordes of *Simba*, who indulged in excesses of brutality and savagery under the influence of narcotics such as hemp, they behaved as though they were in conquered territory. These youths also gave vent to their class-based frustrations by killing large numbers of professionals and medium- to high-level civil servants for the simple reason that they were 'intellectuals' (meaning people with at least secondary education), and presumably reactionaries.

Thus what appeared to be the CNL's main strength, its militarist strategy, turned out to be its greatest weakness. More successful militarily than the Kwilu maquis, the eastern front privileged militarism over politicization, and preferred action to reflection. The result was that its political success was short-lived. The masses, who had welcomed CNL leaders and the *Simba* as liberators, would soon become disenchanted by both the apparent neglect of their pressing needs and, more importantly, the reign of terror unleashed by the revolutionary movement. There were also weaknesses in the military field, in which ill-prepared operations against élite government units and mercenaries showed that adventurism and improvisation often took precedence over serious attention to strategy and tactics. Ernesto Che Guevara has documented these weaknesses in the diary of his disappointing experience in the maquis at Fizi-Baraka in 1965.[15]

The Argentine-born Cuban revolutionary led a contingent of mostly black Cuban volunteers in a clandestine operation designed to rescue the Congolese revolution after its major defeat at the hands of the US-led counterinsurgency in November 1964. During the six months he spent in the mountains alongside Lake Tanganyika, Guevara was usually frustrated by his failure to find revolutionary leaders to help him train fighters with whom to wage a serious liberation struggle. The one possible exception in this regard was Ildephonse Masengwo, Kabila's deputy. As for Kabila himself, he only showed up once in the bush during this entire period, preferring to direct the revolution from afar, in the relative comfort of Dar es Salaam and the social pleasures of Kigoma. Due to the limitations of his own *foco* theory of guerrilla warfare, which minimizes prior political preparation in favour of instant 'armed propaganda', his ignorance of Congolese political realities and Kabila's reluctance to work with him, Che failed to make a difference in the balance of force between the second independence movement and the neocolonial state.

All of these weaknesses helped to undermine the ability of the CNL to protect its gains from the externally led counterinsurgency. In the face of this challenge from imperialism, the leaders of the eastern front lacked an appropriate political strategy. Moreover, they no longer had a political base, as the masses had come to lose faith in these particular heirs of Patrice Lumumba. All top CNL leaders went into exile, but

Mobutu lured most of them back home and gave them the means with which to engage in private business. He knew these politicians well and considered them less dangerous than Mulele, whom he murdered. By the time of the CNS in 1992, Olenga was already dead, Soumialot had abandoned politics for farming, and Gbenye and Kanza were now in Mobutu's camp against the democratic opposition. Kanza was actually the dictator's candidate for prime minister against opposition leader Etienne Tshisekedi.

Alone, Kabila led a low-intensity guerrilla struggle in the Fizi-Baraka area until the early 1980s, when he, too, retired to the world of business, doing cross-border trading in gold and ivory, among other goods. He was brought back from obscurity in 1996 as the inevitable client of Rwandan and Ugandan authorities, who needed a Congolese ally to justify their invasion of the country and their drive to overthrow the Mobutu regime, the best relic of Western neocolonialism in Central Africa.

The Externally Led Counterinsurgency

The second independence movement was the single major threat to Western neocolonialism in the Congo after the elimination of Patrice Lumumba and his followers from the political scene. With external support, the moderates had won the political confrontation with the radicals. Now they were on the first line of defence against a mass-based struggle for radical change. Gérard-Libois describes the reaction of the new ruling class to this ominous danger as follows:

> In order to meet this challenge, it subdued its own internal conflicts and changed its Prime Minister, resorted to the help of South African, Rhodesian, Belgian and German mercenaries, and relied upon Belgian high-ranking officers to organise and coordinate military aid. After the reconquest of Stanleyville and the ruthless repression meted out in rebel zones, the ruling group long seemed to hesitate as to the policy it should pursue – whether to seek a new understanding with the other African states, or to continue repressive policies in the Congo with the help of Mike Hoare's mercenaries. The dilemma was resolved by the Army, whose leaders seek to gain popularity by attacks on corrupt politicians and by some measures of reform.[16]

The change of prime minister, with Tshombe replacing Adoula in July 1964, was engineered by Belgium and the United States.[17] The repeated defeats of Mobutu's army before the *Simba*, the impending departure of UN troops by 30 June 1964, and the continuing threat of an invasion from Angola by Tshombe's Katanga gendarmes called into question the very viability of the Adoula regime. Someone else was needed to provide the leadership required to correct the deteriorating security situation.

The solution adopted by those who controlled the country's destiny was to set up a provisional government of 'public salvation' headed by Tshombe, which would bring together old secessionists, radicals and moderates in the same cabinet. The former Katanga leader had made himself invaluable not only by the implied threat of his army of gendarmes and mercenaries, but also by a clever strategy of contacts with all sectors of political opinion, including the more moderate CNL/Gbenye through Thomas Kanza. André-Guillaume Lubaya, a member of the more radical CNL/Bocheley, became health minister in Tshombe's cabinet. According to Tshombe, Kanza would have become foreign minister had it not been for Kasa-Vubu's objection, due to the Congolese president's long-standing feud in intra-Abako politics with Kanza's father Daniel.[18]

Long before Tshombe and his mercenary army became a useful tool of Western neocolonialism at the national level, the CIA had since early 1964 started to conduct a major paramilitary campaign against the Kwilu and eastern insurrections. Since the CNL received support from Nasser's Egypt and the Eastern bloc countries, the counter-insurgency was led by the United States and included Belgian military experts and white mercenaries, working together with some elite government units such as the Katanga gendarmes, which Tshombe had brought back from their exile in Angola. With Kisangani as the nerve centre and the symbol of the revolutionary movement's success, it was there that the forces of the counterrevolution decided to strike their boldest blow. They did so with Opération Dragon Rouge, a combined land and air offensive that culminated with the US–Belgian paratroop drop on 24 November 1964. This is the operation that broke the back of the eastern insurrection, which never recovered from this knockout punch by the externally led counterinsurgency.

The paramilitary campaign under the CIA Fearing intensified fighting and the probable defeat of the moderates once UN troops left the Congo at the end of June 1964, the CIA began a major paramilitary campaign against the second independence insurrections earlier that year. This campaign continued after November 1964, for the most part against the Mulele maquis in the Kwilu and the Kabila maquis in the east. According to Weissman, it lasted for nearly four years and included the use of anti-Castro Cuban and European mercenaries to fly T–6 training planes, T-28 fighter planes armed with rockets and machine-guns, C-147 military transportation planes, H-21 heavy duty helicopters and B-26 bombers.[19] The US Air Force gave critical air support to government troops and mercenaries, in addition to dropping napalm and other deadly agents on the people. In June 1964, US paratroopers were sent to guard US military transportation aircraft sent to assist the government. Shortly after Tshombe assumed office, the situation became critical for Kinshasa, as the Lumumbists received more support at home and abroad in their struggle against a man universally decried in Africa as a traitor.

After the fall of Kisangani to the insurgents, the pattern of the counterinsurgency changed to include both covert and overt forms. Weissman describes these forms as follows:

> Four American C-130 military transports with full crews and parachutist 'guard' arrived in Léopoldville, along with 4–5 B-26 bombers, ground vehicles, arms and ammunition. The Belgians also supplied equipment as well as 300–400 officers who assumed background roles of command and logistical support. Nearly all this overt assistance was on behalf of a 700 man force of South African, Rhodesian and European mercenaries which did much of the fighting as 'spearheads' of selected Government troops ... The Agency did supply more Cuban pilots for the B-26s which joined the rest of the CIA Air Force in support of the mercenary advance. (By January 1965, two additional T-28s were operating in the Congo as were 3–4 more B-26s apparently provided by International Aviation, a CIA proprietary.)
>
> As certain African countries began to ship arms to the rebels across Lake Tanganyika with apparent promises of Soviet replacement, the CIA engaged pilots and crews, reportedly South African, for patrol boat operations. A CIA front organization, Western International Ground Maintenance Organization (WIGMO) chartered in Liechtenstein, handled maintenance for the boats as well as the fighter planes with a staff of 50–100 Europeans. The WIGMO mechanics and maintenance personnel enabled US and Belgian military personnel to escape direct association with air and sea operations; they also represented an attempt by the CIA to get away from its increasingly visible Cuban connection.[20]

With the CNL in control of Kisangani and over half of the country, attempts were made by African countries to resolve the conflict peacefully. As in the case of the dispute between Lumumba and Kasa-Vubu, the United States and its allies did everything possible to undermine African diplomatic efforts. US President Lyndon Baines Johnson showed his determination to end the crisis by force by increasing the US military presence and activity in the Congo. Using a humanitarian pretext, and one that smacked of racism, Johnson sent US planes to drop Belgian paratroopers on Kisangani and Isiro on 24 November 1964 with the express aim of rescuing whites from the conflict area. However, the real purpose of the intervention was to pave the way for the recapture of those cities by the Congolese government.

Operation Red Dragon With military and financial support from the United States, Belgium, Israel and others, Tshombe used his gendarmes and mercenaries to defeat the CNL regime and its army, and thus succeeded where Mobutu's army had been profoundly humiliated. However, the gendarmes and the mercenaries could not have done the job without external support. A more direct intervention of metropolitan troops was deemed necessary to break the back of the insurrection in the east, by providing better support to the mercenaries and Belgian-officered government troops sent to reconquer Kisangani. Thus, by mid-November 1964, a column of mercenaries and élite units of the Congolese army had already been assembled at the Kamina military base, under the command of none other than Colonel Frédéric Vande-walle of Surêté and Katanga fames, so that its arrival in the Kisangani area could coincide with the Belgo-American military intervention.[21] This is the operation code-named 'Red Dragon' at the end of which some 70 whites held hostage by the *Simba* and well over one thousand Congolese were killed. The Kisangani episode showed how major powers can cynically exploit humanitarianism and the right of humanit-arian intervention as a smokescreen concealing for their real interests. In the case of the Congo of 1964, it was partly a question of the east–west confrontation of the Cold War.

Operation Red Dragon succeeded in ending Gbenye's 'People's Republic' and in opening the way for the final defeat of the Lumumbist-led popular insurrections for a second independence. The magico-religious arsenal that had worked so well against Mobutu's troops proved futile in the face of the more disciplined Katanga gendarmes, and against foreign mercenaries and troops, which did not share the same worldview. Equally futile was the militarist strategy of frontal attacks by thousands of untrained and poorly armed partisans, who became easy targets of a well-armed enemy, using automatic arms, armoured vehicles and military aircraft.

Thus, if it is true that imperialism played a decisive role in the defeat of the second independence movement in the Congo, there is no doubt that the leaders of the movement made it easier for the external forces by their intellectual bankruptcy and political opportunism. Only Mulele and his top lieutenants seem to be above reproach, although they failed to exploit his popularity and mass appeal to the full by breaking out of their isolation in Kwilu and geographically expanding their area of operation. Questions will also remain on the wisdom of establishing the maquis in his own area of origin rather than elsewhere, so as to maximize his role as a national leader.

In the final analysis, the second independence movement was a major event in the popular struggle for democracy in the Congo. By rising up, arms in hand, against an externally backed regime of corrupt and self-serving leaders, the people sought to uphold the egalitarian and developmentalist ideals of independence, together with the political legacy of Patrice Lumumba. Coming on the heels of the political violence and dislocations of the independence struggle, this first war of liberation against the postcolonial state in Africa has taught the Congolese people the value of being sceptical about would-be saviours who seem to thrive in destroying rather than building the country. At the same time, one of the legacies of the second independence movement is that a culture of resistance against illegitimate state authority has become a major feature of Congolese political life

Notes

1. This became known as the 'Léopoldville–Bakwanga–Elisabethville axis', following the colonial names of Kinshasa, Mbuji-Mayi and Lubumbashi, respectively. For details, see Artigue, *Qui sont les leaders congolais?*, pp. 218–19 and 363.

2. Chomé, *L'ascension de Mobutu*, p. 112.

3. Weissman, *American Foreign Policy in the Congo*, p. 208.

4. In his seminal essay on intellectuals, Antonio Gramsci distinguishes between 'traditional intellectuals' or professional philosophers, and 'organic intellectuals', or 'democratic philosophers' who spring from within the popular classes to articulate through intellectual discourse the views, values and interests of the people. See Gramsci, 'On intellectuals'. For an excellent study of the intellectual origins of this concept, see Fontana, *Hegemony and Power*.

5. Cabral, *Unity and Struggle*.

6. Initially a unitarist, Bolikango opted for federalism once he failed to gain an important post in Kinshasa, having lost the election for the ceremonial presidency to Kasa-Vubu. Nendaka claimed for a while to be the leader of a third MNC wing, but his real prominence came later, when he assumed the direction of the security police. Adoula, like Ileo, was nominally a member of the MNC-K. But unlike Ileo, who presided over the Kisantu congress of federalist parties in December 1959, he seems to have remained a unitarist.

7. National Liberation Council.

8. Ziegler, *Sociologie de la nouvelle Afrique*, p. 12. My own translation.

9. Badiou and Balmès, *De l'idéologie*, p. 91

10. On the élitism of university students and the political limitations of UGEC, see Willame, 'The Congo'; Makidi-ku-Ntima, 'The role of Congolese intellectuals in the making of neo-colonialism'.

11. Before Mulele, the Union de populations du Cameroun (UPC), a national independence movement in Cameroon, was involved in such a struggle, but this was a continuation of the armed struggle for independence against the French, who installed Ahmadou Ahidjo in power in 1958 before granting nominal independence in 1960. The French also continued to lead the counter-insurgency drive against the UPC.

12. For a detailed study of the Mulelist experience, see Martens, *Pierre Mulele ou la seconde vie de Patrice Lumumba*.

13. For more information on the social origins of Mulele's partisans and other pertinent analyses of the strengths and weaknesses of the Kwilu maquis, see Coquéry-Vidrovitch et al., *Rébellions-Révolutions au Zaïre 1963–1965*.

14. Gérard-Libois, 'The new class and rebellion in the Congo', pp. 277–8.

15. For details on Che Guevara's adventure on the eastern front in the Congo, see Galvez, *Che in Africa*.

16. Gérard-Libois, 'The new class and rebellion in the Congo', p. 271.

17. The author received something resembling an advanced tip of Tshombe's return in a most improbable way. In late June 1964, I was in Detroit to attend the congress of the USA–Canada section of UGEC. For lodging purposes, I was staying with a Congolese friend, Joncker Biandudi, who was then an International Christian Youth Exchange (ICYE) student in the home of a prominent African American clergyman, the pastor of perhaps the largest black congregation in Detroit. Seeing my interest in politics, the minister took me to a Democratic Party reception at the home of Governor G. Mennen Williams, then the US assistant secretary of state for African affairs. Speaking to me in very bad French, Williams attempted to convince me that what my country needed was someone like Tshombe as head of government. 'Le traître Tshombe?' was my incredulous reply. Although rumours of Tshombe's return were already circulating by then, it was amazing to hear it from the number-one US policymaker on Africa, speaking to a college underclassman. A few days later, a front-page article in the *Detroit Free Press* confirmed Tshombe's return to the Congo.

18. Tshombe, *Quinze mois de gouvernement au Congo*, p. 20.

19. Weissman, 'The CIA and U.S. Policy in Zaire and Angola', pp. 391–2.

20. Ibid, pp. 392–3.

21. See Vandewalle, *L'Ommegang*.

CHAPTER 5

The Mobutu Regime: Dictatorship and State Decay

§ PRESIDENT Mobutu was Congo's head of state from 24 November 1965 until 17 May 1997. For a quarter of a century, between 1965 and 1990, he was the undisputed master of the country. In the very imaginative but apt description by V. S. Naipaul, author of *A Bend in the River*, Mobutu was *the big man*, a new king for the Congo, and the true successor to King Leopold as the owner of the country and its resources.[1] As though to prove that he considered the Congo a personal possession, he unilaterally changed the country's name to 'Zaire' in 1971, and took great pleasure in privatizing the state and its assets for the benefit of his relatives, cronies and clients.

The Mobutu regime began as a military dictatorship with the entire army high command making up the junta. But it soon acquired all the characteristics of personal rule then found elsewhere in Africa: a one-party dictatorship under the authoritarian control of a single individual. Mobutu's power was so absolute that he could do anything his heart desired. An accomplished Machiavellian, he used his ill-gotten wealth and his powers of patronage to outfox potential opponents and to keep wavering officials in line. At the same time, he did not hesitate to use force when it could best serve his purpose. And he did so with such ferocity and regularity that in addition to corruption, gross violations of human rights, including assassinations, extrajudicial executions, massacres of unarmed civilians, and banishment to remote penal colonies became the defining characteristics of the Mobutu regime. He thus succeeded in demobilizing the mass democratic movement, the result being that until 1980 organized opposition to the regime could take place only from outside the country.

Mobutu's ascendancy, as already shown in Chapter 3, was only in part a function of his own personal qualities. For the most part, he owed his rise to power and the astonishing longevity of his regime to external sponsorship and backing by the United States and its Western allies. It is this basic character of his regime as an externally backed autocracy, both distant from its own society and impervious to popular aspirations and loyalties, that eventually led to state decay and collapse. This was due in large part to the increasingly corrupt mode of governance by the president and his large entourage of relatives, senior aides and political associates, plus cabinet ministers and managers of state enterprises. As the *New Nigerian* of 15 June 1978 editorialized in reference to the Shaba II war, the Mobutuist system was a kleptocracy that ruled the country 'at the pleasure of foreign powers to the disadvantage of their own people'.[2]

As a system of absolute power, dictatorship and personal rule, the Mobutu regime ended in 1990, with the official demise of the Second Republic and its party-state system, and the beginning of the transition to multiparty democracy. But the wily dictator was still hanging on to the helm of his sinking ship of state seven years later, when Laurent Kabila and his Rwandan backers dispatched him into exile on 17 May 1997. By the time the CNS voted to establish the political institutions of the transition on 4 August 1992, the ruling clique around Mobutu had been reduced to its bare essentials as a band of bloodthirsty thieves who survived by looting and thuggery. For regime diehards, all that seemed to matter was reliance on a few élite units of the military to maintain control over the mining and other revenue-generating parastatals, the central bank, the customs office and the central tax office. Mobutu, the band's chief, was now afraid to set foot in the capital city, preferring instead to live in his Versailles-type palace at Gbadolite in the far north, on the border between the Congo and the Central African Republic. His was a government that could no longer govern, for lack of legitimacy at home and support abroad, and an administration that could no longer administer, given its lack of essential resources and the disenchantment of civil servants.

The Origins and Nature of the Regime

As an externally backed autocracy, the Mobutu regime was a pure product of the Cold War. It originated in the cold strategic calculation of Western powers that leaders with no social or political base were preferable to those with strong national constituencies, to which they were accountable. Since the latter reflected the militant nationalism and anti-imperialist positions of their supporters, they had to be discredited in the eyes of world public opinion. Eric Rouleau, a distinguished journalist and a former French diplomat, explains that the tactic consisted in imputing madness or erratic personality to leaders such as

Fidel Castro of Cuba, Mohamed Mossadegh of Iran, Gamal Abdul Nasser of Egypt, Kwame Nkrumah of Ghana and the Congo's Patrice Lumumba, among others. They were judged 'unreasonable for defying the logic of *homo occidentalis*, in doing things outside the established norms and, above all, in harming the "vital interests of the free world"'.[3]

To protect and promote these interests in the turbulent countries of the Third World, policymakers in Washington and other Western capitals could trust only a 'strongman' as the ideal ruler. As described by Rouleau, the strongman is supposed to be intelligent, cunning, and independent of any uncontrollable coalition or popular consensus 'that would prevent him from being understanding towards external protectors'.[4] Accordingly, he 'is singularly ambitious and stops at nothing to attain his objectives'.[5] During the first Congo crisis, Mobutu was deemed to possess all of these prized qualities, and his Western protectors groomed him as the perfect candidate for the role of Congo's strongman. He played this role so well and so faithfully that he became extremely bitter for being publicly shunned by his former mentors, friends and allies between 1990 and 1997, until he was left to die on the run like a wandering dog.

Mobutu's emergence as a strongman for the Congo Much of the story about Mobutu's rise to power has already been told in Chapter 3. However, a recapitulation of his political itinerary should help clarify why he became a strongman and Washington's inevitable ally in the Congo. Born in 1930 of a very young woman, who was either unmarried or abandoned by her spouse, Joseph-Désiré Mobutu grew up in the Equator province with the reputation of being an unruly youth. His turbulence was such that he was kicked out of secondary school by Catholic missionaries and conscripted in the Force publique. Since he had not completed two years of secondary education, he had to do seven years of military service, between 1950 and 1956.[6] With his intellectual abilities, he rose to the rank of quartermaster sergeant, and served in this capacity at one of the major military bases in the Belgian Congo, at Kananga in the Kasai province.

In January 1957, Mobutu began a new career as a journalist, taking advantage of the writing and typing skills he had learned in the army. It was during his connection with a Belgian-dominated weekly in Kinshasa, *Actualités africaines*, that he was hired as an informer for the Belgian intelligence service. The following year, he went to Belgium, ostensibly to study social work, but actually for training in intelligence work. A momentous year in Congolese political history, 1958 was the year of the Brussels World's Fair and one in which a record number of

Congolese visited Belgium and Europe for the very first time. With the rising tide of African nationalism having finally hit the Congo, Belgian and US policymakers were anxious to know who was who among the emergent politicians. In the CIA office in Brussels, the Congo case was assigned to Lawrence Devlin, who quickly retained Mobutu's services as an informer as well. After independence, Devlin would become the CIA station chief in Kinshasa and a major player in the fall of Lumumba and Mobutu's rise to power.

Fresh from the Accra meeting and his triumphant public rally of 28 December 1958 in Kinshasa, Lumumba went to Brussels in early 1959 to make himself known to different political circles in Belgium. Mobutu was eager to welcome him to Brussels and to show him the town and its nightlife. Lumumba was so impressed by Mobutu, five years his junior, that he named him the Brussels representative of the MNC. A close bond developed between the two men. To Lumumba, Mobutu was more than just someone who carried his briefcase (*porteur de mallette*), as Mobutu's detractors would have us believe. Lumumba's trust in a man he came to consider a younger brother was such that he had no hesitation naming him one of his top assistants, as a junior minister in the prime minister's office, and as chief of staff of the armed forces. Rejecting information that Mobutu was connected to Western intelligence as baseless rumours, Lumumba thought that by appointing Mobutu to the number two position in the ANC, he had the right man with whom to control the military politically. This was Lumumba's second major political blunder, less than three weeks after his fateful choice in the fratricidal war in Kasai.

As it turned out, Mobutu played a critical role in every step leading to Lumumba's assassination. As ANC chief of staff, he had overall operational control of the military campaign in South Kasai, whose atrocities were blamed on Lumumba by Kasa-Vubu and his backers in the international community. It was he who accomplished what the Cordier–Kasa-Vubu coup of 5 September 1960 had failed to achieve, namely, the effective removal of Lumumba from power. He did so by the coup of 14 September, Lumumba's arrest on 1 December, and his incarceration at the élite military garrison of Mbanza-Ngungu. And Mobutu was among the top Congolese leaders involved in acquiescing to the Belgian plan of sending Lumumba to his death in Katanga, including President Kasa-Vubu, interim Prime Minister Ileo and the Binza Group.

With Lumumba and then his followers eliminated from the political scene, it was Mobutu who took centre stage politically as the leader of the Binza Group. Although remaining in the background until 1965, he was behind every major decision taken in Kinshasa since September 1960. As shown in Chapter 4, the single most important challenge faced by the moderate ruling alliance led by the Binza Group, and a major variable in the rise and nature of the Mobutu regime, was the second independence movement. For the Western powers in general and the United States in particular, this revolutionary movement was an ominous development, all the more so as it was led by the same radical national-ists whom these powers had done their best to eliminate politically. Every possible avenue, including the use of foreign mercenaries and direct military intervention, was pursued to help the moderates crush the popular insurrections.

For the most part, these uprisings confirmed the worst fears of those policymakers in Washington and other Western capitals, who preferred strongmen to democratically elected leaders. With Tshombe as their new leader, the moderates outside the Binza Group wanted to make a fledgling parliamentary democracy work. With a new constitution adopted in 1964, the first national elections since independence were conducted without violence and without foreign observers during the month of May 1965. Of 135 parliamentary districts, the results were contested in five only. In spite of this and other encouraging signs of political maturity, a parliamentary regime was deemed incapable of maintaining peace and protecting Western interests in such a potentially turbulent country. Since the moderate leadership had already shown signs of weakness *vis-à-vis* the popular classes in revolt, parliamentary democracy was seen as 'chaotic' because of the fractional struggles to which it gives rise. A 'strongman' was needed, and one was readily available, in the person of General Mobutu.

Mobutu's dictatorship, underdevelopment and state decay Initially, the Mobutu regime enjoyed what can only be described as an ostensible popular mandate. The coup of 24 November 1965 won approval in nearly all sections of the population. The new regime was apparently popular because it held the promise of peace and stability in a country that had been torn asunder by over five years of civil strife caused in large part by the self-serving actions of politicians. The initial popularity of the regime overshadowed its external dimension, its class base and Mobutu's personal stake in the political life of the country. These were precisely the three most important determinants of the regime's in-ability to serve the interests of ordinary people, and the factors that eventually undermined its credibility in their eyes.

That the coup was engineered by external forces determined to promote Western interests in the context of the Cold War cannot be denied. It will be recalled that the strength of the revolutionary movement had already been broken by the US–Belgian intervention of 24 November 1964, exactly a year earlier, which eliminated the CNL regime at Kisangani. However, resistance was still alive in several areas of the country, particularly in the Mulele and Kabila maquis in Kwilu and South Kivu, respectively. The fact that the national army was incapable of effectively executing its counterinsurgency role made it necessary to retain white mercenaries, whose presence in the Congo revealed the weakness of a neocolonial state and its inability to stand on its own, without imperialist support. President Kasa-Vubu's attempt to please pan-African opinion in promising a speedy repatriation of mercenaries at the Accra OAU summit in October 1965 alarmed Washington and Brussels, and thus triggered Mobutu's second intervention in Congolese politics.

By the time Mobutu took over state power, the country's economy was recovering from the turmoil of five years of political crisis, thanks to popular confidence in Tshombe's management and Belgium's strong support for the former Katanga secessionist leader. The political strife had taken its toll on the economy. The gross domestic product (GDP), which had grown by approximately 6 per cent per annum in 40 years, fell in a drastic manner, only to regain its pre-independence level in real terms by 1967.[7] Agriculture was among the hardest-hit sectors, as commercialized production fell by 40 per cent, and agricultural exports by 50 per cent.[8] Political insecurity, the breakdown of the transportation network, and peasant resistance to colonially imposed cultivation of certain cash crops were among the factors contributing to this decline. Agricultural production had already been abandoned in many areas before independence because of violence. Inter-ethnic rivalry and fighting had resulted in the displacement of thousands of people from some primary food producing areas of the country, notably within the Kasai province.

The major priority in state economic policy was to resolve the dispute with Belgium over the state investment portfolio and the external debt of the colonial state. On the eve of independence, Belgium had robbed the new state of its rightful claim to this portfolio by divesting the colonial state's vast holdings to the benefit of Belgian companies. At the same time, it did its best to overburden its former colony with much of the external debt.[9] Extremely pro-Belgian, Prime Minister Tshombe could not resolve the dispute in Congo's favour, although he pretended otherwise.[10]

This is the point at which Mobutu enters the scene in 1965. Given the external sponsorship and backing of his coup, he understood the need of counterbalancing, or even concealing, his dependence on Western support by projecting a more nationalistic vision for the country and a progressive policy agenda. Such an approach was also useful in his attempt to broaden his political base beyond the Binza Group by uniting the different fractions of moderates behind him and co-opting student and labour leaders. The nationalist offensive that Mobutu launched after the coup served the purpose of minimizing his external dependence, and the more important task of restoring the internal unity of the new ruling class and providing the forcefully retired politicians with an opportunity to develop economically.

Mobutu launched his economic offensive by pressing the claims of the new ruling class for a larger share of the economic pie, now that it had been purged of radical elements likely to threaten Western interests. Soon, it became readily apparent that these interests were not monolithic, given the competition between the different Western countries and their respective transnationals for new sources of raw materials, new markets for their manufactured goods and technical services, and new fields of profitable investment. Thanks to his American connections, Mobutu became the instrument by which a US-led international bourgeoisie sought to break the Belgian colonial monopoly to penetrate nearly all the sectors of the Congolese economy. The newcomers included Italy, Japan, the Federal Republic of Germany and France, while Britain and South Africa were now in a position to further develop their already established foothold in the Congolese market.

Two important decisions by the Mobutu regime were obviously meant to help this penetration. The first was the Bakajika Law of 1966, by which the state established its rightful claim to all land and mineral rights in the country. The second was the nationalization of the giant mining company UMHK in January 1967, transforming it into a state enterprise, the Générale des carrières et des mines, or Gécamines for short. Given its threat to Belgian hegemony, it was the new penetration, rather than the nationalization of land and mineral rights, or the mere fact of changing the legal status of the giant copper mining company from private to public, that caused Belgium to take these matters so seriously.

The Belgian government reacted quickly and vigorously to protect the interests of Belgian capital. It imposed an embargo on copper imports from the Congo and sought to cripple the Congolese economy by seeking the cooperation of its European partners in imposing other economic sanctions on its former colony. The United States offered its good offices in the dispute, with former Kennedy aide Theodore Sorensen acting as the Mobutu government's counsel. The result was that rather than weakening the links of economic dependence, the 'national-ization' of the copper industry strengthened them. The 1967 agreement provided for full compensation and granted management, processing and marketing contracts to a sister company of the UMHK in the SGB group, the Société générale des minerais. Instead of mobilizing mass support for a real strategy of economic independence or self-reliance in the face of the Belgian-initiated economic war, the Mobutu regime settled for compromises and face-saving agreements that its propaganda machine did not hesitate to sell to the people as real victories in the war for 'economic independence'.

The fundamental reality that this episode demonstrates, and the one that the 1973 'Zairianization' of foreign-owned commercial and agri-cultural enterprises was to confirm six years later, is that the basic goal of the Mobutu regime was simply to reinforce its bargaining power *vis-à-vis* foreign capital in order to provide the new ruling class with a relatively solid economic base.[11] Made up of the petty bourgeois leaders of the independence struggle and newer recruits among university graduates, military officers and rich merchants, this class was the main beneficiary of Mobutu's dictatorship and the system of patronage built around him. Owing its existence to the place its members occupy in the upper echelons of the state apparatus and to increased state participa-tion in the economy, this class was, by virtue of its relationship to the state, a *state* bourgeoisie. Operating in an underdeveloped country within the world capitalist system, it was an element, however small and underdeveloped, of international capital and, hence, a capitalist bour-geoisie.[12] As the domestic branch of the international bourgeoisie, the state bourgeoisie constitutes its own capital collectively through the output of state enterprises, royalties, taxes, and so on, as well as individu-ally, for instance, through savings from exorbitant salaries, corruption and the use of state resources for personal ends.

The enrichment of the Congolese bourgeoisie in this way was made easier by the spectacular economic recovery from 1968 to 1974, the only period of real economic growth during the Mobutu era. This recovery was made possible by political stability, the devaluation and change of the currency from Congolese francs to zaires in 1967, and above all by high copper prices due to increased demand because of the Vietnam war. The high level of economic activity and exports, with the GDP growing by about 10 per cent between 1967 and 1970 and about 5 per cent between 1970 and 1973, combined with the very liberal investment code of 1969 to create a favourable climate for foreign investments. However, the bulk of investment was allocated to mining and manufacturing, and to services, which benefited some of the major urban centres in the country. Agriculture, transportation and health received disproportionately small allocations, even when the first sector was officially declared the 'priority of priorities'. At the same time, much of the expenditure for education was spent on salaries.

Long-term economic recovery was jeopardized by the prestige-seeking economic policies associated with the ideology of 'authenticity', the costly and unproductive construction projects to which they gave rise, and the corruption involved. These projects included the new town with an international airport at Gbadolite, Mobutu's village of origin; the extravagant Inga–Shaba power line, a veritable white elephant that never used above 10 per cent of its capacity; the equally under-utilized Maluku steel plant, which relied on imported scrap and skilled workers; and others, too numerous to be mentioned here.[13] The legacy of all this wasteful expenditure for the Congolese state and society consists in a mounting external debt, which had grown to $5 billion by 1970, and an economic débâcle unique for a country so rich in natural resources. From 1975 until its demise in 1997, the Mobutu regime presided over an economic crisis that reduced a once proud people to abject poverty and a daily quest for sheer survival.

The crisis itself can be traced back to the mismanagement of the economy during the years of economic growth, when the Congolese ruling class sought to exercise greater control over the economy in general and the commercial sector in particular. This resulted in the nationalization measures of 1973–75. The first of these measures was called 'Zairianization', in conformity with Mobutu's new name for the country. It consisted in the confiscation of small and medium enterprises owned by foreign nationals, including Belgians, Greeks, Portuguese, Italians, Pakistanis and West Africans, for the benefit of Congolese politicians, senior civil servants and merchants. President Mobutu announced the localization decree on 30 November 1973.

A year later, in December 1974, this policy was declared a fiasco, the new owners or *acquéreurs* having failed to run their freely acquired businesses properly. But what was initially proclaimed as a 'war against the bourgeoisie' by the very leader of this class ended in a victory for the state bourgeoisie, as the recipients of 30 November businesses succeeded in the majority of cases in not having to surrender them to the state. In reality, the so-called 'war against the bourgeoisie' turned out to be an assault on the primarily Belgian industrial sector, a large part of which was integrated into an expanded parastatal sector. Never short on words, the ideologues of Mobutuism found it convenient to crown this second phase of the nationalization process with a revolutionary slogan. They called it 'radicalization'. Unfortunately for them, this new step, like Zairianization, did not enhance the capacity of the Congolese economy to serve the people of the Congo. Only the new managers of state enterprises, who for the most part were already *acquéreurs*, gained from it through exorbitant salaries and expense accounts, embezzled funds, kickbacks and other benefits. The only perceptible radicalization was that of the deterioration of the economic situation of the country, whose major consequence was the increasing misery of ordinary men, women and children.

The nationalization measures clearly demonstrate how the Congolese bourgeoisie was a creation of the state under Mobutu's authoritarian rule and patronage. As a patrimonial ruler for whom the state and its resources were indistinguishable from his own personal possessions, Mobutu rewarded and punished individual members of the ruling class at his own pleasure. New and younger members were recruited to high party and government jobs. But once appointed to any such post, an individual was likely to remain a permanent member of the kleptocracy, as he/she had quickly to find the means with which to maintain a high standard of living, including in most cases European schooling of one's children, during those intermittent periods of time when he/she would be out of a lucrative cabinet or parastatal post. The Mobutu regime thus answered perfectly to Frantz Fanon's characterization of the African head of state as 'the general president of that company of profiteers impatient for their returns',[14] and the screen behind which the leadership group as a whole perpetuated its shameful exploitation of the country.[15]

Mindful of the attention he received from the West, Mobutu took care to be accompanied on his trips abroad by one of the managing directors of state mining companies and/or by the governor of the central bank. These officials were expected to draw on the numerous accounts their organizations maintained in foreign banks for any cash that the Congolese dictator might need for lavish entertainment, expensive gifts for influential friends and other forms of political corruption. What Mobutu did at the top was replicated at each and every level of the system where officials had access to public revenues. This privatization of the state was a major factor in the collapse of the economy and the eventual decay and collapse of the state. For the money so diverted to private use could not be made available for productive investment in the country or for keeping up essential public services. The bulk of it went to foreign bank accounts and real estate holdings abroad. What remained in the country was used for the most part in conspicuous consumption. Meanwhile, the physical infrastructure of production and distribution decayed thoroughly, the health and educational sectors deteriorated beyond recognition, and children died by the thousands each year of preventable and easily curable diseases such as malaria, measles and dysentery.

Under Mobutu, the Congolese ruling class was responsible for an administration that could not administer properly. Lacking the most elementary demographic and other statistical data due to the poor quality of record keeping, the Congolese public administration often worked with fictitious data. Economic regulation was at best limited to the selling of various business licences, while the privileged groups whose activities and businesses often endangered the health and welfare of the public were usually able to frustrate law enforcement. The rich and the influential used their might to evade taxes, while the poor and the powerless suffered a state of permanent insecurity due to the arbitrary nature of revenue collection.[16] Given the generally insufficient revenues available to municipal and national field services together with mismanagement and generalized corruption, the system was totally incapable of maintaining existing services.

The Mobutu regime never failed to bare the primacy of the extractive and repressive functions of the neocolonial state, which proved inferior to the colonial state in terms of meeting the vital needs of the population. In nearly thirty-seven years of national rule, the masses were purely and simply excluded from the fruits of independence, and their standard of living declined steadily from 1975 onwards. As if the increasing cost of living were not enough, the looting incidents of 1991 and 1993 destroyed much of the modern sector of the economy, throwing thousands of wage earners out of gainful employment. The informal sector has until today allowed many to make ends meet, but most of the people involved in it do not realize substantial gains likely to sustain their lives in the long run. They barely manage to survive.

Until 1990, when much of foreign assistance was cut off, none of the measures taken by Mobutu's backers in the international community, including frequent rescheduling of the external debt by the Paris Club and stabilization and adjustment measures by the Bretton Woods institutions, could succeed in reversing the economic decline. In 1978, these external forces even went beyond their usual stabilization and adjustment remedies by placing the country's major economic organs under their tutelage. Erwin Blumenthal, a distinguished German banker, was appointed by the IMF to manage the central bank, while French and Belgian teams of experts were entrusted with running the ministry of finance and the customs agency, respectively.

This experiment failed miserably, as one of its principal actors has described it in the now famous *Blumenthal Report*.[17] The fact that 50 to 75 per cent of foreign exchange continued to elude the IMF-supervised central bank was a good demonstration of the futility of his position in the face of the determination by Mobutu and his kleptocracy to defend their vested interests. The tutelage of foreign experts was based on a major fallacy, the view that mismanagement in the Congo was basically a *technical* problem. This was a false view, for what was wrong with the country under Mobutu, as subsequently under Kabila, was not so much the lack of technical skills among nationals as the use to which the skills available were put. The frequent purges of competent young officers in the armed forces had their parallels in the staffing policies and practices within the other branches of the state apparatus. For those who thrived on corruption and incompetence, mediocrity was preferable to excellence, and immorality to integrity.

The Mobutu regime not only disintegrated rapidly between 1990 and 1997, but also dragged the state itself to its own decay and collapse. Although the seeds of the collapse were laid down long before 1990, the regime's loss of authority during the period of the aborted transition to democracy resulted in greater erosion of the institutional capacity of the state. For a country in which any of Mobutu's words or pronouncements could have the force of law, the rapid decline of this authority was nothing but phenomenal.

For the Congolese people, the major consequences of the Mobutuist system of institutionalized theft and corruption has been the ruin of the country's economy and social fabric, together with state decay and collapse. Mobutu and his retainers succeeded in blocking economic growth and development by destroying or neglecting the economic and social infrastructure inherited from the colonial past, and by depriving the state of basic resources needed to meet the vital needs of the people and to improve their living conditions. In the Congo, as in the rest of the African continent, the persistent economic and state crises have led to a growing realization that a close relationship does exist between the inability of the state to ensure a decent livelihood for its citizens and the lack of democracy. Thus, concurrent with the demand for civil liberties, particularly the freedoms of expression and association, the demand for a quick reversal of the current economic decline is a major part of the struggle for fundamental human rights and democracy in Africa today. The Congolese democracy movement is part of this new African awakening for a second independence.

Instruments of Power

The above description of the origins and nature of the Mobutu regime cannot do justice to a comprehensive analysis of the dictatorship and its role in the decay and collapse of the state in the Congo, in the absence of a close examination of its instruments of rule. For it is these that accentuated its external dimension, its class base and its alienation from ordinary people. Thus, in order to throw more light on the dynamics of Congolese politics under the Mobutu regime, this second part of the chapter looks more closely at how the dictator used various institutions and resources as instruments of power. The five instruments examined here are the security forces, the party, money, external sources of support and the ideological manipulation of popular aspirations and loyalties.

The security forces Of all the five variables identified here, the security forces were the single most important determinant of Mobutu's power and his most decisive instrument of rule. On three separate occasions, 14 September 1960, 24 November 1965 and 1 December 1992, he used the armed forces to remove democratically elected leaders from power by a military coup. He remained in power for nearly thirty-two years thanks to his skilful control of the military organization. The latter consisted of an overlapping network of military and paramilitary forces, none of which was ever in a position to threaten him.

To ensure that no single individual or single force could cause such a problem, the most important or élite units were actually placed under the personal command of loyal and reliable collaborators, most of whom were from the president's own Ngbandi ethnic group and were related to him either directly or by marriage. Presumably a source of strength, this transformation of the military high command into a fraternity eventually led to the collapse of the armed forces as a fighting force. As corrupt military chiefs embezzled funds appropriated for the soldiers' pay, sold military equipment and supplies and paid more attention to their private businesses than to training and discipline, the Congolese military had become a paper tiger.

Nearly half of the estimated 60,000 to 70,000 persons in uniform between 1993 and 1996 belonged to paramilitary forces. The regular military units such as the army (approximately 30,000 soldiers, including the infantry and the gendarmerie or police force), the navy or coast guard (1,000) and the air force (1,000) were barely operational, due to increasing neglect with respect to training, equipment and logistics. After the military-led looting incidents of 1991 and 1993, the two élite units of the regular army that were capable of challenging the paramilitary forces in combat readiness lost their operational capacity. These were the 31st Airborne Brigade, trained by the French until 1991, and the once Chinese-trained 41st Brigade of commandos.

Throughout his tenure, Mobutu relied heavily on the paramilitary forces to repress dissent and to intimidate the population. These forces ranged from heavily armed military units to more or less civilian intelligence and immigration services. The military units were generally autonomous of the armed forces chief of staff, whose official title was chief of the general staff. The different paramilitary forces, together with the information that is available about them, are as follows:

1. La Division spéciale présidentielle (DSP, or Special Presidential Division) was under the command of General Nzimbi Ngbale, a close relative of President Mobutu, until Kabila and his allies showed that there was nothing special about it as a fighting force. As its name implies, the DSP was the unit that was closest and most loyal to the president, whom it was designed to protect. The majority of its approximately ten thousand soldiers in 1996 were Ngbandi, like the president himself, while most of the remainder came from the Ngbaka ethnic group, also from the Equator province. A merger through the years of the initial presidential guard with other élite units such as the Kamanyola Division trained and armed by China and North Korea, it did also benefit from training by Israel. In addition to its presidential guard duty, the DSP was used in repressive and combat activities. Examples of these include its deployment to assist President Juvénal Habyarimana of Rwanda in his campaign against the Rwandese Patriotic Front (RPF) in 1990, and its involvement in the massacre of Christian demonstrators demanding the reopening of the CNS on 16 February 1992 in Kinshasa.

2. La Garde civile (Gaci, or Civil Guard) was the fastest growing of Mobutu's paramilitary forces. Estimates of its strength in 1996 ranged from 15,000 to 20,000 soldiers. It was commanded by Kpama Baramoto, another relative of the president, whose social status rose rather meteorically from a that of a military driver with the rank of sergeant to that of a four-star general with the prestigious title of *élite général de paix*.[18] Initially created as an élite border guard in 1983 with funding and training from West Germany, the unit was taken over by Egyptian trainers who helped transform it into a general-purpose paramilitary force. It replaced the Gendarmerie nationale in performing much of the sensitive police work in crowd and riot control. In the process, it became the main repressive weapon of the Mobutu regime against people demonstrating for democratic change. The Guard was involved in the February 1992 massacre and in the two-day sequestration of members of the provisional parliament, the Haut Conseil de la République (HCR), at the People's Palace without food or water from 24 to 25 February 1993.

3. Le Service d'action et des renseignements militaires (Sarm, or Military Action and Intelligence Service) spent less time in doing mili-

tary intelligence than in suppressing political dissent and opposition. Sarm was the primary instrument of power in this regard before April 1990, as opposition figures could conveniently be accused of colluding with external enemies against the national interest. Less than three weeks after Mobutu's 24 April 1990 speech ending one-party rule, its commandos were involved in the second and deadliest raid of the massacre of students on the campus of the University of Lubumbashi on the night of 11–12 May. The unit was one of the few paramilitary forces to have been headed in the 1990s by a non-Ngbandi officer. General Mahele Lieko, who later became chief of staff twice and died assassinated by Mobutu loyalists on the eve of Kinshasa's fall to Kabila's forces on 17 May 1997, served as Sarm commander until October 1991. A Mbunza, he also came from the Equator province, like the majority of high-ranking military officers in Mobutu's army.

4. La Brigade spéciale de recherche et de surveillance (BSRS, or Special Research and Surveillance Brigade) was the main criminal investigation branch of the gendarmerie. Under the command of General Bolozi, a Ngbandi relative of the president by marriage, the police turned this branch into a veritable paramilitary force. Its detention centre at the headquarters of the Kinshasa military garrison (Circonscription militaire de Kinshasa, or Circo) became notorious for its brutal treatment of political detainees once General Bolozi moved there from the military intelligence post, where he had received nothing but terrible report cards by human rights organizations such as Amnesty International. Rather than handling criminals and criminal investigations, BSRS and Circo dealt primarily with democracy activists.

5. Le Service national d'intelligence et de protection (Snip, or National Intelligence and Protection Service) was the newest incarnation of the colonial branch of the Belgian intelligence service or Sûreté. Before being renamed Snip, it went through two other names: Centre national de documentation (CND) and Agence nationale de documentation (AND). Whatever the nomenclature of the day might be, the service always combined intelligence gathering with repressive activities during the Mobutu regime. Given its relatively successful infiltration of the major arenas of political dissent such as universities and professional associations, it did achieve a high level of intimidation and was widely feared before 1990. Under Honoré Ngbanda Nzambo-ku-Atumba during the late 1980s, the agency began engaging in paramilitary activities. Ngbanda, who is also Ngbandi, was one of the closest aides to President Mobutu, whom he served as intelligence chief, defence minister and national security adviser.

6. L'Agence nationale d'immigration (Ani, or National Immigration

Service) was an autonomous service under Snip. This meant that in addition to controlling population movements across the Congo's borders, Ani also had to engage in intelligence gathering. Like most organs of a parasitic state where any parcel of authority can be exploited for material advantage, Ani agents found it useful to extend their work from border control to social control and political repression inside the country's borders. And it was in fulfilling this role that Gata Lebo Kete, the Ani regional director in Katanga, took it upon himself to lead the first murderous raid of the Lubumbashi massacre in 1990.

7. Les Forces d'action spéciales (FAS, or Special Action Forces), later known as Forces d'intervention spéciales (FIS, or Special Intervention Forces) was a paramilitary unit allegedly set up under the initiative of Ngbanda in his capacities as intelligence chief and security adviser to the president. Although little information is available about this unit, it is widely believed that it is the force whose commandos were known as *les Hiboux*, 'the Owls'. They were so called because they perpetrated their terrorist assaults at night, and drove around in all-terrain Mitsubishi Pajero vehicles with tinted windows. Although the Congo did not reach the level of state terrorism comparable to those of apartheid South Africa and some of the Latin American dictatorships, this is the closest that the country came to experiencing death squads.

From the preceding evidence, it is clear that the security forces under the Mobutu regime were basically a praetorian guard. Their basic goal was to protect the regime and its chief, Field Marshal Mobutu, the supreme military commander. It is interesting in this regard that that in spite of the demise of the party-state, military officers continued to wear a pin with Mobutu's effigy on their uniforms. The message that this seemed to convey, and one that the 1992 walk-out by the military at the CNS two months before it ended did convey, is that this was Mobutu's army and not an army of the people of the Congo. Loyalty to the chief, at least at the higher echelons, was stronger than commitment to the people and respect for their deepest aspirations for democracy and development.

High-ranking military officers, particularly those who commanded paramilitary forces, felt threatened by the democratic transition. They feared the disappearance of a system that had allowed them to enrich themselves, as well as the advent of a new era in which they were likely to become targets of criminal investigations with respect to corruption and human rights abuses. On the other hand, the more disadvantaged officers in the regular military units, including most officers below the rank of colonel, did want political change. Seldom paid regularly, miserably housed, inadequately fed and poorly trained, the rank and file soldiers in these units could no longer be counted upon to defend the status quo. Physically and morally, they were no longer capable of performing their combat and law and order duties in a satisfactory manner. Unable to obtain new uniforms from their commanders, many had to buy their own. In a country where soldiers lived off the civilian population, the uniform was a necessary arsenal for extorting money and goods from innocent people.

The ills that President Mobutu himself identified as eating away at his army in the wake of the First Shaba War in 1977 were even more evident in the twilight of his regime. These included generalized absenteeism, lack of discipline, desertion, abandonment of one's post, cowardliness, treason, disobeying orders, armed rebellion, breach of state security and military revolt.[19] As Romain Yakemtchouk has pointed out, the most profound of the ills afflicting Mobutu's army was its total demoralization. He writes that 'with their starvation wages, officers and soldiers alike [were] affected by the virus of corruption'.[20] Many senior officers were involved in gold, diamond and arms trafficking. Thus, although they constituted an instrument of power as a tool of repression against unarmed civilians, the security forces could no longer perform the normal duties expected of them in a modern state. Throughout the postcolonial era, they generally collapsed when confronted with armed groups: during the popular insurrections of 1964; their Angolan adventure of 1974–75; the Shaba wars of 1977 and 1978; and the pro-Kabila alliance of 1996–97. Given their transformation from the Force publique into the private army of Mobutu and his relatives, they could not survive Mobutu's demise.

Money Since he believed that all of the nation's abundant resources belonged to him, Mobutu did not shy away from using money from the public treasury as an instrument of power. Unlike the countries of advanced capitalism, where the private sector is the primary arena of accumulation, in Africa, it is the state that has served at once as the major source of wealth for the national élite and the means of preserving it.[21] Hence the obsession of powerholders with indefinite tenure of office, resulting in most cases in the privatization of the state and public finances; the expansion of the state sector for the potential rents and prebends it creates; and the decline in the administrative capacity of the state. Servant and protector of the minority in power, the state thus privatized is no longer capable of meeting the people's aspirations for freedom and economic development.

For the Congolese state bourgeoisie, money was useful not only for multiplying the number of clients and keeping them in line, it could also be used by the clients themselves to improve their position in the pecking order built around their patron. As late as 1996, one minister who had reason to believe that he might be dropped from the government in a forthcoming cabinet reshuffle came up with a brilliant idea. He took the prudent step of flying to Gbadolite to see the president and his family. In his briefcase, he carried one million US dollars as a gift to Bobi Ladawa, the president's wife. When the cabinet reshuffle was announced, the minister not only retained his post, he was also promoted to the rank of deputy prime minister. Such was the power of money during the Mobutu era.

The enormous amount of money used by political patrons and clients to ensure their survival, make and keep friends, or neutralize their enemies, was mostly produced locally. It was, as the title of a 1992 bestseller affirms, *Zaire's Money*,[22] and derived mainly from the country's mineral resources, including diamonds and gold. Much of this money did not even go into the state treasury. For example, it was estimated that a sum of $40 to 60 million was generated each month from mining and petroleum revenues. And yet, by 24 July 1996 the government of Léon Kengo wa Dondo claimed to have raised less than $150 million for the 1996 budget exercise, two-thirds of which supposedly came from customs revenue.[23] Where did the rest of the money go?

This disappearing act explains the incredible fact that this country of continental dimensions and so fabulously rich in natural resources had an annual government budget of $300 million in 1996. This was much less than the budget of a smaller country such as Congo-Brazzaville, or even that of a medium-sized university in the United States. Actually, if past experience is a useful guide, there is no doubt that the government spent a lot more than what was provided for in the budget. For example, total expenditure in 1992 and 1993 amounted to $1,541 and $1,001 million respectively, while the corresponding revenue was only $265 and $230 million, respectively. The frequent use of the central bank as a *planche à billets* (or banknote plate) to make up for budget deficits, or simply to provide Mobutu and his entourage with the cash they needed for various purposes, was a major cause of inflation and the constant fall in the value of the national currency. Printing money also became one way of coping with the decline in the state's revenue collecting capacity.

The main beneficiaries of the country's money, both the actually collected revenue and the potential revenue that went uncollected by the state, were found in three groups. The first two groups have already been mentioned here: the politico-administrative élite and senior military officers. The third group was made up of Lebanese merchants in the expatriate business community.

As top managers with financial responsibilities, members of the first group could take *des avantages dans la caisse*, or serve themselves and the president directly from the public till, in addition to receiving kickbacks and gifts in money or in kind from economic operators, both foreign and national. Managers of revenue-producing parastatals, particularly the major utilities such as the water company Régideso and the electricity company Snel, were known to remit a portion of their monthly or quarterly collections to President Mobutu. Money being their only religion, members of the state bourgeoisie had no strong political convictions, and were willing to play any game so long as it ensured for them or their close associates access to lucrative cabinet, parastatal or ambassadorial positions.

Like the politico-administrative élite, senior military officers used state property for private ends, with military vehicles and drivers regularly running errands for them instead of doing their normal tasks. The state housing authorities were seldom successful in collecting rent in many of the publicly owned apartment units occupied by the numerous mistresses or *deuxièmes bureaux* of Mobutu's generals and colonels. With corruptible and demoralized judges and court officers, the judicial system had a very low capacity for upholding the rule of law. In the face of senior military officers, it was totally impotent.

In addition to embezzling much of the pay destined for their troops, military commanders pocketed the pay of hundreds of fictitious soldiers, the names appearing on the payroll having no physical counterparts, as many of these were either military deserters or soldiers long dead. It is no secret that one of the immediate causes of the forced shutdown of the transitional government of Etienne Tshisekedi on 1 December 1992, when the military was used to throw the ministers out of their offices, was the fact that Paul Bandoma, the defence minister, had decided to reduce the payroll by undertaking a head count in all barracks.

An even more lucrative source of income for senior military officers and military commanders in the interior, was their association with the Lebanese merchants. This was a mutually advantageous partnership in which the Lebanese used their money and business know-how to engage in high-risk activities such as the smuggling of gold, diamonds and other goods, by relying on the protection of the military. The Lebanese seemed to prefer such protection to private security companies, especially when it came from the élite paramilitary forces. During the January 1993 incidents, for example, nearly every Lebanese family that went to seek refuge at the Intercontinental Hotel in Kinshasa was escorted there by soldiers from the DSP, Gaci and Sarm.[24]

What gave the money élite a certain cohesion as a kleptocracy was the thread that tied all of its three component parts to a single unifying centre, the neopatrimonial system of rule under President Mobutu. As the chief benefactor and protector of the group, the president was kept abreast of its members' business and other activities by his intelligence chiefs, security advisers and sons. Nearly all of Mobutu's closest advisers worked in the security apparatus and used their positions as intelligence chief or security adviser to make themselves rich. In addition to Ngbanda, who has already been mentioned in connection with Snip, FAS and FIS, the most important of these advisers were Seti Yale, Nkema Liloo, Mokolo wa Mpombo and Nimi Mayidika Ngimbi. Seti was the principal manager of the president's own properties and businesses, while Nkema and Mokolo were among his most trusted aides and served as his roving ambassadors. They are the ones who kept most in touch with Mobutu's external lobbies in Europe and elsewhere. His sons, on the other hand, had business ventures with other members of the money élite, including the Lebanese.

The Congolese state bourgeoisie had done so well for itself under Mobutu's kleptocratic rule that it could not be too excited about the prospects for democracy and the rule of law. For such a political situation involves a clearer distinction between public and private property, obligation by all to pay taxes and customs duties, equality of all citizens and residents before the law, and other requirements of good governance. This is what the democracy movement attempted to achieve from 1990 to 1997 against tremendous odds, including the use of money as a political weapon by Mobutu and his cronies, as well as the indifference of the international community.

External sources of support The role of external forces in Mobutu's rise to power has already been discussed in Chapters 3 and 4. For much of its life, the Mobutu regime also enjoyed strong external support. This came primarily from the United States, France, Belgium and some of their regional allies and clients such as Israel, Egypt, Morocco, Saudi Arabia and apartheid South Africa. The support itself was predicated on three major premises. The first premise, which was consistent with the logic of both Cold War politics and institutional racism in the United States, was that a vast and multi-ethnic country such as the Congo needed a 'strongman' to keep it together and prevent chaos, and therefore communist subversion and/or takeover. The second premise was the need to support loyal friends, regardless of their behaviour towards their own people. It had to do with the so-called 'moral commitment' to US allies in the context of the Cold War, and with the close personal ties between the French ruling class and heads of state in francophone Africa. The third and perhaps the most important premise was the need to use the Congo to promote Western interests in Central and Southern Africa. All of these premises were interdependent, and they played a crucial role in US and Western policy towards the Congo.

That Mobutu was the only person capable of holding the country together was indeed music to his ears, and the dictator played on Western fears of chaos with all the skills and resources he could mobilize for purposes of retaining power. In 1978, for example, his own troops killed whites seeking refuge from Angola-based Congolese rebels at Kolwezi. He disingenuously blamed the killing on the rebels, and used the incident to give France, Belgium and the United States the pretext for intervening militarily in the Shaba II war. Likewise, the looting incidents of 1991 and 1993 by unpaid and poorly paid soldiers, as well as the ethnic cleansing in Katanga and North Kivu in 1992–94, were all his handiwork. When Prime Minister Nguza launched the ethnic cleansing campaign against Kasaians, whom he likened to *bilulu* (or 'insects' in Kiswahili) at a public rally in early August 1992 in Lubumbashi, Ngbanda, the defence minister and one of the president's closest advisers, was on the same platform.[25]

The second premise of Western support for Mobutu revolved around the need to support reliable allies. Both the United States and France justified their pro-Mobutu actions on this basis, in terms of retaining their own credibility as reliable partners. In a 1978 *Foreign Affairs* article on the 'unending crisis' in the Congo, Professor Crawford Young frames the American argument squarely with reference to this Cold War logic. If the US abandons its allies in the Congo, he writes, African leaders elsewhere will perceive identification with the West as a liability.[26] Despite the end of the Cold War, there were policymakers in Washington who clung to this posture. They argued that since the US as a superpower with global interests and obligations needed dependable allies on which to rely, these allies must in turn have a reasonable expectation that they could count on Washington when the chips were down.

Such was the feeling of influential people in the government, particularly at the CIA and the Pentagon, who were still sympathetic to Mobutu for having advanced US interests in Central and Southern Africa.[27] Although he was frequently denounced in the halls of Congress, particularly in the House Subcommittee on Africa, where the move to cut off the modest development assistance programme of approximately $50 million a year was initiated, Mobutu had not lost all of his friends in Washington. With important figures such as Senator Jesse Helms still eager to punish and humiliate former Soviet allies, even after the demise of the Soviet Union, Mobutu was an indispensable partner in a multi-national effort to help UNITA leader Jonas Savimbi in the 1992 elections in Angola.

For the French, support for the Mobutu regime was always conceived in a larger strategic Western calculation favourable to French interests in Central Africa. In an article published in 1979, Jean-Pierre Alaux argued persuasively that, according to this grand strategy, 'the ruin of Zaire is better for Western interests than a strong and indispensable state likely to support the struggle against white Southern Africa'.[28] At the same time, a weak and disorganized state in Congo-Kinshasa would be unable to pose a threat to French hegemony in Central Africa. Jacques Foccart, the Gaullist *éminence grise* of the Africa policy bureau at the Elysée Palace under Charles de Gaulle and Georges Pompidou and Africa adviser to Jacques Chirac, has this to say about the Congo in his memoirs:

> You asked me what was France's interest. On this matter, there is no ambiguity. Congo-Léopoldville, Zaire today, is the largest country in Francophone Africa. It has considerable natural resources. It has the means of being a regional power. The long-term interest of France and its African allies is evident.[29]

What is evident to Congolese patriots and democrats is that France did not want their country to develop into a regional power in Central Africa, and thus become a rival to France for influence in its *chasse gardée*, the resource-rich countries of Cameroon, Central African Republic, Congo-Brazzaville and Gabon. With a significant military presence in the CAR, Chad and Gabon, and a strong corporate presence by trans-nationals such as the oil major Elf-Aquitaine, France was *the regional power* in Central Africa. By supporting a trusted ally such as President Mobutu, whom they had used to further their strategic and economic interests in the region, French authorities were also sending a clear message to their other African allies that they would not be forgotten when the need arose. Towards the end of the Mobutu regime, France also provided the strongest external support to the Kengo government. This was in keeping with the logic of personal ties described before, as the Congolese head of government was well known to French officials, who had already dealt with him as Mobutu's prime minister for nearly six years during the 1980s.

Of the three members of the Western Troika, only Belgium eventually became hostile to Mobutu, Brussels' alienation from the dictator growing more or less proportionately to its loss of influence in its former colony. Not only has the number of Belgian businesses and nationals declined tremendously over the years, many in the Belgian establishment have come to look at the Congo as a liability rather than an asset. In addition to being better informed about developments in the Congo, a major reason for Belgium's continued involvement in Congolese affairs is pressure from civil society organizations, including business, religious and humanitarian lobbies with an important stake in Africa, which do their best to remind their government and fellow citizens of their historical responsibility *vis-à-vis* the Congo.

Belgium took the lead in calling for political change, especially after the Lubumbashi massacre. In order to demonstrate their outrage following this event, both the Belgian and Canadian governments led the successful move to shift the venue of the 1991 summit of French-speaking countries from Kinshasa to another location. While other countries only gave lip-service to the position that the Tshisekedi government was the only legal and legitimate government during the long power struggle between Mobutu and Tshisekedi in 1993, Belgium went beyond words and actually supported the right of the Tshisekedi government to represent the Congo in international gatherings. In this respect, Brussels provided financial support for Tshisekedi's delegations to the 1993 OAU summit in Cairo and the 1993 General Assembly of the United Nations. Although money for the Cairo trip came indirectly through a Belgian NGO, the government was less timid in providing support for the UN meetings in New York, which came directly from the Belgian department of international cooperation.[30]

While Belgium's attitude towards Tshisekedi and the democracy movement was critical but generally positive, that of the other Troika members was clearly negative, if not outright hostile, as in the case of France. As major powers with global and regional interests, the US and France preferred to deal with technocrats, with whom these countries' authorities shared a common world outlook. This outlook, which has been described as *la pensée unique* (single theory),[31] is based on liberalism and its propensity for problem solving based on the requirements of globalization rather than the deepest aspirations and interests of ordinary people. Technocrats are more likely to be accommodating than leaders with a popular base, who are more likely to listen to their national constituencies rather than to their external partners. Whereas Kengo fell into the first category as a technocrat with no popular and social base, Tshisekedi was then leading the largest opposition party in the Congo. The failure of the democratic transition was partly due to the fact that support from the major Western powers went more to the forces of the status quo than to those representing democratic change and popular aspirations.

The party-state However brutal it might be, no political system can sustain its rule with the exclusive use of force. For force, like money, loses its value when it is used in an excessive manner.[32] This is why all ruling classes strive to make use of different political and ideological apparatuses in order to gain compliance without recourse to excessive force. During the colonial period, the rulers used the ideology of racism, which materialized itself economically through the wage/colour bar; politically in the distinction between 'Europeans' and 'natives'; and culturally through the inferiority complex that religious and educational institutions reproduced in the context of the so-called civilizing mission. The African state bourgeoisies, on the other hand, could not rely on colonial-inherited institutions as the primary vehicle of ideological control. They needed an institution of their own creation for purposes of legitimizing their rule. In an Africa where even the parastatal sector had a colonial origin, the one institution they could justifiably claim as their own was the political party. Aristide Zolberg has noted that the party 'was a self-made indigenous institution, and it was an instrument with which the new rulers were familiar'.[33] It was the most appropriate instrument of power for the crisis-ridden states of postcolonial Africa.

Under the Mobutu regime, political party formation began in 1966, with the creation of a government-sponsored youth organization, the Corps des volontaires de la République (CVR).[34] The main purpose of the CVR was to mobilize mass support for the regime. A particular emphasis was placed on the lumpenproletariat. The positive appeal of the CVR to the latter, as well as to obscure politicians of the 1958–65 partisan rivalries in search of a new adventure and to careerist university students seeking senior government positions, encouraged Mobutu to move ahead towards the establishment of a full-fledged political party.

This was accomplished on 20 May 1967, the birthday of the Mouvement populaire de la révolution (MPR).[35] Originally set up as a parallel institution with former CVR cadres and militants as its personnel and effective members, the MPR was progressively integrated within the administrative branch of the state apparatus, with which it eventually made a fusion to create Mobutu's *party-state*.[36] After three years of a *de facto* party-state, the one-party system was finally declared *de jure* in 1970, with the MPR as the supreme institution of the state. Mobutu became the head of all the country's political institutions, and a special provision of the party statutes allowed for his election as party chairman and therefore head of state indefinitely. Implicitly, this made him a life president. And, as befitting to royal dignity, it was a capital offence to insult him. Any of his important public pronouncements could have the force of law, as when he forbade the wearing of Western suits and ties by men and of Western dresses and trousers by women in 1972.

Like the typical ruling party in postcolonial Africa, the MPR became an auxiliary instrument of state propaganda and political control, a task force needed to make up for the administration's deficiencies in law enforcement and intelligence activities. Interestingly, the coercive arm of the youth branch of the party was appropriately called Brigade disciplinaire. This was a most respectable refuge for the worst elements of the lumpenproletariat, which turned their criminal tendencies and street smarts into a formidable weapon of intimidation and of law enforcement without regard to the rule of law. There were moments when the regular police were at their wits' end in a heinous crime of murder, rape or armed robbery, only to see the party's disciplinary brigade produce the culprit without much difficulty.

The drift towards fascism or a 'dictatorship of the national-socialist type' that Fanon had feared did not materialize. Organizational deficiencies and strong ethnic loyalties undermined the move to absolute control, so that the African party-states were authoritarian rather than totalitarian. However, Fanon had correctly observed that the party would become an implement of coercion that 'helps the government to hold the people down'[37] and transforms the militant into an informer.[38] In the Congo, as elsewhere in Africa, his prediction on the party's coercive role has stood the test of time:

> The party plays understudy to the administration and the police, and controls the masses, not in order to make sure that they really participate in the business of governing the nation, but in order to remind them constantly that the government expects from them obedience and discipline.[39]

Popular aspirations and loyalties Popular aspirations and loyalties are an important instrument of power. As indicated above, no rule is sustainable in the long run without popular legitimacy and support. This is why, regardless of how they come to power and whatever their policy objectives might be, all regimes are eager to win popular legitimacy and support. And they strive to do so through socio-economic policies and through ideology. The Mobutu regime went through three distinct periods with respect to popular support: 1965–1975, when it was high; 1975–90, when it was at best lukewarm; and 1990–97, when popular aspirations and loyalties had deserted him in favour of the democracy movement.

The initial popularity of the regime was tied to both general fatigue with the political crisis of the first five years of independence and the renewed strength of the economy between 1967 and 1973. This popularity was genuine, despite massive violations of human rights. It was reinforced by his regime's relative success in winning the people's loyalties by identifying itself with their deepest aspirations. This process of identifying regime objectives and popular aspirations began with the development of the ideology of authenticity. Just as every dominant ideology 'contains features from ideologies other than that of the dominant class',[40] this new ideology began to incorporate in its structure elements of the ideologies of the popular and student movements. Like the people, Mobutu's regime castigated politicians as corrupt and aligned with foreign interests. It depicted Mobutu as a heroic leader who brought an end to chaos, delivered the people from these corrupt and useless politicians, and was the only redeemer who could bring about the long desired second independence. In reality, the presumably nationalistic economic policies of the regime did nothing but reinforce the much-hated alliance between the ruling class and external interests.

Between 1973 and 1977, things fell apart, and the economy began to deteriorate steadily. This was due to the combined effect of the nationalization measures of 1973 and 1974, the crash in copper prices in 1974, and the defeat of Mobutu's army in Angola in 1975. The poor and corrupt management of nationalized businesses resulted in food shortages, a very severe inflation, and popular discontent bordering on rebellion. It is in this context that the first major purge occurred in the armed forces, following what the government alleged was an attempted and failed coup in 1975. Thus began a pattern of purging the military of its ablest and best-trained officers, who were either executed for various offences or prematurely retired from service. It is a pattern that eventually led to a serious decay in the military apparatus of the state, and to its ultimate collapse in 1996–97.

With growing discontent, the regime intensified its repression through the paramilitary forces, but did not neglect the necessity of ideological work. Throughout the 1970s, a great deal of effort went into strengthening a personality cult built around President Mobutu. He was given titles such as 'father of the nation', 'father of the revolution', 'the helmsman', and the 'enlightened guide'. All of this was part of the ideology of authenticity, in which the president was depicted as possessing exceptional wisdom for solving the country's problems, a wisdom based on traditional family and village values. Compared to a household head and a village chief, he and his wife were presumably father and mother to all citizens, and remained on the same wavelength with all good citizens. For wayward children or rebellious citizens, the chief knew not only how to administer the right punishment, but also when and how to forgive.

The task of inculcating this ideology fell to both the repressive and ideological branches of the state apparatus. The party-state organization at all levels of territorial administration played a major role in this regard, with governors, district commissioners and local administrators seeing to it that public and private sector workers began the day with a salute to the flag with songs in honor of Mobutu. At each prefectorial level of administration, one of the deputies was in charge of party mobilization, a task that included the organization of troupes of party cheerleaders whose presence was essential to the success of any public event, particularly visits by the president himself, foreign dignitaries and important Congolese officials. The degree of 'militantism' or commitment to the party could be judged by how well one sang and danced. Fortunes and careers could also change overnight, particularly for those beautiful women who knew how to surrender body and soul to the MPR.[41]

Trying to be as paternalistic as the Belgians before him, Mobutu lacked the organizational capacity to provide real bread and circuses. He was reduced to wishful thinking, in statements such as: 'Happy are the people who sing and dance.' For the majority of citizens, however, there was little to sing and dance about after 1975. Fear of repression rather than enthusiasm for the president and his regime made them comply with administrative orders to attend public rallies and to demonstrate in support of the regime. Until 1990, when it became possible to openly engage in opposition politics, popular resistance to the regime or expression of alienation from it took place primarily in the form of religious sects.

When popular aspirations and loyalties became clearly hostile to the regime, opposition to it and support for the democracy movement were also expressed in religious terms. A leading Congolese historian has shown how, in a popular culture heavily marked by a fundamentalist reading of the Bible, the people had no problem combining the sacred and the profane in their politically inspired music. Melodies and ideas from Christian hymns were used to depict the struggle for democracy as a duel between the forces of evil, which were identified with Mobutu, and the forces of good, represented by 'Tshitshi'.[42] Thus the flipside of the demonization of Mobutu was the elevation of Tshisekedi to sainthood. The faithful called him 'Moses'.

The transfer of popular loyalty from the Mobutu regime to the democracy movement was best exemplified by the hero's welcome Tshisekedi received upon his return home in February 1991. After attending a major conference on the prospects for democracy in the Congo in November 1990 at Howard University in Washington, Tshisekedi made a tour of several North American cities and European capitals. He had, by then, captivated the popular mind by his courage in the face of repression and humiliations by the regime, and his strong commitment to democracy. The cortège from Kinshasa's N'Djili International Airport to his home in Limete, a distance of approximately 12 kilometres, lasted about eight hours. Moses had arrived to deliver his people from Pharaoh.

Between April 1990 and February 1991, the Mobutu regime lost the ability to use its instruments of power for purposes of intimidating the people and keeping them down. As Tshisekedi liked to tell his followers, the effective power of a dictator resides in the fear that people have of him. Consequently, the moment that fear disappears, the regime loses its power of intimidation. The disintegration, in such a rapid fashion, of the authority and the means of coercion of a regime in which the word of the chief used to be tantamount to law was nothing but phenomenal. For Mobutu, the loss of moral authority and the erosion of coercive power deepened as a result of the Lubumbashi massacre, which brought about worldwide condemnation and the suspension of the external military assistance, which helped to sustain his repressive apparatus through training, equipment renewal and moral support. Irregular pay and poor living and working conditions also led to increased discontent within the armed forces, resulting in the looting incidents of 1991 and 1993, which involved serious fighting between the paramilitary forces and the élite airborne division in Kinshasa.

By the time the CNS was debating his future in 1992, Mobutu's authority had been so undermined that he no longer felt at ease in the capital. He first retreated to the presidential yacht, which was for the most part moored on the Congo River at N'Sele, north of Kinshasa, and then to Gbadolite. When he occasionally ventured to visit the capital, as he did in 1992 to attend the funeral of the spiritual leader of the Kimbanguists Joseph Diangenda, his cortège from the airport to town included helicopters, tanks and armoured cars. This display of might was in sharp contrast to the ease with which Tshisekedi could move between his house and the People's Palace, where the CNS was being held. Unarmed UDPS volunteers guarded the Limete residence of the leader of the democracy movement and the people's symbol for radical change.

Notes

1. Naipaul, 'A new king for the Congo'.

2. *New Nigerian*, 15 June 1978.

3. Eric Rouleau, 'Guerre et intoxication au Tchad', *Le Monde diplomatique*, September 1983, p. 1. Emphasis in the original.

4. Ibid, p. 8.

5. Ibid, p. 8.

6. Military service in the Force publique was limited to two years for individuals with at least two years of secondary education. All other Congolese recruits served seven years.

7. Vanderlinden, *Du Congo au Zaïre, 1960–1980*, pp. 182–3.

8. World Bank, *Zaire*, p. 4.

9. For more details on the origins of the Belgo-Congolese economic dispute (*le contentieux belgo-congolais*), see Said, *De Léopoldville à Kinshasa*, pp. 211–32.

10. Tshombe added to his popularity in 1965 when, returning from one of his frequent visits to Brussels, he held high his briefcase at Ndjili Airport in Kinshasa and told the whole country that he had brought home all that Belgium owed the Congo. It was all in the briefcase!

11. See Peemans, 'The social and economic development of Zaire since independence', p. 163.

12. Olivier, 'Afrique: qui exploite qui?'; Hussein, *Class Conflict in Egypt, 1945–1970*, p. 106.

13. The word *Shaba*, which means 'copper' in Kiswahili, was used by Mobutu to designate the copper-rich Katanga province. Thus the electricity transmission line from the Inga Dam to the Katanga mining complex, and the wars that were fought in this province in 1977 and 1978, are known respectively as *Inga-Shaba* and the *Shaba* wars.

14. Fanon, *The Wretched of the Earth*, p. 166.

15. Ibid, p. 168. The national leader, who in this instance can be either a head of state or a warlord, is 'a screen between the people and the rapacious bourgeoisie since he stands surety for the ventures of that caste and closes his eyes to their insolence, their mediocrity, and their fundamental immorality'.

16. Nzongola-Ntalaja, 'Urban administration in Zaire: a study of Kananga, 1971–73', pp. 272–323; Schatzberg, *Politics and Class in Zaire*, pp. 59–80.

17. Blumenthal, 'Le rapport Blumenthal et annexes'.

18. Baramoto is a former driver for General Eluki Monga, with whom he later formed, along with Nzimbi and Admiral Mavua Mudima, the 'gang of four' that, according to Mobutu's last security adviser Honoré Ngbanda, destroyed Mobutu's army. See Ngbanda Nzambo-ku-Atumba, *Ainsi sonne le glas!*

19. Département de la défense nationale, Etat-major-général des Forces armées zaïroises, *Mobutu et la guerre de 'quatre-vingts jours'* (1978), p. 75, cited in Yakemtchouk, 'Les deux guerres du Shaba'.

20. Yakemtchouk, 'Les deux guerres du Shaba', p. 422.

21. See Clapham, *Third World Politics*.

22. Dungia, *Mobutu et l'argent du Zaïre*.

23. Verbal communication from Prime Minister Léon Kengo wa Dondo to the bureau of the National Electoral Commission, Kinshasa, 26 July 1996.

24. I was an eyewitness to these developments.

25. In an interview with the Voice of America in August 1992, I used this incident to show that it was Mobutu himself who was behind the ethnic cleansing, because he did not condemn the actions of his two senior ministers. On 30 August, when Mobutu met Tshisekedi to endorse the latter's government, he complained that the new prime minister had sent Professor Nzongola to level insults at him in Washington.

26. Young, 'Zaire: the unending crisis'.

27. Confidential information from a Congressional source in Washington in October 1993.

28. Alaux, 'L'étonnante longevité du régime Amin Dada'.

29. Foccart and Gaillard, *Foccart parle: entretiens avec Philippe Gaillard*, p. 310. My own translation.

30. I was the number-two person in both delegations, in my capacity as diplomatic adviser to Prime Minister Tshisekedi.

31. See Ignatio Ramonet, 'La pensée unique', *Le Monde diplomatique*, January 1995.

32. The best example of this in recent African history is the heroic image of teenagers boldly confronting with their bare hands the tanks and armoured cars that apartheid South Africa deployed in the townships against the Mass Democratic Movement between 1984 and 1990.

33. Zolberg, *Creating Political Order*, p. 123.

34. Corps of Volunteers for the Republic.

35. People's Revolutionary Party.

36. On the concept of the 'party-state', see Zolberg, *Creating Political Order*.

37. Fanon, *The Wretched of the Earth*, p. 171.

38. Ibid, p. 182.

39. Ibid, pp. 181–2.

40. Poulantzas, *Political Power and Social Classes*, p. 210.

41. One of the party's mottos was that 'in the MPR, one surrenders both the body and the soul'. During my dissertation research in Kananga, I asked one woman party official why she was at the lower end of the hierarchy while many less qualified women were higher than she was. She replied: 'I gave the soul, but not the body.'

42. Ndaywel à Nziem, *La société zaïroise dans le miroir de son discours religieux, 1990–1993*.

. . . .

CHAPTER 6

The Struggle for Multiparty Democracy

§ THE third and longest period of the Congolese resistance to tyranny has comprised two distinct phases. The first phase, from 1969 to 1980, was marked by the absence of overt political opposition internally, as those opposed to the Mobutu regime challenged its policies and not the regime itself. They sought reforms rather than revolution. Externally based groups, on the other hand, sought to overthrow the regime. During the first phase, the banner of freedom and human rights was taken up by civil society organizations internally, particularly the student movement and the Catholic Church, and by two groups in exile, the Mouvement d'action pour la résurrection du Congo (MARC) and the Front de libération nationale congolais (FLNC).[1]

These and other manifestations of resistance to the Mobutu regime did the necessary groundwork for the second and most important phase, that of the struggle for multiparty democracy. This phase, from 1980 to 1997, saw the ascendancy of internally based groups, which transformed their resistance against the worst excesses of Mobutu's dictatorship and reign of terror into one of the first national campaigns for multiparty democracy in the Africa of the party-states. The culminating point of this campaign, which started with a group of dissident members of parliament in 1980, was the CNS in 1992.

The Fight against Mobutu's Dictatorship and Reign of Terror

The struggle for multiparty democracy in the Congo is part of a worldwide rejection of military rule and the one-party system of government. It is also a continuation of the fight for national independence and economic development begun in 1956, and of the resistance against the political and economic crimes of the Mobutu regime. Having already taken part in the country's 'original sin', Lumumba's assassination, Mobutu went on to compile such a lengthy record of criminal deeds to become, in Nguza's words, 'the incarnation of the Zairian sickness'.[2] Following is a brief summary of this tragic record:

- 1966: the unjustified public hanging of four prominent leaders: Jérome Anany, Emmanuel Bamba, Evariste Kimba and Alexandre Mahamba;[3]
- 1968: the assassination of Pierre Mulele;
- 1969: the massacre of university student demonstrators in Kinshasa, which is discussed below;
- 1971: the enrolment of Kinshasa and Lubumbashi university students in the army, for daring to commemorate the 1969 massacre;
- 1971–72: the arbitrary measures associated with the ideology of authenticity, including changing the country's name unilaterally; the ban on 'foreign' names for all citizens; and the ban on Western suits and ties for men, and Western dresses and trousers for women;
- 1974–75: military intervention in Angola as an ally of the CIA and apartheid South Africa, followed by two decades of support to Angolan rebel leader Jonas Savimbi against the best economic interests of the Congo, namely, access to the Benguela Railroad, the best exit route for minerals from Katanga;
- 1975: first major purge of the armed forces, under the pretext of an aborted coup that never was;
- 1977: ceding one-tenth of the national territory to OTRAG, a German missile-making firm, a deal that was later rescinded because of protests by regional states;
- 1979: massacre of artisanal diamond diggers at Katekelayi, in Eastern Kasai province;
- 1990: the massacre of Lubumbashi University students;
- 1991 and 1993: instigation of looting and violence by the military;
- 1992: the massacre of Christian demonstrators demanding the reopening of the National Conference, in Kinshasa;
- 1992–94: the instigation of ethnic cleansing in the Katanga and Kivu provinces;
- 1994–96: refusal to deal with the danger posed to the country by the Rwandan refugee camps under the control of Hutu extremists;
- 1996–97: use of white mercenaries in a last-ditch effort to save the regime; and
- other political and economic crimes, including the burning of entire villages in counterinsurgency zones; the neglect of victims of volcanic eruptions; and the taking of kickbacks to authorize the construction of unproductive ventures and turnkey projects such as the Inga–Shaba Line, the Maluku steel plant and other white elephants.[4]

Since the MPR had been institutionalized in 1970 as the supreme organ of the state, all the political space was now monopolized by the party-state. Women, labour, student and youth organizations lost their independent existence to become branches of the party. Only religious organizations had the possibility of retaining some autonomy. However, this autonomy was threatened by the launching of the authenticity drive in 1971–72, with the banning of Christian names as 'foreign' and the requirement that students in Catholic seminaries take part in the activities of the youth branch of the party, the JMPR. This brought the state and the Catholic Church, perhaps the most important numerically on the African continent, on a collision course. Led by Joseph Cardinal Malula and relying on progressive social analyses done by young priests inspired by the theology of liberation, the Catholic bishops of the Congo became a powerful voice of dissent against the Mobutu regime. Their pastoral letters and other declarations will remain as outstanding works of critical analysis in the historical record, and manifestations of the moral authority and the social importance of the Church as a power centre in the Congo.

In spite of its radical critique of the regime, the Catholic Church as an institution was too conservative to lead a social movement against it. While issuing progressive documents drafted by young priests, the bishops as individuals retained cordial, and even warm, relations with political authorities. Mass political activity, such as the February 1992 demonstration in Kinshasa, was the work of lay groups under the leadership of radical priests and nuns. University and other tertiary-level students were the only civil society group that attempted to go beyond radical critique to political action as a social movement.

Resistance in civil society: the student movement Congolese students, like university students elsewhere, are deeply concerned with the organization and relevance of their education, as well as with their country's politics. In Africa, these two concerns go hand in hand, inasmuch as the state is the major source of funding for higher education and, in most cases still, the major employer. In the Congo, university-specific issues included demands for reforms in admission policies, the curriculum, university governance, the material conditions of student life and career opportunities after graduation. The government's position on these issues was seen as a barometer of its commitment to national independence and the general welfare of the society.

When medical assistants, Catholic priests and agricultural technicians, who had a university-level education, were excluded, the Congo had about twelve university graduates at independence. The Catholic University of Lovanium, founded in 1954 at Kinshasa as an extension of Belgium's Louvain University and the Université officielle du Congo (UOC), the state university established at Lubumbashi in 1956, were the only two universities in existence in 1960. A third university was established by the Protestants in 1963 at Kisangani as the Université libre du Congo (ULC). Under the circumstances, the demand for more graduates reflected not only the interests of the student movement as a pressure group, but also a national need. In addition to this goal, students demanded the democratization of governance in the three universities and the technical institutes, the decolonization and African-ization of the curriculum, and better living and working conditions on the campuses.

Long before the famous French student revolts of 1968 and even before the Berkeley student movement in the United States, Congolese students had taken political action to advance their interests. A major strike with barricades and student occupation of all offices in the administration building took place in March 1964 at Lovanium. It was a classic example of the opposition between the students' democratic ideal and the authoritarianism of the Establishment. In reply to the students' demand for representation on faculty councils, the deans of the various schools were quoted as saying that 'the educative relation-ship is essentially aristocratic'.[5] So when in this case the privileged ruling class was of Belgian origin, it became apparent why the students accused the expatriate staff of being neocolonialist and of behaving in a patronizing, or even racist, manner. They further accused the staff of deliberately striving to slow down the educational development of the country with restrictive admissions policies and a scandalously high failure rate. On this score, the students' complaints had the full weight of statistics behind them.

Between 1958 and 1968, for example, Lovanium awarded only 470 degrees to Congolese, out of a total of 630 degrees, 35 of which went to Belgians and the rest mostly to Africans from other countries. This was the total output for 14 years. For its twelve years of work, including two years and a half under the secessionist regime, UOC awarded 170 degrees to Congolese and 70 to Europeans. Seen in relation to enrol-ment figures, of which it was a very small proportion, the total number of degrees represented an amazingly low productivity. For Congolese students, this was a wastage of criminal proportions, given the massive investment of state revenues in higher education. Even the private universities were heavily subsidized by the state, with Lovanium re-ceiving about 50 per cent of its budget from the public treasury and the ULC about 80 per cent in the late 1960s.

A study mission sent to the Congo in June 1969 by the American

Council on Education to make a survey of educational problems on behalf of the US Agency for International Development reported that the Congo's extremely high attrition rates were the highest of all universities in Africa. The failure rate was high in all departments, and extremely so in the natural sciences. Up to 1968 Lovanium's Faculty of Medicine failed 81 per cent of all students who were enrolled in it. At UOC, the comparable figure was 75 per cent for 1961–68, and 89.5 per cent in pharmacy and agriculture in 1963–68. By 1968, Lovanium had produced fewer than twenty Congolese engineers.[6]

When Mulele took over the education portfolio in the Lumumba cabinet at independence, he did not wait to send clear signals that he intended to transform the higher education system radically. His successors were more timid, and did nothing to use the resources at their disposal to effectively control the universities. With his nationalistic discourse, Mobutu touched the right chord with the students on the question of decolonization and Africanization. Both UGEC, the national student association, and the Association générale des étudiants de Lovanium (AGEL), a separate union for Lovanium University students, welcomed the Mobutu regime. They each declared their support for its programme, AGEL for most of it, and UGEC for those parts of it that seemed to agree with its own national goals. On his first visit to Lovanium, General Mobutu saw himself inducted into the student community by AGEL.

UGEC remained cautious and selective in its support, in spite of the regime's attempt to win it over. Nevertheless, relations between the two remained cordial, and André N'Kanza-Dolumingu, the UGEC national president, accepted President Mobutu's invitation to address the nation at the Independence Day celebration on 30 June 1966. This is the occasion that Mobutu used to proclaim Lumumba the Congo's national hero and to restore to a number of cities their African names.

The apparently growing relationship between the Congo's then most stable political organization and the new regime was based on a basic misunderstanding. Mobutu's friendly attitude towards UGEC seems to have convinced its leadership that, in contrast to previous governments, the Mobutu regime had a clear understanding of the rightness of UGEC's political goals. The union also hoped that the regime would entrust to it the leadership of the entire Congolese youth in order for the latter to be organized on a solid ideological footing. The regime, on its part, seemed to think that by adopting progressive slogans, fighting regionalism and tribalism, renaming Congolese cities, and following UGEC's example in proclaiming Lumumba the country's national hero, it would have met the necessary conditions of co-opting the UGEC leadership into a new national youth movement, stripped of UGEC's ideological garments.

As events up to mid-1967 were to show, both sides were wrong. Two significant happenings had by then demonstrated that there was no basis for a lasting cooperation between UGEC as a social movement and the regime, which by then had created its own political party, the MPR.

The first event was the third national congress of UGEC, held in Kinshasa in October 1966. Following a debate on the president's exhaustive report on the situation in the country, the representatives of Congolese university students at home and in more than eight foreign countries voted unanimously to make the Congo a socialist state, with scientific socialism as the basic ideology, and democratic centralism the organizational principle.

The second was the publication in May 1967 of the MPR manifesto, known as the *Manifeste de la N'Sele* after the name of the location where it was issued, which later became the party's headquarters and conference centre. According to this manifesto, the MPR is against both capitalism and communism. Nationalism is its ideology, and its revolution is genuinely Congolese, because it is not based on borrowed theories and doctrines. This was an obvious reference to UGEC. As in other African countries where progressive ideas are denounced as foreign, the defenders of official ideology are generally oblivious to the fact that 'market economy' or 'mixed economy' are not African, either. Since they are not natural principles, they, too, must have originated from some foreign source.

In spite of the ideological differences, UGEC and the regime maintained an uneasy peace throughout 1967. The regime continued to consider UGEC as a legitimate student trade union, and from time to time its national executive committee was consulted on matters of national interest by the Ministry of National Education. It also served as a mediator between the government and students in disputes at universities and technical institutes. This period of peaceful coexistence came to an end in February 1968, following the arrest of N'Kanza-Dolumingu and other UGEC leaders, student protests at Kinshasa, Lubumbashi and Kisangani, and the banning of UGEC as an organization by the MPR's politburo.

It all began with the visit of US Vice-President Hubert H. Humphrey to Kinshasa. He chose 4 January, the Independence Martyrs' Day and Congo's greatest revolutionary day, to visit the Lumumba monument, where he planned to lay down flowers. UGEC-Lovanium organized a protest demonstration, whose purpose, according to a UGEC communiqué, was to prevent 'a profanation by the same people who, yesterday, had done everything to make the great fighter for Congo's and Africa's freedom disappear'. The demonstration, with the throwing of eggs and tomatoes, greatly embarrassed the regime, then a major recipient of US military and economic assistance in Africa. President Mobutu was so angry that twelve days later he bitterly denounced N'Kanza-Dolumingu, who holds a degree in mathematics from Princeton University, as a marginal element and a foolish troublemaker, when he could put his knowledge at the service of his country in high places.

In a sense, this was a tribute to N'Kanza-Dolumingu's integrity for having until then resisted co-optation into Mobutu's entourage. He paid dearly for this resistance, or what Mobutu saw as insolence, with over a dozen years of banishment to his village of origin. This punishment must have crushed him morally, for he later accepted appointment to the MPR central committee in the 1980s. Long before him, most of the other prominent UGEC leaders had been easily co-opted into the Mobutu regime by 1967. Some of Mobutu's closest collaborators had served as members of the UGEC national executive committee. Joseph N'Singa Udjuu, interim president in 1962–63, served in top party and state positions, including that of prime minister. Henri Takizala, the very first UGEC president, also served in the cabinet and as provincial governor. And Gérard Kamanda wa Kamanda, international affairs secretary in 1963–66, started his political career in Mobutu's office in 1967; 30 years later, he was still serving Mobutu as foreign minister in the government that Laurent Kabila overthrew in May 1997. Of all the top UGEC leaders, only Anatole Malu and Tharcisse Mwamba resisted the co-optation, and went instead to make successful careers in international organizations.[7]

With the banning order, the MPR made two important revelations: the supremacy of its politburo over the government, and a last warning that no political activity would be allowed outside of the single party organization. Students, on the other hand, did not feel that the JMPR sections, whose leaders tended to be opportunists with an eye to postgraduation careers in government, could represent their interests effectively. Convinced that the government was doing too little for them materially and indifferent to their academic and other concerns regarding university governance, they felt compelled to take action, with or without the JMPR. The Mobutu regime's ideology of authenticity and its nationalistic policies were of no consequence in the universities. To the students, the curriculum appeared unnecessarily cumbersome, and much of the instruction devoid of significance for them, given its lack of relevance to Congolese and African realities. Moreover, the rigidly centralized and authoritarian university bureaucracy was seen as an obstacle to educational reforms. Having defined themselves as 'intellectual workers', the students felt that they should participate in the planning and management of their work.

During the university crises of 1967 and 1968, the government almost invariably sided with university administrators. The situation worsened in 1969, as the monthly allowance of $12 to $16 was inadequate for satisfying the student's basic needs in books, food and clothing. With all the display of wealth and privilege around them by the nouveaux riches of the Mobutu regime, the students definitely shared a sense of relative deprivation. Books were particularly needed as the final, comprehensive, examinations for the academic year were approaching. At Lovanium, there was fear that university authorities and professors were more than willing to use the exams as a means of eliminating all those they considered politically undesirable. Since the failure rate was expected to be as high as 90 per cent, a climate of uneasiness and frustration pervaded the entire student community in Kinshasa.[8] This is the background to the massacre of 4 June 1969.

Early that Wednesday morning, the students gathered to carry out a peaceful demonstration, planned some three or four days earlier, in favour of increased support for their academic and social needs. They easily broke through two police roadblocks, before coming into confrontation with the army. In order to disperse them, the army first used tear-gas grenades, which some students picked up and flung back to the soldiers. Then the soldiers opened fire, and this resulted in many casualties among the students, of whom more than sixty were dead. The government immediately imposed a strict censorship, and it was General Mobutu himself who gave the first lengthy public account of the events to the nation. Among other measures, all the students from the Institut Pédagogique National (IPN), the national teachers college, and 86 from the Ecole Nationale d'Administration (ENA), the national school of administration, were expelled. Lovanium students were sent home until further notice. A similar measure was taken at Lubumbashi, where UOC students had marched on the provincial governor's residence, bare-chested and bare-footed, to show their solidarity with their peers in Kinshasa.

Violence erupted again two years later, when Lovanium students held a memorial service for their fallen comrades. This time, the punishment for them and for students at UOC who held a sympathy demonstration was to enrol all of them in the armed forces. The MPR then moved to nationalize Lovanium and ULC to create a single national university with campuses at Kinshasa, Lubumbashi and Kisangani. These have once again become separate state universities, but the harm done in 1971 to the system of higher education in the Congo will take a long time to repair.

Once enrolled in the armed forces, the students became a danger to the regime. For the soldiers who were indoctrinated to hate them developed a lot of respect for these intellectuals in uniform. Given their intellectual skills and relatively good health, the students excelled at tasks that soldiers had considered difficult. Rather than being effete snobs, the students turned out to be physically fit to challenge career soldiers at anything, including physical exercise and hand-to-hand combat. To the soldiers' bewilderment, the students explained how better fed they were, compared to the soldiers, and took pleasure in politicizing the latter in discussions concerning inequality and injustice in the Congo. When his intelligence services informed him of rumblings of discontent in the armed forces, Mobutu understood that it was time for the students to leave military service.[9]

As already shown in Chapter 4, the student movement was incapable of assuming the leadership of the mass democratic movement. Eloquent in its radical critique of the Mobutu regime and bold in promoting its own corporate interests, it could not defend these and the general societal interest at the same time. Another limitation to its ability to act in this way was ideological. Lovanium, the oldest and academically the best-established university, did set standards for the entire higher education community in the Congo. The élitist philosophy on which it was founded was so pervasive that it penetrated the minds of all its constituents, including radically oriented students. These failed to see the contradiction between their constant reference to themselves as an élite and their profession of faith in scientific socialism. When careerism reared its ugly head at graduation, such a profession was simply a sham. However, in spite of its political and ideological limitations, the student movement was the single most important civil society organization to challenge the Mobutu regime at the height of its power, and it made a positive contribution to the fight against the dictatorship and its reign of terror.

Externally based political opposition: MARC and the FLNC With the party-state monopolizing virtually the entire political space, the main opposition to the Mobutu regime between 1969 and 1980 came from groups in exile. The externally based opposition was made up of a number of exile groups and personalities. Unlike the internal opposition, which fought to change some concrete conditions inside the country as part of an overall struggle for political change, the exile groups and personalities tended to be lobbyists searching for external support to overthrow Mobutu. Instead of seeking to organize people at home, as more successful opposition movements have done elsewhere, they were content with issuing manifestoes and communiqués or holding press conferences and talking to American and European legislators. At the same time, they kept hoping and waiting for a spontaneous mass revolt or a military coup, which would prepare the way for their return home to occupy high government positions.

The externally based opposition would not have attracted much attention had it not been for the presence within its ranks of former dignitaries of the Mobutu or previous regimes. The two most famous figures from the First Republic were Moïse Tshombe, the former Katanga secessionist and Congolese prime minister, and Antoine Gizenga, former deputy prime minister under both Lumumba and Adoula. Of the two men, it was Tshombe who represented a real threat to the Mobutu regime, given his fortune, his European connections, and his reserve army of mercenaries and gendarmes, some of whom had returned to Angola to help the Portuguese fight the national liberation movement. This threat ended when his plane was hijacked over the Mediterranean on 30 June 1967. Kidnapped to Algiers, he died in an Algerian jail exactly two years later, on 30 June 1969, reportedly of a heart attack. Gizenga posed virtually no threat, as he quietly enjoyed the hospitality of socialist comrades in Sofia, Luanda and Brazzaville, before returning home after nearly twenty-eight years of exile to attend the CNS. His political antics since then clearly demonstrated that he had lost touch with the country and its realities.

A third but lesser figure of the pre-Mobutu era was Cléophas Kamitatu Massamba, who had gone into exile after having been named as a minor conspirator in the so-called 'Pentecostal Plot', a trap set by Mobutu to consolidate his power. Released from jail after the first year of a five-year prison sentence, Kamitatu lived and studied in France for ten years. He made a name for himself by publishing a scathing attack against Mobutu, *La grande mystification du Congo-Kinshasa: les crimes de Mobutu*.[10] Curiously, within a year of a second book in which he proclaimed that power was now within the Congolese people's reach, he returned home in 1977, where he eventually joined Mobutu's cabinet as agriculture minister.[11] Later, as the Congolese ambassador to Japan, he sold the chancery building, and did not account for how he used all the proceeds.[12]

Tshombe's younger relative Nguza turned out to be a political chameleon like Kamitatu and Bernardin Mungul-Diaka, with whom he formed the club of leading practitioners of what the Congolese would call *vagabondage politique* (or 'political vagrancy').[13] After eight years as a career diplomat, Nguza rose to the post of foreign minister in 1972 and that of prime minister in 1980, after intervals as director of the politburo and a prisoner condemned to death for treason. He earned the latter distinction in 1977, when he was accused of knowingly withholding from Mobutu information that Katangese exiles in Angola, many of whom identified as former Tshombe loyalists, were to invade the country in what became known as the Shaba I war. From 1981 to 1985, he became the most famous exiled opponent to the Mobutu regime. Like Kamitatu, he also wrote a sensationalist anti-Mobutu book, in which he identified his former boss as the personification of evil.[14] Nguza shocked the uninitiated when he returned home to rejoin Mobutu's service, first as ambassador to Washington, and then as foreign minister once again. In 1990, he left the Mobutu camp for the opposition, only to return to the fold in 1991 as prime minister, ten years after he had abandoned the post for exile in a Brussels villa that Mobutu had bought for him.

Of the groups that did rise independently of such personalities, only two are worth mentioning, for their significant contribution to the fight against Mobutu's dictatorship and, consequently, to the evolution of the political situation in the country. MARC, the first group, was actually founded in 1974 in Brussels by deserters from the Mobutu regime, Kanyonga Mobateli and Ali Kalonga, who were former leaders of the Belgian section of the JMPR, the most important section of the youth branch of the party abroad. Initially, these former Mobutu cheerleaders called their group the 4th of June Movement, in memory of the 1969 massacre, before changing its name to MARC in 1976. This attempt to reclaim student radicalism as a political foundation and the 1969 martyrdom as their banner revealed MARC leaders' desire to minimize their collaborationist past and to appeal to a student population deprived of a political platform since the banning of UGEC in 1968.

Events were to show, however, that this attempted identification of MARC with UGEC was a total mystification. As reflected in the pages of its monthly, *Miso Gaa*,[15] whose propaganda value *vis-à-vis* the Mobutu regime was invaluable, MARC's political theory and practice had nothing in common with UGEC's revolutionary programme. Personal attacks against Mobutu and members of his family, rather than deeper analyses of the structures within which they operated, and moralistic sermons rather than a materialistic diagnosis of society's ills and a revolutionary prescription for curing them, characterized a political discourse that derived more from nineteenth-century European liberalism than contemporary social theories, including the African Socialism that MARC itself espoused. With respect to resurrecting the Congo,

MARC's programme consisted in a twofold strategy: (1) establishing close ties with Western governments in order to win their confidence and support; and (2) taking power through a *putsch*.

It is partly because of their sentimentalism, and their penchant for sensationalism, that MARC leaders easily agreed to collaborate with all those holding a personal grudge against Mobutu. One such person was Daniel Monguya Mbenge, a former provincial governor until his dismissal on charges of corruption in July 1972. That a corrupt regime should dismiss one of its prominent members on such charges is certainly dubious, but Monguya's performance as a provincial administrator was hardly exemplary.[16] Author of a sensational book entitled *Histoire secrète du Zaïre*, in which no earthshaking revelations were made,[17] Monguya became MARC's president in 1977, and he was expected to exploit the close ties he developed with the expatriate business élite during his tenures as governor in Katanga and Kasai to mobilize support for the group within the Belgian business community.

Left to itself, the group would have been quickly forgotten, as were so many others. But in a party-state in which a presidential monarch seeks unanimity and where serious criticism and nasty remarks or insults against the chief and his family are crimes of *lèse majesté*, the work of MARC amounted to more than a little nuisance for the regime. As with all banned reading materials, issues of *Miso Gaa* were regularly smuggled into the country and widely read by the informed public. Whatever its real penetration or influence within the Congolese state apparatus might have been, MARC's strategy and propaganda played into the hands of Mobutu's intelligence services. The regime implicated the group's leaders in the February 1978 alleged plot to overthrow the government, and for which at least thirteen people were executed in March. MARC's leaders Monguya, Kanyonga, and Kalonji Mpinga were condemned to death *in absentia*.

Several weeks later, Kanyonga was found shot in a Brussels apartment, allegedly by a female agent of Mobutu's paramilitary forces. His death raised fears in exile circles as possibly marking the Mobutu regime's entry into the sinister world of international terrorism, with death squads on the trail of opposition leaders. Whatever the true circumstances of this episode, it served as a warning to political exiles of the danger they faced while attempting to blemish Mobutu's reputation in the West.

The second and most important of the two exile groups was the FLNC, which made history in a big way with the two Shaba wars of 1977 and 1978. It distinguished itself from all externally based groups by waging an armed struggle, and it was the only group to have seriously threatened Mobutu's hold on state power before the CNS. In fact, the FLNC was basically a military organization of Congolese refugees in Angola. Its origins go back to the end of the Katanga secession in 1963, when many of Tshombe's gendarmes went into exile in Angola. This is why the group was usually identified as 'Katanga gendarmes', although most of its original members would have been too old to engage in military adventure in 1977–78. Besides, many of them were killed in the Congo, where they had returned to help Tshombe fight the second independence movement in 1964–65. Unsure of their loyalty after Tshombe's fall from power, Mobutu neglected to pay them regularly, and used white mercenaries to crush their revolts in eastern Congo in 1966.

Those who succeeded in fleeing back to Angola were joined by new recruits from among members of the local police and young people targeted for repression during the reign of terror by Mobutu's henchman, Governor Prosper Manzikala, in 1967–68. One of those who fled Katanga for Angola at this time was a police commissioner by the name of Nathanaël Mbumba, who would later became president and military commander of the FLNC. In Angola, the refugees, and later their sons, did not remain idle. They were first recruited by the Portuguese to fight against the Angolan independence movement. After the revolution of April 1974 in Portugal, progressive military officers were more sympathetic to the MPLA than to UNITA and the FNLA.[18] Given the fact that the last two groups were backed by Mobutu, their nemesis, the Katangese went to the side of the MPLA. The latter used them in late 1974 to repel the joint invasion of Mobutu and FNLA troops from the north, at the very time that South African troops were marching on Luanda from the south. Having survived this attempted strangulation, the MPLA government was just as happy to let the 'tigers' loose to do whatever they felt needed to be done to return and live in peace in their homeland.[19] For the FLNC, this objective could not be accomplished without the overthrow of the Mobutu regime.

Unfortunately, FLNC leaders did not organize their offensive in a manner conducive to reaching this strategic objective. In each instance, their basic approach was to seize control of the strategic mining centre of Kolwezi, expand their control to the entire mineral-rich province of Katanga, and thus strangulate Kinshasa economically. The assumption was that once this was done, it would be easy for popular discontent and urban insurrections to lead to Mobutu's overthrow. In both instances, Mobutu's army was decisively routed, leaving the FLNC in control of Kolwezi and threatening to enlarge its perimeter of operations. Moreover, people all over the country were enthusiastic about the invasions and hoping that they would succeed in driving Mobutu from power.

At the same time, the FLNC, like the CNL in the 1960s, did not take sufficient account of the length to which imperialism was prepared to go in protecting Mobutu and his regime. With US support, Morocco in 1997, and France and Belgium in 1978, intervened to keep him in power. It is a mystery as to why Mbumba and his top lieutenants opted in 1978 for the same strategy that had failed in 1977. They do not seem to have given much thinking to either a frontal attack on Kinshasa, the capital, which could have been achieved with support from Luanda with Brazzaville turning a blind eye on it, or a long-term strategy of people's war, which requires prior political training and organization.

Internal political opposition: the Group of 13, UDPS and the Sacred Union From 1975 on, the deteriorating economic situation combined with the Congo's military defeat in Angola and increased repression at home to create more pressure for political change. This is the context in which the Shaba wars intervened to demonstrate the relative weakness of the Mobutu regime, its inability to maintain itself in the face of armed opposition without foreign military backing. This is the time when Mobutu's external patrons started putting pressure on him to liberalize the system. Jimmy Carter, the US president, was the first to do so, in the wake of Shaba I. He sent Ambassador Donald McHenry to Kinshasa to urge Mobutu to implement meaningful political reforms. About the same time, the IMF and other external donors asked him to leave the day-to-day management of the economy to a prime minister. Weakened by internal dissent within the regime and by open popular support for the FLNC invasions, Mobutu gave in to these pressures.

As a result, the 1977 parliamentary elections were the freest vote possible under a one-party dictatorship. For the first time, candidates did not have to be hand-picked by the MPR politburo, thus encouraging many independent-minded people to run for office. The parliament that emerged from these elections was relatively autonomous of the executive, particularly during the liberalization experiment, from 1977 to 1980. It was more assertive of its legislative authority and its oversight role than its predecessors. Until it was muzzled in February 1980, this parliament attempted to monitor the work of the executive closely, with members taking advantage of the question and answer periods (or *interpellations*) to ask cabinet ministers and other high-ranking officials embarrassing questions about government policies and finance. Members also denounced the Katekelayi massacre and demanded an independent inquiry in the matter. More importantly, it is out of this parliament that the leaders of the third period of the Congolese democracy movement would emerge in 1980.

Thirteen members of parliament sent a 52-page letter to President Mobutu in December 1980 demanding political reforms. By this time, Mobutu had already managed to clip the parliament's wings, thanks to diminished concern with the human rights situation in the Congo by Washington, then distracted by its Cold War priorities in the Horn of Africa and in Afghanistan, as well as by the Iranian hostage crisis. For their audacity, members of the Group of 13, as the dissident parliamentarians became known, were jailed, tortured and banished to remote detention centres. In spite of this repression, most of them continued to fight for democracy.

Their determination in this regard was best exemplified by Etienne Tshisekedi wa Mulumba, the man who eventually emerged as the leader of the democracy movement. He was so stubborn in his opposition to the Mobutu regime, and so provocative in his defiance, that some thought that he had lost his sanity. For someone who was so close to Mobutu during the 1960s, and whom he served as interior and justice minister before becoming ambassador to Morocco and vice-president of the National Assembly, his break with Mobutu was total and irretrievable. Hard feelings between the two did play a part, however small, in the repeated failed attempts at cohabitation during the transition period.

In spite of repeated jailing and the defection of some of its original members, the Group of 13 persisted in its opposition to the Mobutu regime. During a brief release from detention in 1982, the remaining members of the group defied the party-state and its ban on opposition parties by founding a party of their own, the Union pour la démocratie et le progrès social (UDPS).[20] Although illegal, the new party became instantly popular with the masses. In 1988, UDPS leader Tshisekedi chose 17 January, the anniversary of Lumumba's assassination, to launch a pro-democracy demonstration in Kinshasa with a rally at the Kasa-Vubu Bridge. Thousands of ordinary people answered the call to join the march, as it was steeped in two important symbols of the democracy movement in the Congo. Thus, long before Mobutu was compelled by internal and external pressure to accept multipartyism in April 1990, the UDPS had become associated in people's minds with the struggle for multiparty democracy.

By January 1990, Mobutu had been so overwhelmed by internal and external pressures for change that he decided to launch an exercise called 'popular consultations' on the country's future. Individuals and groups were asked to send memoranda to a special commissioner stating what was wrong with the system and what should be done about it.

Over six thousand memoranda were recorded. Unfortunately, the public was never told what they said. What is clear from those that were leaked to the press and from the public forums that Mobutu himself attended briefly as part of the consultation exercise before he was forced to abandon the idea for fear of further embarrassment is that the popular verdict was against him. The problem, he was frequently told at public forums by people who no longer feared him, 'is you, Citizen President'. The solution was his departure and the establishment of a multiparty democratic system.

Were Mobutu a patriot who loved his country and a dignified ruler who respected himself, he would have resigned. The problem is that we are dealing here not with a normal type of political regime, but with a kleptocracy based on state-sponsored banditry and bent on promoting its narrow group interests to the detriment of the general welfare. The pathological character of the regime was evident whenever Mobutu sent tanks to encircle the central bank, the customs head-quarters and the general tax office to ensure that they remain his private cash boxes. In the face of an overwhelming popular desire for radical change, Mobutu and his entourage decided to pretend that they were in favour of democratic reforms, while doing everything possible to obstruct the democratization process.

On 24 April 1990, Mobutu announced to the nation that he was abandoning the single-party system. Within a few months, most of his well-known collaborators, including former prime ministers, ministers and other high-ranking officials, felt compelled to abandon him to reposition themselves for political office in the new order. By identifying themselves with the people's desire for radical change, they also hoped to be spared of popular justice and/or eventual legal pursuits for crimes committed during the Mobutu era. They, too, founded their own political parties and sought to become full partners in the democratic opposition. For the most part, these parties were simple cliques of ambitious individuals, with no popular base. The only exception to this was Nguza's Union des fédéralistes et des républicains indépendants (Uferi), whose chauvinism and ethnic cleansing appeals found a favourable echo among all those Katangese who were eager for a takeover of all jobs held and properties owned by Kasaians in their province. Of the other parties created by the 'dinosaurs', as former members of Mobutu's *nomenklatura* were now known, only the PDSC of Ileo and Boboliko was seen as being genuinely a legitimate member of the democratic opposition, along with the UDPS and Gizenga's Parti lumumbiste unifié (PALU).

At Nguza's initiative, the PDSC, UDPS and Uferi joined hands in July

1991 to create an opposition united front known as Union sacrée (Sacred Union), which became the major rallying point for the democracy movement. Under its leadership, the democratic opposition rejected the regime's plans to set up a constitutional conference, and won a major victory by successfully pressuring Mobutu to allow for the holding of a sovereign national conference. PALU did not join the alliance, rejecting its leaders as Lumumba's enemies and hoping to spearhead a more radical counterweight to the moderate and conservative ideologies represented in the Sacred Union: social democracy (UDPS), Christian democracy (PDSC) and liberalism (Uferi). This counterweight did not emerge, for two major reasons. The first is the fact that PALU remained clothed in its original PSA garb as a regional party, and failed to transform itself into a truly national party. The second reason has to do with the breakdown of the MNC/L into a dozen of factions and cliques, some of which were led by opportunists who finally ended up in the Mobutu camp.

Two other parties of former Mobutu dignitaries joined the Sacred Union as full-fledged members of the democratic opposition. Like Uferi, they were simply wolves in sheep's clothing. The first of these was the Union des démocrates indépendants (UDI), whose top leaders were Kengo and Alexis Thambwe Mwamba. This club of technocrats beholden to foreign interests included some of the richest people in the Congo. In their wisdom, Kinshasa's free press and *radio trottoir* – street radio or rumour-mill – saw no democrats among them. To popular delight, they read the acronym UDI as really representing either the *union des dinosaures impunis* or the *union des détourneurs incorrigibles*, both of which were apt descriptions of this group.[21]

The other party was the Front commun des nationalistes (FCN), founded by Gérard Kamanda wa Kamanda and Mandungu Bula Nyati. These so-called nationalists had made a long career as defenders of Mobutu's anti-patriotic policies at home and abroad. As events were to show, they each represented separate but complementary wings of Mobutu's political family, Kamanda with the more sophisticated and technocratic wing headed by Kengo, and Mandungu with the hardcore loyalists led by Mobutu's inner circle. When the formal establishment of bipolarization in Congolese politics took place in 1993, the two wings of the FCN were clearly evident, with Kamanda joining Kengo and the leaders of the real opposition in the Union sacrée de l'opposition radicale (Usor), while Mandungu joined Nguza as leaders of the pro-Mobutu Forces Politiques du Conclave (FPC).[22]

The seeds of bipolarization were already sown during the 1980s in the struggle by the UDPS for legal recognition and against the monopolization of the political space by the MPR. As a matter of fact, the UDPS was the only party that Mobutu himself could name when asked by the press on 24 April 1990 which two parties he had in mind besides his own MPR for the three-party system he had proposed. As expected, the political class rejected the three-party system in favour of unlimited or open multipartyism. As so many parties were being created, the regime found it useful to dilute the strength of the real opposition by setting up its own opposition parties. Financed by the regime, these artificial creations consisted of a few individuals who were mostly interested in money, hence the derogatory label they were given as *partis alimentaires*, meaning that they were created for purposes of earning a living. Legally registered, they had no real existence as political parties.

By July 1991, the number of parties, real and fictitious, increased tremendously, as preparations were under way for the sovereign national conference. Each registered party had the right to send four delegates to the conference. The exceptionally large number of parties, with 204 of them represented at the CNS,[23] did create the need for some sort of regrouping or coalitions based on ideological, programmatic, or other affinity. Eventually, as shown above, two major blocks did emerge: the Mobutu camp, initially known as the *mouvance présidentielle*, or presidential tendency; and the democratic opposition under the Sacred Union.

The opposition alliance had barely been established when Mobutu made the first of his many politically savvy moves to destabilize it. During the same month of July 1991, everyone was surprised to hear an announcement on national radio and television that Mobutu had appointed Tshisekedi prime minister. Secret negotiations had apparently been going on between the two men through trusted aides. Needless to say, all of this was in flagrant contradiction with Tshisekedi's long-held view, and the Sacred Union's official position, that Mobutu's departure from office was a precondition for genuine change and democratization. This was also the only position that the politicized masses of Kinshasa and presumably other major cities were prepared to accept. Immediately after the announcement, demonstrators descended on Tshisekedi's residence in Limete to force him to back down. For the masses, their 'saviour' should not cohabit with the 'devil'.

Although bowing to popular pressure, Tshisekedi made it clear that he was prepared to accept the post, as it would have given him the opportunity to organize and manage the sovereign national conference that the whole country wanted held. While attempting to protect his democratic credentials, he damaged his reputation, perhaps irreparably, among those powerful external forces which are distrustful of leaders who are accountable to their own national constituencies. Forgetting their own definition of democracy as 'a government of the people, by the people, and for the people', some Africa specialists at the US Department of State insisted that 'a leader must lead'. For them, Tshisekedi was weak and useless.

The incident also created strained relations between Tshisekedi and his senior partners in the Sacred Union, who accused him of having failed to consult with them. While this was a legitimate complaint, all of these gentlemen were jealous of him, and any of them would have jumped at the opportunity to head the government had the offer been made to him. As it turned out, this is exactly what Nguza did four months later. More importantly for Congolese political culture, the incident revealed the élitist and undemocratic strain of bourgeois politics worldwide, as politicians prefer to solve leadership and other important issues through deal-making, rather than through open democratic processes. Thus, each time that the democratic process seemed to be going forward, something would happen to bring the politicians back to deal-making behind closed doors, away from the watchful eyes of the people. It is with this unresolved tension between the people's aspiration for democracy and the politicians' concern for their narrow class interests that Congolese political and social forces went to the CNS in August 1991.

The Sovereign National Conference

The long-awaited conference opened on 7 August, 1991, only to be disrupted in September as a result of looting and violence by poorly paid soldiers. The conference itself was so mired in procedural disputes that the new crisis seemed to offer the politicians an opportunity they needed to go back to the negotiating table. This they did at Mobutu's Marble Palace in Binza, Kinshasa. Under foreign pressure, it was agreed that cohabitation by Mobutu and Tshisekedi was essential to peace, economic recovery and progress in the democratization process. Disappointed, but hopeful that their Moses would after all find a way to eventually get rid of Mobutu, those who had demonstrated in July reluctantly accepted the fact that Tshisekedi was going to serve as Mobutu's prime minister. It did not take long for things to fall apart. No longer able to have access to ready cash at the central bank, Mobutu dismissed Tshisekedi and his government shortly after they took office in October, ordering his army to lock them out of their ministries.

Tshisekedi was replaced by Mungul-Diaka, who proved totally incapable of managing the political crisis. A month later, in November

1991, Mobutu sprang yet another surprise on the opposition by naming Nguza, then chair of the Sacred Union, prime minister. Acting on Mobutu's orders, Nguza arbitrarily closed the conference on 19 January 1992. As in the past, ordinary people stepped in to change the situation. Responding to a call by Catholic priests and other religious groups, thousands of people left church on Sunday 16 February 1992, candles and Bibles in hand, to join a massive demonstration all over Kinshasa in a Christian march for reopening the national conference. Similar marches also took place in other cities. In Kinshasa, the paramilitary forces opened fire, killing over thirty people. To the martyrs of independence who fell on Sunday 4 January 1959 were now added the 'martyrs of democracy'. Their sacrifice would compel the dictator to give in to internal and external pressures by reopening the conference.

The Conférence nationale souveraine (CNS) met uninterrupted between 6 April and 6 December 1992. A total of 2,842 delegates, representing all classes and strata of Congolese society, qualified to sit as the 'people in conference'. Their task was to interrogate their country's history in order to determine how and why things had not worked out as expected at independence, and to find a way to get out of the multidimensional crisis – political, economic, social, cultural and moral – facing the country. This was to lead to the establishment of the political institutions needed to manage the transition to multiparty democracy. The discussion that follows attempts to present a succinct description of the nature and functioning of the CNS, the major problems and obstacles confronting it, and its historical legacy for the Congo.

The nature and functioning of the national conference National conferences became popular in Africa in 1990, following the example set earlier that year in Benin. In only ten days of serious deliberations on the political crisis in their country, between 19 and 28 February, delegates at Benin's Sovereign National Conference succeeded in stripping the then dictator Matthieu Kérékou of his executive powers, making him a ceremonial head of state, and appointing Nicéphore Soglo, a World Bank official, as the interim prime minister and the executive head of government.

That Kérékou accepted the conference's resolutions as expressing the will of the people and chose to comply, and that the whole affair passed without violence, did have a great appeal all over the continent, particularly in francophone Africa. The impact was greater here because of the commonality in political experience and the wide publicity given to the event by the media such as Radio France Internationale and *Jeune Afrique*. National conferences were also held in other francophone

African countries with variable results, including Niger, Mali, Gabon, Congo-Brazzaville and, later on, Chad. In anglophone countries, the only thing to come close to a national conference was CODESA, the Conference for a Democratic South Africa. In Nigeria, the democracy movement is still demanding the holding of a sovereign national conference, in spite of the return to civilian rule in 1999.

From the experience of the various countries that have held one, a national conference can be defined as a democratic forum of all the relevant social forces of a nation designed to take stock of what has gone wrong in the past and to chart a new course for the future. In examining the wrongs of the past, including political and economic crimes, the forum is akin to a truth and reconciliation commission, with all the investigative powers necessary for shedding light on the past and preparing the groundwork for both reconciliation and justice. In this regard, it is supposed to serve as a national catharsis in the African tradition of conflict resolution through the *palaver*, as well as a modern rule of law mechanism of compensatory justice for the victims of state-sponsored crimes.

With respect to the present and the future, the national conference is a constituent assembly, whose tasks include defining a new vision for the country, designing the institutional and legal framework of the democratic transition, drafting the constitution for a new and democratic form of state, and formulating policy guidelines for the new regime. The sovereign character of the conference resides in its nature as the embodiment of the popular will – as the 'people in conference' – and its exceptional status as the supreme organ of state authority in a crisis situation. Consequently, its decisions are meant to be authoritative or binding on everyone. Finally, the national conference is designed to serve as a school of democracy for the country as a whole, through live television and radio coverage.

The Congo's CNS holds the record with respect to number of participants and duration. Because of the interruptions mentioned above, it effectively met for a little over eight months. When it resumed its work on 6 April 1992, it proceeded in a very methodical way to organize itself for tackling the important tasks facing it. A whole month was devoted to determining who would sit as a delegate, with credentials challenges against controversial figures sometimes taking up an entire day. The following month and a half, May to mid-June, turned out to be a lot more pleasant. The CNS and, through the national radio and television network the nation as a whole, listened to over one hundred general policy statements by political parties, civil society organizations, representatives of state institutions and distinguished citizens. These speeches were meant to provide the CNS with the raw materials needed for its central task of taking stock of the past in order to chart a new course for the future.

An agenda commission was charged with sorting out the major themes from the speeches in order to propose a comprehensive agenda to the CNS. The result was the constitution of 23 commissions and over one hundred sub-commissions, to study, investigate and debate the record of the past in order to make recommendations for the country's future. Every conceivable subject or aspect of our national life was dealt with by at least one sub-commission. Subjects ranged from assassinations and ill-gotten property to economic policy, political structures and minority rights, including those of Pygmies and immigrants. Once completed, the report of each commission – itself a synthesis of the reports by its different sub-commissions – was distributed to each of the 2,842 delegates for examination, publicly read by the commission's rapporteur-general, and debated in plenary session. Once a report was debated, amended and approved by the plenary, matters arising from it could be presented in the form of resolutions for state policy that were also handled in the same manner as the report until their approval by the CNS.

On the basis of commission reports and conference resolutions, the CNS had to adopt two important documents, a constitution for the Third Republic, and a provisional constitution for the period of transition to democracy. It also had to establish the political institutions of the democratic transition, including a provisional parliament, a transitional government of national unity, and an independent electoral commission. Very successful in taking stock of the past, with some commissions producing truly outstanding reports in their assigned areas, the CNS was not so successful in terms of setting the democratic transition into motion.

Major problems and obstacles A major problem for the CNS was that Mobutu and his entourage had not accepted it in good faith. Having been forced by internal and external pressure to let the CNS take place, they set out to destabilize it and made it clear throughout its duration that they were not prepared to accept an outcome that would go against their monopoly of power, particularly with respect to vital resources such as money and the security forces. For reasons of which he alone knows the secret, the CNS president for his part made it clear by his acts that he was prepared to go to any length to be accommodating to Mobutu. For Laurent Monsengwo Pasinya, the Roman Catholic Archbishop of Kisangani, any compromise was necessary if it were the only way of getting the dictator to implicate himself in the democratization process. This is why he went so far as to betray the trust that CNS delegates and the nation as a whole had placed in him by managing a democratic forum in an authoritarian manner. Three unilateral actions by the prelate are worth mentioning in this regard.

First, Monsignor Monsengwo blocked the audition of the reports of the assassination and ill-gotten property commissions by the CNS, for the purposes of sparing President Mobutu any further embarrassment. Second, he interrupted the public reading of the political affairs commission report for the same reason. Third and more importantly, he suspended the conference's audition of commission reports in late July 1992 for purposes of conducting extra-CNS negotiations on the constitutional and institutional framework of the transition with Mobutu's representatives. That such negotiations were a violation of the CNS rules of procedure and an evident way of calling into question the sovereignty of the conference did not seem to disturb the prelate and those who supported him on this course, including the UDPS leadership. The Sacred Union did participate in these negotiations over a power-sharing formula originally proposed by Herman Cohen, then US assistant secretary of state for African affairs. Cohen himself went to Kinshasa at the end of the month to give a final push for this formula and to broker an agreement to this effect between the three key political players of the moment: Mobutu, Monsengwo and Tshisekedi.

The agreement, known as *le compromis politique global* (comprehensive political compromise), provided for a two-year transition under a government elected by the CNS and responsible to a provisional parliament also elected by the CNS, and a ceremonial presidency that would be filled by the incumbent head of state, Mobutu. The compromise was presented to the CNS as a *fait accompli* on 3 August 1992, but it was broadly incorporated in the transitional charter or provisional constitution adopted the next day. In the compromise and the charter, crucial issues of transitional politics were left extremely vague, with loopholes that the wily dictator could and would later exploit to his advantage. These included the fate of Mobutu's old parliament, which the compromise sent into recess; the status of his party-state constitution, which was still in effect except for multipartyism; and the concrete mechanisms of collaboration between the president and the prime minister in foreign affairs and national security matters. The leadership of the democratic opposition was so preoccupied with gaining a parcel of power by winning the post of prime minister that they paid little or no attention to these crucial issues.

As a delegate to the CNS, I took the floor on 3 August to denounce the compromise and call for its rejection. My argument was that the compromise was undemocratic, since it had not been subjected to public debate and full scrutiny and approval by conference participants; that it gave Mobutu a legitimacy he did not deserve, given his political and economic crimes; and that a dictator cannot be expected to become a democrat overnight. Monsengwo did not bother to ask for a formal vote on my motion. Like many conference members and those who supported his initiative in the opposition press, he believed that such a compromise would avert a bloody confrontation with the dictator. Many who shared this view considered my position extremist.[24]

That Mobutu and his entourage were not prepared to accept giving up even a limited parcel of power became clear on 4 August, the very day the compromise was transformed into the provisional constitution. The president's representatives were quick to register their disapproval of several provisions of the charter, including changing the country's name from 'Zaire' back to 'Congo' and the transformation of the political system from a presidential to a parliamentary regime. Subsequently, Mobutu and his entourage decided to subvert, if not obstruct, the democratic transition. But before adopting their final line of action, they attempted to bar Tshisekedi from the post of prime minister, either by disrupting the electoral process or by finding a candidate likely to defeat him.

The firebombing of UDPS headquarters and home of its co-president Frédéric Kibassa-Maliba in Limete on the night of 12–13 August was a ploy to disrupt the election of prime minister at the CNS, then planned for 14 August. The Mobutuists had hoped that UDPS militants would react violently to this crime, giving Mobutu the excuse he needed to declare a state of emergency, suspend the conference and regain control over the political situation. Fortunately, here is a case in which a cellular phone may have prevented a violent crisis in the Congo in 1992. Living some two blocks away from Kibassa's home, I used my phone to reach Washington, where the Voice of America became the first broadcasting system to learn of the event. It was also the first to announce it to their Congolese audience in the early morning hours of 13 August. Idrissa Fall of the VOA had also interviewed Kibassa, who called on his party's followers to remain calm and not respond to the regime's provocation.

Having failed to achieve their immediate aim through terror, Mobutu and his entourage sought to defeat Tshisekedi, the 'people's candidate' for prime minister, with an attractive candidate of their own, Thomas Kanza, and by pouring money for the buying of votes into the People's Palace, the CNS venue.[25] But from 5 p.m. on Friday 14 to 5 a.m. on

Saturday 15 August, the Congolese people witnessed the freest and most transparent election ever held in the country's history. Nearly 71 per cent of the delegates voted for Tshisekedi, as against 27 per cent for Kanza. Few in Kinshasa slept that night. At dawn, hungry and exhausted honourable members of the CNS were met by enthusiastic crowds of citizens, who thanked them for having respected the popular will in choosing Tshisekedi. Like Kinshasa, the whole country erupted into a joyful victory dance from dawn to sunset on 15 August 1992.

Less than four months later, the people's victory turned out to be hollow. After his friend and ally Savimbi defied international public opinion and went back to war after losing a free and fair election in September 1992, Mobutu did not see why he should live with a situation he disliked. He carried out the third coup of his political career on 1 December 1992. He also ordered Monsengwo to bring the CNS to an end, and this was done on 6 December. In March 1993, he named a rival government, which took effective control of the state away from Tshisekedi; went back to his old constitution; and convened his old parliament. In all this, he was encouraged by the fact that his former patrons in Washington, Paris and Brussels talked tough but did nothing. They called upon the Congolese political class to go back to the negotiating table, as though a sovereign national conference had never taken place.

Rather than defending the institutional framework adopted by the CNS over which he had presided, Monsignor Monsengwo showed his true colours by adopting the Western call for more negotiations. As his subsequent actions were to show, particularly that episode in May 1997 when he rushed back home from Rome with the hope of being appointed interim president, the prelate was primarily interested in promoting his own career. In addition to being a brilliant intellectual and one of the few Catholic bishops then assigned to serve outside their own province of origin, he was a past president of the Episcopal Conference of the Congo.

Monsignor Monsengwo was very effective as the presiding officer in plenary sessions. But if the conference is judged to have lasted too long, this was not the fault of CNS delegates, as many commentators have abusively condemned them of prolonging it for *per diem* purposes.[26] Members had no control over the work calendar, which was badly managed by Monsengwo and his conference bureau. A lot of time was wasted in detailed discussions of matters of law, which should have been left for the future parliament. The CNS role was to adopt the directive principles of state policy, and not specific and detailed laws. At the same time, important issues such as the election of the High

Council of the Republic (HCR), the provisional parliament, were done in a hurry, while others, such as the setting up of provincial authorities and the electoral commission, were altogether relegated to later action by the HCR.[27]

Monsengwo was chosen to preside over the CNS with the assumption that, being a religious leader, he would play a neutral role and reconcile the warring political camps. Such a role had been played with great success by the bishops who presided over the national conferences in Benin and Congo-Brazzaville. Although he did attempt to play this role, he was constrained by his own political agenda and his contempt for democracy. A politician under the cassock, Monsengwo was no ordinary priest. Anonymous tracts at the CNS recounted his rise in the Catholic hierarchy through means fair and foul, as well as his political ambitions, including his alleged feud with the late Cardinal Malula.

More importantly, Monsengwo saw his role as taming the passions of what he saw as the ignorant CNS majority, to spare the country from further disrepute in the eyes of the international community.[28] For him, important decisions on a country's future had to be made by the political class rather than a representative people's assembly such as the CNS. In going along with this élitist thinking, the Congolese political class, including the so-called radical opposition represented by the Sacred Union, showed its utter contempt for democratic procedures and for democracy itself. Deal-making among politicians made more sense to them than decisions reached through a democratic process such as the national conference.

The historical legacy of the CNS For the Congolese people, who had invested so much hope in it, the CNS failed to achieve the goal for which they gave it their full support, namely, getting rid of Mobutu as Congo's ruler. The CNS also failed to achieve its own short-term objective of setting up a viable political framework for the transition to democracy. This failure was due to internal and external factors, particularly the multiple obstacles and blockages to the democratization process that I have described elsewhere for Africa as a whole.[29] These include the political immaturity of the democratic opposition, the growing impoverishment of the salaried middle classes, the monopoly of the public media by the incumbent regime, and state-sponsored violence against the democracy movement. In the Congo, the many mistakes made by the opposition, the duplicitous role of Monsignor Monsengwo, and the many incidents of violence instigated by the regime in the major cities and in Katanga and North Kivu helped to derail the democratic transition. The lack of strong support from the international community also strengthened the hand of the dictator in his resistance and violence against democracy.

On the other hand, the CNS did accomplish a lot. More than any other national conference in Africa, the CNS did a rather thorough job in examining the country's past and in adopting a new vision or societal project for the future. Most of its 23 commissions produced solid and well-documented reports on the country's history, resources, institutions, social problems and economic performance. These are extremely useful documents that will enrich the Congo's national archives. Moreover, the fact that conference proceedings were broadcast live on national radio and television turned the CNS into a great educational experience for the country as a whole. It also gave ordinary people the ability to influence the proceedings through letters, public forums and, unfortunately, occasional acts of popular justice.[30] The people became better informed about their country's realities, and this had the effect of strengthening Congolese civil society.

Discussing politics on the sidewalks near newspaper stands became so popular that it gave rise to a novel political phenomenon in Kinshasa, a political organization of young people calling themselves *parlementaires-debout*, which is best translated as 'street parliamentarians'.[31] Organized in each municipality in Kinshasa and with a central organ for the city as whole, these forums debated current issues, took decisions and sought ways of implementing them. Major actions involved publicly denouncing opposition politicians who were seen as faltering in their resolve for democratic change, and organizing rallies and demonstrations in support of the various demands of the democracy movement. Although supportive of Tshisekedi and providing him with whatever protection they could for his safety, the 'street parliamentarians' were independent of him and the UDPS.

In sum, the CNS marks a major watershed in Congolese history. It has become such a major historical landmark and a defining moment in the political life of the nation that there can be no serious discussion of the future political and institutional framework of the country without reference to it. Moreover, the CNS strengthened the bonds of citizenship and the commitment to national unity among the Congolese. While there is strong commitment to a large decentralization of political authority in this vast land, including a passionate belief in federalism within the political class, nearly everyone wants to keep the country within its colonially inherited boundaries. Finally, the CNS reaffirmed the ideals that the democracy movement had championed in earlier periods, and introduced some new ones. Among these is the revolutionary idea, legally enshrined in the provisional constitution and the draft constitution for the future, that Congolese citizens have the *obligation* to rise up against any group of people who seize state power illegally.

With this new civic duty, the culture of resistance against illegitimate state authority, which the second independence movement helped keep alive, has been given legal sanction as a moral imperative. In defence of fundamental human rights, including the rights to self-determination and to choose one's own rulers, the Congolese are called upon to become, as Cabral said of national liberation fighters, *anonymous soldiers for the United Nations*,[32] fighting and dying to promote the ideals for which the UN was established.

Politics and the Institutions of the Democratic Transition

The political situation following the end of the CNS was characterized by both a formal bipolarization of Congolese political life between the FPC and Usor, and the breakup of the opposition into antagonistic factions. Of the two tendencies, it was the latter that had a major impact on political life, since it gave added strength to the forces of the status quo. There were prominent individuals claiming to be part of the opposition, and even holding leadership positions in Usor, who were in actual fact collaborating with the FPC against the real opposition led by Tshisekedi. For most of these opportunists, politics and, above all, the quest for higher state positions, was basically a game of jockeying for advantageous placement on the winning side depending on the respective strengths of each of the main protagonists, Mobutu and Tshisekedi. Thus, when Mobutu seemed so vulnerable during the halcyon days of the CNS, Tshisekedi became the main pole of attraction for office seekers. But once Mobutu used his considerable resources to regain the upper hand, *vagabondage politique* reared its ugly head again.

As a consequence, the post-CNS period was rife with conflicts and endless negotiations to resolve them in a situation of acute political instability. The power struggle between Mobutu and Tshisekedi revolved around the former's *imperium* and the latter's legitimacy. The party-state president could use his effective power to deny the democratically elected prime minister control over important state organs such as the central bank, but was unable to have his edict obeyed by the population. For example, as already noted, when the central bank issued a 5 million zaire note on 2 December 1992, the prime minister declared it null and void, and people obeyed him by refusing to accept the invalidated note as legal tender. The outbreak of violence and looting by elements of the military between 28 and the 30 January 1993 in Kinshasa was triggered by vendors' refusal to accept this note from soldiers.

In the end, it was Mobutu who emerged victorious. There were three main reasons for this outcome. The first and most important reason was Mobutu's exploitation of the loopholes in the transitional charter to resist change. The second reason, already mentioned above, was the lack of adequate support for the democratic transition in the international community, which strengthened Mobutu's hand. The third reason was Tshisekedi's own failure to seize the moment to advance the radical change agenda. He, too, must share the blame for the failure of the democratic transition in the Congo. For those who might react to this affirmation as a case of blaming the victim, it must be admitted that the prime minister did not take full advantage of the exceptional circumstances that history and the CNS had thrust upon him to neutralize the forces of the status quo.

Tshisekedi and the aborted transition, 1992–93 A great deal of optimism was generated following Tshisekedi's election as prime minister and his acceptance speech at the CNS. There were two important messages in his speech. The first, which was addressed to the people, promised that his transitional government would mark a radical break with the past, *changement* (or change) being its guiding principle.[33] The second message was addressed to his political adversaries, to whom he extended pardon for any wrong or pain they had inflicted on him. During the three months in which his government was formally unchallenged as the executive power of the state, from 30 August to 30 November 1992, he was unable to start fulfilling his promise to the people. His adversaries, the forces of the status quo, responded to his olive branch with utter contempt, and exploited his patience to obstruct his administration.

During these three months, Tshisekedi and his cabinet functioned more like a caretaker government than a regime entrusted with the mission of preparing the groundwork for a new vision of society. They did not live up to a major guiding principle of the CNS, that the transition itself be a prefiguration of Congo's future, and they failed to exploit the political momentum created by Tshisekedi's election to effect radical change. His entourage conducted state business in the usual Congolese way, with much of the time devoted to dealing with an endless stream of visitors seeking government jobs, contracts or redress, and doing the paperwork to authorize disbursement from the central bank. Heinous crimes such as ethnic cleansing in Katanga went on unpunished, with the prime minister taking no action to suspend the governor involved, or even to denounce his criminal behaviour publicly.[34] The only attempt made at personnel change in the vast state apparatus was the appointment of a new governor for the central bank, a move that Mobutu blocked by sending élite troops to encircle the bank with tanks.

What this episode and the entire 'go slow' approach of the transitional government indicate is that Tshisekedi had no clear-cut political strategy for a successful transition. For such a strategy must include as a central component the rapid control of the levers of state power such as the security forces, law enforcement agencies, diplomacy, revenue-generating state enterprises and the regional administration. The new government was expected to make a clean sweep in all of these areas. To do so successfully, it needed ministers with a strategic vision and a good knowledge of their respective departments, and a comprehensive plan for retiring all top military commanders and replacing them with younger and more competent officers. The Tshisekedi government did not meet the first requirement, and the prime minister and his entourage did not give serious thought on how to deal with the security forces.

The cabinet named on 30 August 1992 was unusual in the sense that it did not have the qualifications for implementing radical change. A number of portfolios were given to people with absolutely no knowledge of the field. A former leader of an NGO specializing in agricultural cooperatives was named foreign minister, and the important ministries of defence, justice and the interior went to individuals with no background in these areas. The most unusual appointment was that of a total unknown, politically or otherwise, as a super-minister in charge of three critical portfolios: budget, finance and state enterprises. If this had been a government in an established parliamentary democracy, in which the permanent bureaucracy serves any cabinet with loyalty, there would have been no problem. In a country emerging from 27 years of a corrupt dictatorship, it was nothing but a disaster.

Since Mobutu's power relied heavily on the security forces, it was amazing that little thought went into the matter of how to manage the transition with military chiefs who were against it. The political rift between the latter on the one hand, and younger officers and the rank and file, on the other, was an open secret. In the policy statement that he read on the behalf of the armed forces to the CNS in May 1992, General Mahele, then chief of staff, declared that as a people's army and not an army belonging to an individual, they were prepared to abide by all the decisions of the CNS. A day after Mahele's speech, General Eluki Monga, then ambassador to Israel, came dressed in a military uniform and delivered another speech 'on behalf of the armed forces' in which he warned that the real power relations outside the People's Palace were quite different than those at the CNS. When asked which of the two generals spoke for the armed forces, Ngbanda, then defence minister, said that it was Mahele. What is evident is that Mahele's speech, which was written by young officers on his staff, reflected the majority view, while Eluki spoke on behalf of the hardliners, including the defence minister.

The hardliners eventually prevailed, as they forced all military delegates to walk out of the CNS four months later, thus stating openly that they were not prepared to accept its decisions. They were prepared to work with Mobutu's civilian advisers to obstruct change in every way possible, and they did so throughout Tshisekedi's tenure.

The prime minister apparently had one more chance to get rid of them, but it seems to have quickly passed away. When violence erupted again in January 1993 in Kinshasa, French and Belgian paratroopers flew to Brazzaville to rescue their nationals and other foreigners. With approximately seven hundred paratroopers across the river, the Belgian government was in the position to disarm Mobutu's paramilitary forces and help the legitimate government consolidate its power. There are unconfirmed reports that the Belgians were prepared to do so if Tshisekedi had requested such assistance.[35] It is possible that since such a request did not materialize quickly and in time to make a difference, the Belgians got cold feet, especially in view of opposition by Mobutu, France and the United States.[36] France's position was all the more astonishing, in view of the cold-blooded murder of the French ambassador by Mobutu's soldiers on the very first day of the incidents, 28 January 1993.[37]

In addition to exploiting Tshisekedi's lack of control over the state apparatus, Mobutu and the status quo forces used the loopholes of the Comprehensive Political Compromise referred to earlier to frustrate and obstruct his actions. These loopholes or ambiguities, which were known in the Congo as *zones d'ombre* (grey areas), played a significant role in the confusion and chaos that marred Congolese politics between August 1992 and July 1994.

The first grey area had to do with the constitution. Contrary to expectations, the CNS did not take a clear-cut decision abrogating the constitution under which the country was governed during the Mobutu regime or the Second Republic. Rather than stipulating clearly that the old constitution was no longer valid, the Transitional Charter states simply that 'all constitutional provisions contrary to the present act are abrogated'. When legal and political experts told opposition leaders that this language could be interpreted as meaning that there were provisions of the old constitution that could still be applicable, they were dismissed as intellectuals who paid too much attention to legal texts rather than to the more important political dynamics.

As it turned out, Mobutu and his entourage took advantage of this ambiguity to insist that the old constitution was still applicable. In his ordinance of 19 August 1992 naming Tshisekedi prime minister, he referred not only to the latter's election by the CNS and the political compromise, but also to the old constitution. He did not make reference to the Transitional Charter. The fact that Tshisekedi accepted to start his mandate under this cloud, even if on his part he felt that it was a way of reconciling himself with Mobutu, meant that he easily fell into the trap prepared for him by Mobutu's strategists. The logic here was that if he could be named prime minister by presidential ordinance, surely he could also be dismissed by the same. And yet this was in contradiction with the Transitional Charter, according to which the prime minister was elected by the national conference and could be dismissed from office only by the HCR, the transitional parliament.

The second grey area concerned the institutional framework of legislative power during the transition. Once again, and contrary to the recommendation of its political affairs commission, the CNS did not take a decision to abolish Mobutu's parliament or national assembly, even though its mandate was due to expire in December 1992. Whereas the Transitional Charter created the HCR, the political compromise declared the old assembly to be in recess; it was to disappear only after a referendum was held on the constitution of the Third Republic.[38] But – and experts warned the opposition leaders only to be dismissed again – a parliament in recess is one that can be recalled any time. And that is exactly what President Mobutu did in March 1993. There were now two parliaments.

With two constitutions and two legislatures, it was inevitable that for it to be complete, the dual authority structure would include two governments as well. Part of the problem originated in the political compromise, according to which the president and the prime minister were to share power in the areas of foreign affairs and internal security. The text remained silent as to how this was to work out in practice. At the same time, the Transitional Charter was drafted on the parliamentary model and it gave the prime minister full governmental powers, including the control of all organs of state sovereignty such as the ministries of foreign affairs, defence and the interior, the intelligence and immigration services, the central bank, customs and other revenue generating parastatals. This was the third grey area.

Unable to impose his will on Tshisekedi, the president decided to ignore him, with his domestically legitimate and internationally recognized government. He named a government of his own, with former UDPS national organization secretary Faustin Birindwa as prime minister. His nomination came as a result of a conclave by the MPR and its political allies between 9 and 19 March 1993 at the National Palace in Kinshasa. Although it did have effective control of the reins of power, the Birindwa government remained unpopular internally and was never formally recognized internationally. Coming in the wake of the January incidents in Kinshasa and amidst inter-ethnic violence in Katanga and North Kivu, it was incapable of ending the crisis of legitimacy and stopping the breakdown of the social and institutional orders.

Mediation efforts to resolve the political crisis came from both internal and external sources. Internally, initiatives to end the power struggle between Mobutu and Tshisekedi were taken by, among others, resident African diplomats under the Togolese dean of the diplomatic corps, leaders of the major religious communities (Roman Catholic, Protestant, Kimbanguist, Orthodox and Islamic), and the bureau of the HCR under Monsignor Monsengwo. The major external mediators were the OAU secretary-general, Salim Ahmed Salim, and the Algerian diplomat Lakhtar Brahimi, who served as the special envoy of the UN secretary-general, Boutros Boutros-Ghali. These efforts were eventually successful in bringing the rival camps to the negotiating table in September 1993. Nine months of intermittent and confusing negotiations ended in 1994 with the victory of the Mobutu camp, now composed of both reactionaries and the moderates who deserted Tshisekedi.

Kengo and the restoration of the Mobutu regime, 1994–97 A single institutional framework was finally adopted following negotiations initially held in September 1993 at the People's Palace in Kinshasa. The first step at ending the dual authority structure was the establishment on 23 January 1994 of a single legislature composed of members of the HCR and of Mobutu's national assembly, plus those participants in the above negotiations who were not members of either house. The new legislature of over seven hundred members was called Haut conseil de la République-Parlement de transition (HCR-PT). In the second place, a single fundamental law, the Constitutional Act of the Transition, was promulgated on 9 April 1994.

As one would have expected, the most difficult task in completing the framework was the selection of the prime minister. Mobutu's political recovery was such that since Tshisekedi was not acceptable to him, most of the prominent members of the political class were ready to dump him. Despite the popular mandate he had won at the CNS, Tshisekedi had become a liability to opportunists in the opposition whose major goal was to gain or return to a ministerial post. A new break occurred in Usor between the 'radicals' who remained loyal to Tshisekedi, and the 'moderates' who wanted someone else. The latter coalesced with the Mobutu camp to pick Léon Lobitch Kengo wa Dondo as prime minister. The prime minister of the last party-state government on 24 April 1990 was sworn into office as the prime minister of the transition to democracy on 6 July 1994. *Plus ça change, plus c'est la même chose!*

Born in the Belgian Congo of a Polish-Belgian father and a Tutsi mother from Ruanda-Urundi, Kengo was raised among the Ngbandi, Mobutu's ethnic group, and was considered a member of the 'white Ngbandi clan' in Mobutu's entourage.[39] According to people who worked or played tennis with Kengo, he was very close to Mobutu and spoke to his mentor several times a day, in the Ngbandi language. Kengo's third mandate as prime minister was in many ways the restoration of the Mobutu regime. Three of the four deputy prime ministers were Mobutu's men, and they controlled the key ministries of defence, the interior and mines.[40] Other past and current members of the MPR *nomenklatura* were at justice, budget, parastatals and other important ministries. That such a government could be considered as led by the opposition to bring about democratic change demonstrates just how successful Mobutu's followers and sympathizers were at mystifying political reality in the Congo.

Kengo was Mobutu's most trusted and longest-serving prime minister, with two previous tenures from 1982 to 1986 and 1988 to 1990. By way of comparison, the average term of office for the other five prime ministers who served in 1978–82 and 1986–88 was less than one year. A Mobutu protégé, Kengo also enjoyed strong support from France, the United States and the Bretton Woods institutions as a supposedly competent technocrat who did a good job in economic governance. This assessment flies in the face of reality, as it was during Kengo's long tenure in the 1980s that the most systematic and greatest pillage of the country's wealth by the prime minister and his associates took place.[41] All this escaped the attention of institutions and people who were mostly interested in debt recovery, and who were easily misled by Kengo's tricks and lies.[42] The composition and the actions of the government he headed as a coalition of FPC loyalists and the more sophisticated technocrats associated with him, Kamanda and former prime minister N'Singa Udjuu left no doubt that Kengo and President Mobutu remained close political allies.

The failure of the democratic transition Three institutions were established to manage the transition to a multiparty system of democratic government in the Congo: a provisional parliament, a transitional government, and an independent electoral commission. All three failed to make substantial progress towards a democratic transition by the time war erupted in the Great Lakes region in October 1996. In contrast to the crucial role they played in supporting the CNS and influencing its deliberations, the mass democratic movement remained passive with regard to the transitional institutions. A possible explanation of this is that the transitional process did revert to business as usual, with politicians making self-serving decisions in negotiations held behind closed doors. In fact, the attempted transition to liberal democracy undermined the participatory features of the Congolese democracy movement.

The provisional parliament was originally set up in December 1992 as a legislative body of 435 councillors elected by the CNS to carry on the mission of political reforms and to oversee the work of both the government and the electoral commission until the establishment of the Third Republic. Due to the objections of the Mobutu camp, which found itself in the minority, the HCR was eventually restructured as the HCR-PT in January 1994, with a shift of parliamentary majority to the FPC side. The Constitutional Act of the Transition, the modified provisional constitution adopted to legalize this change, provided clear procedural rules for legislative activity. One of these rules stipulated that all matters of national importance had to be decided only by consensus. This rule was seldom observed, as the FPC violated it frequently by imposing its majority through voting. Decisions of utmost importance, such as the election of Kengo as prime minister, were taken in this manner.

The public had a very low opinion of the HCR-PT. Its meetings usually started three or four hours behind schedule, and decisions were taken even when the required quorum was not attained. The law provided for two annual sessions: a general legislative session from the first Monday in April to the first Monday in July; and a budgetary session from the first Monday in October to the first Monday in January. These sessions were held regularly, but important matters were generally put off until the end of the session. The distinction between general and budgetary sessions was never observed, as any issue was taken up whenever the parliament got to it. For example, on Sunday 31 December 1995, the HCR-PT did wonders by debating and adopting the 1996 government budget within four to five hours before moving on to approving the final composition of the electoral commission, the Commission nationale des élections (CNE). Members of the commission present were sworn in between 4 and 5 a.m. on New Year's Day 1966, the final day of the session. Begun around 1 p.m. on Sunday, the parliament's most productive day of the entire session ended at 5 a.m. on Monday, as legislators and CNE members happily sang the national anthem.

Very little was achieved at the next two sessions, the legislative session from April to July, and a special session from July to October. The latter was called to deal with the adoption of legislative texts essential for the organization and holding of national elections in 1997. As war erupted in the east, the HCR-PT could only sit and take notice of its irrelevance and impotence.

Even more than the legislature, the executive arm of the transitional framework went through several incarnations. It started out in conformity with the law as a government formed by a prime minister elected by the CNS. With the advent of a parallel and *de facto* government led by Birindwa, the transition process virtually came to a halt. And it is only after Kengo took over in July 1994, with a mandate to hold elections by July 1995, that the process was presumably put back on track. However, the Kengo government failed to meet this deadline, and obtained a two-year extension from the HCR-PT, whose members were equally happy to prolong their own tenure in office. The lack of urgency that both the legislature and the executive displayed with regard to elections was evident in the fact that this extension took place some six months before the electoral commission was established.

The overall political climate, and the shortcomings of both the HCR-PT and the government made the goal of holding free, democratic and transparent elections by the end of June 1997 a very elusive one indeed. The electoral commission, or CNE, was composed of 44 members, 22 from each of the two political camps, and four for each of the eleven provinces. Given this political mode of selection, the CNE could not succeed in the absence of a political consensus within the political class on respect for the legal texts governing the transition, the rules of the game and the autonomy of the commission. For internal dynamics were often influenced by the country's political realities. For example, the CNE could not conduct its business for six weeks because of an impasse over the selection of its president. Claiming that the FPC had promised to let Usor choose the president, the opposition insisted on having the presidency. Since Mobutu did not like the opposition candidate, he instructed his camp to take the presidency.[43]

Having adopted bylaws according to which the six-member bureau of the commission was to make decisions collegially, CNE members decided to emancipate themselves of their political tutelage by the 'political families' in order to honour their oath of office as election commissioners. On 17 March, Professor Bayona ba Meya, a former Supreme Court justice and minister of justice, was elected president. As the leader of the democratic opposition group in the CNE, the author was elected to the number-two position as deputy president. This decision brought the CNE opposition members on a collision course with Tshisekedi, the head of the opposition camp, who finally and publicly withdrew his support from the CNE at a rally in Kinshasa on 21July. In addition to lacking the backing of the then recognized leader of the democracy movement, the commission was unable to discharge its obligations effectively because of sabotage from the Kengo government.

This sabotage took two major forms. The first was the government's usurpation of the powers of the commission. Between January and July 1996, the government appeared determined to control the electoral process, by marginalizing the CNE. An interministerial commission on elections headed by Kamanda, deputy prime minister and interior minister, had withdrawn money from the CNE allocation in the state budget and engaged in electoral preparation activities that were clearly part of the CNE mandate. Moreover, the government drafted an electoral bill and a decree on the electoral census without having consulted the CNE. These actions brought the government into direct conflict with the CNE.[44] It also increased suspicions in some quarters that being dominated by FPC loyalists and by technocrats with no political base, the Kengo government was not really committed to holding free and fair elections.

The second form of sabotage had to do with the parsimonious manner in which the government released funds for CNE activities. Between January and August 1996, the CNE received only 52 billion zaires out of its 1996 budget allocation of 1,207 billion zaires, or only 4.35 per cent of the total.[45] This, from a government that had made it known internationally that it was allocating $51 million to the electoral effort in 1996. While it is true that the government had serious problems with revenue collection, it could not explain where all the petroleum and minerals revenue went to, nor justify that frequent and costly trips abroad by the prime minister were more important than its constitutional mandate of leading the country to national elections. In spite of its weaknesses in other respects, the HCR-PT supported the CNE in its demands that the government stop interfering with its work and release the funds the parliament had voted for the commission. Unfortunately, the legislature was powerless *vis-à-vis* the government, as many honourable members had taken the habit of receiving from it envelopes filled with green banknotes (i.e., US dollars).

Thus, by mid-August 1996, eleven months away from the long expected birth of the Third Republic, it was evident that the electoral
commission and the other two institutions responsible for managing
the transition would fail to fulfill their respective mandates. Tshisekedi's
repudiation of the CNE, the sabotage of its work by Kengo and Kamanda, and the lack of principled commitment to its mission by many
commission members, made it pointless for me to remain in the CNE.
After careful reflection, I decided to resign from it as a way to protest
against the undermining of the democratization process by the political
class, on 3 September 1996.[46]

One by one, each of the major components of the institutional
framework of the transition – the legislature, the executive and the
electoral commission – failed to help effect the democratic transition in
the Congo. The original framework adopted at the CNS was called into
question by the Mobutu camp, which used its control of the security
forces and other organs of state power to block the democratization
process. Once the framework was restructured in a manner acceptable
to Mobutu and the forces of the status quo, it was incapable of implementing democratic change. By the time Laurent-Désiré Kabila's Alliance
des forces démocratiques pour la libération du Congo (AFDL) started
its march to Kinshasa in October 1996, the democracy movement had
lost confidence in the capacity of the transitional framework to perform
successfully the tasks for which it was created, but was too weak to do
anything about it. The transition to a democratic political order had
been derailed by Mobutu and his allies. A new effort was needed to put
it back on the rails.

Notes

1. Respectively, Action Movement for the Resurrection of the Congo and
Congolese Liberation Front.

2. Nguza, *Mobutu ou l'incarnation du mal zaïrois*. Nguza served Mobutu as
prime minister in 1980–81 and again in 1991–92.

3. In what became known as the 'Pentecostal Hanging', Mobutu had one
of his colonels lure to his house former prime minister-designate Kimba and
the three other former ministers, initiate a discussion about the possibility of a
military coup, and then later denounce them as coup instigators. After a mock-
ery of a trial by a military tribunal, they were hanged in Kinshasa before a
crowd of over 50,000 spectators.

4. The Inga–Shaba Line is an ambitious project involving the transportation
of electric current from the Inga Dam on the Congo River in the southwest to
the mining industry in Katanga, over a distance of approximately 2,000 km. It
is the longest such transmission line in the world. According to an investigation

by the US business daily the *Wall Street Journal*, the president of the construction firm, Morrison Knudsen of Idaho, was a personal friend of Sheldon Vance, the US ambassador who sold Mobutu on the deal. Several expert testimonies, including one by Congolese geologist Wa Nsanga Mukendi before a US Senate subcommittee in May 1979, showed that this line was not necessary, inasmuch as there are other important energy sources in the Katanga province. Moreover, the line was not being equipped to provide power to all the territory between Inga and Kolwezi, the result being that it was operational at only 10 per cent of its capacity. The Brussels-based Centre d'Etudes et de Documentation Africaines (CEDAF) has done excellent studies on the Congo's 'white elephants'. The most outstanding is Willame's *Zaïre, l'épopée d'Inga*.

5. Ilunga-Kabongo, 'Crise à Lovanium', p. 74.

6. American Council on Education, *Survey of Higher Education in the Congo*.

7. Of the AGEL leaders, the best known is Hubert Makanda Kabobi. After resisting for some time, he, too, succumbed to the virus of co-optation in 1969, becoming secretary-general of the JMPR in 1970 and a member of the politburo in 1972. He died in 1973, reportedly of poisoning.

8. I owe this information to Professor Crawford Young, who visited Kinshasa shortly after the June 1969 incidents, as a member of the USAID study group mentioned above. Yamvu Makasu a M'teba and Jacques Katuala, who were Lovanium students at the time, have corroborated this version of events.

9. Personal information from Yamvu.

10. Kamitatu Massamba, *La grande mystification du Congo-Kinshasa*.

11. Kamitatu Massamba, *Zaïre: le pouvoir à la portée du peuple*.

12. Several subcommittees of the CNS had to deal with this issue in 1992. Kamitatu was also asked to explain the misappropriation of state property during his tenure as minister of agriculture and rural development.

13. In 1980, Mungul-Diaka became head of an oppositon front in Brussels, after tenures as Mobutu's ambassador and minister of education. He later went back to the fold, and served Mobutu as prime minister in October and November 1991, and much longer as governor of Kinshasa.

14. See note 2 above.

15. *Miso Gaa*, in Lingala, can be translated as 'Open your eyes' or 'Be vigilant'.

16. The balance sheet of his tenure as governor of Western Kasai at Kananga in 1970–71, where the author conducted his field research for the doctoral dissertation between 1971 and 1973, was generally negative, according to interviews with provincial and city officials.

17. Monguya Mbenge, *Histoire secrète du Zaïre*.

18. The full names of the three Angolan nationalist movements are, respectively, Movimento popular de libertacão de Angola (Popular Movement for the Liberation of Angola), União nacional para a independência total de Angola (National Union for the Total Independence of Angola) and Frente nacional de libertação de Angola (National Front for the Liberation of Angola).

19. The Angola-based Congolese military refugees called themselves *les Tigres* (tigers).

20. Union for Democracy and Social Progress.

21. Either 'union of unpunished dinosaurs' or 'union of incorrigible embezzlers'.

22. Political Forces of the Conclave, so-called because these parties of the presidential tendency (*mouvance présidentielle*) constituted themselves into a formal political alliance at a conclave held in March 1993 to ratify Mobutu's illegal removal of Tshisekedi as prime minister and his replacement by Faustin Birindwa, a renegade member of the UDPS directorate.

23. According to Kabungulu Ngoy-Kangoy, *La transition démocratique au Zaïre*, 381 parties were registered at the ministry of internal affairs by 27 November 1993.

24. To its credit, the newspaper *Le Potentiel* published the full text of my motion in its edition of 4 August 1992, although it took issue with my position. Although the motion was endorsed beforehand by several MNC/L factions, including the MNC/L of the Diaspora to which I belonged, none of the MNC/L comrades spoke in its favour at the CNS. Support in this regard came from three or four speakers, including a student leader and Dr Kabamba Mbwebwe of the Front patriotique.

25. Some honourable colleagues told me that they took the money but still voted for Tshisekedi, since the vote was by secret ballot. They saw no impropriety in their act, they said, since they were simply taking back the people's money stolen by Mobutu!

26. This charge of prolonging sessions for the sake of accumulating the *per diem* has also been made against the High Council of the Republic, the provisional parliament, in Filip Reyntjens's *La guerre des grands lacs*, p. 12. There is no doubt that the *per diem* received by the conference and council members appeared scandalous in a context of growing poverty in which even civil servants and law enforcement officers were not regularly paid. But what could conference delegates and legislators coming from the interior and abroad living in Kinshasa hotels do if they had no means of subsistence?

27. The electoral commission was finally established three years later, on 1 January 1996, but nothing was done concerning the setting up of new provincial authorities for the transitional period.

28. He strongly emphasized this point to me when I went to see him to protest the way he attacked my general policy statement or formal speech to the CNS on 14 May 1992. Despite the prelate's displeasure, nearly all Kinshasa newspapers printed the full text of the speech, with some of them devoting to it editorial comment and guest columns.

29. See my 'The state and democracy in Africa'.

30. A few CNS delegates were molested, and some had their houses looted, by young people in Kinshasa for statements and/or behaviour deemed uncharacteristic of a democratic opposition. These acts of intimidation and violence

were few and could not justify the irresponsible charges made before the Subcommittee on Africa of the US House of Representatives on 26 October 1993 by Herman Cohen that Tshisekedi used an armed militia to keep opposition politicians in line.

31. See the excellent study of this phenomenon by Kalele-ka-Bila, 'La démocratie à la base: l'expérience des parlementaires-debout au Zaïre', in Nzongola-Ntalaja and Lee, *The State and Democracy in Africa*, pp. 64–73. See also Mulambu-Mvuluya, 'Les masses populaires et les préalables d'une transition démocratique au Zaïre (1990–1992)', in ibid, pp. 53–63, for a more comprehensive analysis of the role of the masses in the democratic transition during this period.

32. Amilcar Cabral, 'Anonymous soldiers for the United Nations', in Cabral, *Revolution in Guinea*, pp. 50–2.

33. The word *changement* came up several times in the course of the speech, to wild applause by the CNS and millions who were following the historic event on radio and television.

34. When, in my presence in early November 1992, the US ambassador Melissa Wells asked Maître Jean-Joseph Mukendi, Tshisekedi's political adviser, why no action was being taken by the government on the situation in Katanga, he replied that being from the same ethnic group as the victims, the prime minister did not want to get involved for fear of being accused of tribalism. The ambassador found the explanation ludicrous, as I did.

35. Personal communication from Colette Braeckman, the renowned correspondent of the Brussels daily *Le Soir*, on 1 March 2000 in Addis Ababa. However, in an e-mail message dated 22 August 2000, Gauthier de Villers, director of the African Institute at Tervuren, Belgium, maintains that the Belgians were not ready to intervene militarily in support of Tshisekedi and the democratic opposition in January 1993. Erik Kennes, another African Institute researcher, writes in an e-mail message dated 23 August 2000 as follows: 'You don't send 700 commandos just to evacuate a few Belgians. I know that Colonel De Smet, who led the operation, wanted to intervene. Delcroix (the defence minister) wanted to cross over, but Dehaene and Claes were against. Another piece of information we received later: people close to Mobutu (Nguz?) warned Herman De Croo (Liberal, pro-Mobutu, currently president of parliament) that the DSP would immediately attack Belgians, thus they became afraid.' My own translation from French. Dehaene and Claes were respectively prime minister and foreign minister.

36. Nancy Ross, executive director of Rainbow Lobby, was among the foreigners then evacuated from Kinshasa. One of the American agents who escorted her from the Intercontinental Hotel told her that the Belgians wanted to intervene but the French and the Americans opposed such a move. Personal communication, February 1993.

37. Officially, the ambassador was killed by a stray bullet, while standing in front of the window on the fifth floor of the French Embassy building. Another

stray bullet, according to this account, killed a Congolese telephone operator on the second floor. According to *Radio trottoir*, the French ambassador was part of a plot to liquidate Tshisekedi, whom he had called to come seek refuge at the French Embassy. The American ambassador, Melissa Wells, had got wind of the plot and sent an ambulance to get Tshisekedi from the prime minister's office to the safety of the US Embassy. When the execution squad arrived at the French Embassy and found that Tshisekedi was not there, they killed the ambassador and the telephone operator. No independent inquiry has been made concerning this bizarre affair. Will Tshisekedi and Wells ever tell what really happened?

38. When asked to explain this strange provision, those who negotiated the political compromise maintained that this was a simple face-saving formula that allowed for members of the old national assembly to be kept on the payroll. But why not pay them until the expiration of their mandate in December 1992? Or simply give them a retirement package? As some of us suspected, the main reason was elsewhere.

39. There were two Ngbandi clans around Mobutu, a black clan, with Ngbanda, Professor Vunduawe Te Pemako and the generals, identified in Chapter 5; and a 'white clan' or that of mulattos, which included Kengo and Seti Yale.

40. Respectively, Admiral Mavua, Kamanda, and Mutombo Bakafwa Nsenda.

41. See Willame, *L'Automne d'un despotisme*. Wa Bilenga Tshishimbi lost his job as finance minister after two months in 1995 following a report he prepared for Mobutu on how Kengo and his associates stole the country's money.

42. As deputy president of the National Electoral Commission in 1996, I was able to see and appreciate at close range these tricks and lies, particularly in manipulating statistics and distorting facts.

43. Personal communication from Parastatals Minister Mboso in June 1996, who informed me that Mobutu was adamantly opposed to my becoming president of the commission.

44. For details on this conflict, see, among other press reports, 'Elections: c'est très mal parti. Bagarre au sommet entre Kamanda et Nzongola', *Le Phare*, 9 July 1996; 'La Cne dénonce l'ingérence du "gouvernement" Kengo dans le processus électoral', *La Tempête des tropiques*, 9–10 July 1996; 'La Cne dénonce la tricherie du gouvernement', *Le Compatriote*, 16 July 1996; 'La Cne dénonce les immixtions de Kengo dans ses attributions', *Le Journal Tshiondo*, 16–22 July 1996.

45. As one US dollar was exchanged for 15,000 zaires at the beginning of the year and for over 55,000 zaires by the end of August 1996, this amounted to less than $2 million.

46. For the next several days, the Kinshasa press had a field day with all kinds of commentary on my resignation. Several newspapers, including *La Référence plus* (4 September) and *Le Soft* (5 September) published the full text of the prepared text of my press conference. So many lies were told about my departure in the pro-Mobutu press that, regrettably, some of them ended up in

reputable places such as Filip Reyntjens's excellent book *La guerre des grands lacs*, p. 12, where it is insinuated that I left the CNE because I was not chosen president. If that were the case, I should have left shortly after 17 March and not bothered to request an extension of my leave of absence from Howard University in May 1996 for purposes of serving on the commission.

. . . .

CHAPTER 7

Conflict in the Great Lakes Region

§ MOBUTU's propaganda machine and his external backers had created the image of a strongman without whom the Congo could not be held together. On 16 May 1997, Mobutu's generals dispelled the myth when they informed the field marshal that they could no longer guarantee his own security in the country. Mobutu left Kinshasa, where he had returned from prostate cancer surgery in Europe for negotiations with the Rwandan- and Ugandan-backed rebel leader Laurent Kabila, for the relative security of Gbadolite. On the next day, he suffered the double indignity of refusal by the crew of his presidential jet to fly him out of the country, as they insisted, rightly, that the plane was state property, and his attempted lynching by some of his own soldiers, who blamed him for the assassination the night before of General Mahele in Kinshasa.[1] The soldiers fired on the military transportation plane carrying Mobutu and his family into exile, as it was taking off from the Gbadolite airport. The strongman had become a weak and lonely man. The helmsman had lost his grip on the helm of the ship of state; he could no longer steer it out of trouble or find the anchor to keep it secure.

The major determinant of the present conflict and instability in the Great Lakes region is the decay of the state and its instruments of rule in the Congo. For it is this decay that made it possible for Lilliputian states the size of Congo's smallest province, such as Uganda, or even that of a district, such as Rwanda, to take it upon themselves to impose rulers in Kinshasa and to invade, occupy and loot the territory of their giant neighbour. Such a situation would have been unthinkable if the Congolese state institutions were functioning in a normal way as agencies of governance and national security, rather than as Mafia-type organizations serving the selfish interests of Mobutu and his entourage, particularly his generals. The Congo under a capable and responsible government could have stopped the genocide of 1994 in Rwanda, the second major determinant of instability in the region, or at least prevent the genocidal forces from using Congolese territory to launch raids into Rwanda. The disintegration of the Mobutu regime and the state decay associated with it made both possibilities academic, while Kabila's sponsorship by Rwanda and Uganda made it possible for these countries to feel entitled to determine the Congo's destiny. The power vacuum created by state decay reinforced their determination to fish in troubled waters and to maximize their resource extraction from the Congo.

This is the background to the violent conflict in the Great Lakes region at the turn of the century. The region entered the twenty-first century still embroiled in a major war unleashed in 1998 and involving all of the countries comprising it, except Tanzania, plus Angola, Zimbabwe, Namibia and, for a while, Chad. Burundi, Rwanda, Uganda and the Congo were also at war internally against rebel groups, and the first three had invaded the Congo under the pretext of protecting themselves against rebel incursions, while they were actively involved in looting the Congo's natural resources.

This chapter provides an analysis of this regional war with reference to both its historical context and its connection to the long-standing interest of external forces in plundering the Congo's riches. After an examination of these two factors, the chapter concludes with a brief look at the political situation in the country from the standpoint of resistance to tyranny with respect to both the struggle for national liberation and the fight for democracy.

The Historical Context

The most salient variables of the historical background to the war in the Great Lakes region are the Rwandan genocide of 1994 and Mobutu's fall from power in 1997. No region of the African continent has known as much political strife, loss of life and social dislocation during the last 42 years as the Great Lakes region. This is a region whose name is derived from the system of lakes and tributaries draining the central section of the Great Rift Valley of Africa. The great lakes in the system, some of which were named after European monarchs by the first white travellers to see them, are Victoria, Albert, Edward, Kivu, Tanganyika, Mweru and Malawi. Lake Victoria is the second largest lake in the world and the largest in Africa, while Tanganyika is the second largest in Africa and the fifth largest in the world.

Geographically, the region can be said to comprise nine countries: Congo-Kinshasa, Uganda, Kenya, Rwanda, Burundi, Tanzania, Zambia, Malawi and Mozambique. However, the label 'Great Lakes region' is conventionally restricted to the core of the region, whose members are Congo, Uganda, Rwanda, Burundi and Tanzania. With Lakes Victoria and Albert being the sources of the White Nile – while Ethiopia's Lake Tana is the source of the Blue Nile – the countries of the core have a major stake in the larger political economy and geopolitics of the Nile River Basin, whose partners include Egypt, Sudan, Ethiopia and Eritrea. Together, the five countries of the region constitute an area of 3,582,746 square kilometres, representing 12 per cent of the African landmass. In the year 2000, their total population was estimated at 124 million, or 15.5 per cent of the total population of Africa, about 800 million. Most of the inhabitants speak Bantu languages, and Kiswahili, the national language of Tanzania, is also a lingua franca throughout the region.

The high level of cultural integration and informal economic transactions has been superseded by political and social cleavages, which have caused a lot of turmoil since 1959. The defining moment in the history of the region during the last decade of the twentieth century was the 1994 genocide in Rwanda. This cataclysmic event was a logical outcome of an ideology and a politics of exclusion that had generated earlier episodes of large-scale massacres and the flight of Rwandans of Tutsi origin into exile. But the roots of the genocide ideology lie deep in the history of ethnic identity construction and mobilization under colonial rule.

The construction of ethnic identity in Rwanda and Burundi Both Rwanda and Burundi are two major precolonial kingdoms to have survived European conquest and occupation as more or less viable political entities in Africa. From 1898 until Germany's defeat in the First World War, the two territories formed part of German East Africa, which also included the mainland portion of present-day Tanzania. Having occupied Rwanda and Burundi in 1916, Belgium formally took over their administration as a mandatory power under the League of Nations mandates system in 1921, and remained as the administrative authority under the United Nations trusteeship system from 1945 to 1962. Although Belgium had to submit annual reports on its administration of the trust territory to the United Nations and deal with periodic inspections from the UN Trusteeship Council, the territory was already administratively annexed to the Belgian Congo in 1925. Thus, from then on until Congolese independence in 1960, Belgium governed the three territorial units as a single colonial entity known as Le Congo Belge et le Ruanda-Urundi, with a single army, the Force publique, and a single governor-general in Kinshasa.

As already shown in Chapter 1, Belgian colonialism was characterized by a close working alliance between the state, the Catholic Church and large business enterprises, particularly the mining companies. Born out of the brutal legacy of primitive accumulation by the Leopoldian state and concessionary companies, the colonial trinity sought to impose its hegemony through paternalism, white supremacy and administratively enforced ethnic divisions among Africans. The Hutu–Tutsi conflict is in large part a result of the grafting of the colonial ideology of racism and paternalism on the precolonial social system of both Rwanda and Burundi.

Unlike the typical ethnic map in Africa, this system was quite unique in that three social groups, identifiable in part by differences in physical characteristics and interrelated through clientship ties, shared the same homeland, language and culture. Although the distinctions in status and occupation tended to go hand in hand with differences in physical characteristics, the social cleavages thus created were never rigid, since they were not based on differences of race, caste or religion. As the whole social order revolved around the institutions of kingdom and the patron–client relations associated with them, proximity and/or service to the royal court and its representatives in the provinces were an overriding factor in an individual's rank, whether the latter was Hutu, Tutsi or Twa.

The Twa are a pygmoid people, who also have important settlements west of the Great Lakes in the equatorial forest of Central Africa, including the nearby Ituri Forest in the Congo. Hunter-gatherers and undoubtedly the first occupants of the territory before its settlement by the Bantu, they were renowned for their martial skills and musical talents. This explains the important roles they played as soldiers in the king's regiments and as entertainers at the royal court. Thus, in spite of the low status and social discrimination that were the lot of the Twa as a group, male individuals could gain titles of nobility and wives of royal blood.[2] In the traditional system, these ennobled Twa became 'Tutsi'. Today, the Twa are said to represent about one per cent of the population in each country, as against 14 per cent for the Tutsi and 85 per cent for the Hutu.[3]

The Hutu occupied an intermediate position on the social pyramid as agriculturalists and clients of Tutsi chiefs and nobles. They were also recruited into the army and in other areas of public service. Owing perhaps to the fact that they had settled in both countries before their Tutsi compatriots, numerous were those among them who held the position of land chief, one of the many subordinate chiefly roles in the traditional system. Like the Twa, ennobled Hutu men took daughters of Tutsi aristocrats for wives. Intermarriage between Hutu and Tutsi as part of patron–client ties and, more generally, social climbing for the Hutu have progressively led to the decreasing importance of physical characteristics as a reliable guide for distinguishing between Hutu and Tutsi today.

The 1994 genocide and its aftermath have revived interest in the debate concerning Tutsi origins. Impressed by the social, political and military organization of ancient Rwanda and Burundi, nineteenth-century European adventurers and missionaries invented 'theories' that resulted in the construction of a cultural mythology about the Tutsi. Among the origins attributed to them by their Western admirers were the following: (1) descendants of ancient Egyptians; (2) black Caucasians of 'Hamitic' or 'Semitic' origin; (3) survivors from the lost continent of Atlantis; (4) immigrants from Melanesia, Tibet, India or Asia Minor; and (5) according to one highly imaginative Catholic priest, people who came straight out of the Garden of Eden.[4] Of all these labels, it was the Hamitic myth that stood out, partly because of its importance in colonial anthropology, and partly because of its systematization and popularization by a Rwandan Catholic priest, Alexis Kagame.[5]

Generally, the Tutsi were cattle-owners, many of them associated with the royal court and the territorial expansion of its power throughout the land. Obviously, all the Tutsi were not of noble rank – there were poor and ordinary Tutsi as well – and all cattle-owners were not Tutsi. In her study of Kinyaga, a peripheral region in southwestern Rwanda, Catharine Newbury points out that cattle-owners who would have been considered Tutsi in central Rwanda had arrived in Kinyaga during the eighteenth century. For the people of Kinyaga, however, being 'Tutsi' was 'associated with central government power and institutions, and particularly with the exactions of chiefs backed by central government'.[6] With the intensification of oppression under colonialism, 'ethnic categories came to be even more rigidly defined, while the disadvantages of being Hutu and the advantages of being Tutsi increased significantly. Passing from one ethnic category to the other was not impossible, but over time it became exceedingly difficult and, consequently, very rare.'[7]

According to René Lemarchand, 'ethnic identities are not pure invention' and the social categories *Hutu* and *Tutsi* 'are not figments of the colonial imagination'.[8] This is to say that although these identities have been invested with a normative load they did not have before colonialism, the potential for ethnic mobilization and conflict was inherent in the historically grounded relations of inequality in the precolonial social order. What the colonial system did was to take advantage of these relations by making them more rigid, and then to help intensify the antagonism between the privileged Tutsi and the disadvantaged Hutu. The Belgian colonialists effectively ended the internal dynamic of social equilibrium by which individuals could pass from one social category to the other, including the mechanism of ennoblement, through administrative acts and practices such as the issuance of identity cards with ethnic labels and preferential treatment for the Tutsi with respect to education, white-collar jobs and chiefly positions in local colonial administration.

Having served as faithful auxiliaries of the colonial order for more than thirty years, the Tutsi élite became expendable when its members began to advocate self-determination and independence in the 1950s.[9] The missionaries, colonial anthropologists and other Belgian ideologues who had created the myth of Tutsi superiority suddenly found it expedient to portray the Tutsi as an aristocracy of alien origins that should relinquish power to the oppressed Hutu indigenous majority. Although there is no evidence of systematic violence between Tutsi and Hutu during the precolonial period, this ideological reconstruction of their history sought to depict them as antagonistic groups with centuries-old enmities. Unfortunately, just as the old myth of Tutsi superiority had fallen on receptive ears among the Tutsi élite, the new myth of Hutu as slaves in need of emancipation was warmly embraced by the rising Hutu counter-élite in its quest for the social advantages to which Hutu intellectuals felt entitled.

The process of ethnic identity construction and mobilization thus gave rise to a dichotomous vision of society that did not exist in precolonial Rwanda and Burundi. If the Tutsi, like the Twa, have non-Bantu origins, the same cannot be said of the political and cultural institutions within which relations between all three groups were articulated. For the monarchy that governed them, the cultural matrix in which they lived and the language they spoke were all of Bantu creation and indigenous to the Great Lakes region. It is for this reason that contemporary scholarship maintains that whatever their past origins might be, the Tutsi are a Bantu people by virtue of the fact that they share a common Bantu culture with the Hutu, with whom they speak a common Bantu language, Kinyarwanda or Kirundi, depending on the country.

However, this commonality of language and culture has failed to stem the rise of an ethnic consciousness nurtured in the competition for power and privilege between Hutu and Tutsi élites, and to put an end to a catastrophic process of ethnic mobilization involving *final solution* scenarios of genocide in both Rwanda and Burundi. It is that history of ethnic identity politics as a source of conflict that constitutes one of the root causes of the crisis in the Great Lakes region.

Ethnic conflict and genocide in Rwanda The rise of Hutu ethnic consciousness as a political force in Rwanda resulted from the emergence of a Hutu counter-élite in the midst of a divorce between the colonialists and their erstwhile Tutsi allies in the 1950s. The Catholic Church played a key role in this process, as the new sympathies of the white clergy for the Hutu made the Church shift its support from the Tutsi élite to the Hutu, whom it sought to help build a new middle class.[10] In the context of the then ongoing struggle for decolonization and independence, economic and social advancement for Africans ultimately implied the conquest of political power.

The flexing of Hutu political muscles began in earnest in 1957. On 24 March, in anticipation of an inspection visit by the UN Trusteeship Council, nine Hutu intellectuals published a 'Hutu manifesto' in which they denounced a political, economic and social monopoly by the Tutsi and rejected the idea of abolishing ethnic labels on identity papers. 'Their suppression', they argued, 'runs the risk of *preventing the statistical law to account for the reality of the facts.'*[11] This is the intellectual origin of the idea of identifying democracy and majority rule with Hutu rule. Ethnically based political mobilization for attaining this goal was launched in June and November through the creation of two Hutu political parties: the Mouvement social muhutu (MSM), led by a Catholic intellectual, Grégoire Kayibanda; and the Association pour la promotion sociale de la masse (APROSOMA), established by a businessman, Joseph Gitera.[12]

Of the two men, it was Kayibanda who succeeded in mobilizing the masses for fulfilling the dream of a Hutu republic. Between 1952 and 1956, he served as secretary of the Amitiés Belgo-Congolaises, the discussion circles of Europeans and the *évolués,* and as editor of a Catholic monthly, *L'Ami.* In 1956, he became editor of an influential Catholic weekly, *Kinyamateka,* and also served as private secretary to Monsignor André Perraudin, the Swiss vicar apostolic of Rwanda. With strong support from the Catholic Church and Belgian colonial authorities, Kayibanda became a major opponent of Tutsi royalists, who organized themselves in 1959 under the banner of a political party, the Union nationale rwandaise (UNAR). Also in 1959, Kayibanda renamed the MSM as Mouvement démocratique rwandais/Parti du mouvement de l'émancipation hutu (MDR-Parmehutu).[13]

Within the context of the politics of decolonization, the crystallization of ethnic tensions intensified unrelentingly. The explosion came in November 1959, with the Hutu uprising generally known as the 'Rwandan Revolution'. This was a peculiar revolution, in that it took place under colonialism, with the tacit consent and support of Belgian officials, and left the basic colonial power structure standing intact. It is reported that 'Belgian authorities were very partial in favor of the Hutu, letting them burn Tutsi houses without intervening'.[14] Furthermore, the colonial authorities rewarded Hutu violence by installing mostly Hutu administrators in the communes to replace the Tutsi chiefs and administrators who had either been killed or fled away.

To the people of Rwanda, the events of November 1959 were truly revolutionary in the sense that they ultimately resulted in the overthrow of the monarchy and the transfer of political power from one ethnic group to another. In Kinyarwanda, what happened is referred to as the *muyaga*, a word normally used to describe a strong but variable wind, with unpredictable and destructive gusts. Although independence came nearly three years later, on 1 July 1962, the basic framework of the Hutu republic was already being established in 1959. Another major consequence of the *muyaga* was the large number of refugees and internally displaced persons it generated. At the time of independence, the number of refugees in the neighbouring countries and abroad was estimated at about 120,000.

The number of refugees continued to grow, due to both natural increase and new outflows resulting from episodic outbursts of inter-ethnic violence and the politics of exclusion by both Kayibanda and his successor, Juvénal Habyarimana. A career army officer who had quit medical school at Lovanium University in Kinshasa to enrol in the newly created Rwandan army in 1960, Habyarimana overthrew President Kayibanda in 1973 and subsequently established a military and one party-dictatorship. In over twenty years of personal rule, he steadfastly refused to allow Tutsi refugees to return home. In August 1988, a world congress of the Tutsi diaspora was held in Washington, DC, with delegates adopting very strong resolutions on the 'right of return'. Meanwhile, the Tutsi diaspora in Uganda had gained positions of responsibility and influence in Yoweri Museveni's National Resistance Army (NRA), after having helped the latter come to power in Kampala in January 1986.

Of these Rwando-Ugandans of Tutsi origin in Museveni's entourage, the most prominent were Fred Rwigyema and Paul Kagame. Recruited in Museveni's guerrilla organization as a teenage secondary school boy in the mid-1970s, Rwigyema rose in ranks to become second only to Museveni in the NRA and the Ugandan military establishment, as deputy commander-in-chief and deputy minister of defence. Mahmood Mamdani describes his position and that of other future leaders of the Rwandese Patriotic Front (RPF) as follows:

When the NRA entered Kampala in 1986, Rwigyema was its Deputy Commander. In 1987, he was appointed Deputy Minister of Defense in

Kampala. Paul Kagame became the Acting Chief of Military Intelligence of the NRA. Peter Baingana was head of NRA medical services. Chris Bunyenyezi was commander of the notorious 306th Brigade, accused of gross rights violations in Teso. The senior officers who under the command of Major-General Rwigyema formed the leadership of the RPF when it crossed into Rwanda, included six other senior NRA officers: Lt. Col. Wasswa, and Majors Kagame, Baingana, Kaka, Bunyenyezi, and Nduguta. These senior officers were just the tip of the iceberg.[15]

In fact, Kagame did not take part in the initial military offensive by the Rwandan Patriotic Army (RPA), the armed wing of the RPF, against the Habyarimana regime in October 1990. He was then in the United States as a Ugandan military officer in a staff training course at Fort Leavenworth. He abandoned the training to join the front as RPA commander following Rwigyema's death in battle. The offensive did not attain its objective, as France, Belgium and Mobutu's Zaire came, with variable degrees of assistance, to the dictator's rescue and prevented a victory by the RPF.

Under the auspices of the Organization of African Unity (OAU) and subregional actors, negotiations over two years between Habyarimana's government and the RPF to end the civil war led to the signing of the Arusha Accords in 1993. These included the Arusha Peace Agreement of 4 August 1993, a ceasefire agreement, and six protocols on a variety of subjects, including the rule of law, power sharing, integration of the two armed forces, repatriation of refugees and resettlement of dispersed persons. In spite of having signed these accords, President Habyarimana did his best to undermine them, and thus played into the hands of Hutu extremists bent on exterminating the Tutsi. He was killed upon his return to Kigali on 6 April 1994 from a one-day subregional summit in Dar es Salaam on the implementation of the accords.

The shooting down of Habyarimana's plane, which triggered the genocide, remains clouded in mystery. No international inquiry has been carried out, and reports by UN and OAU panels on the genocide have failed to throw any light on the matter.[16] A critical element of the puzzle that is of interest to the Congo is why both President Mobutu and his foreign minister, Professor Honoré Mpinga Kasenda, failed to show up at the Dar es Salaam summit. Only Congo's ambassador to Tanzania represented his country at the meeting, and he was unable to explain to President Habyarimana why his 'big brother' Mobutu did not come to give him moral support. Habyarimana reportedly kept looking at his watch all the time, hoping that Mobutu would show up.

Mobutu was tipped off, allegedly by the French, not to attend the meeting, for something was bound to happen. He instructed his foreign minister to represent him at the meeting. Informed by a friend in Mobutu's entourage that something dreadful could happen, Mpinga flew from Gbadolite to Goma, on the border with Rwanda, and stayed there. He pretended to be sick. Mobutu apparently tried to warn Habyarimana, but when he called Kigali, it was Madame Agathe Habyarimana who answered the phone. She never gave her husband Mobutu's message. The original plan was for Mobutu's presidential jet, a Boeing 727, to bring back to Kigali the Rwandan president and his aides, so that Habyarimana's plane could take the president of Burundi back home to Bujumbura. Since neither Mobutu nor Mpinga went to Dar es Salaam, Habyarimana took the Burundian with him, and they died together.[17] The plane in the missile's path could have been Mobutu's.

The genocide that took place after the shooting of the plane was planned in advance and executed by hardliners in President Habyarimana's entourage, as part of their violent backlash against the democratization process in Rwanda. Led by members of the *akazu*,[18] who included the First Lady and her brothers, the hardliners or advocates of Hutu Power unleashed their genocidal machine against the Tutsi and moderate Hutu leaders who were campaigning for democratization and national reconciliation. In the absence of conclusive evidence and a thorough international investigation into Habyarimana's death, a strong hypothesis remains that the plane was shot down by the extremists in the president's own entourage. This speculation exists because they were the ones who stood to lose the most from a process of national reconciliation involving the return of Tutsi exiles and power sharing between Habyarimana, the RPF and Hutu moderates. On the other hand, there is a second hypothesis, which cannot be excluded either, that the assassination was carried out by the RPF as a calculated move on their part to create a war situation likely to help them take over state power.[19]

In three months, between 800,000 and one million people were killed in a genocide spearheaded by elements of the Forces armées rwandaises (FAR), the national army, and the extremist Hutu militia known as *interahamwe*, or 'those who work together'. The act of killing was so generalized that even priests and nuns are said to have taken part in it. As Philip Gourevitch points out, killing 'was not regarded as a crime in Rwanda; it was effectively the law of the land, and every citizen was responsible for its administration'.[20] Obviously, the definition of who a citizen was in Hutu Power ideology did not include the Tutsi, as the latter could not be expected to carry out the civic duty of killing against themselves. Since they did not belong to the 'Hutu nation' they were defined as outsiders to be ethnically cleansed from Rwanda. Consistent with the demonization peculiar to final solution scenarios of ethnic cleansing and genocide, Tutsi were depicted as being less than human. They were called *inyenzi*, or 'cockroaches', and thus troublesome insects to be crushed or burned without mercy.[21] With the international community looking on, the genocide ended only with the victory of the RPA over the FAR and the *interahamwe*.

Once the RPF victory seemed certain, France obtained UN approval for a supposedly humanitarian intervention in Rwanda, the Opération Turquoise (June–August 1994). If we must acknowledge the good deeds of its soldiers in caring for and burying cholera victims in Kivu, it is imperative to affirm that there was nothing humanitarian in France's intent, given its own role as an accessory to crime in Rwanda.[22] As Jean-François Médard, a renowned French Africanist, told *Newsweek* magazine in 1994, French policy in Africa was 'erratic and criminal', as Paris operated 'not on principle, but on cynicism'.[23] The cynicism was evident in that having supported the Habyarimana regime and trained its genocidal machine, including the extremist Hutu militia, the French were more anxious to erase the traces of their own involvement in Rwanda by rescuing their former allies than in helping the victims of genocide inside the country. In April, the French had evacuated regime dignitaries, including known organizers of the genocide, while even Tutsi employees of the French Embassy were left behind to be killed.

The defeated forces fled together with over a million people across the border into the Congo. Protected by the French, the *génocidaires* were able to relocate their regime on Congolese soil, with the entire Rwandan state treasury and virtually all of the military arsenal at their disposal. All this allowed them to regroup for purposes of reconquering Rwanda and finishing off their genocidal enterprise. They then used the refugee camps in Kivu to raid Rwanda on a regular basis and to organize the slaughter of Tutsi citizens and residents of the Congo. For two years and a half, the Mobutu–Kengo regime and the international community watched and did nothing to stop this, while the UN and the donor community continued to be more preoccupied with feeding the refugees, rather than trying to remove the killers among them and find a lasting solution to the whole crisis.

On 6 October 1996, the RPF launched the final offensive to destroy the UNHCR refugee camps in Kivu and, consequently, the bases of the FAR and *interahamwe* in the Congo.[24] The victorious march of Kabila and his AFDL could not have taken place without the RPF drive against the genociders. The alleged massacres of Hutu non-combatants (old men, women and children) during the seven-month war against the

Mobutu regime remain a hotly debated subject, whose resolution should provide answers with respect to the prospects for peace and national reconciliation in Rwanda.

The fall of Mobutu and Kabila's rise to power in the Congo The fall of Mobutu came as a consequence of the drive by the new Rwandan authorities against Hutu extremists in the Congo. In order to deal with the threat posed by the *interahamwe* and ex-FAR soldiers who had taken refuge across the border, the Rwandans had already recruited and trained Congolese Tutsi from both South Kivu (the Banyamulenge) and North Kivu who would comprise their Trojan horse in the fight against Hutu extremists and their Congolese backers. Congolese Tutsi youths had either joined the RPA as part of Tutsi solidarity or were forced by anti-Tutsi chauvinism in the Congo to prepare themselves to fight for their national rights as Congolese citizens.

To legitimize the move by a coalition of African states, including Angola, Eritrea, Rwanda, Tanzania, Uganda and Zimbabwe, to get rid of Mobutu,[25] Museveni and Kagame proposed the idea of using Kabila, a former guerrilla chief turned ivory and gold trader, as the leader of an instant Congolese liberation struggle.[26] A failed revolutionary, Kabila had also served as an intermediary between Mobutu and John Garang, the leader of the Sudanese People's Liberation Movement (SPLM), and trained the Juféri, the youth wing of Uféri that Governor Gabriel Kyungu wa Kumwanza later used as his ethnic cleansing militia, in 1991.[27] According to Erik Kennes, 'Kabila's statement that "Mobutu only allowed the less competent and weaker opposition leaders to survive" may just as well apply to him'.[28]

By 1996, Kabila had neither an autonomous and credible organization nor a coherent political vision for the country. He was propelled to power by a regional dynamic of which the Congolese people did not know the ins and outs. The AFDL was created on 18 October 1996 at Lemera in South Kivu, nearly two months after the beginning of the offensive from Rwanda. It was a coalition of four groups: Kabila's own PRP, which was now reduced to a few exiles in Europe and America; the Conseil national de résistance pour la démocratie (CNRD),[29] a small Lumumbist guerrilla group established in 1993 in eastern Congo by André Kisase Ngandu; the Alliance démocratique des peuples (ADP),[30] a grouping of Congolese Tutsi led by Déogratias Bugera; and the Mouvement révolutionnaire pour la libération du Zaïre (MRLZ),[31] an opposition group centred around the Bashi of South Kivu led by Anselme Masasu Nindaga.

At its birth, the Alliance had two major leaders: Kabila as *porte parole* or spokesperson, and Kisase Ngandu as military commander. It is evident that Kabila and his new Congolese associates did not have the kind of military organization capable of defeating the otherwise weak and demoralized army of Field Marshal Mobutu. The *kadogo* or child-soldiers whom they recruited during the long march from Goma to Kinshasa were valuable only for purposes of intimidation against civilians. The one solid Congolese faction in the seven-month war was made up of the *Tigres* or mostly Katangan auxiliaries of the Angolan army who where brought back home for the good cause. They engaged in serious combat against Mobutu's white mercenaries, his praetorian guard, and Jonas Savimbi's men at Kisangani, Lubumbashi and Kenge, respectively.

All other military operations were the work of Rwandan soldiers and units of Congolese Tutsi trained in Uganda and Rwanda. General Kagame himself has boasted about the crucial role Rwanda played in the 1996–97 war.[32] That role, which included acts of genocide against Hutu refugees in the Congo, has yet to be investigated thoroughly for crimes against humanity and gross violations of international humanitarian law by Rwandan military officers and their field commander, James Kabarebe. Like most of the Rwandan authorities today, Kabarebe is a product of the Tutsi diaspora in Uganda. Until 13 July 1998, he served as chief of staff of the Forces armées congolaises (FAC), the new Congolese national army, and many of his trusted unit commanders were equally officers of the RPA.

Commander Kisase Ngandu did not live to see the AFDL victory. He died in mysterious circumstances in January 1997, apparently assassinated by those who did not feel comfortable with his Lumumbist sense of nationalism and patriotic duty.[33] After his death, the remaining leaders decided to fuse their groups into one, with Kabila as AFDL president, Bugera as secretary general, and Masasu as military commander.

Commander Masasu was out of the picture before the end of the year, arrested and jailed for 'indiscipline' on 25 November 1997. After Masasu's arrest, Kabila spoke of him disparagingly as 'a simple corporal from the Rwandan army that we picked up along the way ... he was never associated with the strategic centre of military operations during the liberation war'.[34] Ironically, this was a recognition of the central role that outsiders, and not the AFDL, played in these operations. What is of interest today is why this 'simple corporal' should pose such a threat to the Kabila regime that, after being released from detention in April 2000, he was arrested again in November 2000 and taken to an unknown location. Having initially denied a human rights group's report that Masasu had been summarily executed on 24 November at Pweto, in Katanga, the government later acknowledged the fact.[35]

Bugera was removed from his AFDL post in May 1998 and sidelined as minister of state in the president's office, with no particular duties, and then excluded himself in late July as his plotting failed to remove Kabila from power. History was repeating itself, with the advent of yet another one-man rule in the Congo. Even before the second Congo war increased his chances of political survival, Kabila had already established himself as *'l'homme seul'* in the Mobutuist tradition. The AFDL would eventually disappear in 1999, and personal rule under a new 'enligthened guide' was consolidated in the Congo.

The War of Partition and Plunder

Rwanda and Uganda, later on joined by Burundi, took advantage of the disintegration of the Congolese state and armed forces to create territorial spheres of interest within which they could plunder the Congo's riches. They had hoped to find in Laurent Kabila and the AFDL a useful cover for their strategic interest in creating a buffer zone of economic and political security in eastern Congo. Since Kabila had not lived up to their expectations, Rwanda and Uganda were determined to find a new Congolese puppet, to fulfill their desire of having 'another Bizimungu in Kinshasa'.[36] Their flagrant aggression in the Congo was made possible by three factors. The first was their clever attempt to depict the war that erupted on 2 August 1998 as a civil war in which they were simply providing support to Congolese rebels to ensure security on their own borders. The second factor was the indifference of the international community, within which Rwanda and Uganda appeared to have the support of their superpower ally, the United States. The third and no less important factor was the logic of plunder in the new era of globalization, which has to do with the growing tendency of states, Mafia groups, offshore banks and transnational mining companies to enrich themselves from crises.

The invention of a civil war   There is no truth to the widely held view that Uganda and Rwanda intervened in support of a rebellion by Congolese Tutsi and their allies against President Kabila. As already indicated above, it is true that a plot to topple Kabila had existed at least since February 1998, and was masterminded by Bugera, then secretary-general of the AFDL. It took on added urgency on two occasions, first in May, when Bugera was removed from the AFDL job and moved up to a useless position of minister of state at the presidency; and then in July, when Commander James was relieved of his post as armed forces chief of staff and named adviser to the president. This was a move by Kabila to free himself from the cumbersome Rwandan military tutelage in order to assert his independence as president of a sovereign state. His 27 July 1998 decision to send Commander James and his Rwandan comrades-in-arms back home, apparently to preempt a coup, was the immediate cause of the rebellions that shook Goma and Kinshasa six days later. Although the leaders of the Goma rebellion turned out to be Congolese, Commanders Jean-Pierre Ondekane and Sylvain Buki were trusted lieutenants of Commander James, who had placed them in charge of this strategic military location.

Since the inside job had failed, the initiative to remove Kabila from power had to come from the outside. Just as Rwanda had done in 1996, by first invading the Congo and then setting up the AFDL to legitimize its action, Rwanda and Uganda initiated the war that erupted on 2 August 1998, prior to the founding of the Rassemblement congolais pour la démocratie (RCD), the rebel movement. In addition to eye-witness reports of Rwandan troops crossing the border into the Congo on that day, the author received confirmation of this initiative within two weeks of the war. On 6 August, Ernest Wamba-dia-Wamba called me from Kigali, asking me to join him there as soon as possible so we could go to Goma and lead the rebellion against Kabila. Wamba, who had been in Brussels at the end of July for a consultation on Belgian development policy organized by the Belgian secretary of state for development cooperation, had just arrived in Kigali by way of Kampala. My initial reaction was negative. However, in view of 33 years of a close friendship and association, I asked him to give me a few days of reflection and a telephone number at which I could reach him once I decided what to do. When I called back a week later, on 13 August, a man who did not speak French answered and identified himself as 'Don'. When I told him that my name was Georges Nzongola, the conversation went like this:

Don: Professor Nzongola-Ntalaja? We are waiting for you.
GNN: Who are you and how can you be waiting for me, you don't even speak French? Here is my message for Wamba: tell him I cannot join something guided from the outside.
Don: But this is not guided from the outside, it is a Congolese affair.
GNN: You are not Congolese, and you're waiting for me in Kigali, and then you have Mobutuists like Alexis Thambwe Mwamba financing the war.
Don: There are no Mobutuists, and Thambwe has no major role here.[37]

Upon checking with Congolese compatriots, I learned that the Don in question was none other than Commander Don, the Rwandan military officer who was second in command to James Kabarebe, and who is alleged to be responsible for the massacre of Hutu civilians at Mbandaka.[38] While James was then hijacking planes to take troops and equipment to Kitona for the march on Kinshasa, Don was serving as liaison officer with the new Congolese leadership in Goma.

So who are the Congolese rebels and why did they choose to become Rwanda's or Uganda's puppets? The rebels are a disparate group with nothing in common except their opposition to Kabila.[39] Except for the individuals who worked in Bugera's AFDL office, there is no past linkage between the different factions, and no coherent ideology and societal project. With the possible exception of Jean-Pierre Bemba in the Equator province, they have no popular support in the country. Rebel subgroups include Kabila's former Tutsi allies, most of whom are close to the RPF regime in Rwanda; left-wing intellectuals dreaming of revolutionary change; members of the Mobutu *nomenklatura* seeking to return to power; mostly junior officers from Mobutu's army, the Forces armées zaïroises (FAZ),[40] bent on avenging their humiliation by Kabila; and little-known political figures in search of new adventures.

The first and most powerful subgroup within the rebellion is made up of Congolese Tutsi with close ties to the RPF. They have dominated the main rebel group, the RCD-Goma, which has seen four different non-Tutsi presidents since its creation in August 1998. In addition to Bugera, the kingmakers include Moïse Nyarugabo, Azarias Ruberwa and Bizima Karaha. Bugera has already been identified as a minor political leader in North Kivu who rose to become the number 2 AFDL official thanks to his ties to the RPF. Nyarugabo grew up in urban and mining centres of Katanga, where his parents were among the Rwandan immigrants brought over to work for the UMHK. A brilliant lawyer from Lubumbashi, he occupied the strategic position of Kabila's private secretary before becoming head of the anti-corruption parastatal, the Office de Biens Mal Acquis (OBIMA). Ruberwa, another Lubumbashi lawyer, served as top adviser to Bizima Karaha when the latter was Kabila's foreign minister.

Little is known about Karaha himself, whose real name is supposed to be Bizimana Karahato. The only undisputed fact is that he did complete his general training in medicine at the Medical University of South Africa (MEDUNSA).[41] His claims of being a native of the Banyamulenge hills are generally disputed, making him a person of 'questionable nationality' in Congolese political discourse. What is most disturbing about the Congolese Tutsi close to the RPF is that they and Kigali have taken it upon themselves to speak in the name of the entire Tutsi community in the Congo, by assimilating its interests with those of the RPF regime in Rwanda. This is a danger for Congolese Tutsi, who became victims of officially inspired hatred and violence,[42] and some of the biggest losers of the second Congo war.[43] The authentic leaders of the Banyamulenge understood this from the very beginning of the war, and this is the reason why they refused to join the Rwandan- and Ugandan-backed Congolese rebels.[44]

The left-wing intellectuals include Wamba and his close friend and associate Jacques Depelchin. They have both taught at the University of Dar es Salaam, and are known to hold President Museveni of Uganda in high esteem. When Wamba was removed from the presidency of the RCD in May 1999, the group broke into two wings, with Wamba and the progressives moving to establish themselves as RCD-Kisangani in Congo's third most important city. Following the bloody confrontation between Rwandan and Ugandan troops in Kisangani from 14 to 17 August 1999 and in which more than two hundred innocent Congolese civilians died, the Wamba wing of the RCD moved to Bunia, a district town close to the border with Uganda. Since then, the Ugandan tutelage of what is officially known as Rassemblement congolais pour la démocratie – Mouvement de liberation (RCD-ML) has grown to such an extent that the group has no autonomy. The level of dependence on Uganda was such that to settle a leadership dispute between Wamba and his deputy in November 2000, the two factions had to go to Kampala. Before the trip to the imperial capital, a spokesperson for the Wamba faction kept complaining in radio interviews that Ugandan troops were supporting the rebellion, in spite of clear signals from President Museveni that he still favoured Wamba as the RCD-ML leader. It seems unlikely that Wamba and his associates can succeed in building a new and progressive mode of politics under foreign bondage.

In the third and fourth subgroups, former Mobutu ministers and former FAZ junior officers, the most prominent members were Vincent de Paul Lunda Bululu, Alexis Thambwe Mwamba, Kin-kiey Mulumba and Commanders Ondekane and Buki. All of these men were members of the RCD-Goma, the Rwandan-controlled group, in which they served at some point as head of governmental affairs, head of the foreign affairs department, spokesperson, military commander and second vice-president, and head of military intelligence, respectively. A former prime minister, Lunda Bululu held the same post under Wamba, and this dual executive led to so many conflicts between the two that it was dropped when Emile Ilunga succeeded Wamba in May 1999. One of the richest men in the Congo, Thambwe Mwamba served in several ministries under Mobutu and Kengo. During the aborted transition, he was president of Kengo's political party and a minister in both Tshisekedi's and

Kengo's cabinets. Kin-kiey Mulumba, the third prominent Mobutuist in the group, was editor of the conservative Kinshasa daily *Le Soft* and the information minister in Mobutu's last government.

Also connected to the Mobutu regime through his father, the millionaire businessman Bemba Saolana, Jean-Pierre Bemba is unique among the anti-Kabila rebels. Here is a man with no previous political or military experience, a political creature of Museveni, and yet a person who seems capable of erasing the stigma of external sponsorship to establish himself as a credible political actor in the Congo. The Mouvement de liberation du Congo (MLC), the third rebel group after the two wings of the RCD, was created by Uganda in November 1998 as a response to the lack of popular support for the RCD in the Congo. The choice of northwestern Congo, his own region of origin, as the theatre for his rebellion seems to have worked in Bemba's favour by mobilizing popular support among people who had known nothing but neglect and repression at the hands of Kabila's regime. However, Bemba could not establish himself nationally as an alternative to Kabila, given his external backing by Uganda and the reported support of his enterprise by some of Mobutu's former generals.

Finally, the fifth and last subgroup of rebel leaders is made up of hitherto little-known political figures, such as Bemba, in search of new adventures. The most prominent individuals in this category are Arthur Zahidi Ngoma and Dr Emile Ilunga. A former UNESCO official who had just been freed from Kabila's jails for engaging in banned political activities, Zahidi Ngoma was the first choice of the Rwandans to preside over the rebel movement. In the second half of August 1998, when the group assumed the RCD label, he was replaced by Wamba. After a couple of months in Goma, Zahidi Ngoma quit the RCD, denouncing a group that he once headed as being controlled by Rwanda. Most Congolese observers could not understand why it took him so long to see this reality. Actually, the real reason seems to lie elsewhere, in the fact that he had lost the presidency of the RCD.

As for Dr Ilunga, he is a medical doctor who had once represented Kabila's PRP in Europe. Until 1996, he was known as the political leader of the *Tigres* in Angola. It is apparently he and Déogratias Symba who played a key role in having these troops join the AFDL drive against Mobutu.[45] According to Symba, an agreement was reached in Luanda that once Mobutu was overthrown, Kabila would become president and Ilunga vice-president. Since Kabila proclaimed himself president and proceeded to set up personal rule, Ilunga became one of his major political enemies. But how was Kabila able to tame the *Tigres* and keep them under his control? Ilunga served as president of RCD-Goma from

May 1999 until he was replaced on 28 October 2000 by Dr Adolphe Onusumba, a total unknown.

With this new development and the ongoing squabbles in Bunia, the disintegration of both wings of the RCD was progressing steadily in early 2001. As a well-informed news digest on the DRC has observed, the RCD-Goma had become a mere shadow of its former self, with most of its prominent leaders leaving one by one, while the RCD-ML was by then mostly a fiction. As for the MLC, its image was still tarnished 'because it is in part financed by the dinosaurs of the deposed regime'.[46] The inevitable result was the forced merger of the two Ugandan-sponsored organizations into a single group, the Front de libération congolais (FLC), with Bemba as president and Wamba as vice president. Unable to accept the accumulating humiliations, Wamba refused to acknowledge his demotion.

The indifference of the international community The myth that what was going on in the Great Lakes region was a civil war gave comfort to the aggressors and excuse for inaction by those responsible for upholding international peace and security, particularly the United Nations Security Council. It took the Council nearly two years, until June 2000, before it accused Rwanda and Uganda of aggression in the Congo, and ordered them to withdraw their troops from the DRC, in Resolution 1304. The responsibility of the major world powers generally and of the United States particularly in the regional war is best described in the following excerpts from the independent Ugandan newspaper *The Monitor* of Kampala:

> In August 1998, the Western world in general and the US in particular, looked on as Uganda and Rwanda invaded the DRC with the aim of overthrowing the very government they had been instrumental in bringing to power. The Western powers readily bought the propaganda of the Ugandan and Rwandan governments to the effect that they had occupied the DRC to safeguard their security interests.
>
> The interests of the people of the DRC never featured anywhere on the agenda. The Lusaka agreement treated Rwanda and Uganda with kid gloves. It was only when their armies turned their guns on each other, and in the process killed and maimed hundreds of thousands of DRC civilians, that the world woke up to the carnage in Kisangani. ...
>
> The US and its Western allies had kept quiet all this time the Rwandan and Ugandan armies were engaged in the gross abuse of human rights of the innocent people of the DRC. The US and the West must bear the responsibility for the deaths of the Congolese people, since

they have the capacity to prevent those deaths if the political will is there.

The US has trained and armed both Rwanda and Uganda ostensibly to counter the Islamic fundamentalist state of Sudan. Although the US is the only remaining super power, its world leadership role has sadly been marred by its continued cold-war behaviour, especially where its interests are concerned.

As a result, the US together with the other Western democracies have invariably failed to uphold the internationally accepted norms and principles for parochial interests. Hence their rogue allies like Rwanda and Uganda can, with impunity and arrogance, occupy a sovereign state and cause massacres and destruction.[47]

The 'parochial interests' of the United States and other major powers include maintaining access to the strategic resources of the Congo, selling weapons of war and, in the particular US case, supporting allies such as Uganda and Rwanda, which may ensure this access in addition to being guardians on the frontline *vis-à-vis* the Islamist threat from Sudan. Given the inability of the dying Mobutu regime to provide an effective response to this and other transnational threats such as terrorism, drug trafficking, arms proliferation and humanitarian disasters, Washington supported its clients' sponsorship of Kabila to remove former ally Mobutu from power. One of the reasons for this support was the fact that Mobutu's generals were known to be involved in narcotrafficking and in selling arms to rebel groups, including the ex-FAR and the *interahamwe*. Some of the arms taken from these groups to be returned to Rwanda were actually resold to them by Congolese military officers. Kabila's incompetence, erratic behaviour and friendship with states to which the US is hostile such as Cuba, Libya and Sudan did not endear him to American policymakers. Until July 1998, US military personnel were training Rwandan troops in counterinsurgency, and a US military and diplomatic team was sighted at the Rwanda–Congo border when the war broke out on 2 August 1998. Officially, the team was there 'to assess the Rwandese government's ability to prevent another genocide'.[48] There could be no better expression of support for Rwanda's aggression in the Congo, which Kigali justified in terms of preventing another genocide.

Having prevented UN action to stop the genocide, US policymakers and other major players in world politics feel so guilty with respect to Rwanda that they seem prepared to let the Tutsi-dominated regime there get away with murder. Add to this the seal of approval granted to Museveni and Kagame as two of Africa's 'new breed of leaders', and you understand why they feel so bold in taking actions such as invading the Congo. No sanctions have been taken against them for their aggression against the sovereignty and territorial integrity of the DRC, while Mugabe's Zimbabwe has been punished for its costly war effort, exerted in support of an internationally recognized regime. On the contrary, and despite their lack of democratic credentials nowadays required of others as conditions for economic assistance, Uganda and Rwanda continue to obtain US foreign aid and loans from the Bretton Woods institutions. Given the punishment administered to Iraq for its invasion of Kuwait and the billions of dollars spent in the Balkans to stop Serb aggression against other national groups, the people of the Congo cannot but feel bitter about the double standards in international response to aggression and state-sponsored terrorism.

The only countries to dare attempt to 'uphold the internationally accepted norms and principles' as outlined in the UN and OAU charters were Angola, Zimbabwe, Namibia and, for a while, Chad. While there is no doubt that the personal motivations of the leaders involved as well as the economic and geopolitical interests of their countries did influence the decision to intervene, their intervention saved the Congo from the expansionist aims of its neighbours. On the other hand, the peace process since the Lusaka Agreement of 10 July 1999 reflects the lack of a strong international commitment to a just and fair settlement of the Great Lakes conflict. In the first place, the Agreement itself is flawed in several respects. The true nature of the war as an external aggression is not acknowledged, and the external actors are treated equally, whether they came to commit aggression or to Kabila's rescue. Burundi, a major belligerent, is not a signatory to the Agreement. Even more shocking is the fact that rebels from Uganda, Rwanda and Burundi are outlaws who must be disarmed, while the Congolese rebels are *interlocuteurs valables* with a seat at the negotiating table. The Agreement seems to legitimize the *de facto* partition of the country by inviting the signatories themselves, the states involved minus Burundi plus the Congolese rebels, to disarm the illegal militias.

In the second place, Africa and the international community have not provided an adequate response to two key provisions of the Agreement, which deal with UN assistance in establishing peace by disarming rebels, particularly those committed to genocide, and the OAU role in national reconciliation in the Congo. Without an UN force with Chapter VII powers of peace enforcement, the countries involved will, like Sierra Leone, be hard put to accomplish by themselves the task of disarming the *interahamwe* and other extremist militias. Failure to do so would not remove the very pretext that Rwanda has used for intervening in the

Congo. The OAU made an extremely poor choice in picking Ketumile Masire, the former president of Botswana, as the facilitator for the inter-Congolese dialogue. Despite his outstanding qualities as a statesman and a man of integrity, President Masire had two major handicaps. In the first place, he does not speak French, which is essential for a full grasp of the complex nuances of Congolese political discourse. In the second place, the fact that he served as chair of the OAU Eminent Personalities Panel on the Rwandan Genocide was bound to offer to those Congolese officials opposed to the dialogue the pretext that he is likely to be sympathetic to Rwanda because of the genocide.

The indifference of the international community *vis-à-vis* aggression in the Congo represents a tacit approval of the attempt by Rwanda and Uganda to modify existing state boundaries or, failing that, to establish *de facto* control in eastern Congo, by those for whom the idea that the Congo is too vast and ungovernable in the absence of strong-arm rule has long been an article of faith. Thus, even though current developments may not result in the breakup of the Congo into smaller and more manageable sovereign entities, it ensures both control of some of its richest and strategic regions by trusted allies and undisturbed access to mineral and other resources by transnational corporations.

Transnational networks of pillage and corruption With state decay and the breakdown in law and order, the Congo has once again become a wild frontier in which everyone is free to fetch whatever they can. The ease with which money can be moved in the new global markets and invested in offshore banks has made crisis areas such as the Great Lakes region opportunity zones for arms merchants, money launderers, and other types of unscrupulous business entrepreneurs out to make quick profits. The abundance and diversity of Congo's minerals had given the country its colonial-era distinction as a 'geological scandal'. Since Leopold's days, the national wealth is monopolized by the country's rulers and their foreign business partners to the detriment of the mass of the people, who remain among the poorest of the poor in the world today. This is the real scandal of the Congo. The scandal is all the more shocking today in that the plunder of the country's wealth is not limited to foreign merchants who trade weapons of destruction for the gold, diamond and other minerals of the Congo, which they obtain on the cheap. It also involves sovereign states, the aggressors as well as those allied with the Kabila regime.

All of this activity is taking place at a time when there is renewed interest by mining transnationals in Africa's minerals. Transnationals from all over the world have joined their South African counterparts in a new scramble for mining concessions and exploration rights all over Africa. They are hopeful of cashing in on the new opportunities of the post-Cold War era, including the push towards privatization and the fact that Africa does possess a large supply of resources that by and large have been depleted in the developed countries.[49] One of the main reasons for their attraction to the Congo – in spite of the economic ruin of the country and its political turmoil – is the mineral contents of Congolese copper, cobalt and gold ores, which are among the highest in the world.[50] Thus, although their long-term interests require political stability, investors seeking mining contracts do not seem to shy away from war-ravaged countries with a fabulous resource endowment.

While many of the foreign enterprises do engage in legitimate business, there are rogue groups and individuals who would stop at nothing to achieve their aims. The intricate networks and lobbies of legitimate and rogue operators, together with the assistance and protection they often receive from their national governments, have been described in great details by Wayne Madsen for the United States and by Stephen Smith and Antoine Glazer for France.[51] While these networks and lobbies are an important factor of the crisis and a major contributor to the repression of the Congolese people, their role should not be overly exaggerated. For they cannot operate without the willing complicity of Congolese nationals and the rulers of neighbouring African states, who together have allowed mercenaries, merchants of death and adventurers of all kinds to continue plundering our land and plunging our people into deeper poverty and destitution. If it is true that the corrupted cannot exist without corrupters, it is in the former group that the major culprits are to be found.

The corrupters, of course, have no respect for diplomatic niceties such as national sovereignty and territorial integrity that may stand in the way of short-term profitability. They make deals with whoever controls a mineral-rich territory, including warlords and invaders, as they have done in the Congo with the AFDL, Rwanda, the Ugandan warlord Brigadier James Kazini, both wings of the RCD and the MLC.[52] For the African partners, all that does matter is the amount of money foreign businesses are prepared to pay up front to win lucrative contracts, and the percentage of earnings that will later go back to political authorities or warlords.

Rebel groups, beginning with Kabila's AFDL, have discovered that making deals in this manner is a good way of raising money for warfare. In one transaction in May 1997, the AFDL received an initial payment of $50 million from Consolidated Eurocan Ventures of the Lundin

Group of Vancouver, Canada, for a copper and cobalt investment deal worth $1.5 billion, with the remainder $200 million to be paid over four years.[53] Jean-Raymond Boule, the principal owner of American Mineral Fields, a company registered in Canada but operating from the State of Arkansas in the USA, even loaned his executive jet to then rebel leader Kabila for his visits to liberated cities in the Congo and diplomatic missions in Africa.

Rwanda and Uganda have been deeply involved in mining and other economic activities in the Congo since 1996. For President Museveni of Uganda, dividing up the Congo among rival warlords was the best way of maintaining political influence in the country and access to its vast resources. Kampala's support for Jean-Pierre Bemba and its strong backing for the Wamba faction of the RCD, are indicative of a strategy aimed at the Somalization of the Congo. Museveni's generals and other military commanders were more successful in making business deals than in waging war in the Congo. Thus, beginning with his half-brother, General Salim Saleh, and the army chief of staff, Brigadier Kazini, the major activity of the Ugandan Peoples Defence Forces (UPDF) in northeastern Congo was the systematic looting of natural resources and consumer durables.

A regime of pillage was established, with Ugandans and Rwandans dividing up among themselves the gold, diamonds, timber, coffee and tea of the northeast. Entire factories and a lot of machinery and tools have also been plundered from the Congo. For example, the Montreal-based *Info-Congo/Kinshasa* has reported that in July 2000, RCD-Goma transferred what was left of the equipment of the Congolese Bureau of Roads in the area under its nominal control to Rwanda.[54] The military clashes of 1999 and 2000 between Rwandan and Ugandan troops in Kisangani were basically a case of fighting over turf and resources.[55] In a comment on this bloody row between the UPDF and the RPA, the Ugandan daily *The Monitor* has written that 'though the Ugandans made money, they got crumbs as Rwanda took the lucrative deals'.[56]

The Rwandans are said to have awarded mining concessions for rare metals such as nobium and tantalum in the occupied territory to foreign firms,[57] and by making sure that Rwanda, and not Uganda, takes the lion's share of Congo's resources. Rwanda is also the main beneficiary of the current boom in the artisanal exploitation of columbium-tantalite (or coltan), for which the city of Bukavu serves as the major trading centre. It follows, then, that the need to end rebel incursions from the Congo that Uganda and Rwanda use as a justification for their aggression is a pretext for hiding their expansionist aims in northeast Congo. As pointed out above, RPA officer Kabarebe was the chief of staff of the

FAC. With respect to Uganda, President Kabila had authorized the stationing of a UPDF battalion on Congolese soil to police the Congo–Uganda border. How, then, can Kampala and Kigali accuse Kabila for having failed to put an end to rebel incursions when they were directly involved in the management and activities of Congolese security forces until July 1998?

Burundi, the third partner in the anti-Kabila coalition in the region, has also sought to justify its limited military involvement as arising out of the need to stop incursions of Hutu extremists based in the Congo. Until the imposition of economic sanctions in the wake of the coup of July 1996 by Major Paul Buyoya, the Bujumbura Free Trade Zone was the major market for gold smuggled from the Congo.[58] With Kampala and Kigali deeply involved in the gold trade, Bujumbura could not afford to be left out of the new scramble for Congo's riches.

The plunder of Congo's riches was not limited to the aggressors. Kabila's allies, too, took their share of the loot. Of the three Southern African Development Community (SADC) intervening states, Angola was the only one with genuine security interests in the Congo. For Angola, these interests were basically twofold. First, Luanda needed to protect its petroleum and diamond exploitation zones, particularly the oil-rich area from the northwest to Cabinda, which is partitioned by a slice of Congolese territory. The occupation of the Atlantic region of the Congo by the anti-Kabila alliance in August 1998 was a clear and present danger for Luanda, not only for its potentially negative impact on industry and commerce, but also in view of the alleged collaboration between the alliance and Savimbi's UNITA. Second, the Luanda government feared that Savimbi would once again use the Congo as a rear base for his rebellion, as he did during the Mobutu regime. More than the other two countries, Angola has an evident interest in the stability of the Congo, a country with which it shares a long land border of 2,511 km. Having already intervened in the Congo through the Katanga gendarmes in 1977 and 1978, and more decisively in 1997 in both Congos by helping to put Kabila in power in Kinshasa and restoring the *ancien régime* of Denis Sassou-Nguesso in Brazzaville, the Angolan government was eager to establish its credentials as a regional power in Central Africa.

Both Angola and Namibia followed Zimbabwe in advocating a military role for the SADC in the Congo. Zimbabwe took the initiative in making their intervention a collective defence action against an external threat through the SADC Organ for Politics, Defence and Security, chaired by President Robert Mugabe.[59] In spite of objections by some SADC members on identifying his intervention with the regional organization and growing opposition to Zimbabwean involvement at home, Mugabe did not hesitate to commit the largest military contingent of all of Kabila's allies, with as many as 11,000 to 12,000 troops. While a lot of attention has been given to a leadership rivalry between Zimbabwe and South Africa, perhaps more important in the decision to intervene were the economic interests of the country and its governing élite.

It is widely reported that the Kabila government owed millions of dollars to Zimbabwe for military equipment and supplies obtained during the seven-month war of 1996–97. After the regime change in Kinshasa, a number of Zimbabwean businesses and state enterprises extended credit to the Congo for the purchase of goods in various sectors, but did not receive payments as expected from the Congolese. With its population of approximately 60 million people, the Congo represents an attractive market for Zimbabwean goods and services, inasmuch as Zimbabwean textile, agro-industrial and other enterprises are losing ground, even at home, to competition from South Africa and suffering from the detrimental effects of globalization. In the area of clothing, for example, the textile factories of Bulawayo are having a hard time competing with better-quality imports.

The Zimbabwean governing élite is determined to make good on its investment in the Congo. During the civil war in Mozambique, Zimbabwe sent thousands of troops to help the Frelimo government fight the Renamo rebels.[60] After the civil war, there were no dividends for the sacrifices made, as South Africa, the very country that had armed Renamo and tried to destroy Mozambican society and economy, reaped the lion's share of the benefits of peace. Zimbabweans were determined not to be short-changed this time around. They made sure of reaping some concrete benefits from their military intervention in the Congo.

Billy Rautenbach, a Zimbabwean businessman with interests in transportation and automobile assembly, served for a while as the managing director of Gécamines, the Lubumbashi-based state mining company specializing in copper and cobalt.[61] With a strong military presence in Mbuji-Mayi, Zimbabweans were said to be shipping diamonds home on a regular basis, by air.[62] A diamond-mining venture involving Mugabe's and Kabila's associates was also set up in Kasai. Zimbabwe, like Rwanda and Uganda, was determined to finance its war effort with the Congo's resources, but much of the loot went into private hands. By the end of August 2000, Zimbabwe had spent $200 million for the Congo war effort, according to Simba Makoni, the finance minister.[63] Leo Mugabe, the Zimbabwean president's nephew, and General Vitalis Zvinavashe,

Commander of the Zimbabwean Defence Force (ZDF), are among a select group of individuals who have personally benefited from the war. The general's trucking company was used to carry supplies for Zimbabwean troops in the Congo from Harare to Lubumbashi.[64]

Only Namibia and Chad could make a strong claim for an intervention for which economic motives were not paramount. It is true, and the Namibian authorities themselves are quick to admit, that they would like to have access to the water and hydroelectric resources of the Congo.[65] From a strategic perspective, Namibia has legitimate concerns with its vulnerability to any security threat posed by Savimbi's UNITA to Angola, as there may be spillover into Namibia. In fact, UNITA has given material support for secessionist activity in Namibia's Caprivi Strip, and Windhoek has every right to make sure that this does not recur.[66] This, of course, does not mean that no Namibian entrepreneurs or military officers have made economic gains in the Congo as a result of their country's involvement in the war.

Chad withdrew its troops from the Congo following the April 1999 Sirte (Libya) ceasefire agreement between Kinshasa and Kampala. Chadian authorities have explained their intervention as a form of gratitude for military support from Kinshasa during their own troubles in the 1980s. However true this might be, there is no doubt that the geopolitical interests of France and its Central African allies were a factor, particularly through pressures exerted by President Omar Bongo of Gabon, the dean of heads of state in Central Africa. The countries of the subregion would like to see the Congo remain engaged with them, rather than turn eastward and southward to English-speaking countries.[67] The aborted meeting of Kabila with other Congolese political and social forces outside the Lusaka Agreement framework, which was planned to take place in Libreville, Gabon on 21 December 2000, represents yet another attempt by France and the francophone states of Central Africa to claim ownership of the Congolese crisis to the detriment of the SADC countries.

Resistance and Repression in Kabila's Congo

The victory of the AFDL and the fall of the decadent and dictatorial Mobutu regime were a major event in the annals of the history of postcolonial Africa. The involvement of other African states in the liberation of the Congolese people from Mobutuism was applauded all over the continent as a legitimate affirmation of the Pan-African right of interference in the internal affairs of a sovereign state.[68] In the wake of the genocide in Rwanda, a consensus has emerged that Africa as a whole cannot remain indifferent to flagrant violations of human rights, simply for the sake of respecting the legal principle of non-interference. While this principle remains a major component of African international law, the Pan-African right of intervention in exceptional circumstances has been added to this legal regime by the 2000 summit of the OAU in Lomé as part of the African Union project. In this light, the intervention by Angola, Rwanda and Uganda, as well as the assistance of other countries of Eastern and Southern Africa, in overthrowing the Mobutu regime was salutary, like the earlier intervention of Mwalimu Julius Nyerere of Tanzania against the sanguinary regime of Field Marshall Idi Amin Dada of Uganda in 1979.

However, it is equally established as a maxim of inter-African relations that as soon as assistance to the liberation of an oppressed people is over, all regional actors should return home and let the liberated people manage their own affairs. In the Congo case, this maxim was respected by Angola, but flagrantly violated by Rwanda and Uganda, whose leaders had motives other than liberating the Congolese from Mobutu's already crumbling rule. The expansionist aims of these two countries were soon to put them in conflict with Kabila, the man they had imposed as Congo's new ruler, and with the Congolese people. At the very time that popular discontent against Kabila was rising because of his authoritarianism and lack of direction, the second invasion of the Congo by Rwanda and Uganda in August 1998 gave a new breath of fresh air to his new political adventure. For the Congolese democracy movement, the resulting political situation called for fighting on two fronts, with a double strategy of resistance against external aggression and new forms of dictatorship by the Kabila regime.

Popular resistance against external aggression From its inception, the war was waged principally against the civilian population. Major Kabarebe had commandeered aircraft to carry troops and supplies from Goma on the Congo–Rwanda border to the military base of Kitona in the southwest, with the aim of marching on Kinshasa from the south. His blockade of the port of Matadi and the interruption of electricity and water supply to Kinshasa by the repeated switching off of the Inga power dam resulted in shortages of basic necessities, an outbreak of waterborne diseases and numerous deaths. This was a major miscalculation, because it earned nothing but contempt and hostility for the Congolese rebels in alliance with the invaders. Angola ended the blockade of Matadi and, with help from Zimbabwe, defeated Rwandan and Ugandan troops before they could take over Kinshasa.

Except for the battle for Kinshasa and a few major confrontations in the Equator province and in North Katanga, the state armies involved seldom faced each other in combat, even before the signing of the Lusaka ceasefire agreement in July 1999. The regional war was thus peculiar in that it remained mainly a war against unarmed civilians, with repeated massacres of innocent men, women and children, particularly by Rwandan troops and their Congolese auxiliaries, and with HIV-positive soldiers passing on the deadly virus to the thousands of women they raped or, occasionally, to those whose services they purchased. According to five mortality surveys conducted in eastern Congo for the International Rescue Committee (IRC) between 18 April and 27 May 2000, it is estimated that of the 2,300,000 people who died between August 1998 and May 2000, 1,700,000 died as a result of the war.[69] While only 200,000 of these deaths were attributable to violence, the vast majority were due to hunger, malnutrition, the breakdown of the health infrastructure, and the vulnerability of internally displaced persons to the hazards of seeking refuge in the dense equatorial forest.

Of all the occupied areas, North and South Kivu were the hardest hit in terms of massacres and acts of daily violence against innocent civilians by the RPA and their surrogates, the RCD-Goma. It is also in these two provinces that resistance to external aggression has been highly organized, in two major forms. The first is a nonviolent campaign against the occupation by civil society organizations, and involves acts of civil disobedience, refusal to recognize and deal with the RCD as legitimate rulers, and a courageous public denunciation of human rights violations through local, national and international communication channels. A great deal of courage has been shown by individuals and groups in this effort, which resulted in summary executions, disappearances and other crimes. Even religious leaders have not been spared, as evidenced by the persecution of Monsignor Emmanuel Kataliko, the Roman Catholic Archbishop of Bukavu, who spent much of 2000 banished to Butembo in North Kivu, away from his ministry in South Kivu. His sudden death on 4 October 2000 while attending a meeting in Rome, less than three weeks after he was allowed to return to Bukavu on 14 September, is believed by many to have been caused in one way or another by the occupation regime.

The second form of resistance to the invaders in the east is armed struggle by the Forces d'autodéfense populaire (FAP),[70] which are better known under their African names of Mai-Mai, Simba and others.[71] Their rise in 1993 was tied to conditions of political turmoil and economic crisis in which the increasingly large number of school drop-outs and other young men with nothing to do and no hope for further education or wage employment found a life of excitement in armed bands. Originally local militias organized to defend their lands against encroachment by outsiders, these fighters have grown so much in both organization and operational capacity that they have become a major social force. Unfortunately, they lack the kind of leadership and training necessary to acquire political discipline and a scientific understanding of reality; to liquidate what Cabral has referred to as 'remnants of tribal mentality'; and to abandon those 'rites and practices which are incompatible with the rational and national character of the struggle'.[72]

These organizational resources are needed for the FAP to become more discerning in their definitions of friend and foe, as well as their targets. Collaborating with Kabila and the *interahamwe* on the assumption that 'the enemy of my enemy is my friend', and using indiscriminate violence against innocent Banyamulenge and other Congolese Tutsi who have nothing to do with Rwanda's invasion and occupation of our country, are practices that are not compatible with the national character of the resistance. Working with the Mai-Mai and the Simba to correct these errors, to minimize the loss of life in their ranks, and to make them more effective in providing security to their respective local communities is a patriotic duty of the highest order.

Civil society and the struggle for peace and democracy In an article written in early November 1996 on the AFDL adventure, I indicated that Laurent Kabila had no strategic vision for the Congo's future and no organizational capacity to govern a modern state.[73] This was due to the fact that in over thirty years of a sporadic campaign of armed struggle, he 'had for all practical purposes become a typical African warlord rather than a revolutionary guerrilla leader. If he and his allies are to be congratulated for once again showing to the whole world the bankruptcy of the Mobutu regime ... they are far from being the liberators they hope to be.'[74]

The International Crisis Group aptly described Kabila as 'a ruler by default', and one who 'prefers sharing the country to sharing power'.[75] In a system of personal rule marked by the absence of statesmanship and regime building, Kabila relied for political control on a multiplicity of intelligence agencies and close relatives. These include his son Joseph, who served as deputy FAC chief of staff and commander of the land forces; Gaëtan Kakudji, the regime's number-two official and interior minister; and Mwenze Kongolo, a former Philadelphia (USA) bail-processing clerk who has served as minister of justice since leaving the interior ministry in 1998. Of Kabila's long-serving ministers, these two cousins of the president were the only two to avoid the frequent humiliation of spending a few weeks in prison for misbehaviour. As the

ICG pointed out, Kabila ran the country 'like the autocratic father at the head of a family enterprise', with leadership methods that did not differ 'fundamentally from those he practiced as a militia leader in Fizi-Baraka or while running his many Tanzanian businesses'.[76]

With political parties unable to function legally and incapable of working clandestinely, much of the fight against both external aggression and internal dictatorship has been led by civil society organizations, which have campaigned against the war; denounced the violation of human rights by the invading forces and their local allies, as well as by the Kabila regime; and kept the flame of the CNS alive. As reflected in the nine workshops at the nationwide gathering of civil society organizations held in Kinshasa from 6 to 9 October 1999, there are at least nine types of organization:

- human rights and civic education NGOs;
- development NGOs;
- humanitarian and relief organizations;
- women's organizations;
- religious organizations;
- youth organizations;
- labour unions;
- professional organizations; and
- press and cultural associations.

Within a few months of the outbreak of the war in 1998, these organizations formed a Campaign for Peace and launched a process of consultation and lobbying around the world to mobilize Congolese, African and world public opinion for peace in the Congo. Among the major consultations on building peace and democracy in the DRC are meetings held in Morat, Switzerland (November 1998), Antwerp, Belgium (January 1999), Montreal, Canada (February 1999), Kinshasa (October 1999), Paris (May 2000) and Cotonou, Benin (October 2000). As reflected in the final report of the Cotonou Conference, the basic positions of Congolese civil society on peace and democracy have remained more or less constant and include the following:[77]

- The inter-Congolese dialogue provided for in the Lusaka Agreement is the most appropriate forum for negotiating peace and for putting the democratization process back on track.
- The expected outcome of the national dialogue is a consensual legal and institutional framework for a peaceful transition to democracy, which includes the provisional institutions of the transition, a minimum government programme of action for the transitional

period, and a broad-based government of national unity to implement it.[78]

- The CNS framework should serve as the basis for governance during
  the transition and the subsequent regime.
- A constitutional commission should be set up to draft a new and
  permanent constitution for the country.
- An independent electoral commission should be established to organize all aspects of the electoral process.
- Taking power by the force of arms should not be allowed.
- Civil society should play an important role in the peace process, as
  well as in the management of the transition and the establishment
  of a new political order.

Congolese civil society organizations are by no means perfect. As social
actors in a country that for long has been marked by kleptocracy,
nepotism and dictatorship, they are not immune from corruption, opportunism and anti-democratic values and practices. Some of their
leaders are autocrats who do not tolerate dissent and internal democracy, while others see the setting up of NGOs as a means of satisfying
their pecuniary interests through foreign donations. There are those
who seek to curry official favours in order to be allowed to operate
without trouble, while others would challenge the regime only to be
noticed in order to gain appointment to senior government positions.
A recent example of this is Mme Marie-Ange Lukiana, who has been
politically active in women's organizations since the CNS, and who
entered the Kabila government as deputy minister of labour and social
security on 1 September 2000. Opportunism, it seems, is not an exclusively male phenomenon.

From Laurent Kabila to Joseph Kabila In spite of its evident limitations,
Congolese civil society was a major actor in the resistance to Kabila's
dictatorship, arbitrary rule and totalitarian project of governance based
on the Comités de pouvoir populaire (CPP).[79] These neighbourhood
groups, to which lumpen elements were greatly attracted, were supposed to serve as basic units of grassroots democracy and state power.
Doing everything to pre-empt the inter-Congolese dialogue according
to the Lusaka Agreement, Kabila proceeded to set up a hand-picked
legislative assembly in July 2000. A great admirer of the Ugandan model
of 'democracy without parties', Kabila also showed strong interest in
Mobutuism, from which he borrowed a number of features. These
included using Mobutu's pre-party organization, the CVR, as a model
for his CPP; military courts for trying civilians accused of violating the

ban on political activities; a reign of terror orchestrated by intelligence and paramilitary units; and a personality cult directed by the former chief architect of Mobutu's propaganda machine in the 1970s and 1980s, Dominique Sakombi Inongo.

Kabila's totalitarian project was diametrically opposed to the social and political democracy that has been on the national agenda since 1956, and to the democratic vision and legacy of the CNS. It could not satisfy the deepest aspirations of the Congolese people who, according to a well-informed observer, 'have succeeded in creating for themselves, during this period of aborted democratization, a space of freedom of which they have the right to be proud today'.[80] Whether it is the power monopoly of a single party, Chinese-style, or people's power committees with a providential leader at the apex in the Libyan or Ugandan fashion, the consequences for democracy and the rule of law are likely to be the same. They include considerable erosion of fundamental rights and liberties, the aggravation of poverty and social inequalities, and the persistence of the political crisis in the Congo.

Instead of going forward, this was a move backwards. Kabila squandered the political capital he earned in overthrowing Mobutu. On two separate occasions, he failed to seize a rare historic opportunity to unite the country behind him: in a collective effort to rebuild the social and economic infrastructure destroyed under the previous regime following his rise to power in May 1997; and in a patriotic war against the foreign invaders in August 1998. Instead of making common cause with the democratic forces that emerged from the CNS and thus merging the revolutionary legitimacy of overthrowing Mobutu with the democratic legitimacy of the CNS, he opted for personal rule in typical African fashion, with reliance on relatives and cronies. His death, apparently at the hands of Rachidi Kasereka, a bodyguard belonging to the corps of *kadogo* or child-soldiers, is symptomatic of the life of an adventurer who lacked any sense of statecraft and who was neither a wise patrimonial ruler nor a modern statesman. It is reported that his child-soldiers had no regular pay, and that when associates warned him of the danger that this represented, he dismissed their concerns with the saying that those kids were like his children. Although we may never know which of the different hypotheses about his assassination on 16 January 2001 is credible, it is evident that he will not be greatly missed by his compatriots and even by those governments that supported his war effort.

There are two main reasons for this, which Joseph Kabila must heed. Internally, the regime he inherited was lacking in vision, competence and concern with the plight of the Congolese people. It is partly for this reason that his father's associates found it convenient to designate him as successor. They did this as part of building a heroic myth around which they could hang on to power, the myth of an indefatigable fighter for national liberation and unity, whose exceptional legacy would be carried on under the leadership of his son. Externally, Laurent Kabila had become a great burden to his backers, who were annoyed by his lack of sincerity, or even simple manners. It was evident that he was a major stumbling-block to peace negotiations, and particularly the inter-Congolese dialogue, at the end of which new political institutions were to be established in the Congo. This is why the first preoccupation of the powers-that-be in Kinshasa was to establish his successor's credibility *vis-à-vis* the United Nations, major world powers and prominent African leaders such as Nelson Mandela and Thabo Mbeki.

Thus, after barely two weeks in office, Joseph Kabila set out on his first diplomatic mission, to Paris, Washington, New York and Brussels, where he seduced the international community with his apparent willingness to change course. As in the halcyon days of neocolonialism, a regime with no legitimacy at home, and itself a veritable insult to the Congolese people, rushed to seek legitimacy abroad. In any case, it remains to be seen whether this young man of 29 years of age with less than five years of permanent residence in the country can overcome the vested interests of his father's entourage to be able to negotiate peace and national reconciliation in good faith. Given his lack of political experience, he is vulnerable to all kinds of manipulation by his father's cousins and other relatives making up the regency in Kinshasa today.

What Laurent Kabila did not seem to understand, but ought to become crystal clear to Joseph Kabila, is that the current crisis of the state can be checked only with a legitimate and responsible government. This means a government with which the people can identify and consider as the one that best expresses their aspirations and best defends their interests. Such a government is possible only when it is constituted not by people co-opted on basis of kinship, friendship or blind allegiance to an 'enlightened guide' or providential man, but rather by women and men representing veritable democratic forces, imbued with patriotism and enjoying the people's confidence. With the upsurge of tribalism and regionalist tendencies, and given the interests at stake economically and strategically in the larger world, these women and men must of necessity be irreproachable nationalists, and personalities who would defend against all odds the highest interests of the Congolese nation.

If the elder Kabila was truly a tragedy and a real disaster for the Congo, it is not historically inevitable that his heir and successor in this new Congolese dynasty should turn out as a farce.[81] To avoid this fate, the young man should go to the school of the people who, in their political songs, 'street parliament' debates and carefully argued position papers by civil society organizations, continue to rally around the banner of the historical legacy of the Sovereign National Conference. For the foreseeable future, this popular and progressive legacy will remain the alpha and omega of democratic politics in the Congo.

Notes

1. As chief of staff of Mobutu's army, the general had positively responded to American pressures to avoid a battle for Kinshasa, and he was already collaborating with the incoming pro-Kabila forces.

2. Sebudandi and Richard, *Le drame burundais*, pp. 147–8.

3. Widely accepted as such, these population estimates are suspect, because of their fixed and unchanging nature.

4. Prunier, *Rwanda, 1959–1996*, pp. 13–19.

5. On Alexis Kagame and his influence as a historian of ancient Rwanda, see Newbury, *The Cohesion of Oppression*, note 13, pp. 247–8; Prunier, *Rwanda*, pp. 52–3.

6. Newbury, *The Cohesion of Oppression*, p. 52.

7. Ibid, p. 52.

8. Lemarchand, *Burundi*, p. 34.

9. See Prunier, *Rwanda*, pp. 59–72; Sebudandi and Richard, *Le drame burundais*, p. 156.

10. Prunier, *Rwanda*, p. 61.

11. *Manifeste des Bahutu*, cited in Prunier, *Rwanda*, p. 63. Italics in the original.

12. Respectively, Hutu Social Movement and Association for Mass Social Promotion.

13. Or Rwandan Democratic Movement/Party for the Emancipation of the Hutu.

14. Prunier, *Rwanda*, p. 66.

15. Mamdani, 'The political diaspora in Uganda and background to the RPF invasion', p. 321. According to Mamdani, nearly a quarter of the 16,000 NRA guerrillas in January 1986 were Banyarwanda (p. 317).

16. I was consulted by the OAU Secretariat in the setting up of the International Panel of Eminent Personalities on the Genocide in Rwanda, and I served as one of the experts invited to Addis Ababa in February 2000 to review and edit the preliminary report of the panel.

17. I have two reliable sources for this plan. The first is a group of Habyarimana's aides, including a legal adviser in the president's office, who were left behind in Dar es Salaam because there was not enough space for them on their president's plane once he decided to take the Burundi party with him. I met them in July 1994 while watching a World Cup match on television in the lobby

of the Kilimandjaro Hotel. The second source is a close friend of Mpinga's, to whom he had confided that had he gone to Dar es Salaam, he would have probably died with Habyarimana. Mpinga died a month later in a plane crash near N'Djili Airport in Kinshasa, while returning from Gbadolite. While there is no conclusive evidence, sabotage cannot be ruled out as a cause of the crash.

18. *Akazu*, or 'little house' in Kinyarwanda, refers to a clique of insiders who call the shots at the royal or presidential court.

19. A Canadian newspaper, the *National Post*, is a champion of this thesis.

20. Gourevitch, *We wish to inform you that tomorrow we will be killed with our families*, p. 123.

21. According to Prunier, *Rwanda*, p. 482, *inyenzi*, or 'cockroaches' in Kinyarwanda, was the word used to designate Tutsi rebels in 1960–63, 'in part by contempt and in part because they moved mostly at night'. In the demonization logic of Hutu Power ideology, the label was extended to all Tutsi.

22. See Krop, *Le génocide franco-africain*, pp. 71–108.

23. *Newsweek*, International Edition, 21 November 1994, p. 30.

24. According to Erik Kennes, 'La guerre au Congo', in Reyntjens and Marysse, *L'Afrique des grands lacs*, p. 238, low-intensity skirmishes 'to test the resistance capacity of Zairian troops' began in early August 1996, while the first major attack on the camps with heavy artillery from Rwandan territory took place in September.

25. On the regional role in the fall of Mobutu, see Charles Onyango-Obbo, 'So who really did overthrow Mobutu?', *The East African*, July 1997; and Gérard Prunier, 'Forces et faiblesses du modèle ougandais', *Le Monde diplomatique*, February 1998.

26. On Kabila's past as a guerrilla leader and his business ventures, see Cosma, *Fizi 1967–1986*. According to the author, Kabila retained interest in his maquis between 1980 and 1985 to have access to the rich natural resources of the Fizi area, including gold, ivory and leopard skins. He resided in Tanzania under the name of Francis Mutware (pp. 75, 101 and 110–11).

27. Erik Kennes, 'L.-D. Kabila: a biographical essay', in Goyvaerts, *Conflict and Ethnicity in Central Africa*, p. 149, reports that this training took place in the Kasenga area.

28. Ibid., p. 152.

29. National Council for Resistance and Democracy.

30. People's Democratic Alliance.

31. Revolutionary Movement for the Liberation of Zaire.

32. See articles based on Kagame's interviews with John Pomfret in the *Washington Post*, 9 July 1997, and with Mahmood Mamdani in *The Mail & Guardian*, 8 August 1997.

33. To my knowledge, Kabila made no public statements about Kisase Ngandu, and no public inquiry was made concerning the circumstances of his death.

34. *Bulletin Quotidien de l'Agence Congolaise de Presse*, 28 January 1998. My own translation.

35. The report on the execution came from the Congolese human rights group Association africaine de défense de droits de l'homme (Asadho), through e-mail messages sent around the world and a statement by Asadho Vice-President Pascal Kambale to Radio France Internationale on 15 December 2000.

36. The expression 'another Bizimungu in Kinshasa' belongs to President Kabila, who provoked much laughter at the OAU special summit on conflicts held in December 1998 in Ouagadougou, Burkina Faso. He was referring to the nominal or figurehead role of Pasteur Bizimungu as Rwandan president between 1994 and 2000.

37. The record from our Bell Atlantic statement of 13 September 1998 (Account No. 301–847–3477–363–99) shows on p. 18 a call to Rwanda, number 250–85116, on 13 August at 2.48 p.m. EDT, and lasting exactly four minutes.

38. Oral communication from civil society organizations in the Congo.

39. See 'Une alliance hétéroclite sans dynamique intérieure', my interview with *Jeune Afrique Economie*, No. 270 (31 August to 13 September 1998), pp. 102–3.

40. The best-known exception to this was General Félicien Ilunga, former aide-de-camp to Mobutu and interior minister in Mobutu's last cabinet, who joined the rebellion in 1999 as the RCD-Goma defence minister. He died, apparently of heart failure, in June 2000.

41. But Dr Karaha, who did not even finish his internship as a general practitioner there, presents himself as a paediatrician!

42. President Kabila and some of his aides launched a hate campaign against the Tutsi in August 1998, resulting in indiscriminate violence by security forces and ordinary citizens against anyone thought to be a Tutsi and the detention of hundreds of Tutsi, allegedly 'for their own safety'.

43. Colette Braeckman, 'Les Tutsis congolais ont déjà perdu la guerre', *Le Soir*, 24 August 1998.

44. Personal communication from Joseph Mutambo and Müller Ruhambika.

45. Personal communication from Déogratias Symba.

46. *Info-Congo/Kinshasa* (Montreal), No. 161, May–June 2000. My own translation from the French.

47. *The Monitor* (Kampala), 3 July 2000.

48. Amnesty International, *Democratic Republic of the Congo*, p. 10.

49. Denis Tougas, 'Les transnationales minières à l'assaut du Zaïre comme du Congo', *Info-Zaïre*, No. 127, May 23, 1997.

50. Ibid. p. 3. At Tenke-Fungurume, the mineral content for copper is 4.42 per cent, while the one for cobalt is 0.33 per cent.

51. See Madsen, *Genocide and Covert Operations in Africa, 1993–1999*; Smith and Glazer, *Ces messieurs Afrique*.

52. See 'The rise of a new colonial power: Uganda's Brigadier Kazini sets up a system of governance for Ituri and Haute-Uele districts in the Congo', http://www.marekinc.com/NCNNews081902.html (19 August 1999); *The Monitor* (Kampala), 11 August 11 and 14 August 1999; *New Vision* (Kampala), 16 August 1999; and the *New York Times*, 16 August 1999. A splinter group from the Congolese Rally for Democracy led by Professor Wamba was set up in 1999 as the Rassemblement congolais pour la démocraite-Mouvement de libération (RCD-ML).

53. Tougas, 'Les transnationales minières', pp. 3–4.

54. *Info-Congo/Kinshasa*, No. 162, August–September 2000.

55. See particularly *The Monitor* of 11 August 1999. *New Vision* of 16 August 1999 quotes spokespersons for both governments stating that they have no intention of fighting each other and attributing the clashes to 'the confusion in Kisangani'.

56. 'What're Uganda, Rwanda beefing over in DRC?', *The Monitor* (Kampala), 11 August 1999.

57. See http://www.marekinc.com/NCNSpecialTantalum3.html

58. Tougas, 'Les transnationales minières', p. 6.

59. For Zimbabwe's role in the SADC peacekeeping strategy, see Michael Nyambuya, 'Zimbabwe's Role as Lead Nation for Peacekeeping Training in the SADC Region', in Malan, *Resolute Partners*, pp. 90–6. General Nyambuya later served as the first field commander of Zimbabwean troops in the Congo.

60. Frelimo and Renamo stand for, respectively, Frente de libertação de Moçambique (Mozambique Liberation Front) and Resistência nacional de Moçambique (Mozambique Resistance Movement).

61. Although Rautenback is reported to be close to Mugabe's entourage, a senior Zimbabwean cabinet minister told me on 11 August 1999 in Harare that he did not understand why President Kabila would appoint such a rogue entrepreneur to head the Congo's number-one parastatal.

62. Personal communication from Mbuji-Mayi.

63. International press reports, 31 August 2000.

64. Robert Block, 'Zimbabwe's elite turn strife in nearby Congo into a quest for riches', *Wall Street Journal*, 9 October 1998.

65. President Sam Nujoma made this point to the Tshisekedi government delegation at the 1993 OAU summit in Cairo, and he subsequently signed an agreement with President Kabila for the collection and transport to Namibia by pipeline of Congo River waters before they flow into the Atlantic.

66. Personal communication from Prime Minister Hage Geingob of Namibia in Ijebu-Ode, Nigeria, 21 December 2000.

67. Although it has joined the SADC and the Common Market for Eastern and Southern Africa (COMESA), the Congo remains a member of the Communauté économique des Etats de l'Afrique centrale (CEEAC, or the Economic Community of Central African States) and its security organs, the Comité

consultatif permanent des Nations uniés sur les questions de sécurité en Afrique centrale (United Nations Standing Advisory Committee on Security Questions in Central Africa) and the Conseil pour la paix et la sécurité (COPAX, or Council for Peace and Security).

68. President Alpha Oumar Konaré of Mali is one of the major defenders of this *droit d'ingérence*. His latest statement on the subject was made in his address to the 4th International Conference of New or Restored Democracries, organized by the Government of Benin with technical assistance from the United Nations and held in Cotonou from 4 to 6 December 2000.

69. See 'Mortality study, Eastern Democratic Republic of Congo', in http://www.theIRC.org/mortality.htm

70. Popular Forces of Self-Defence, also known as Popular Forces of Resistance.

71. These include *Bangilima, Batiri, Kasindiens* and *Katuku*, which 'are nothing more than different names for the same phenomenon', according to Koen Vlassenroot, 'Identity and insecurity: buildinjg ethnic agendas in South Kivu', in Doom and Gorus, *Politics of Identity and Economics of Conflict in the Great Lakes Region*, pp. 263–88, cited in René Lemarchand, 'Exclusion, marginalization and political mobilization: the road to hell in the Great Lakes', *L'Observatoire de l'Afrique centrale*, Vol. 3, No. 45, in http://www.obsac.com/OBSV4N45-LemarchandEng.html

72. Amilcar Cabral, 'National liberation and culture', in Cabral, *Unity and Struggle*.

73. Georges Nzongola-Ntalaja, 'Crisis in the Great Lakes Region', *Southern African Political and Economic Monthly*, November 1996, pp. 5–7. Also posted online by zaire-news listserve (André Kapanga); the Africa Policy and Information Center (APIC); and http://www.geocities.com/Capitol Hill/Lobby/1243/Nzongola.text; and reprinted as 'Conflict in Eastern Zaire', in *Africa Insight*, Vol. 26, No. 4 (1996), pp. 392–4.

74. *SAPEM*, November 1996, p. 7.

75. International Crisis Group, *Scramble for the Congo*, p. 40.

76. Ibid., p. 47.

77. *Rapport final de la Conférence de la société civile de la RDC à Cotonou, du 19 au 21 octobre 2000*.

78. One of the resolutions of the Cotonou conference is to exclude from public office all individuals 'directly implicated in war crimes, crimes against humanity, crimes of an economic character and others'.

79. People's Power Committees.

80. Gérard Papy of the Brussels daily *La Libre Belgique*, cited in Lejeune, *Laurent-Désiré Kabila, militant nationaliste congolais*, p. 83. My own translation.

81 Following the Marxian adage, quoted in the Introduction (n. 20) that history repeats itself, 'the first time as tragedy, the second time as farce'.

CHAPTER 8

Conclusion

§ SINCE 1956, the people of the Congo have waged a major struggle for freedom, development and other democratic rights, with the hope of improving their lot and ensuring a better future for their children. The struggle has gone through four periods, corresponding to the fight for independence (1956–60), the revolt against the failure of the post-colonial state to fulfill the expectations of independence (1963–68), opposition to one-party dictatorship and support for multiparty democracy (1969–97), and the current resistance against external aggression and new forms of dictatorship internally. This book provides a survey of these struggles, in which ordinary people have played a crucial role in the resistance against repression, and explains why the ultimate objectives for which they have made numerous sacrifices are yet to be achieved. The book attributes the failure of the Congolese democracy movement in this regard to its own weaknesses, particularly the political culture and class interests of those who have assumed its leadership, and the constraints of the international environment.

A tradition of popular resistance to illegitimate power and arbitrary rule had grown out of primary resistance to colonial domination and repression, of the prophetic religious movements, and of peasants' and workers' revolts during the first half of the twentieth century. Areas in which these manifestations of anticolonial resistance occurred became very receptive to the propaganda of radical nationalist parties such as Abako, Balubakat, Cerea, MNC/L and PSA. Once the political agitation for independence was launched in 1956, the initiative passed progressively from the *évolués* to the masses of the people, who transformed Kasa-Vubu's oratorical slogan of *indépendance immédiate* into a nonnegotiable demand on 4 January 1959. The attainment of national independence in 1960 is the single most important achievement of the democracy movement in the twentieth century. Unfortunately, the major outcome of this momentous event was to allow the petty bourgeois leadership of the independence movement to become a part, however small and underdeveloped, of the international bourgeoisie. Members of the political class became more preoccupied with increasing and protecting their acquired privileges than with helping to meet the popular expectations of independence. They betrayed the deepest aspirations of the people.

This betrayal of the anticolonial alliance formed the basis of the next period of the struggle, in which it was once again ordinary people who coined the strategic objective as the attainment of a 'second independence'. Under the leadership of politicians from the progressive coalition of former Prime Minister Patrice Lumumba, the mass democractic movement posed a serious threat to the neocolonial state under the control of moderate leaders led by the Binza Group. While Mulele's revolutionary experiment held some promise, it was too isolated and too limited in its impact to give a significant impetus to the effort to dismantle the neocolonial state. CNL leaders, on the other hand, behaved in the same manner as the Western-backed politicians in Kinshasa, being concerned above all with serving their own narrow class interests. Thus, due to its own political limitations and an unfavourable international environment dominated by the Cold War, the second independence movement was in the end crushed by a counterinsurgency effort led by the United States. Resistance against the neocolonial state was met head on by the Western-led repression against progressive forces.

Mobutu, who had betrayed his mentor Lumumba in the service of Uncle Sam and the West, was the main beneficiary of this effort. From 1965 to 1990, he ruled the Congo as a private preserve, building in the process a system of personal rule, nepotism and corruption that eventually resulted in state decay. The fragile nature of his seemingly omnipotent regime was already exposed in 1977 and 1978, during the two Shaba wars, in which his armed forces proved incapable of fighting an armed group, in this case the FLNC. Once again, he had to rely on external support to repress the resistance against his dictatorship and reign of terror. When that support wavered following the end of the Cold War, he was forced to give in to the democratic opposition's demand for a sovereign national conference.

The struggle for multiparty democracy gave a new impetus to the mass democratic movement, whose weight was felt in the CNS deliberations, including the 1992 election of Tshisekedi as prime minister of the government charged with managing the democratic transition. The transition itself was a tragic failure, thanks to the errors and weaknesses of the opposition, the violent backlash against democracy by Mobutu and his entourage, and the indifference or even hostility of the major powers in the international community, particularly France and the United States. While Paris was openly hostile to Tshisekedi, Washington preferred a strongman to a democratically elected leader accountable to his national constituency. This is why they both embraced Kengo, a technocrat who had no political base, and who was equally backed by the Bretton Woods institutions.

When the United States finally resolved to let go of Mobutu, he was unceremoniously removed from power by a coalition of regional states led by Uganda and Rwanda. Having ignored, and even disparaged, the remarkable expression of the popular will through the CNS, Washington gave its green light to Museveni and Kagame to invade the Congo and install Kabila as president. Once the latter proved his incompetence and sought to be independent of godfathers, big and small, the very governments that had imposed him on the Congolese people once again invaded the country with the aim of replacing Kabila with a more pliable puppet. For the Congolese democracy movement, the new situation calls for a double assault on the external aggressors and their local allies, on the one hand, and on the internal forces of dictatorship, on the other. The popular forces of resistance known as Mai-Mai and Simba have taken up the first challenge, but they cannot be expected to prevail under their present level of material and political organization. With political parties and activities banned, civil society organizations became the last rampart against the flagrant violation of human rights by both the invading forces and the Kabila regime. They held high the banner of democracy in the Congo.

How do we explain the failure of resistance against oppression and the prevalence of repression in Congolese history? Why, in other words, has the democracy movement failed to eradicate the persistence of personal rule in the Congo? What lessons have we learned in 45 years of struggle for freedom and development? Answers to these questions may be found by examining the internal and external environments in which the Congolese democracy movement has evolved.

Internal Political Limitations

Of the two, it is the internal environment that is crucial as the principal stage of the confrontation between the forces of change and those of the status quo. While this is the primary contradiction, a secondary contradiction exists between the deepest aspirations of the masses, who constitute the rank and file of the movement, and the political culture and class interests of its leadership, however well meaning it might be. Generally, the people have sought a radical or fundamental change likely to impact on their lives in a positive way. On the other hand, the politicians who arise to lead the movement are for the most part self-centred seekers of political power and material benefits. They are not interested in transforming the state radically by democratizing it and increasing its capacity to serve the people. This was the case with the *évolués*, who were fighting to integrate the top layers of colonial society; the Lumumbists, who wanted to regain the power they had lost to the Binza Group; and the so-called radical opposition under Tshisekedi, which was more preoccupied with getting rid of Mobutu and his cronies than with dismantling the system he had created in order to make the state responsive to the basic needs of the people.

With the possible exception of Mulele, the major leaders of the democracy movement were élitist, and their conception of democracy did not go beyond the bourgeois liberal brand of representative democracy in which the people choose members of the élite who are going to govern them. Parliamentarism was so appealing as a mode of politics that even the most radical form of urban-based grassroots politics, the *parlementaires-debout* phenomenon of the 1990s, was inspired by it. However, this and other popular forms of politics were not welcomed by the élite, because they were independent mass initiatives, which the leaders could not control. Most of the prominent politicians then seemed to agree with Monsignor Monsengwo that important matters of state should be decided by leaders behind closed doors, away from the watchful eyes of the people.

This is a reflection of a political culture in which opportunism takes precedence over principle, in such a way that decisions taken at democratic gatherings like the national conference could easily be overturned through horse-trading or deal-making. Moreover, most leaders also fail to honour the agreements to which they subscribe in negotiations. Even signed agreements are simply ignored when they no longer conform to one's interests. Interminable negotiations over the spoils of the political game, endless splits within parties, and the shameless shifting from one political camp to another (*vagabondage politique*) are typical manifestations of this political culture in the Congo.

The cultural and material conditions of life among the masses are also a factor in the success and failure of the democracy movement. The growing poverty in which the majority of workers and the lower petty bourgeoisie find themselves since the breakdown of much of the modern sector of the economy in 1991 makes it very difficult to sustain resistance through political mobilization and organization. It has, in other words, contributed to sapping the combativeness, resiliency and other strengths of the mass democratic movement. With so many essential public services broken down, and so much time spent on finding food or making ends meet generally, it is difficult, if not impossible, to organize and sustain a general strike, even in a politically sophisticated city such as Kinshasa. The stay-at-home strikes (*opérations ville morte*) that were so successful in undermining Mobutu's authority between 1990 and 1992 are not likely to have the same effect today. Although the modern sector of the economy and the public infrastructure of social services have collapsed, traditional solidarity mechanisms continue to help people survive. This also helps to diminish the urgency of organized action against the state.

As for cultural factors, it can be shown that the very elements that help to weaken the enemy and give the movement its basic strength in the short term also undermine it in the long run. For example, resort to cultural values and symbols, including memories of the precolonial past, may be effective in politically mobilizing people. On the other hand, it can also be effectively exploited by the enemy to divide people along ethnic lines. This tactic was successfully used by the Belgian colonialists to fan ethnic hatred during the pre-independence period, and by the counterinsurgency against the second independence movement. It is being used by the occupying forces in the northeast to weaken resistance to their aggression, as in the case of the Hema–Lendu conflict. Similarly, reliance on religious beliefs tends to undermine recourse to sound strategy and tactics in guerrilla warfare, as well as active political work, as people have placed their faith in magical water, words and charms when facing the enemy in battle, or entrusted their political deliverance to a saviour called 'Moises'. In addition to Mulele and Tshisekedi, other heroes with saintly credentials include the prophet Kimbangu, the officially proclaimed national hero Lumumba and the late Cardinal Malula, who were often called upon in prayer meetings to intercede with God for Congo's deliverance from Mobutu.

In a society in which hero worship is not incompatible with traditional culture, a single charismatic individual emerged as the standard-bearer of the democracy movement in each of the first three periods: Lumumba, between 1958 and 1960; Mulele, from 1963 to 1968; and Tshisekedi, from 1988 to 1997. But the hopes raised by each of these men ended up being dashed. For, however successful they were in mobilizing the masses, their victories over the enemy were short-lived. They were incapable of delivering the goods to their followers, since they were defeated before they could govern effectively. Both Lumumba and Tshisekedi lost to their enemies in the political class, who relied on their control over the key organs of state power such as the repressive apparatus and the central bank, as well as on Western support, to win the power struggle. Mulele, of course, never managed to lay his hands on the reins of power.

The three leaders failed in part because they were politically isolated. They did not succeed in building a strong political organization likely to wrestle political power from the enemy so as to govern effectively, on the one hand, and to protect themselves from external interference and aggression, on the other. Mass support and adulation in the absence of a strong organization and an appropriate political strategy are not enough for effective political change. Lumumba, Mulele and Tshisekedi were also weakened by the deals and compromises they were forced to make as part of a political culture that puts less emphasis on respect for the democratic process of open debate and transparent decision-making than on deal-making among politicians.

External Constraints

Throughout the 116 years of Congo's existence as a state, external interests have always been a major factor of the political equation. The strategic position of the country in the centre of Africa and its enormous natural wealth have made it a prime candidate for imperial ambitions and the envy of adventurers, mercenaries and looters of all kinds. The presence on its territory of armies from at least seven African states at the end of the twentieth century had its antecedents in the European and African armies that came to pacify Katanga in the wake of the Shaba wars of 1977 and 1978; white mercenaries from all over Europe and Southern Africa during much of the 1960s; the first major UN peacekeeping force of the postcolonial era, with a civilian component of Dag Hammarskjöld's nation-builders; and the Leopoldian occupation force with officers from Europe and America and soldiers from West Africa between 1885 and 1908. These armies were nothing but foot soldiers in a long chain of command behind which sat the dominant economic interests of the contemporary world. For the Congo, the articulation of the dialectic of resistance and repression with respect to both the major powers and the networks of transnational criminality involving mercenaries and other merchants of death is not a new phenomenon.

The strategic objective since 1884 has remained the same. It is, above all, to prevent the country from falling into the wrong hands, politically speaking, so as to maximize the extraction of its bountiful natural wealth to the benefit of these dominant interests. Thus, to prevent one of them from gaining undue advantage over the others by owning this precious piece of the 'African cake', the major powers of the day agreed to bestow ownership on King Leopold II of little Belgium. While France expected the vain and overly ambitious monarch to fail and thus that France could reap the spoils, Britain, Germany and the Unites States were primarily interested in using the Congo Free State as a test in the Congo River basin for free trade and an open-door policy on investment. In order to succeed and maintain his international credibility as a legitimate member of the world capitalist club, the king and his men on the ground set up a brutal exploitation regime that resulted in a major holocaust at the end of the nineteenth century and the beginning of the last century. The holocaust gave rise to two movements whose legacy is particularly positive with regard to human rights, namely, the Congo Reform Association, the first international humanitarian organization of the twentieth century, and the first nationwide inter-ethnic resistance to repressive and arbitrary rule in the Congo between 1895 and 1908.

The successor colonial state followed in the king's footsteps, by attempting to monopolize control over the Congo's economy. However, Belgium was too small and too weak to stand up to the hegemonic interests, particularly in the mining sector, in which Britain and the United States had each an interest, the first as a major investor through its South African partners in UMHK and TCL, and the second with the aim of acquiring strategic minerals like cobalt and uranium. The supply by the UMHK of the uranium used in the first atomic weapons, the bombs that were dropped on Hiroshima and Nagasaki, made the Congo an important element of Washington's geopolitical strategy in the context of the Cold War.

Consequently, the mass democractic movement was perceived less as a struggle for fundamental human rights than as an opportunity for communists and fellow travellers to infiltrate the movement and indoctrinate unsophisticated Africans. Lumumba's militant independence day speech, which told truths that were obvious to Africans, and his request for Soviet military assistance to counter Belgian aggression and the Katanga secession, earned him the label of 'communist' or 'communist sympathizer' from American policymakers, and a presidential assassination order from Dwight D. Eisenhower, the US president, in August 1960. Politicians were automatically classified into 'pro-Western' and 'anti-Western' or 'pro-communist', and those thought to be in the second category were targeted for elimination from the political scene. This is what happened to Lumumba's colleagues and coalition partners under the rule of the 'moderates' led by Mobutu and the Binza Group.

Having used the UN umbrella as a cover for its own initiatives between 1960 and 1964, the US responded to the internal security gap created by the departure of UN troops with a paramilitary campaign under the CIA against the second independence movement. This included a CIA-operated air force with anti-Castro Cuban pilots. While the newly created OAU was attempting to resolve the Congo crisis peacefully under the mediation of Jomo Kenyatta, the Kenyan president, the USA and Belgium intervened militarily on 24 November 1964, to break the back of the movement at the CNL command and control centre in Kisangani. A year later, Mobutu staged his second coup with US and Western support, and proceeded to build an externally backed kleptocracy.

The external constraints on the post-Cold War democratization process are also described in the book. The lack of support for the CNS and the celebration of the managerial talents of the 'new breed of African leaders' do clearly indicate that the Western powers and the international financial institutions under their control are not sincere in their avowed support for 'democracy' in Africa. Since it is no longer politically correct to say that Africa 'is not ready for democracy', those who support incumbent regimes prefer to say that 'Africans will democratize at their own pace and their own rhythm'. For the moment, democracy seems to be identified with the holding of elections, while emphasis is placed on good governance, particularly the strengthening of the rule of law, enhancing the capacity of the public sector to manage the nation's affairs effectively and efficiently, and improving the administration of justice. These are also seen as conditions likely to create an enabling environment for private investment.

Thus the need to adapt Africa to the logic of global capitalist expansion may not necessarily be compatible with the requirements of democracy as a process of expanding the realm of freedom and capability for human beings to lead meaningful lives. Governments that are responsive to mass democratic movements need to spend more rather than less on basic social services, provide more employment opportunities than lay off those already employed, and be more attentive to their constituencies than to the donor community. For democracy is meaningless without economic and social rights. It means nothing to people who cannot eat properly, have a roof over their heads, find a job, send their children to school, and have access to a minimum of decent healthcare. These are some of the basic social services and economic opportunities that only governments can help provide in times of economic crisis.

One of the reasons for the Western reluctance to support the CNS was precisely the difference in vision concerning state policy in the post-Mobutu era. A major bone of contention concerned Western responsibility in political crimes such as Lumumba's assassination and the destruction of entire villages through counterinsurgency activities. Were reparations to be paid for these crimes against humanity, and who would be responsible for them? More importantly, there was the question of Western complicity in economic crimes, such as the construction of so many white elephants that have increased indebtedness without contributing to economic growth, and the loaning of money to a regime that everyone knew did not spend it on development. The CNS adopted the principle that 'odious debts', or those debts that did not benefit the country and its people, and one-sided contracts (*contrats léonins*) had to be repudiated. In other words, the Congo was not obligated to repay those debts that did not benefit the economy in a tangible manner, and all outstanding debts and contracts had to be renegotiated with a view to determining where the money went and who owed whom as far as the balance was concerned. This was seen as an ominous and precedent-setting development with negative consequences for international finance capital. It is one of the reasons why Monsignor Monsengwo did not allow the public reading and discussion of the reports of the assassination and ill-gotten property commissions in plenary session.

The conference also challenged one of the cardinal tenets of the current *pensée unique* of liberal capitalism, according to which the state should radically reduce its role in the economy. The CNS voted against a wholesale privatization of state enterprises, as this meant selling them on the cheap to foreign interests and to wealthy Congolese who had actually destroyed these formerly successful ventures through systematic pillage. The radical tone of plenary discussions on this matter, which were influenced by representatives of parastatal employees and of trade unions, did not please Western embassies in Kinshasa and those elements of the political class who sought to be imposed as rulers from the outside rather than be chosen by the people.

Although Tshisekedi did nothing with respect to implementing the radical economic agenda of the CNS, the Western powers and the Bretton Woods institutions did not trust him. Recalling his refusal of the post of prime minister in July 1991 because of popular pressure, they renewed their faith in technocrats with no national constituency who could be counted upon to implement anti-labour, anti-people, and therefore anti-democratic policies. They rejected the democratically elected prime minister, and one who had more votes than most prime ministers elected in parliament worldwide, because their interests would be better served by Mobutu, Monsengwo, and the technocrats associated with Kengo wa Dondo. When he returned to the post of prime minister in 1994, Kengo had no problem with letting civil servants go unpaid for months, so he could please his Western patrons by making regular payments on the external debt and making deals with Canadian and other foreign interests for the eventual privatization of parastatals.

Kengo's return to the prime minister's office constituted in a way the restoration of the Mobutu regime, whose power and authority had been deeply eroded by the CNS. In the eyes of the people, his close identification with Mobutu doomed his chances of legitimacy. As one of the longest-serving members of the *nomenklatura*, he also understood the limits of his power in the Mobutu system. Duplicitous and artful with words and figures, he enjoyed fooling both foreign emissaries and members of the political class. He and Kamanda, the interior minister, did their best to sabotage the very mission with which his government was entrusted, namely, the organization of national elections. In the end, he had nothing to show for his two and a half years in office, except the criminal hiring of Serbian and Croatian mercenaries to fight against the AFDL and its Rwandan, Ugandan and Angolan backers. Along with Mobutu's generals, he had helped erode the capacity of the state for governance, creating a vacuum that Museveni and Kagame were ready to fill, for reasons that have already been described and need not be repeated here.

The Way Forward

By the end of the twentieth century, the Congolese democracy movement had been so weakened that it could no longer hope to realize the high levels of mass mobilization as in 1959–60, 1963–64 and 1991–92. As a movement of the working people (peasants, workers, the lumpen-proletariat and the lower petty bourgeoisie), it was incapable of throwing up its own organic leaders to lead the political struggle nationally, as the mass democratic movement has at times succeeded in doing in Southern Africa. With opposition political parties and activities banned by the Kabila regime, civil society organizations have attempted to fill the void, but they lack the capacity to provide the necessary leadership to the movement.

Why did a movement that seemed to be on the brink of victory in 1992 descend to such a low level of activity by the end of the decade? What can be done to reverse the trend so that the mass democratic movement can once again mobilize the Congolese people to realize their dream of freedom and material prosperity? This book has attempted to offer answers to these questions.

Hope and despair are two words that best explain the difference in the levels of mass mobilization between the earlier three periods and the fourth. During the first period, the winds of change characteristic of the decolonization era in Africa led to the rising expectations associated with independence. Although the latter failed to meet these expectations, hope was soon rekindled by the second independence movement. The success of the popular rising against a neocolonial regime in Congo-Brazzaville and the great inroads of the national liberation struggle in East and Southern Africa provided an added impetus for the war against the neocolonial state in Congo-Kinshasa. In the early 1990s, great expectations for freedom and development were once again possible as a result of the new democratization wave then sweeping Africa.

The situation changed drastically in the Congo, first with the failure of the transitional framework adopted at the CNS, and then with the disillusionment with Laurent Kabila, whose rise to power had temporarily raised new hopes for the future. Instead of joining hands with the democratic forces energized by the CNS, Kabila proceeded to ignore and even disparage the legacy of the national conference. Bent on imposing his own mode of governance borrowed chiefly from Museveni's 'movement regime' or 'no-party democracy', he sought to make the lumpenproletariat his social base. In 1998, the war of aggression by Rwanda and Uganda gave him a second chance to put together a national united front with the democratic opposition and civil society organizations against the invaders and their Congolese lackeys. Instead of uniting the country and defending its honour with its own daughters and sons, he was so concerned with his own selfish interests that he preferred to entrust the country's defence to foreign armies, whose presence was no less detrimental for its inhabitants than that of the invading forces.

Thus, from 1994 to the end of the decade, the prevailing sentiment was that of despair. Under the circumstances and given the growing economic crisis, the organic intellectuals of workers, peasants and the lower petty bourgeoisie were less inclined to mobilize their followers to fight for the promised land of milk and honey in Central Africa, than to lead them into a heavenly city of peace, abundance and everlasting joy. Religion took over politics, and the mass democratic movement lacked the political and organizational resources required to fight both the Kabila dictatorship and the external aggression. The only exceptions to this sombre picture were the Mai-Mai, who took up arms against the aggressors and their local puppets, and civil society organizations, which resisted against the violation of human rights by Kabila, the rebels and the invaders. Due to their political and organizational limitations, the popular forces involved in armed resistance can easily be led astray, as in their unfortunate collaboration with Kabila, the *interahamwe* and Hutu extremists from Burundi. As for civil society organizations, they can play useful political roles in consciousness raising through civic education and in political mobilization though human rights campaigns. However, most of them are incapable of providing leadership to the mass democratic movement because they are too issue-specific, have no nationwide organization, and are too comfortable in their well-equipped downtown offices to develop close ties with the urban and rural masses.

For the moment, the most urgent task on the road to political recovery in the Congo is the holding and successful completion of a national dialogue as stipulated in the Lusaka Agreement. With the death of Laurent Kabila and the apparent willingness of his son and successor Joseph to let the peace and reconciliation processes go forward, hope has once again been revived concerning the Congo's future. By bringing together the Kabila government, the rebels, the unarmed opposition and civil society organizations, the dialogue represents yet another attempt since the CNS to put the democratization process back on track. Such a process should lead at the very minimum to the restoration of the liberal democratic regime of the early 1960s, which is far better than the absence of any democracy. For democratic governance is not only essential for addressing the peace and security needs of the country. It is also indispensable for laying down the foundations for increasing the freedom and capabilities people need to lead meaningful lives, or for social and economic democracy. Increasing capacity for freedom and a better standard of living cannot be obtained under an undemocratic government, however young and new its breed of leaders might be, or under a government that excludes other political and social forces from equitable participation in running the country's affairs. For the Congo, as for Rwanda, Burundi and Uganda, this implies the resolution of the crises of democratic transition by putting an end to governments established by the force of arms, and embarking on the path of genuine national reconciliation, justice and inclusiveness. That would be a fitting fulfilment of the objectives of the Congolese democracy movement in the twentieth century.

Chronology

1400   The Kongo kingdom, whose name would eventually be adopted for the country as a whole, arose as a major state in Central Africa during the fifteenth century due in part to a prosperous economy based on agriculture and long-distance trade.

1482   First known encounter between the Kongo and Europe, when the Portuguese traveller Diego Cão arrives at the mouth of the Congo River and mistakes the latter's local name of 'Nzadi' for 'Zaïre'.

1665   The Battle of Ambuila, in which the Portuguese defeat the Kongo, would eventually lead to the disintegration of the Kongo kingdom into autonomous chiefdoms.

1700   Kimpa Vita, a young woman prophet, leads resistance to foreign domination in an effort to restore the unity and integrity of the Kongo kingdom.

1855   Msiri, a Nyamwezi trader, brings his caravan west of the Luapula river and settles in Katanga, where he establishes the state of Garenganze with its capital at Bunkeya.

1871   Henry Morton Stanley, an American journalist, finds Dr David Livingstone, the British missionary, at Ujiji on the Tanzanian shores of Lake Tanganyika, and rekindles through his reports European interest in colonizing Africa.

1874   Stanley begins his travel across the continent from Zanzibar, and is accompanied through eastern Congo by the Zanzibari slave trader Hamed bin Muhammed el-Murjebi, who is better known by his caravan name of Tippu Tip.

1876   King Leopold II of the Belgians convenes the Brussels International Geographical Conference, which decides to establish the Association internationale africaine (AIA).

1877   Stanley reaches the mouth of the Congo River, and returns to Europe with the aim of reclaiming the Congo basin for his native Great Britain.

1878   Taking advantage of Britain's lack of interest in the Congo, King Leopold sets up the Comité d'études du Haut-Congo (CEHC) with Belgian banker Léon Lambert, British shipping magnate William

Mackinnon and others, for a feasibility study on colonizing the Congo basin.

1879   The CEHC becomes the Association internationale du Congo (AIC), an international organization with its own flag, a blue standard with a single gold star in the middle, and Stanley leads its expedition to acquire for the Belgian monarch 'a slice of this magnificent African cake' between 1879 and 1884.

1882   Tippu Tip establishes a Swahili political estate east of the Lualaba River.

1884   22 April: The United States becomes the first country in the world to recognize King Leopold's claims to the Congo.

15 November: The Berlin West African Conference is convened to discuss the freedom of navigation and commerce in the Congo basin, with the AIC interests being represented by the Belgian delegation.

1885   26 February: At the closing ceremony of the Berlin Conference, German Chancellor Otto von Bismarck reads a letter from the AIC informing the conference of its recognition as a sovereign state by the major powers, and the delegates respond with a standing ovation and wild applause.

29 May: The Congo Free State (CFS) is officially established by royal decree.

1 August: King Leopold's official accession as king-sovereign of the Congo.

1888   John Dunlop, a Scottish veterinary surgeon, invents the pneumatic or inflatable rubber tyre, leading to Edouard Michelin's patent of a tyre in 1891, a growing world market in rubber tyres and high demand for natural rubber in Europe.

1890   George Washington Williams, an African American historian and journalist, travels across the Congo and brings to the world the first detailed account of rubber-related and other atrocities, which he characterizes as 'crimes against humanity'.

Tippu Tip returns to retire in his native Zanzibar and leaves control over his political estate to his son Sefu and other Swahili-Arab lieutenants.

1891   18 April: The Reverend William Henry Sheppard, an African American, and the Reverend Samuel Lapsley found the American Presbyterian Congo Mission (APCM) at Luebo, in the Kasai region.

28 December: King Msiri's resistance against Leopold's rule is ended by his assassination by a CFS military officer.

1892   Resistance to the colonial conquest in the Swahili-Arab estate east of the Lualaba River, until 1894.

1893   Ngongo Lutete, former Tippu Tip's Tetela auxiliary turned CFS collaborator, is summarily executed by a Force publique (FP) officer.

1895   Kanyok uprising, led by Chief Kalenda, is put down by the FP.

        4 July: First major FP mutiny under Sergeant Kandolo at the Kananga (Luluabourg) garrison, would eventually lead to 13 years of armed resistance led by Corporals Kimpuki and Yamba-Yamba and Luba chief Kapepula.

1897   14 February: Second major mutiny of the FP at Ndirfi in northeastern Congo, results in a major anticolonial resistance in the east lasting until 1900.

1898   The Lower Congo railroad (between Kinshasa and the sea) is completed, at the cost of thousands of lives, including those of labourers from West Africa, Barbados and China.

1900   17 April: Third major FP mutiny, at the Shinkakasa garrison at Boma, is quickly repressed, thanks to the collaboration of West Africans under the leadership of Nigerian businessman Hezekiah Andrew Shanu.

        Outbreak of resistance by the Shi kingdom, which was not brought under control until 1916.

1901   Edmund Dene Morel, a young British shipping clerk, decides to devote himself to full-time investigative journalism on the gross violations of human rights in King Leopold's Congo.

1903:   Shanu begins to collaborate with Morel by sending him documents and other relevant information on atrocities in the Congo.

1904:   23 March: First meeting of the Morel's Congo Reform Association (CRA) is held in Liverpool's Philharmonic Hall.

        Shanu is entrapped by the police chief of Boma, denounced as Morel's accomplice and ostracized by Europeans, who boycott his businesses.

1905:   July: Facing economic ruin, Shanu commits suicide.

1906   18 October: Establishment of the Union minière du Haut-Katanga (UMHK), the giant mining company, with Belgian and British capital.

1907   Outbreak of resistance in the Luba-Katanga kingdoms of Kabongo and Kasongo Nyembo, which were not 'pacified' until 1917.

1908   The 23-year Leopoldian regime ends, as the Congo Free State becomes the Belgian Congo, a colony of Belgium.

1909   Dr William Sheppard's trial and acquittal in the libel suit by the Compagnie du Kasai, a rubber collection monopoly in western Kasai.

1916   The FP defeats German troops and occupies Rwanda and Burundi.

1921   6 April: Simon Kimbangu, a Baptist catechist and onetime manual worker, begins a prophetic ministry in Lower Congo, which leads to his arrest and life imprisonment, and gives rise to religious protest as one of the means of anticolonial resistance.

1923   Kitawala, a religious movement born out of the Watch Tower movement in Malawi and Zambia, quickly begins to spread in the eastern half of the Congo.

     As Ruanda-Urundi, Rwanda and Burundi become a mandated territory of the League of Nations under the administrative control of Belgium.

1925   Belgium annexes the mandated territory to the Congo to create a single administrative entity known as Congo belge et Ruanda-Urundi.

1931   Pende uprising, one of the major rural revolts in the Belgian Congo, takes place in the Kwilu region against the economic hardships imposed by the colonial state and the concession companies.

1941   4–9 December: UMHK mineworkers' general strike begins in Likasi and ends with the massacre of over one hundred strikers in Lubumbashi.

1944   February to May: Insurrection by soldiers, workers, peasants and white-collar employees along the line of rail from Kananga to Lubumbashi, begins on 20 February as a mutiny at the FP garrison in Kananga.

1945   Dockworkers' strike and demonstration at Matadi.

     Ruanda-Urundi becomes a UN trust territory under Belgian supervision.

1946   Joseph Kasa-Vubu, a Kongo intellectual and middle-level civil servant, gives a lecture in Kinshasa on 'the right of the first occupant'.

1948   The process of assimilating educated Africans or *évolués* begins in the Belgian Congo with the introduction of the 'social merit card'.

1950   Abako is established as an association for the promotion of Kongo language and culture.

1951   Simon Kimbangu dies in jail at Lubumbashi after 30 years of detention, a world record for a political prisoner.

1952   Another step in the assimilation process is taken with the introduction of the status of 'matriculation' or the designation of a certain category of *évolués* as honorary Europeans.

1954   The controversy over the establishment of public schools in the Congo plays a major role in politicizing the *évolués*, who are now beneficiaries of the importation of Belgian political organizations and quarrels in the colony.

Kasa-Vubu takes over the presidency of Abako with a determination to go beyond its original cultural agenda to deal with more general issues of social and political emancipation in the Congo.

1955   King Baudouin's visit to the Congo and his willingness to listen to the voices of the *évolués* help to strengthen those advocating political liberalization and power sharing with the African élite within a 'Belgo-Congolese community'.

1956   February: Professor A. A. J. Van Bilsen's pamphlet with a 'thirty-year plan for the political emancipation of Belgian Africa' is published in French translation.

2 July: A group of Catholic intellectuals known as Conscience africaine responds favourably to the Van Bilsen plan, with a manifesto published in *Courrier d'Afrique*, a Kinshasa newspaper.

23 August: A counter-manifesto by Abako rejects the plan and in presenting the group's position, Kasa-Vubu calls for 'immediate independence'.

1957   Abako wins an impressive victory in the municipal elections in Kinshasa.

1958   20 April: At his inauguration as the mayor of the Dendale *commune* or municipality in Kinshasa, Kasa-Vubu calls for the recognition of the Congo as a nation.

October: Patrice Lumumba, Joseph Ileo, Cyrille Adoula and Joseph Ngalula found the Mouvement national congolais (MNC), a nationwide political party.

December: Lumumba, Ngalula and Gaston Diomi attend the All-African People's Conference in Accra, Ghana.

28 December: Lumumba holds a mass rally in Kinshasa, to report to the nation on the Accra conference and to agitate for independence.

1959   4 January: Popular uprising for independence in Kinshasa.

13 January: The Belgian king and government announce their willingness to consider independence for the Congo.

April: First conference of Congolese political parties is held in Kananga.

July: King Mutara Rudahigwa of Rwanda dies in mysterious circumstances.

August: Violence erupts in Kananga, and Albert Kalonji, the MNC provincial leader, is relegated to Kole, in the Sankuru district.

October: Adoula, Ileo and Ngalula cause a split in the MNC, resulting in two wings, respectively led by Lumumba (MNC-Lumumba) and Kalonji (MNC-Kalonji).

11–12 October: The Luba–Baluba war erupts in the Kasai province.

29–30 October: The MNC-Lumumba Congress in Kisangani is followed by a popular insurrection, Lumumba's arrest and his relegation to the infamous underground prison at Likasi.

2 November: The Hutu uprising turns into a veritable pogrom against the Tutsi in Rwanda, and the FP occupies the territory.

December: Most political parties boycott elections for local government councils.

1960 20 January to 20 February: The Roundtable Conference on Congolese independence is held in Brussels, resulting in the decision for the Congo to obtain a total and unconditional independence on 30 June 1960.

26 April to 16 May: The Economic Roundtable Conference, held in Brussels to determine the economic future of the country, is virtually relegated to secondary importance by most political parties.

May: Elections for provincial assemblies and the national parliament are held.

June: Political jockeying following national elections results in Lumumba becoming prime minister and Kasa-Vubu the ceremonial head of state.

30 June: At the national independence ceremony, Prime Minister Lumumba responds to a patronizing speech by King Baudouin, with an unscheduled speech on the meaning of independence for the Congolese.

5–9 July: Mutiny of FP soldiers plunges the new state into crisis, but Lumumba attempts to control the situation with promotions and the restructuring the force into a national army, the Armée nationale congolaise (ANC).

10 July: Unilateral Belgian military intervention worsens the crisis.

11 July: With Belgian support, Moïse Tshombe, president of the Katanga provincial government, declares the secession of the province from the Congo.

12 July: President Kasa-Vubu and Prime Minister Lumumba appeal to the United Nations for UN troops to protect the country against external aggression and to restore its territorial integrity, an appeal to which the UN would later respond favourably.

8 August: Albert Kalonji proclaims the secession of South Kasai.

18 August: US President Dwight D. Eisenhower authorizes the assassination of Prime Minister Lumumba.

August–September: ANC troops on their way to Katanga are given orders to end the secession of South Kasai, and their actions result in large-scale massacres at Mbuji-Mayi and Kasengulu.

5 September: Using the Mbuji-Mayi massacre and its characterization as 'genocide' by UN Secretary-General Dag Hammarskjöld, President Kasa-Vubu dismisses Lumumba as prime minister, illegally.

14 September: With parliament having refused to endorse Kasa-Vubu's decision and renewed its confidence in Lumumba, ANC Chief of Staff Joseph-Désiré Mobutu stages his first military coup and replaces the legitimate government with a college of commissioners composed of university graduates and students.

24 November: In a credentials vote, the UN General Assembly favours Kasa-Vubu's delegation over the one representing the democratically elected government, thus endorsing Lumumba's dismissal.

27 November: A virtual prisoner in his own official residence in Kinshasa, Lumumba tries to break out of his isolation by fleeing to his political stronghold of Kisangani, where Deputy Prime Minister Antoine Gizenga had already established the legitimate government.

1–2 December: Lumumba is captured at Lodi, on the left bank of the Sankuru River, denied UN protection by the Ghanaian contingent at Mweka, and flown back to Kinshasa.

3 December: Lumumba is taken to the armoured brigade camp at Mbanza-Ngungu.

1961　16 January: Acting on behalf of the Congo Committee chaired by Prime Minister Gaston Eyskens and including African Affairs Minister Harold d'Aspremont Lynden and Foreign Minister Pierre Wigny, d'Aspremont Lynden issues an order to transfer Lumumba to the custody of secessionist leaders in Katanga.

17 January: Lumumba and two companions, Senate Vice-President

Joseph Okito and Youth and Sports Minister Maurice Mpolo, are severely beaten on the aeroplane flight to Katanga, tortured and assaulted by Katanga officials at a villa not too far from Lubumbashi's Luano Airport, and shot by an execution squad made up of Belgian military and police officers.

August: US and UN officials succeed in arranging for the formation of a government of national unity, with Adoula as prime minister and Gizenga as deputy prime minister.

1962   January: Gizenga is dismissed from the government, arrested and relegated to the Congo River island prison of Bula-Bemba.

September: Kalonji's own chief of staff ends the South Kasai secession, acting on instructions and with help from Kinshasa.

1963   January: After a month of fighting, UN troops defeat Tshombe's soldiers and white mercenaries to end the Katanga secession.

July: Pierre Mulele returns home after 15 months of guerrilla training in China and begins making preparations for a revolutionary struggle in Kwilu.

13–15 August: A popular uprising known as 'Three Glorious Days' ends the reactionary regime of the priest-president Fulbert Youlou in Congo-Brazzaville, and creates space for political organization by progressive forces across the river.

29 September: Kasa-Vubu dismisses parliament for the second time during his tenure, in a move intended to weaken the Lumumbist forces.

3 October: The Lumumbists establish the Conseil national de libération (CNL), an umbrella organization designed to coordinate their struggle to regain power, and move to establish its headquarters in Brazzaville.

1964   January: Mulelist forces begin a full-fledged guerrilla war in Kwilu, while Gaston Soumialot and Laurent Kabila start preparations for the armed struggle in the east.

15 April: The CNL's eastern front insurrections begin under the leadership of Soumialot and Kabila.

15 May: The CNL takes over the city of Uvira and begins expanding its operations geographically.

30 June: UN troops leave the Congo, as their peacekeeping mandate expires.

July: Tshombe returns home from exile in Spain to become prime minister of the Congo.

4 August: The CNL scores its biggest victory by taking over the city of Kisangani.

September: Establishment of the People's Republic of the Congo in Kisangani, with Christophe Gbenye as president, Soumialot as defence minister, and Thomas Kanza as foreign minister.

24 November: Operation Red Dragon, with US planes dropping Belgian paratroopers at Kisangani and providing air cover for a column of mercenaries and élite units of the Congolese army led by Belgian Colonel Frédéric Vandewalle, ends the People's Republic and demoralizes the CNL.

1965   May: Free and fair elections are held in the Congo, with the results widely accepted nationwide and Tshombe's popularity on the increase.

24 November: Using as pretext the row between Tshombe and Kasa-Vubu, Mobutu stages his second coup and becomes Congo's ruler.

1966   May: Four prominent leaders – Jérome Anany, Emmanuel Bamba, Evariste Kimba and Alexandre Mahamba – are publicly hanged in Kinshasa on trumped-up charges of plotting a coup.

The Bakajika Law establishes the state's rightful claim to all land and mineral rights in the country, thus ending all colonially inherited concessionaire system.

1967   January: Using the Bakajika Law, Mobutu nationalizes UMHK by transforming it into a state enterprise.

May: Mobutu's establishes his own political party, the MPR.

1968   3 October 1968: Pierre Mulele is assassinated by Mobutu's generals, after returning to Kinshasa under a false promise of amnesty by the Congolese president.

1969   4 June: Massacre of university students in Kinshasa, following a peaceful demonstration.

1970   Mobutu reneges on his promise to step down after five years of military rule and establishes a single-party regime.

1971   June: Kinshasa and Lubumbashi university students are forcibly enrolled in the army, for daring to commemorate the 1969 massacre.

July: The Catholic University of Lovanium and the Protestant Congo Free University are nationalized to create a single state university with campuses at Kinshasa, Lubumbashi and Kisangani.

27 October: Mobutu unilaterally changes the country's name from 'Congo' to 'Zaire'.

1972   Arbitrary measures associated with the policy of 'authenticity' are announced and include the ban on 'foreign' or Christian names and the ban on Western suits and ties for men and Western dresses and trousers for women.

1973   30 November: By his 'Zairianization' measures, Mobutu expropriates foreign-owned small and medium businesses and gives them to members of his *nomenklatura*.

1974   Mobutu intervenes in Angola as an ally of the CIA and apartheid South Africa.

1975   The military débâcle in Angola is followed by the first major purge of the armed forces against young and well-educated officers, under the pretext of an aborted coup that never was.

1977   March: First Shaba War is ended by Moroccan troops with French logistical support.

       November: Parliamentary elections are relatively free, with candidates not having to be endorsed by the MPR Politburo.

1978   March: Several officers are executed in the second major purge of the armed forces.

       May: Second Shaba War is ended by French and Belgian paratroopers.

1979   Massacre of artisanal diamond diggers at Katekalayi, in Eastern Kasai province brings forth calls for an international inquiry by some parliamentarians.

1980   December: 13 parliamentarians send a 52-page letter to Mobutu demanding democratic change.

1982   The Group of 13, under the leadership of Etienne Tshisekedi, establishes an opposition political party, the UDPS.

1988   17 January: Tshisekedi leads a major pro-democracy demonstration in Kinshasa.

1990   24 April: Bowing to internal and external pressure, Mobutu announces the end of the one-party regime.

       11–12 May: Massacre of university students at Lubumbashi.

1991   July: Mobutu's nomination of Tshisekedi as prime minister is vetoed by the population, as demonstrators convince the latter to decline.

       7 August: The Sovereign National Conference (CNS) begins in Kinshasa.

       September–October: Looting and violence by poorly paid soldiers around the country.

       October: Tshisekedi is once again named prime minister, but is dismissed after a few days due to disagreements with Mobutu.

1992   19 January: The Mobutu regime suspends the CNS.

16 February: Christian demonstrators march in Kinshasa and in other cities to demand the reopening of the CNS, and security forces commit a massacre in Kinshasa.

6 April: The CNS resumes its work.

4 August: The CNS adopts a provisional constitution for the transition and votes to give the country its original name of 'Congo'.

14–15 August: The CNS elects Tshisekedi as prime minister, with 71 per cent of the vote cast by the 2,842 delegates.

1 December: Mobutu carries out the third coup of his political career by shutting all of Tshisekedi's ministers out of their offices; demanding the naming of a government acceptable to the head of state; and ordering Mgr Laurent Monsengwo, the CNS president, to bring the conference to an end.

6 December: The CNS closes prematurely.

1993   28–30 January: During the second wave of looting and violence by soldiers, the French ambassador is assassinated and hundreds of people are killed in Kinshasa.

9–19 March: A political conclave by the MPR and its political allies results in the establishment of a dual constitutional framework, a dual legislature, and a dual executive, with Tshisekedi and the CNS related institutions as legitimate, while Mobutu's illegal government under Faustin Birindwa has effective control of the reins of power.

September: Negotiations between the forces of the status quo and those of change agree on ways of ending the dual authority structure.

1994   23 January: A single legislature of over seven hundred members is established as the provisional parliament, Haut conseil de la République-Parlement de transition (HCR-PT).

April-July: Genocide in Rwanda results in over one million Hutu refugees fleeing into the Congo, including remnants of the former national army (FAR) and the *interahamwe*, the extremist Hutu militia.

9 April: A single fundamental law is adopted as the Constitutional Act of the Transition.

6 July: Léon Kengo wa Dondo, the longest-serving prime minister of Mobutu's party-state (1982–86 and 1988–90) is once again sworn into office as the prime minister of the transition to democracy.

1995   June: The HCR-PT prolongs the Kengo government for two years, until 30 June 1997, to allow it to fulfill its mandate of holding free and fair elections.

1996   1 January: The National Electoral Commission (CNE) is inaugurated, with 44 members, 22 for each of the two political 'families', the Mobutu camp and the democratic opposition.

17 March: After weeks of political wrangling, the CNE finally elects its six-member bureau.

3 September: The deputy president of the CNE and head of the opposition group resigns.

6 October: Rwandan troops begin to dismantle the Hutu refugee camps in North and South Kivu and to pursue those refugees and fighters fleeing westward.

18 October: AFDL is established at Lemera, with Laurent-Désiré Kabila as its spokesperson, with the aim of overthrowing the Mobutu regime.

1997   17 May: With Rwandan and Ugandan backing, the AFDL takes over Kinshasa; Kabila changes the country's name to 'Congo' and proclaims himself its president.

1998   13 July: Kabila removes Commander James Kabarebe, a Rwandan military officer, as chief of the staff of the Congolese army.

27 July: Kabila decides to send Commander James and his comrades-in-arms back home to Rwanda.

2 August: War erupts once more, as Rwandan and Ugandan troops cross the border into the Congo, and Rwandan officers and their Congolese allies stage rebellions inside the Congo.

6 August–1 September: Rwandans and their allies seize Kitona and start march on Kinshasa, are beaten back by Angola and Zimbabwe, whose intervention saves the Kabila regime. Meanwhile, Congolese rebels in Goma are organized first under Arthur Zahidi Ngoma and then under Professor Ernest Wamba-dia-Wamba as the Rassemblement congolais pour la démocratie (RCD).

November: Disappointed with the lack of popular support for the RCD, President Yoweri Museveni of Uganda sponsors the establishment of another rebel group, the Mouvement pour la libération du Congo (MLC) under Jean-Pierre Bemba, son of millionaire businessman Bemba Saolano, a close associate of Mobutu.

1999   18 April: Presidents Kabila and Museveni sign a ceasefire agreement in Sirte, Libya, but the RCD and Rwanda do not accept it.

20 April: Kabila dissolves the AFDL, which is to be replaced by people's power committees.

16 May: Wamba is replaced as RCD president by Dr Emile Ilunga, but refuses to step down and then moves to Kisangani to form his own faction of the RCD, backed by Uganda.

26 May: After heavy losses, Chad takes advantage of the Sirte agreement to pull out of the DRC.

10 July: Lusaka Agreement is signed by all the state belligerents (Angola, DRC, Namibia, Rwanda, Uganda and Zimbabwe), but rebels refuse to sign.

1 August: MLC leader Bemba signs the Lusaka Agreement.

7–17 August: Fighting over turf between Rwandan (RPA) and Ugandan (UPDF) troops in Kisangani kills over two hundred innocent civilians and destroys much of the city's infrastructure.

31 August: 50 RCD 'founding members' sign the Lusaka Agreement.

1 October: Following its flight from Kisangani, the Wamba faction of the RCD establishes its headquarters at Bunia, a district town close to Uganda's border.

15 December: Sir Ketumile Masire, the former president of Botswana, is appointed as the neutral facilitator of the inter-Congolese dialogue by OAU Secretary-General Salim Ahmed Salim.

2000 25 January: A UN mini-summit is held in New York on the Congo peace process.

31 January–6 February: Civil disobedience against the RCD in Goma and Bukavu. The RCD-Goma responds by preventing Roman Catholic Archbishop Emmanuel Kataliko to return to his parish in Bukavu.

5–22 May: A second wave of heavy fighting breaks out between RPA and UFDF troops in Kisangani.

5–11 June: A third wave of heaving fighting between RPA and UPDF in Kisangani.

9–14 June: Violent demonstrations take place on 9, 10 and 14 June outside the Mission des Nations unies au Congo (MONUC) headquarters in Kinshasa to protest UN inaction during the destruction of Kisangani by the RPA and the UPDF.

16 June: UN Security Council passes Resolution 1304, which designates Rwanda and Uganda as aggressors in the Congo, condemns their actions in Kisangani and calls upon the two countries to withdraw their troops from the Congo.

19 July: Brigadier Edward Katumba Walumba replaces Brigadier James Kazini, the UPDF chief of staff, as the commander of the UPDF operation in the DRC.

21 August: Kabila installs his hand-picked constituent and legislative assembly in Lubumbashi.

28 October: Emile Ilunga is replaced as RCD-Goma president by Dr Adolphe Onusumba, a political unknown.

November: Challenge to Wamba's leadership by his deputy, Mbusa Nyamwisi, turns violent and the two factions are summoned to Kampala to resolve the dispute.

2001   16 January: President Laurent Kabila is assassinated by Rachidi Kasereka, one of his bodyguards.

17 January: Major-General Joseph Kabila, the dead president's 29-year-old son, is chosen by his father's entourage as the new head of state.

31 January to 3 February: The new president visits Paris, Washington, New York and Brussels, where he seduces his interlocutors by his apparent readiness to change course.

Bibliography

Abemba Bulaimu, *Pouvoir politique traditionnel et islam au Congo oriental*, Brussels: CEDAF, 1971.

Alaux, Jean-Pierre, 'L'étonnante longevité du régime Amin Dada', *Le Monde diplomatique*, April 1979.

Almond, Gabriel A. and James S. Coleman, *The Politics of the Developing Areas*, Princeton, NJ: Princeton University Press, 1950.

American Council on Education, *Survey of Higher Education in the Congo*, Washington, DC: USAID, 1969.

Amin, Samir, *The Arab Nation*, London: Zed Books, 1978.

Amnesty International, *Democratic Republic of the Congo: A Long Standing Crisis Spinning out of Control* (AI Report AFR 62/33/98, 3 September 1998).

Anstey, Roger, *King Leopold's Legacy: The Congo under Belgian Rule, 1908–1960*, London: Oxford University Press for the Institute of Race Relations, 1966.

Artigue, Pierre, *Qui sont les leaders congolais?*, 2nd edn, Brussels: Editions Europe-Afrique, 1961.

Asch, Susan, 'Contradictions internes d'une institution religieuse: l'EJCSK au Zaïre', *Archives de Sciences Sociales des Religions*, Vol. 52, No. 1, July–September 1981.

— *L'Eglise du prophète Kimbangu: de ses origines à son rôle actuel au Zaïre*, Paris: Karthala, 1983.

Ascherson, Neal, *The King Incorporated: Leopold the Second in the Age of Trusts*, Garden City, NY: Doubleday, 1964.

Badiou, Alain and François Balmès, *De l'idéologie*, Paris: Maspero, 1976.

Bakonzi Agayo, 'The gold mines of Kilo-Moto: 1905–1960', 2 vols, unpublished Ph.D. dissertation, University of Wisconsin-Madison, 1982.

Bastin, Jean-François, 'Le maréchal Mobutu, allié obligé de l'Amérique', *Le Monde diplomatique*, September 1983.

Belgium, Belgian Congo and Ruanda-Urundi Information and Public Relations Office, *Belgian Congo*, Vol. II, Brussels, 1960.

Bender, Gerald J., James S. Coleman and Richard L. Sklar (eds), *African Crisis Areas And U.S. Foreign Policy*, Berkeley and Los Angeles: University of California Press, 1985.

Bénot, Yves, 'Amilcar Cabral and the international working class movement', translated from the French by Georges Nzongola-Ntalaja, *Latin American Perspectives*, Issue 41, Vol. 11, No. 2, Spring 1984.

Bézy, Fernand, *Problèmes structurels de l'économie congolaise*, Louvain: Ed. Nauwelaerts for the Institut des Recherches Economiques et Sociales of Lovanium University, Léopoldville, 1957.

— 'Problems of economic development of Congo', in E. A. G. Robinson (ed.), *Economic Development of Africa South of the Sahara*, New York: St Martin's Press, 1964.

Bézy, Fernand et al., *Accumulation et sous-développement au Zaïre 1960–1980*, Louvain-la-Neuve: Presses Universitaires de Louvain, 1981.

Bilsen, A. A. J. Van, 'Un plan de trente ans pour l'émancipation politique de l'Afrique belge', *Les dossiers de l'action sociale catholique*, No. 2, February 1956, reprinted in Van Bilsen, *Vers l'indépendance du Congo et du Ruanda-Urundi*, Kraainem, Belgium, 1958.

Birmingham, David, *Central Africa to 1870: Zambezia, Zaire and the South Atlantic*, chapters from *The Cambridge History of Africa*, Cambridge: Cambridge University Press, 1981.

Birmingham, David and Phyllis M. Martin (eds), *History of Central Africa*, Vol. One, London and New York: Longman, 1983.

Blumenthal, Erwin, 'Le rapport Blumenthal et annexes', *Info-Zaïre*, No. 36, October 1982.

Boissonnade, Euloge, *Le mal zaïrois*, Paris: Ed. Hermé, 1990.

— *Kabila clone de Mobutu?*, Paris: Ed. Moreux, 1998.

Braeckman, Colette, *Le dinosaure: le Zaïre de Mobutu*, Paris: Fayard, 1992.

— *Terreur africaine, Burundi, Rwanda, Zaïre: racines de la violence*, Paris: Fayard, 1996.

— *L'enjeu congolais: l'Afrique centrale après Mobutu*, Paris: Fayard, 1999.

Brausch, Georges, *Belgian Administration in the Congo*, London: Oxford University Press for the Institute of Race Relations, 1966.

Bustin, Edouard, 'The Congo', in Gwendolen M. Carter (ed.), *Five African States: Responses to Diversity*, Ithaca, NY: Cornell University Press, 1963.

— *Lunda under Belgian Rule: The Politics of Ethnicity*, Cambridge, MA and London: Harvard University Press, 1975.

Cabral, Amilcar, *Revolution in Guinea: Selected Texts by Amilcar Cabral*, trans. and ed. Richard Handyside, New York: Monthly Review Press, 1972.

— *Unity and Struggle*, New York: Monthly Review Press, 1979.

Caprasse, Pierre, *Leaders africains en milieu urbain (Elisabethville)*, Elisabethville: Centre d'Etudes des Problèmes Sociaux Indigènes (CEPSI), 1959.

CEDAF, *Contribution à l'étude des mouvements d'opposition au Zaïre: le cas FLNC*, Brussels: CEDAF, 1980.

Chomé, Jules, *Le drame de Luluabourg*, Brussels: Ed. Remarques Congolaises, 1959.

— *L'ascension de Mobutu: du sergent Joseph Désiré au général Sese Seko*, Brussels: Ed. Complexe, 1975.

Clapham, Christopher, *Third World Politics: An Introduction*, Madison: University of Wisconsin Press, 1985.

Comité Zaïre, *Zaïre: dossier de la recolonisation*, Paris: L'Harmattan and Brussels: Vie Ouvrière, 1978.

Coquery-Vidrovitch, Catherine, Alain Forest and Herbert Weiss (eds), *Rébellions-Révolution au Zaïre, 1963–1965*, 2 vols, Paris: L'Harmattan, 1987.

Dayal, Rajeshwar, *Mission for Hammarskjöld: The Congo Crisis*, Princeton, NJ: Princeton University Press, 1976.

De Boeck, Guy, *Baoni: les révoltes de la Force publique sous Léopold II, Congo 1895–1908*, Antwerp: Ed. EPO, 1987.

De Craemer, Willy and Renée C. Fox, *The Emerging Physician*, Stanford, CA: Hoover Institution, 1968.

Demunter, Paul, 'Structure de classes et lutte de classes dans le Congo colonial', *Contradictions*, No. 1, January–June 1972, pp. 67–109.

— 'Le régime de Mobutu (1965–1971)', *Les Temps Modernes*, No. 308, 1972, pp. 1448–81.

— *Masses rurales et luttes politiques au Zaïre: le processus de politisation des masses rurales au Bas-Zaïre*, Paris: Anthropos, 1975.

Denis, Jacques, *Le phénomène urbain en Afrique centrale*, Brussels: Académie Royale Des Sciences d'Outre-Mer (ARSOM), 1958.

Depelchin, Jacques, *De l'Etat indépendant du Congo au Zaïre contemporain (1885–1974)*, Dakar: Codesria, 1992.

De Villers, Gauthier, *Zaïre 1990–1991: faits et dits de la société d'après le regard de la presse. Zaïre, années 90*, Vol. 2, Brussels: Institut Africain-CEDAF, 1992.

De Villers, Gauthier and Jean Omasombo Tshonda, *Zaïre: la transition manquée, 1990–1997. Zaïre, années 90*, Vol. 7. Brussels: Institut Africain-CEDAF, 1997.

De Villers, Gauthier and Jean-Claude Willame, in collaboration with Jean Omasombo and Erik Kennes, *République democratique du Congo: chronique politique d'un entre-deux guerres, Octobre 1996-juillet 1998*, Brussels: Institut Africain-CEDAF, 1998.

De Vos, Pierre, *Vie et mort de Lumumba*, Paris: Calmann-Lévy, 1961.

De Witte, Ludo, *L'assassinat de Lumumba*, Paris: Karthala, 2000.

Digekisa Piluka, Victor, *Le massacre de Lubumbashi, Zaïre 11 et 12 mai 1990: dossier d'un témoin-accusé*, Paris: L'Harmattan, 1993.

Doom, Ruddy and Jan Gorus (eds), *Politics of Identity and Economics of Conflict in the Great Lakes Region*, Brussels: VUB University Press, 2000.

Dungia, Emmanuel, *Mobutu et l'argent du Zaïre*, Paris: L'Harmattan, 1992.

Durch, William J., 'The UN operation in the Congo', in William J. Durch (ed.), *The Evolution of Peacekeeping: Case Studies and Comparative Analysis*, New York: St Martin's Press, 1993.

Emerson, Rupert, *From Empire to Nation: The Rise to Self-Assertion of Asian and African Peoples*, Boston, Beacon Press, 1962.

Fanon, Frantz, *The Wretched of the Earth*, New York: Grove Press, 1963.

First, Ruth, *Power in Africa*, New York: Pantheon Books, 1970.

Foccart, Jacques and Philippe Gaillard, *Foccart parle: entretiens avec Philippe Gaillard*, Vol. 1, Paris: Fayard/Jeune Afrique, 1995.

Fontana, Benedetto, *Hegemony and Power: On the Relation between Gramsci and Machiavelli*, Minneapolis and London: University of Minnesota Press, 1993.

Fox, Renée C., Willy de Craemer and Jean-Marie Ribeaucourt, '"The second independence": a case study of the Kwilu rebellion in the Congo', *Comparative Studies in Society and History*, Vol. 8, No. 1, October 1965, pp. 78–110.

Franck, Louis, 'La politique indigène, le service territorial et les chefferies', *Congo*, Vol. 1, No. 2, 1921, pp. 189–201.

Fried, Robert C., *The Italian Prefects: A Study in Administrative Politics*, New Haven, CT: Yale University Press, 1963.

Galvez, William, *Che in Africa: Che Guevara's Congo Diary*, trans. Mary Todd, Melbourne and New York: Ocean Press, 1999.

Gérard-Libois, Jules, *Sécession au Katanga*, Brussels: Centre de Recherche et d'Information Socio-Politiques (CRISP), 1963, translated into English by Rebecca Young as *Katanga Secession*, Madison: University of Wisconsin Press, 1966.

— 'The new class and rebellion in the Congo', in Ralph Miliband and John Saville (eds), *The Socialist Register 1966*, New York: Monthly Review Press, 1966, pp. 267–80.

Gibbs, David N., *The Political Economy of Third World Intervention: Mines, Money, and U.S. Policy in the Congo Crisis*, Chicago and London: University of Chicago Press, 1991.

Gilis, Charles-André, *Kasa-Vubu au coeur du drame congolais*, Brussels: Ed. Europe-Afrique, 1964.

Gould, David J., *Bureaucratic Corruption and Underdevelopment in the Third World: The Case of Zaire*, New York: Pergamon Press, 1980.

Gramsci, Antonio, 'On intellectuals', in Antonio Gramsci, *Selections from the Prison Notebooks of Antonio Gramsci*, New York: International Publishers, 1971, pp. 5–23.

Gourevitch, Philip, *We Wish to Inform You that Tomorrow We will be Killed with our Families: Stories from Rwanda*, New York: Farrar, Strauss and Giroux, 1998.

Goyvaerts, Didier, *Conflict and Ethnicity in Central Africa*, Tokyo: Institute for the Study of Languages and Cultures of Asia and Africa, Tokyo University of Foreign Studies, 2000.

Heinz, G. and H. Donnay, *Lumumba Patrice: les cinquante derniers jours de sa vie*, 2nd edn, Brussels: CRISP, and Paris: Le Seuil, 1976, English trans. *Lumumba: The Last Fifty Days*, New York: Grove Press, 1969.

Higginson, John, *A Working Class in the Making: Belgian Colonial Labor Policy, Private Enterprise, and the African Mineworker, 1907–1951*, Madison: University of Wisconsin Press, 1989.

Hill, Stephen M. and Shahim P. Malik, *Peacekeeping and the United Nations*, Aldershot: Dartmouth, 1996.

Hochschild, Adam, *King Leopold's Ghost: A Story of Greed, Terror, and Heroism in Colonial Africa*, Boston and New York: Houghton Mifflin, 1998.

Hodgkin, Thomas, *Nationalism in Colonial Africa*, London: Frederick Muller, 1956.

— 'The relevance of "Western" ideas for the new African States', in J. Roland Pennock (ed.), *Self-Government in Modernizing Nations*, Englewood Cliffs, NJ: Prentice-Hall, 1964.

Hussein, Mahmoud, *Class Conflict in Egypt, 1945–1970*, New York: Monthly Review Press, 1973.

Ilunga Mbiye Kabongo, 'Ethnicity, social classes, and the state in the Congo, 1960–65: the case of the Baluba', unpublished Ph.D. dissertation, University of California, Berkeley, 1973.

Ilunga-Kabongo, A. R., 'Crise à Lovanium', *Etudes Congolaises* (Kinshasa), Vol. 6, No. 4, April 1964.

Institut de Recherches Economiques et Sociales, *Indépendance, inflation, développement: l'économie congolaise de 1960 à 1965*. Paris and The Hague: Ed. Mouton-IRES, 1968.

International Crisis Group, *Scramble for the Congo: Anatomy of an Ugly War*, Nairobi and Brussels: ICG Africa Report No. 26, 2000.

Janssen, Pierre, *A la cour de Mobutu*, Paris: Ed. Michel Lafon, 1997.

Janssens, Emile, *J'étais le général Janssens*, Brussels, 1961.

Jewsiewicki, Bogumil, 'La contestation sociale et la naissance du prolétariat au Zaïre au cours de la première moitié du XXième siècle', *Revue Canadienne des Etudes Africaines*, No. 1, 1976, pp. 47–71.

Joye, Pierre and Rosine Lewin, *Les trusts au Congo*, Brussels: Société Populaire d'Editions, 1961.

Kabungulu Ngoy-Kangoy, *La transition démocratique au Zaïre*, Kinshasa: CIEDOS, 1995.

Kalb, Madeleine G., *The Congo Cables: The Cold War in Africa, from Eisenhower to Kennedy*, New York: Macmillan, 1982.

Kalele-ka-Bila. 'La démocratie à la base: l'expérience des parlementaires-debout au Zaïre', in Georges Nzongola-Ntalaja and Margaret C. Lee (eds), *The State and Democracy in Africa*, Harare: AAPS Books, 1997; Trenton, NJ: Africa World Press, 1998, pp. 64–73.

Kamitatu Masamba, Cléophas, *La grande mystification du Congo-Kinshasa: les crimes de Mobutu*, Paris: F. Maspero, 1971

— *Zaïre: le pouvoir à la portée du peuple*, Paris: Maspero, 1977.

Kankonde Luteke, J.-M. *Massacres et déportation des Kasaïens au Katanga: Chronique d'une épuration programmée*, Brussels: Pistes Africaines, 1997.

Kankwenda Mbaya (ed.), *Le Zaïre, vers quelles destinées?*, Dakar: Codesria, 1992.

Kanyinda-Lusanga, Théodore, *Institutions traditionnelles et forces politiques au Congo: le cas de la société luba du Kasaï*, Brussels: CRISP, 1970.

— *Le phénomène de la colonisation et l'émancipation des institutions socio-politiques traditionnelles au Zaïre*, Brussels: CEDAF, 1975.

Kanza, Thomas, *Conflict in the Congo: The Rise and Fall of Patrice Lumumba*, Baltimore, MD: Penguin, 1972.

Kelly, Sean, *America's Tyrant: The CIA and Mobutu of Zaire*, Washington, DC: American University Press, 1993.

Kestergat, Jean, *Du Congo de Lumumba au Zaïre de Mobutu*, Brussels: P. Legrain, 1986.

Kinkela vi Kans'y, 'Rapport final des travaux de la Conférence nationale souveraine', *Zaïre-Afrique*, No. 273, March 1993, pp. 135–99.

Kodi, M. W., 'The 1921 Pan-African Congress at Brussels: a background to Belgian pressures', in Joseph E. Harris (ed.), *Global Dimensions of the African Diaspora*, 2nd edn, Washington, DC: Howard University Press, 1993, pp. 263–88.

Krop, Pascal, *Le génocide franco-africain: faut-il juger les Mitterrand?*, Paris: Editions Jean-Claude Lattès, 1994.

Kwitney, Jonathan, *Endless Enemies: The Making of an Unfriendly World*, New York: Penguin, 1984.

Lacroix, Jean-Louis, *Industrialisation au Congo: la transformation des structures économiques*, Paris and The Hague: Mouton, 1967.

— 'Evolution de l'économie et transformation des structures économiques au Congo depuis 1960', *Revue Française d'Etudes Politiques Africaines*, No. 58, October 1970, pp. 48–68.

La Fontaine, J. S., *City Politics: A Study of Leopoldville, 1962–63*, Cambridge: Cambridge University Press, 1970.

Lejeune, Emile, *Laurent-Désiré Kabila, militant nationaliste congolais*, Tubize, Belgium: Gamma Press, 1997.

Lekime, Fernand, *La mengeuse de cuivre: la saga de l'Union minière du Haut-Katanga 1906–1966*, Brussels: Didier Hatier, 1992.

Lemarchand, René, *Political Awakening in the Belgian Congo*, Berkeley: University of California Press, 1964.

— *Burundi: Ethnic Conflict and Genocide*, New York: Woodrow Wilson Press and Cambridge University Press, 1996.

Leslie, J. Winsome, *The World Bank and Structural Transformation in Developing Countries: The Case of Zaire*, Boulder, CO: Lynne Rienner, 1987.

Lewis, David Levering, *The Race to Fashoda: European Colonialism and African Resistance in the Scramble for Africa*, New York: Weidenfeld & Nicolson, 1987.

Lindquist, Sven, *'Exterminate all the Brutes'*, trans. from Swedish by Joan Tate, New York: The New Press, 1996.

Lokomba Baruti, *Structure et fonctionnement des institutions politiques traditionnelles chez les Lokele*, Brussels: CEDAF, 1972.

Lumumba, Patrice, *Le Congo, terre d'avenir, est-il menacé?*, Brussels: Office de Publicité, 1961, English trans. *Congo, My Country*, London, 1962.

Lux, André, 'Migrations, accroissement et urbanisation de la population congolaise de Luluabourg', *Zaire*, Vol. 12, No. 7, 1958, pp. 675–724; and Vol. 12, No. 8, 1958, pp. 819–77.

— *Le marché du travail en Afrique noire*, Louvain: Ed. Nauwelaerts for the Institut des Recherches Economiques et Sociales of Lovanium University, 1962.

McCabe, James L., 'Distribution of labor incomes in urban Zaire', *Review of Income and Wealth*, Vol. 20, No. 1, March 1974, pp. 71–87.

MacGaffey, Janet et al., *The Real Economy of Zaire: The Contribution of Smuggling And Other Unofficial Activities to National Wealth*, Philadelphia: University of Pennsylvania Press, 1991.

MacGaffey, Wyatt, 'Kongo and the King of the Americans', *Journal of Modern African Studies*, Vol. 6, No. 2, June 1968, pp. 171–81.

— *Modern Kongo Prophets: Religion in a Plural Society*, Bloomington: Indiana University Press, 1983.

Mabika Kalanda, Auguste, *Baluba et Lulua: une ethnie à la recherche d'un nouvel équilibre*, Brussels: Ed. Remarques Congolaises, 1959.

— *La remise en question, base de la décolonisation mentale*, Brussels: Ed. Remarques Africaines, 1962.

— *Tabalayi*, Kinshasa, 1963.

Madelin, Philippe, *L'or des dictatures*, Paris: Fayard, 1993.

Madsen, Wayne, *Genocide and Covert Operations in Africa, 1993–1999*, Lewiston, NY: Edwin Mellen Press, 1999.

Magotte, J., *Les circonscriptions indigènes*, La Louvière: Imprimerie Louviéroise, n.d.

Mahaniah, Kimpianga, 'The presence of black Americans in the Lower Congo from 1878 to 1921', in Joseph E. Harris (ed.), *Global Dimensions of the African Diaspora*, 2nd edn, Washington, DC: Howard University Press, pp. 405–20.

Mahoney, Richard D., *JFK: Ordeal in Africa*, New York: Oxford University Press, 1983.

Makidi-ku-Ntima, 'The role of Congolese intellectuals in the making of neo-colonialism: U.G.E.C.–Mobutu alliance or the story of the odd couple', paper presented at the 28th Annual Meeting of the African Studies Association, New Orleans, 23–26 November 1985.

Malan, Mark (ed.), *Resolute Partners: Building Peacekeeping Capacity in Southern Africa*, ISS Monograph Series, No. 21, Halfway House, South Africa: Institute for Strategic Studies, 1998.

Mamdani, Mahmood, 'The political diaspora in Uganda and background to the RPF invasion', in Didier Goyvaerts (ed.), *Conflict and Ethnicity in Central Africa*, Tokyo: Institute for the Study of Languages and Cultures of Asia and Africa, Tokyo University of Foreign Studies, 2000.

Marchal, Jules, *L'Etat Libre du Congo: paradis perdu. Histoire du Congo 1876–1900*, 2 vols, Borgloon, Belgium: Ed. Paula Bellings, 1996.

— *E.D. Morel contre Leopold II. L'Histoire du Congo 1900–1910*, 2 vols, Paris: L'Harmattan, 1996.

— *Travail forcé pour le cuivre et l'or. Histoire du Congo 1910–1945*, Vol. 1, Borgloon, Belgium: Ed. Paula Bellings, 1999.

Marrès, Jacques et Pierre de Vos, *L'équinoxe de janvier*, Brussels: Ed. Euraforient, 1959.

Martens, Ludo. *Pierre Mulele ou la seconde vie de Patrice Lumumba*. Antwerp: Ed. EPO, 1985.

Marx, Karl, *Class Struggles in France (1848–1850)*, New York: International Publishers, 1964.

— *Capital*, vol. 1 New York: International Publishers, 1967.

— *The Eighteenth Brumaire of Louis Bonaparte*, New York: International Publishers, 1972.

Marx, Karl and Frederick Engels, *The German Ideology*, New York: International Publishers, 1970.

Maurel, Auguste, *Le Congo de la colonisation belge à l'indépendance*, 2nd edn, Paris: L'Harmattan, 1992.

Mayo-Mokelo, Justin, 'Instabilité dans les institutions communales de la ville de Kisangani (ex-Stanleyville), 1958–1968', unpublished senior thesis in political science and public administration, Congo Free University, Kisangani, 1971.

Minter, William, *King Solomon's Mines Revisited: Western Interests and the Burdened History of Southern Africa*, New York: Basic Books, 1986.

Monguya Mbenge, Daniel, *Histoire secrète du Zaïre*, Brussels: Editions de l'Espérance, 1977.

Monheim, Francis, *Mobutu, l'homme seul*, Brussels, 1962.

Morel, E. D., *Red Rubber: The Story of the Rubber Slave Trade which Flourished in the Congo for Twenty Years, 1890–1910*, New York: B.W. Huebsch, 1919.

Mouvance Progressiste du Congo (Zaïre). *Congo (Zaïre): démocratie néo-coloniale ou deuxième indépendance?*, Paris: L'Harmattan, 1992.

Mpinga-Kasenda, *L'Administration publique du Zaïre*, Paris: Ed. Pedone, 1973.

Mukendi, Germain and Bruno Kasonga, *Kabila, le retour du Congo*, Ottignies, Belgium: Quorum, 1997.

Mukenge, Léonard, 'Croyances religieuses et structures socio-familiales en société luba: "Bena Muntu", "Bakishi", "Milambu"', *Cahiers Economiques et Sociaux*, Vol. 5, No. 1, 1967.

Mulambu Mvuluya, *Contribution à l'étude de la révolte des Bapende, mai–septembre 1931*, Brussels: CEDAF, 1971.

— *Cultures obligatoires et colonisation dans l'ex-Congo belge*, Brussels: CEDAF, 1974.

— 'Les masses populaires et les préalables d'une transition démocratique au Zaïre (1990–1992)', in Georges Nzongola-Ntalaja and Margaret C. Lee (eds), *The State and Democracy in Africa*, Harare: AAPS Books, 1997; Trenton, NJ: Africa World Press, 1998, pp. 53–63.

Naipaul, V. S. 'A new king for the Congo', *New York Review of Books*, 26 June 1975.

Ndaywel è Nziem, Isidore, *La société zaïroise dans le mirroir de son discours religieux, 1990–1993. Zaïre, années 90*, Vol. 3, Brussels: Institut Africain-CEDAF, 1993.

— *Histoire générale du Congo. De l'héritage ancien à la République démocratique*, Paris and Brussels: Duculot, 1998.

Newbury, Catharine, *The Cohesion of Oppression: Clientship and Ethnicity in Rwanda, 1860–1960*, New York: Columbia University Press, 1988.

Ngbanda Nzambo-ku-Atumba, Honoré, *Ainsi sonne le glas! Les derniers jours du Maréchal Mobutu*, Paris: Ed. Gideppe, 1998.

Ngoy-Kangoy, Kabungulu, *La transition démocratique au Zaïre*, Kinshasa: CIEDOS, 1995.

Nguza Karl-I-Bond, *Mobutu ou l'incarnation du mal zaïrois*, London: Rex Collins, 1982.

Nicolaï, Henri and Jules Jacques, *La transformation des paysages congolais par le chemin de fer: l'exemple du B.C.K.*, Brussels: Académie Royale des Sciences Coloniales, 1954.

Nimtz, August G., Jr., 'The Qadiriyya and political change: class, race, and ethnicity on the East African coast', in Robert Olson (ed.), *Islamic and Middle Eastern Societies: A Festschrift in Honor of Professor Wadie Jwaideh*, Brattleboro, VT: Amana Books, 1987, pp. 189–208.

Nkrumah, Kwame, *Challenge of the Congo*, London: Nelson, 1967.

Northcote Parkinson, C., *The Evolution of Political Thought*, Boston, MD: Houghton Mifflin, 1958.

Nzongola-Ntalaja, Georges, 'Confrontation in Congo Kinshasa', *Mawazo*, Vol. 2, No. 2, December 1969, pp. 19–24.

— 'Les classes sociales et la révolution anticoloniale au Congo-Kinshasa: le rôle de la bourgeoisie', *Cahiers Economiques et Sociaux*, Vol. 8, No. 3, September 1970, pp. 371–88, English version: 'The bourgeoisie and revolution in the Congo', *Journal of Modern African Studies*, Vol. 8, No. 4, December 1970, pp. 511–30.

— 'Urban administration in Zaire: a study of Kananga, 1971–73', unpublished Ph.D. dissertation, University of Madison-Wisconsin, 1975.

— 'The authenticity of neocolonialism: ideology and class struggle in Zaire', *Berkeley Journal of Sociology*, No. 22, 1977–78, pp. 115–30.

Nzongola-Ntalaja, Georges, 'The continuing struggle for national liberation in Zaire', *Journal of Modern African Studies*, Vol. 17, No. 4, December 1979, pp. 595–614.

— 'Class struggle and national liberation in Zaire', in Bernard Magubane and Nzongola-Ntalaja (eds), *Proletarianization and Class Struggle in Africa*, San Francisco: Synthesis Publications, 1983, pp. 57–94.

— 'The national question and the crisis of instability in Africa', *Alternatives*, Vol. 10, No. 4, 1985.

— (ed.), *The Crisis in Zaire: Myths and Realities*, Trenton, NJ: Africa World Press, 1986.

— 'Le mouvement pour la seconde indépendance au Congo-Kinshasa (Zaïre) de 1963–1968', in Peter Anyang' Nyong'o (ed.), *Afrique: la longue marche vers la démocratie*, Paris: Publisud, 1988, pp. 208–52, English version 'The second independence movement in Congo-Kinshasa', in Peter Anyang' Nyong'o (ed.), *Popular Struggles for Democracy in Africa*, London: United Nations University and Zed Books, 1987, pp. 113–41.

— *Le mouvement démocratique au Zaïre 1956–1996*, Mexico City: Center for Interdisciplinary Research in Sciences and Humanities, National Autonomous University of Mexico, 1997.

— *From Zaire to the Democratic Republic of the Congo*, Uppsala: Nordiska Afrikainstitutet, 1998.

— 'The state and democracy in Africa', in Georges Nzongola-Ntalaja and Margaret C. Lee (eds), *The State and Democracy in Africa*, Harare: AAPS Books, 1997; Trenton, NJ: Africa World Press, 1998, pp. 9–24.

O'Brien, Conor Cruise, *To Katanga and Back: A UN Case History*, New York: Grosset and Dunlap, 1966.

Olivier, 'Afrique: qui exploite qui?', *Les Temps Modernes*, No. 347, June 1975.

Peemans, Jean-Philippe, 'The social and economic development of Zaire since independence: an historical outline', *African Affairs*, Vol. 74, No. 295, April 1975.

— 'Imperial hangovers: Belgium – the economics of decolonization', *Journal of Contemporary History*, Vol. 15, No. 2, April 1980, pp. 257–86.

Pons, Valdo, *Stanleyville: An African Urban Community under Belgian Administration*, London: Oxford University Press for the International African Institute, 1969.

Poulantzas, Nicos, *Political Power and Social Classes*, London: New Left Books and Sheed and Ward, 1973.

Prunier, Gérard, *Rwanda, 1959–1996: Histoire d'un génocide*, Paris: Dagorno, 1997.

Ranger, T. O., 'Connexions between "primary resistance" movements and modern mass nationalism in East and Central Africa', *Journal of African History*, Vol. 9, No. 3, 1968, pp. 437–53; Vol. 9, No. 4, 1968, pp. 631–41.

Ratner, Stephen R., *The New UN Peacekeeping: Building Peace in Lands of Conflict After the Cold War*, New York: Council on Foreign Relations, 1995; paperback edn. New York: St Martin's Press, 1996.

Raymaekers, Paul, *L'organisation des zones de squatting*, Leopoldville: IRES, 1963.

Reader, John, *Africa: A Biography of the Continent*, New York: Alfred A. Knopf, 1998.

Reefe, Thomas Q., *The Rainbow and the Kings: A History of the Luba Empire to 1891*, Berkeley and Los Angeles: University of California Press, 1981.

Reyntjens, Filip, *La guerre des grands lacs*, Paris: L'Harmattan, 1999.

Reyntjens, Filip and Stefan Marysse (eds), *L'Afrique des grands lacs: annuaire 1997–1998*, Paris: L'Harmattan, 1998.

Rikhye, Indar Jit., *Military Advisor to the Secretary General: U.N. Peacekeeping and the Congo Crisis*, London: Hurst, 1993.

Rodney, Walter, *How Europe Underdeveloped Africa*, Washington, DC: Howard University Press, 1974.

Rymenam, Jean, 'Comment le régime Mobutu a sapé ses propres fondements', *Le Monde diplomatique*, May 1977.

Saïd, Shafik-G., *De Léopoldville à Kinshasa: la situation économique et financière au Congo ex-belge au jour de l'indépendance*, Brussels: Centre National d'Etude des Problèmes Sociaux de l'Industrialisation en Afrique Noire, 1969.

Schatzberg, Michael, *Politics and Class in Zaire: Bureaucracy, Business, and Beer in Lisala*, New York: Africana Publishing, 1980.

— *The Dialectics of Oppression in Zaire*, Bloomington: Indiana University Press, 1988.

Schwar, Harriet Dashiell and Stanley Shaloff (eds), *Foreign Relations of the United States, 1958–1960, Vol. XIV: Africa*, Washington, DC: Government Printing Office, 1992.

Sebudandi, Gaëtan and Pierre-Olivier Richard, *Le drame burundais: hantise du pouvoir ou tentation suicidaire*, Karthala, Paris, 1996.

Shillington, Kevin, *History of Africa*, rev. edn, New York: St Martin's Press, 1995.

Simons, E., R. Boghossian and B. Verhaegen, *Stanleyville 1959: Le process de Patrice Lumumba et les émeutes d'octobre*, Bussels: Institut Africain-CEDAF and Paris: L'Harmattan, 1995.

Slade, Ruth, *King Leopold's Congo: Aspects of the Development of Race Relations in the Congo Independent State*, London: Oxford University Press for the Institute of Race Relations, 1962.

Smith, Stephen and Antoine Glaser, *Ces messieurs Afrique*, Paris: Calmann-Lévy, 1992.

— *Ces messieurs Afrique 2: des réseaux aux lobbies*, Paris: Calmann-Lévy, 1997.

Spitzer, Alan B., 'The bureaucrat as proconsul: the Restoration prefect and the Police Générale', *Comparative Studies in Society and History*, Vol. 7, No. 4, July 1965, pp. 371–92.

Stengers, Jean, *Combien le Congo a-t-il coûté à la Belgique?*, Brussels: Académie Royale des Sciences Coloniales, 1957.

— 'The Congo Free State and the Belgian Congo until 1914', in L. H. Gann and Peter Duignan (eds), *Colonialism in Africa 1870–1960. Vol. I: The History and Politics of Colonialism 1870–1914*, Cambridge: Cambridge University Press, 1969.

— *Congo mythes et réalités*, Paris and Louvain-la-Neuve: Duculot, 1989.

Stockwell, John, *In Search of Enemies: A CIA Story*, New York: W.W. Norton, 1978.

Suret-Canale, Jean, *French Colonialism in Tropical Africa*, New York: Pica Press, 1971.

Thornton, John K., *The Kingdom of Kongo: Civil War and Transition, 1641–1718*, Madison: University of Wisconsin Press, 1983.

Tshombe, Moïse, *Quinze mois de gouvernement au Congo*, Paris: Table Ronde, 1966.

Tucker, Robert C. (ed.), *The Marx–Engels Reader*, New York: Norton, 1972.

Turner, Thomas, 'A century of political conflict in Sankuru', unpublished Ph.D. dissertation, University of Wisconsin-Madison, 1973.

— *La politique indigène du Congo belge: le cas du Sankuru*, Brussels: CEDAF, 1973.

— 'Peasants, rebellion and its suppression in Sankuru, Zaire', *Pan-African Journal*, Vol. 7, No. 3, Fall 1974, pp. 193–215.

Tutashinda, N. 'Les mystifications de l'authenticité', *La Pensée*, No. 175 (May–June 1974), pp. 68–81.

Twain, Mark, *King Leopold's Soliloquy*, New York: International Publishers, 1970.

U.S. Congress, Senate, *Interim Report: Alleged Assassination Plots Involving Foreign Leaders*, by the Select Committee to Study Government Operations with Respect to Intelligence Activities, 94th Congress, 1st Session, 20 November 1975.

— *Final Report: Foreign and Military Intelligence*, Book I, by the Select Committee to Study Government Operations with Respect to Intelligence Activities, 94th Congress, 2nd Session, April 26, 1976.

— *U.S. Loans to Zaire*, Hearing before the Subcommittee on International Finance of the Committee on Banking, Housing, and Urban Affairs, 96th Congress, 1st Session, 24 May 1979.

Vanderlinden, Jacques (ed.), *Du Congo au Zaïre 1960–1980: Essai de bilan*, Brussels: CRISP, 1980.

Vanderstraeten, Louis-François, *De la Force publique à l'Armée nationale congolaise: histoire d'une mutinerie, juillet 1960*, Brussels: Académie Royale de Belgique; Paris-Gembloux: Duculot, 1985.

Vandewalle, Frédéric, *L'Ommengang: odyssée et reconquête de Kisangani 1964*, Brussels, 1970.

Vangroenweghe, Daniel, *Du sang sur les lianes: Léopold II et son Congo*, Brussels: Didier Hatier, 1986.

Van Lierde, Jean (ed.), *La pensée politique de Patrice Lumumba*, Brussels: Editions des Amis de Présence Africaine, 1963.

Vansina, Jan, *Kingdoms of the Savanna*, Madison: University of Wisconsin Press, 1966.

— 'Du royaume kuba au "territoire des Bakuba"', *Etudes Congolaises*, Vol. 12, No. 2, 1969, pp. 3–54.

— *The Children of Woot: A History of the Kuba Peoples*, Madison: University of Wisconsin Press, 1978.

— 'The peoples of the forest', in David Birmingham and Phyllis M. Martin (eds), *History of Central Africa*, Vol. One, London and New York: Longman, 1983.

— *Paths in the Rainforests: Toward a History of Political Tradition in Equatorial Africa*, Madison: University of Wisconsin Press, 1990.

Van Zandijcke, A., *Pages de l'histoire du Kasayi*, Namur: Collection Lavigerie, 1953.

Vellut, Jean-Luc, 'Rural poverty in Western Shaba, c. 1890–1930', in Robin Palmer and Neal Parsons (eds), *The Roots of Rural Poverty in Central and Southern Africa*, Berkeley and Los Angeles: University of California Press, 1977, pp. 294–316.

Verhaegen, Benoît, *Rébellions au Congo*, Brussels: CRISP, Vol. 1, 1966; Vol. 2, 1969.

— 'Les associations congolaises à Léopoldville et dans le Bas-Congo avant 1960', *Cahiers Economiques et Sociaux*, Vol. 8, No. 3, September 1970, pp. 389–416.

— *Les premiers manifestes politiques à Léopoldville*, Brussels: CEDAF, 1971.

— 'Impérialisme technologique et bourgeoisie nationale au Zaïre', in Catherine Coquery-Vidrovitch (ed.), *Connaissance du tiers-monde*, Col. 10/18, Paris: Laboratoire du Tiers-Monde, 1978, pp. 347–79.

— *L'association des évolués de Stanleyville et les débuts politiques de Patrice Lumumba, 1944–1958*, Brussels: CEDAF, 1983.

Wagoner, Fred E., *Dragon Rouge: The Rescue of Hostages in the Congo*, Washington, DC: National Defense University, 1980.

Weiss, Herbert F., *Political Protest in the Congo: The Parti Solidaire Africain During the Independence Struggle*, Princeton, NJ: Princeton University Press, 1967, French trans. *Radicalisme rural et lutte pour l'indépendance au Congo-Zaïre: le Parti Solidaire Africain (1959–1960)*, Paris: L'Harmattan, 1994.

— *War and Peace in the Democratic Republic of the Congo*, Uppsala: Nordiska Afrikainstitutet, 2000.

Weissman, Stephen R., *American Foreign Policy in the Congo 1960–1964*, Ithaca, NY: Cornell University Press, 1974.

— 'The CIA and U.S. policy in Zaire and Angola', in René Lemarchand (ed.), *American Policy in Southern Africa: The Stakes and the Stance*, Washington, DC: University Press of America, 1978, pp. 382–432.

Wesley, Michael, *Casualties of the New World Order: The Causes of Failure of UN Missions to Civil Wars*, New York: St Martin's Press, 1997.

Willame, Jean-Claude, 'The Congo', in Donald K. Emmerson (ed.), *Students and Politics in Developing Nations*, New York: Praeger, 1968, pp. 37–63.

— *Patrimonialism and Political Change in the Congo*, Stanford, CA: Stanford University Press, 1972.

— *Zaïre, l'épopée d'Inga: chronique d'une prédation industrielle*, Paris: L'Harmattan, 1986.

— *Chronique d'une opposition politique: l'UDPS, 1978–1987*, Brussels: CEDAF, 1987.

— *Patrice Lumumba: la crise congolaise revisitée*, Paris: Karthala, 1990.

— *De la démocratie 'octroyée' à la démocratie enrayée, 24 avril 1990–22 septembre 1991. Zaïre, années 90*, Vol. 1, Brussels: CEDAF, 1991.

— *L'Automne d'un despotisme: pouvoir, argent et obéissance dans le Zaïre des années quatre-vingt*, Paris: Kathala, 1992.

Williams, G. Mennen, 'U.S. objectives in the Congo 1960–65', *Africa Report*, Vol. 10, No. 8, August 1965, pp. 12–20.

Williams, Vernon J., Jr., *Rethinking Race: Franz Boas and his Contemporaries*, Lexington: University Press of Kentucky, 1996.

Williams, Walter L., *Black Americans and the Evangelization of Africa, 1877–1900*, Madison: University of Wisconsin Press, 1982.

Wilungula, B. Cosma, *Fizi 1967–1986: le maquis de Kabila*, Brussels: Institut Africain-CEDAF, 1997.

World Bank, *Zaire: Current Economic Situation and Constraints*, Washington, DC: World Bank, 1980.

Yakemtchouk, Romain, 'Les deux guerres du Shaba: les relations entre la Belgique, la France et le Zaïre', *Studia Diplomatica*, Vol. 41, Nos 4–6, 1988, pp. 375–742.

Yambuya, Pierre, *Zaïre: l'abbatoir*, Brussels: Ed. EPO, 1991.

Yoka Lye, *Lettre d'un Kinois à l'oncle du village. Zaïre, années 90*, Vol. 5, Brussels: Institut Africain-CEDAF, 1995.

Young, Crawford, *Politics in the Congo: Decolonization and Independence*, Princeton, NJ: Princeton University Press, 1965, French trans. *Introduction à la politique congolaise*, Kinshasa, Kisangani, Lubumbashi: Editions Universitaires du Congo, and Brussels: CRISP, 1968.

— 'Rebellion and the Congo', in Robert I. Rotberg and Ali A. Mazrui (eds), *Protest and Power in Black Africa*, New York: Oxford University Press, 1970, pp. 969–1011.

— 'Zaire: the unending crisis', *Foreign Affairs*, Vol. 57, No. 1, Fall 1978, pp. 169–85.

— 'Zaire: the shattered illusion of the integral state', *Journal of Modern African Studies*, Vol. 32, No. 2, June 1994, pp. 247–64.

— 'Zaire: the anatomy of a failed state', in David Birmingham and Phyllis M. Martin (eds), *History of Central Africa: The Contemporary Years since 1960*, London and New York: Longman, 1998.

Young, Crawford and Thomas Turner, *The Rise and Decline of the Zairian State*, Madison: University of Wisconsin Press, 1985.

Ziegler, Jean, *Sociologie de la nouvelle Afrique*, Paris: Gallimard, 1964.

Zolberg, Aristide R., *Creating Political Order: The Party-States of West Africa*, Chicago: Rand McNally, 1966.

Index